6

My Love
Mix-Up!

Art by **Aruko**
Story by **Wataru Hinekure**

Contents

Aoki borrows an eraser from his unrequited crush, Hashimoto. He finds the name "IDA♡" written on the eraser, and his hopes are dashed. Then Ida sees him holding that very eraser, and thinks Aoki is in love with him. While attempting to resolve the misunderstanding, Aoki ends up falling for Ida. Aoki is still reeling from his own emotions when he musters up the courage to confess to Ida. He's ready for rejection...only to find the feelings are mutual?! The two hesitantly start dating and, though they have their troubles, they keep moving forward. Aoki starts working to earn money to buy Ida a birthday present. Meanwhile, things seem to be going swimmingly between Hashimoto and Akkun since Valentine's Day, but...!!

Chapter 22

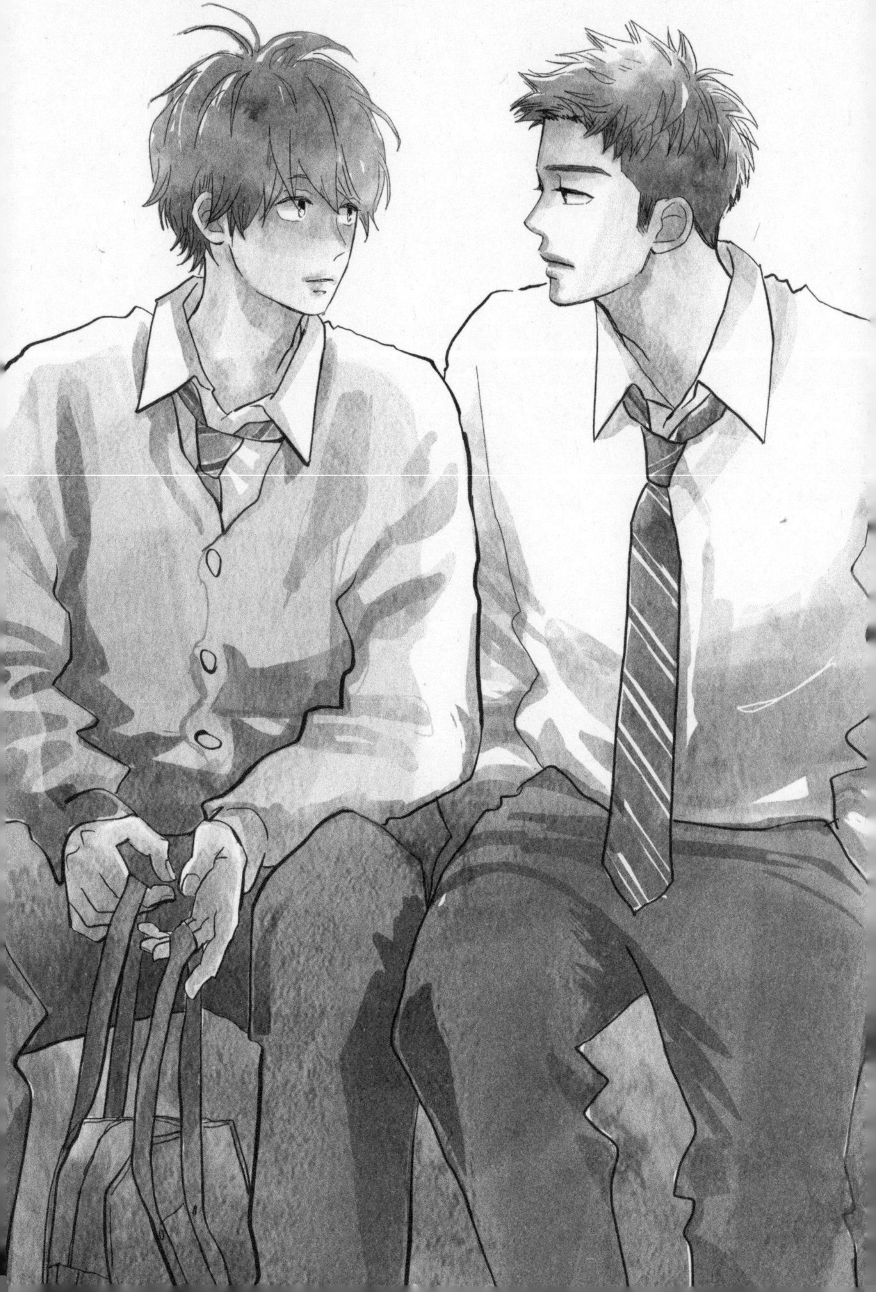

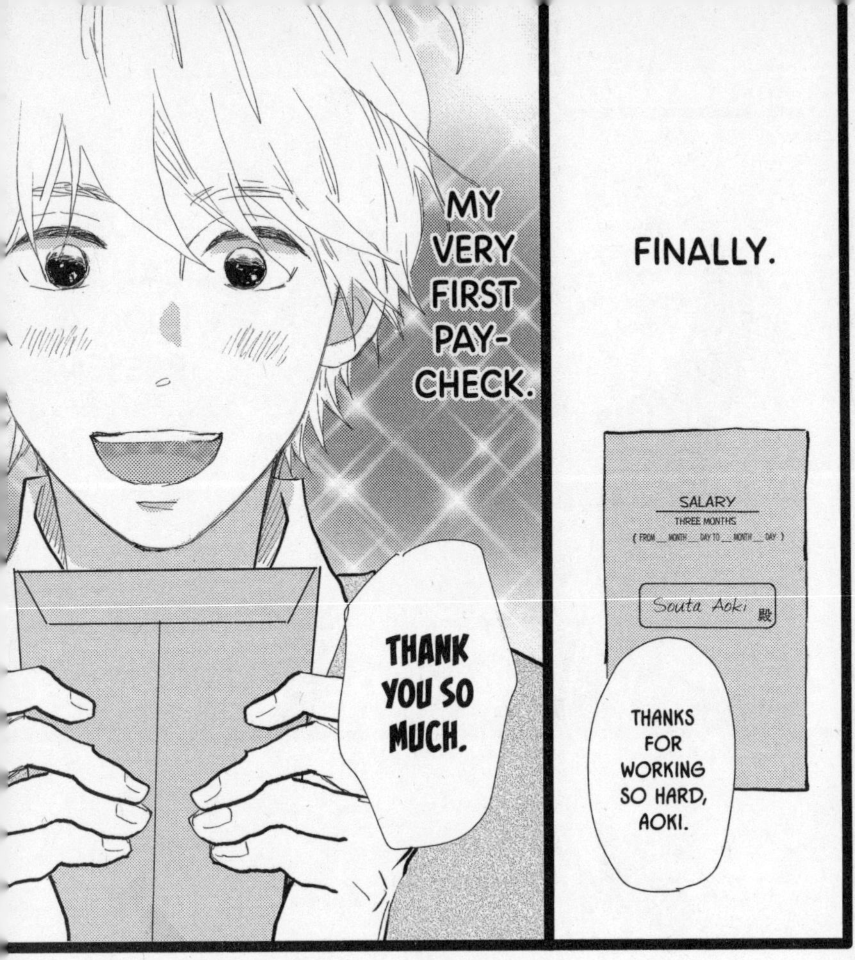
FINALLY.
SALARY
THREE MONTHS
(FROM __ MONTH __ DAY TO __ MONTH __ DAY)
Souta Aoki 殿
THANKS FOR WORKING SO HARD, AOKI.
MY VERY FIRST PAY-CHECK.
THANK YOU SO MUCH.

My Love Mix-Up!

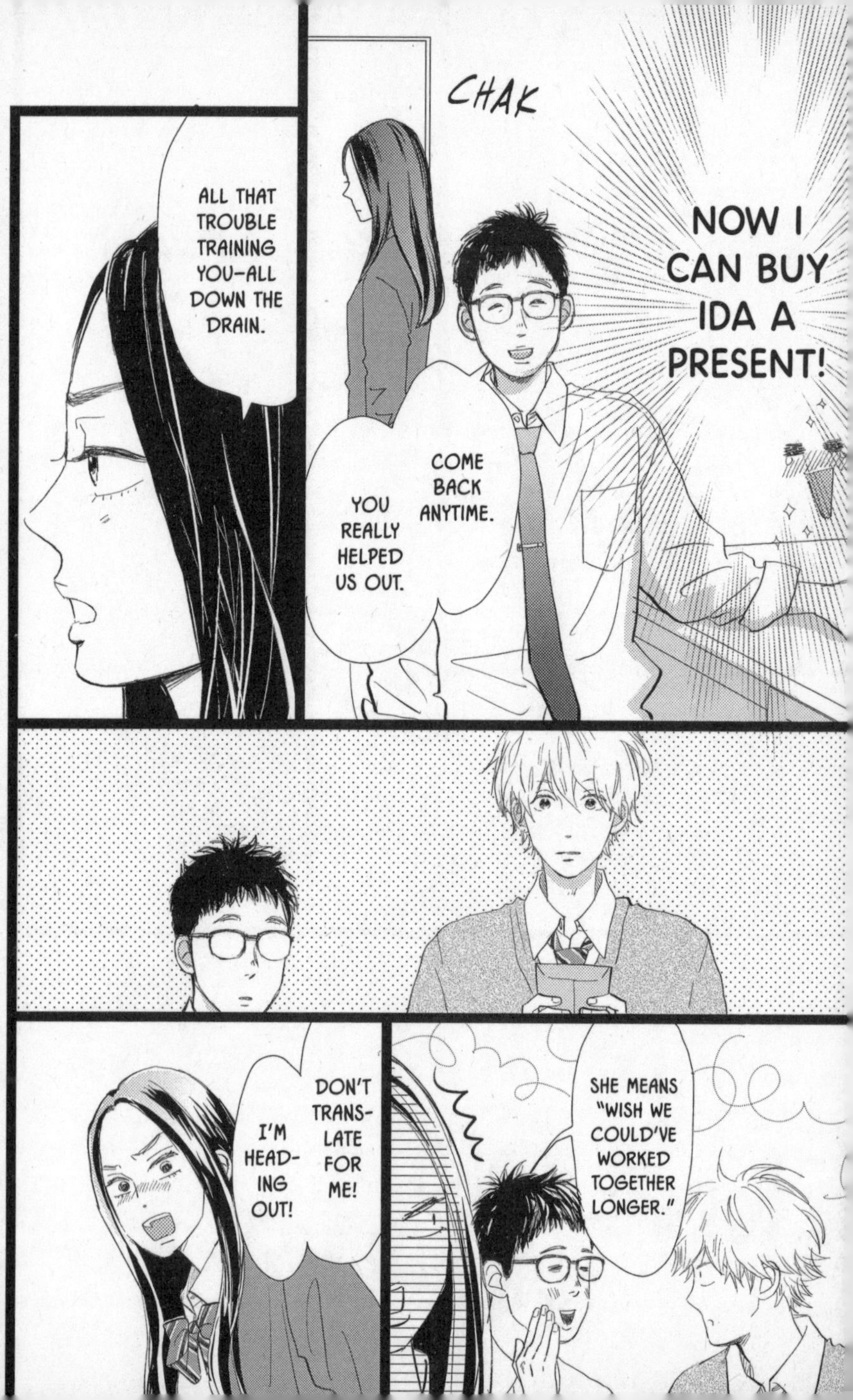

CHAK
NOW I CAN BUY IDA A PRESENT!
COME BACK ANYTIME.
YOU REALLY HELPED US OUT.
ALL THAT TROUBLE TRAINING YOU—ALL DOWN THE DRAIN.
SHE MEANS "WISH WE COULD'VE WORKED TOGETHER LONGER."
DON'T TRANSLATE FOR ME!
I'M HEADING OUT!

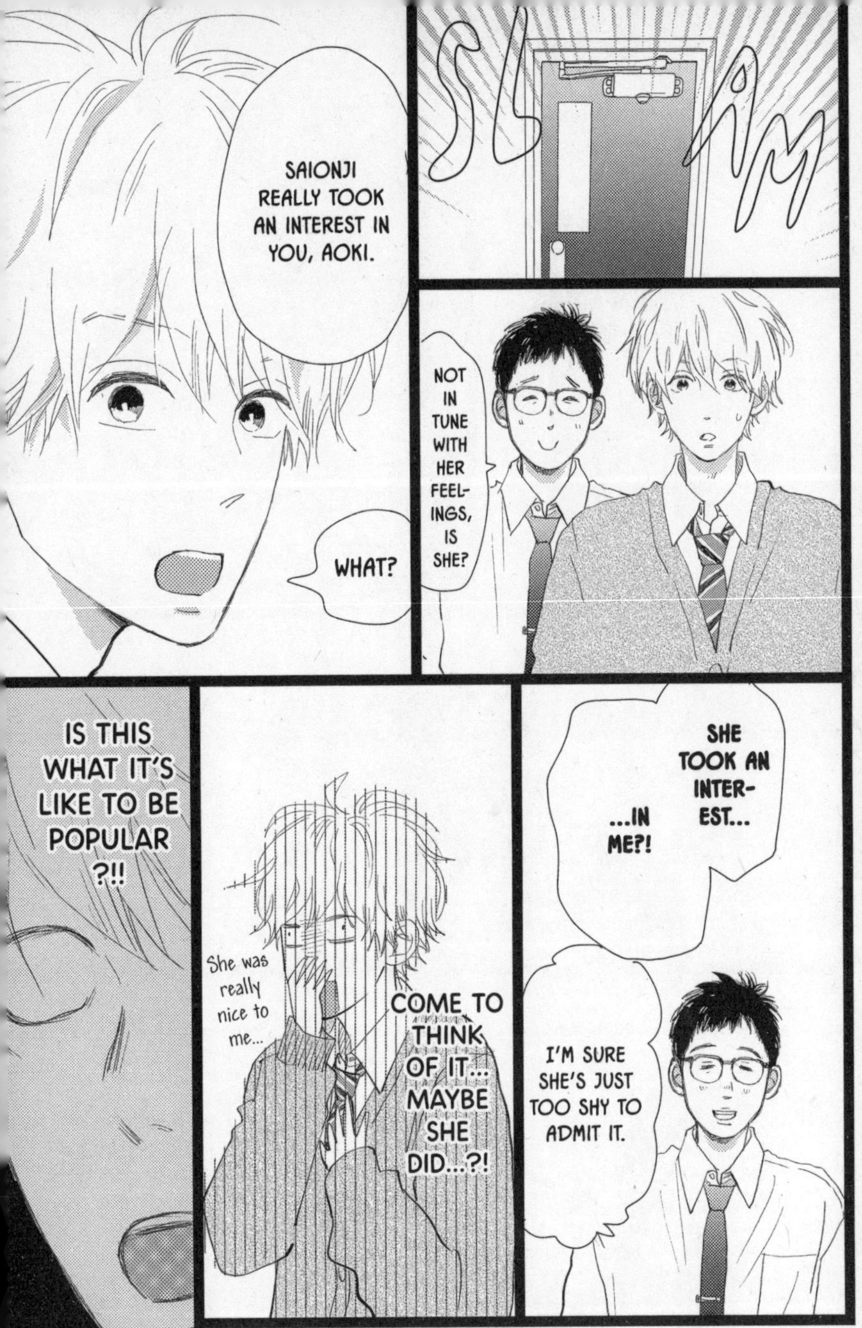
SLAM
NOT IN TUNE WITH HER FEELINGS, IS SHE?
SAIONJI REALLY TOOK AN INTEREST IN YOU, AOKI.
WHAT?
SHE TOOK AN INTEREST...
...IN ME?!
I'M SURE SHE'S JUST TOO SHY TO ADMIT IT.
COME TO THINK OF IT... MAYBE SHE DID...?!
She was really nice to me...
IS THIS WHAT IT'S LIKE TO BE POPULAR?!!

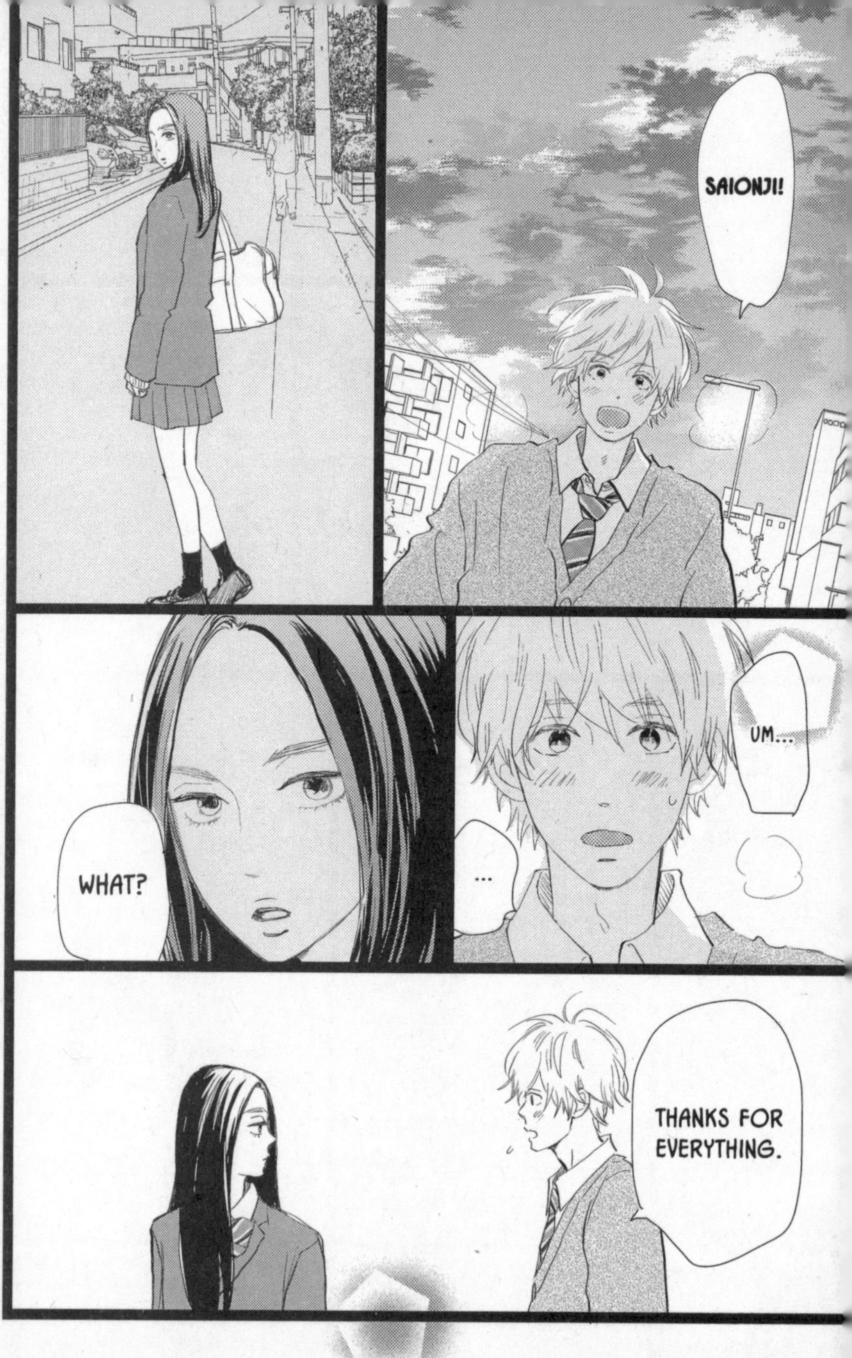
SAIONJI!
UM...
...
WHAT?
THANKS FOR EVERYTHING.

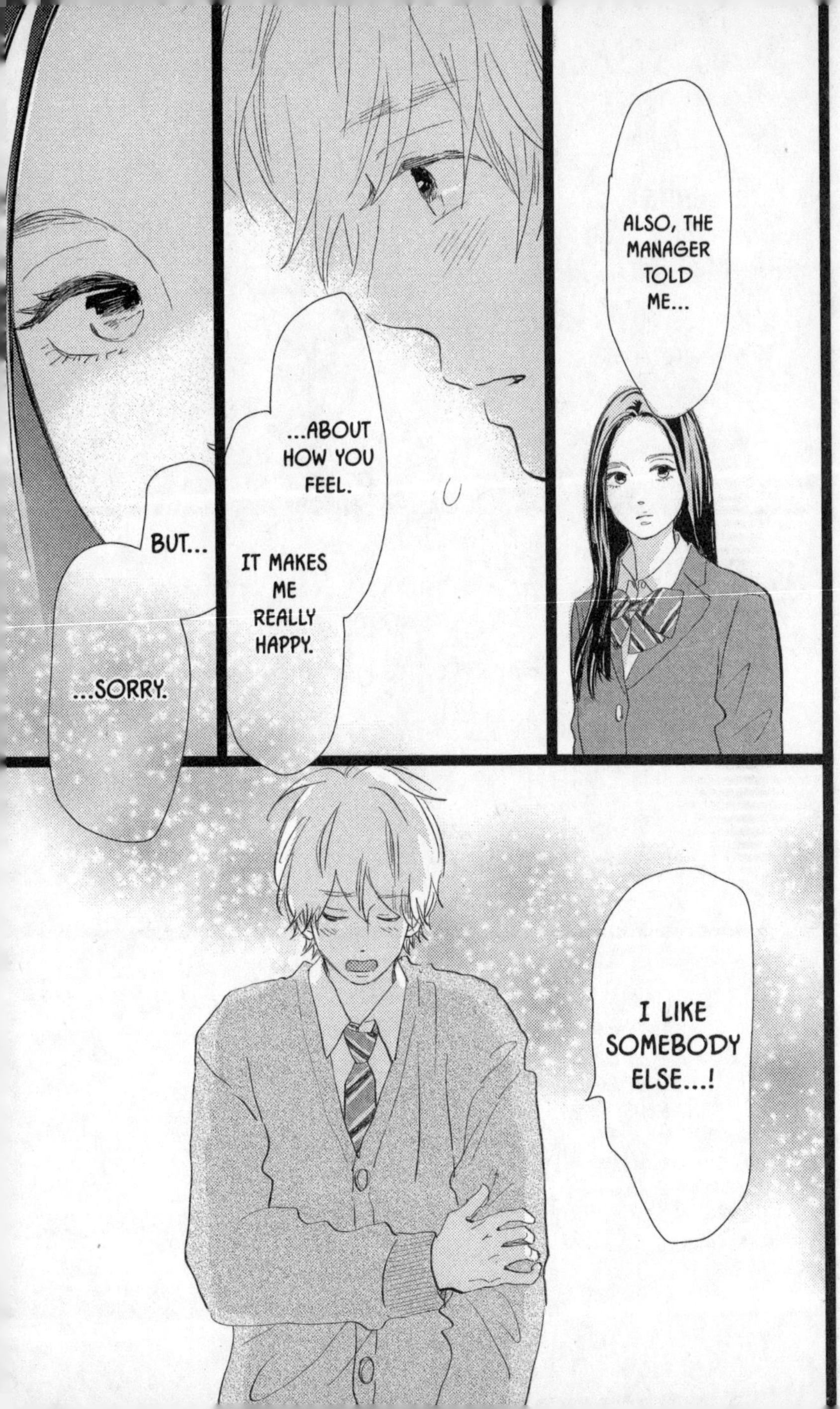
ALSO, THE MANAGER TOLD ME...
...ABOUT HOW YOU FEEL.
IT MAKES ME REALLY HAPPY.
BUT...
...SORRY.
I LIKE SOMEBODY ELSE...!

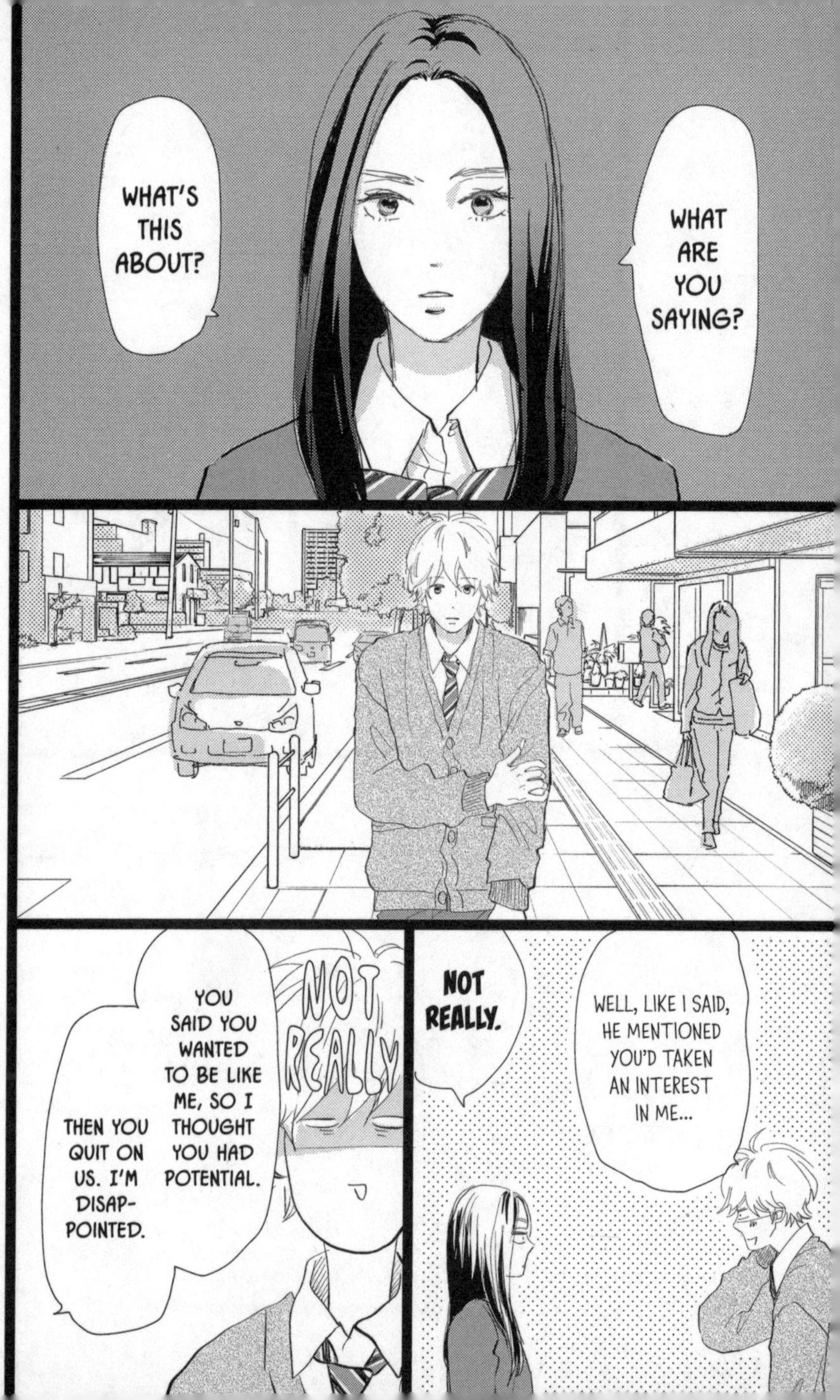
WHAT ARE YOU SAYING?
WHAT'S THIS ABOUT?
WELL, LIKE I SAID, HE MENTIONED YOU'D TAKEN AN INTEREST IN ME...
NOT REALLY.
NOT REALLY
YOU SAID YOU WANTED TO BE LIKE ME, SO I THOUGHT YOU HAD POTENTIAL.
THEN YOU QUIT ON US. I'M DISAPPOINTED.

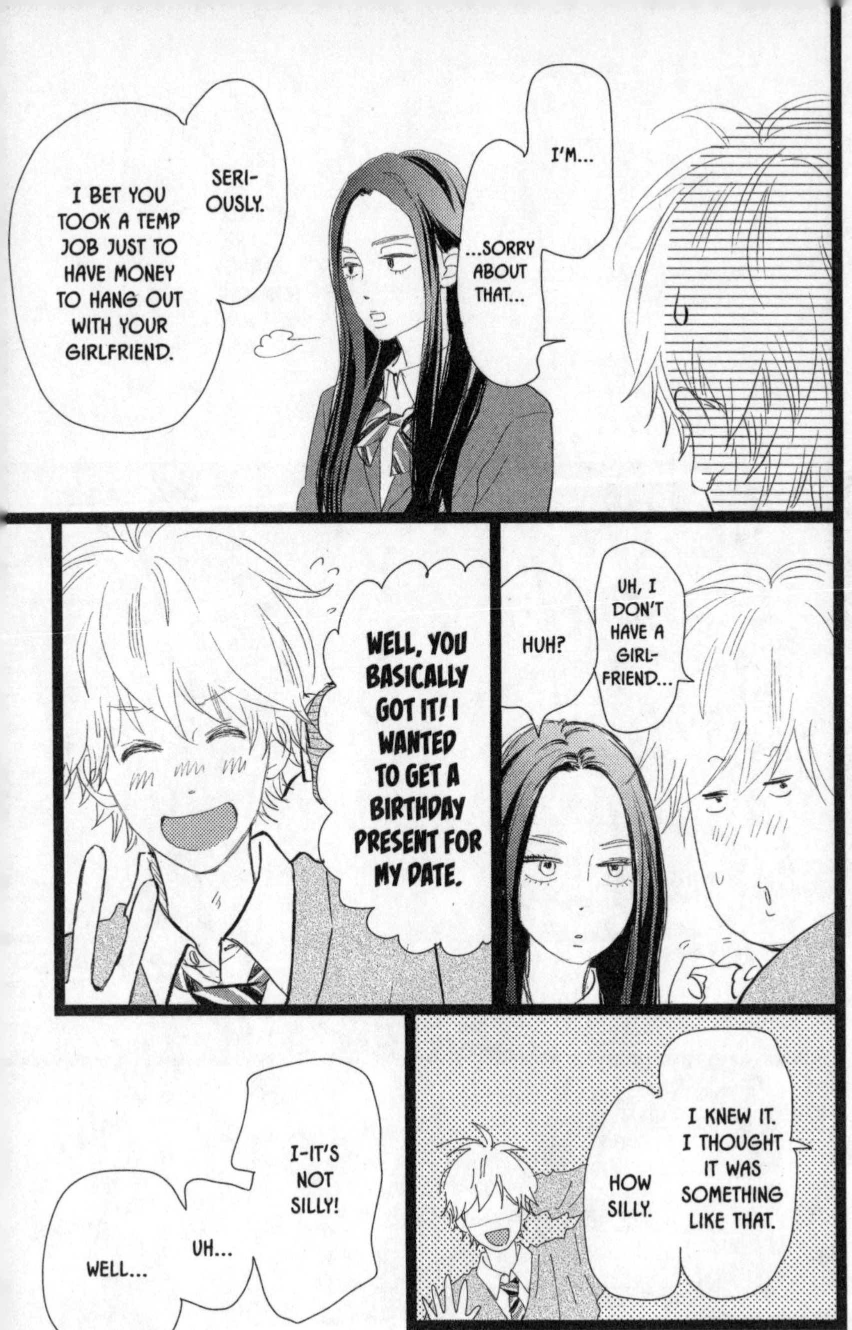
I'M...
...SORRY ABOUT THAT...
SERI-OUSLY.
I BET YOU TOOK A TEMP JOB JUST TO HAVE MONEY TO HANG OUT WITH YOUR GIRLFRIEND.
UH, I DON'T HAVE A GIRL-FRIEND...
HUH?
WELL, YOU BASICALLY GOT IT! I WANTED TO GET A BIRTHDAY PRESENT FOR MY DATE.
I KNEW IT. I THOUGHT IT WAS SOMETHING LIKE THAT.
HOW SILLY.
I-IT'S NOT SILLY!
UH...
WELL...

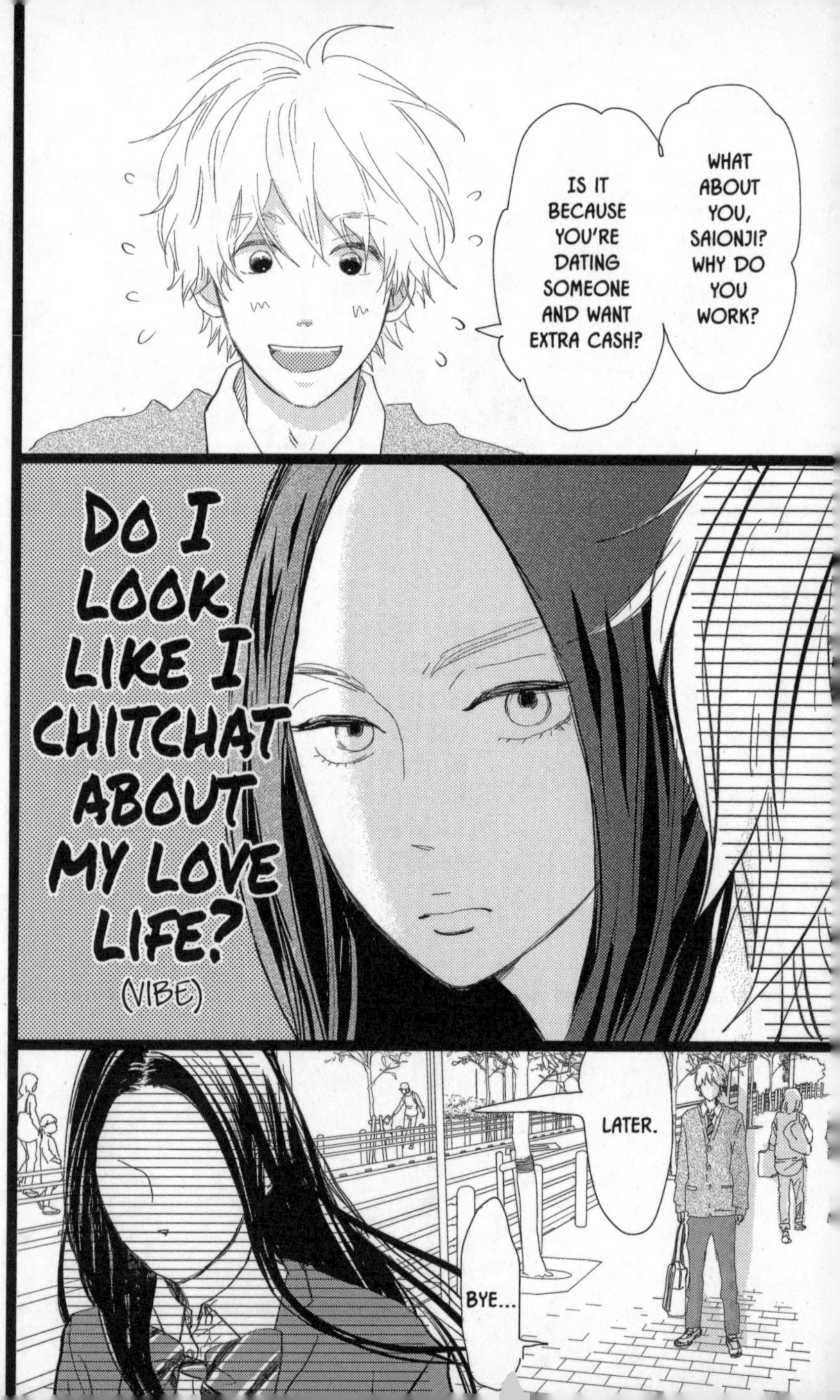
WHAT ABOUT YOU, SAIONJI? WHY DO YOU WORK?
IS IT BECAUSE YOU'RE DATING SOMEONE AND WANT EXTRA CASH?
DO I LOOK LIKE I CHITCHAT ABOUT MY LOVE LIFE?
(VIBE)
LATER.
BYE...

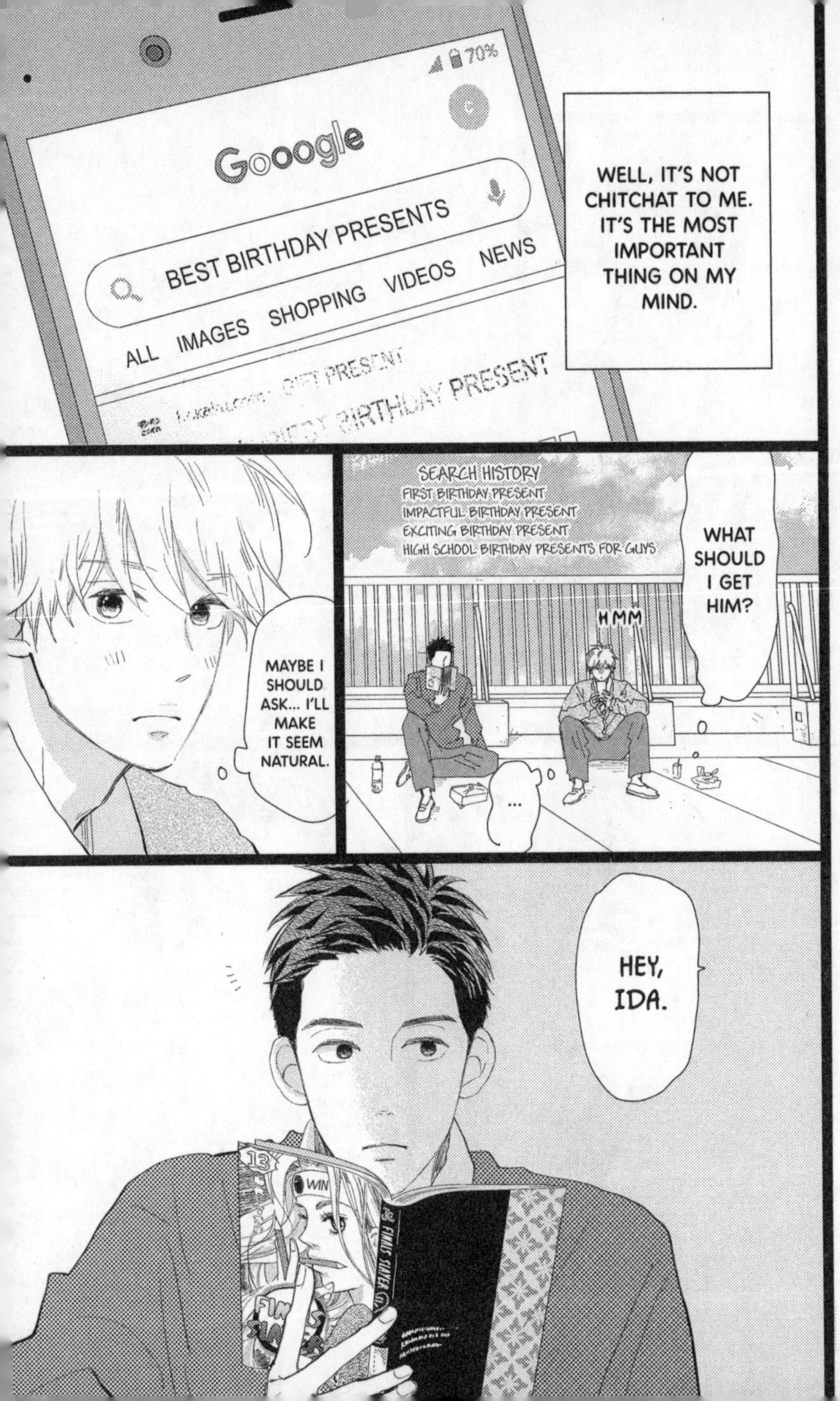
WELL, IT'S NOT CHITCHAT TO ME. IT'S THE MOST IMPORTANT THING ON MY MIND.
70%
Gooogle
BEST BIRTHDAY PRESENTS
ALL IMAGES SHOPPING VIDEOS NEWS
GIFT PRESENT
BIRTHDAY PRESENT
WHAT SHOULD I GET HIM?
SEARCH HISTORY
FIRST BIRTHDAY PRESENT
IMPACTFUL BIRTHDAY PRESENT
EXCITING BIRTHDAY PRESENT
HIGH SCHOOL BIRTHDAY PRESENTS FOR GUYS
HMM
...
MAYBE I SHOULD ASK... I'LL MAKE IT SEEM NATURAL.
HEY, IDA.
13
WIN

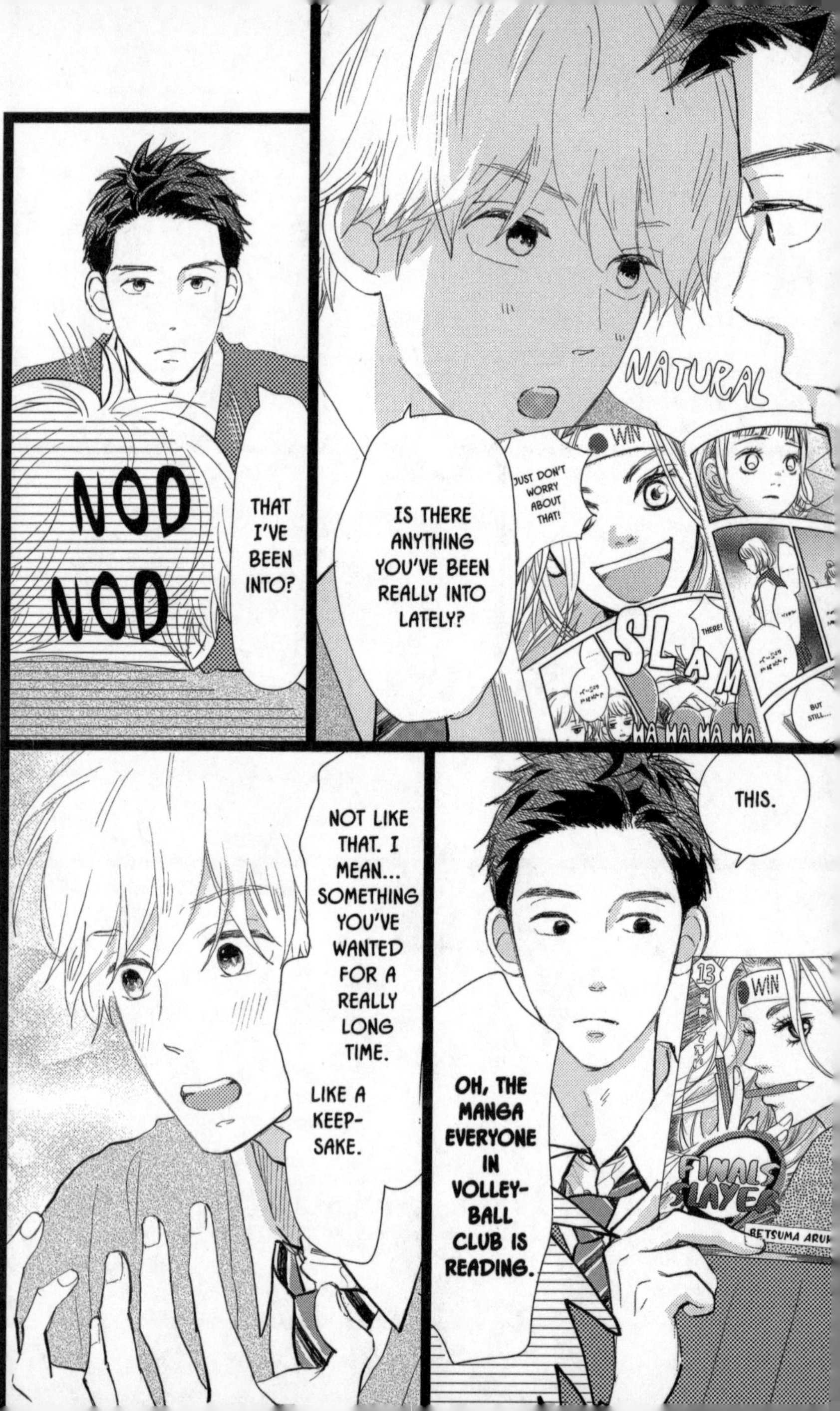
NATURAL
WIN
JUST DON'T WORRY ABOUT THAT!
IS THERE ANYTHING YOU'VE BEEN REALLY INTO LATELY?
SLAM
THERE!
BUT STILL...
HA HA HA HA
THAT I'VE BEEN INTO?
NOD NOD
THIS.
13
WIN
FINALS SLAYER
OH, THE MANGA EVERYONE IN VOLLEY-BALL CLUB IS READING.
NOT LIKE THAT. I MEAN... SOMETHING YOU'VE WANTED FOR A REALLY LONG TIME.
LIKE A KEEP-SAKE.

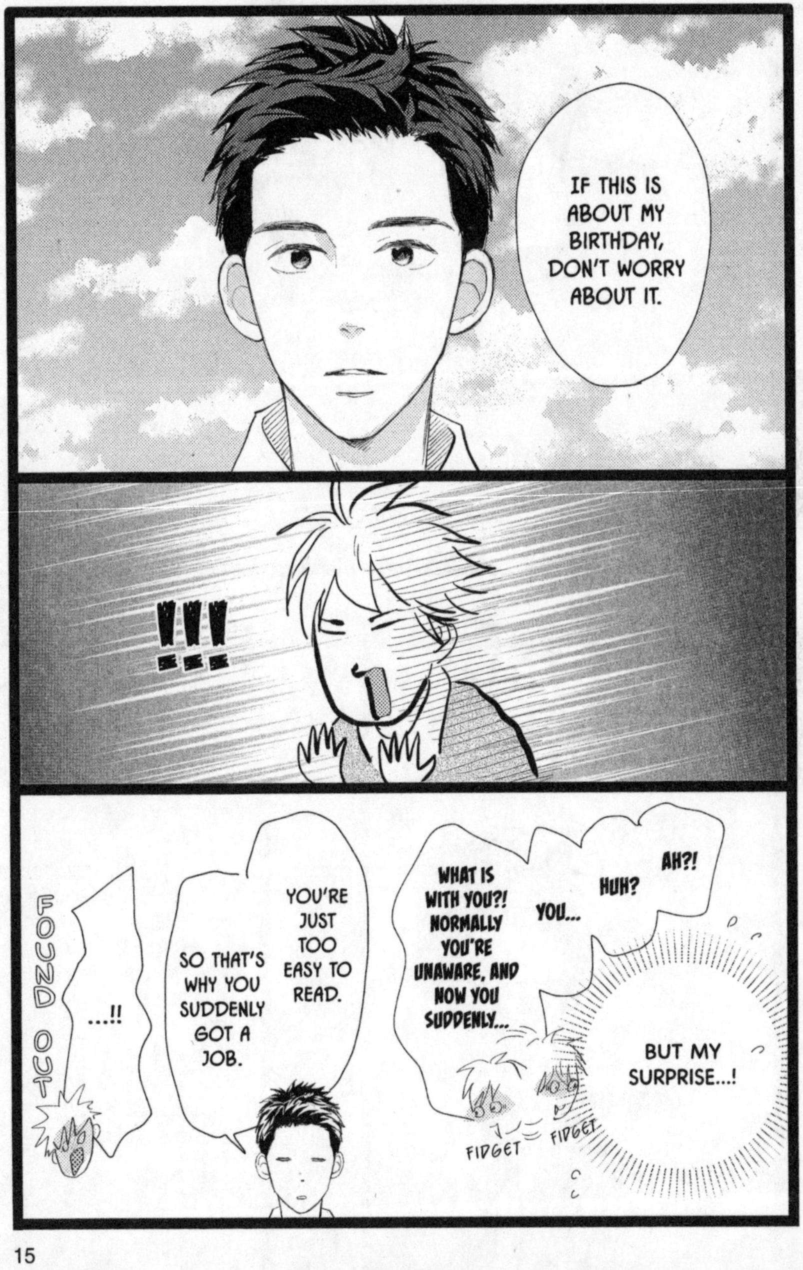
IF THIS IS ABOUT MY BIRTHDAY, DON'T WORRY ABOUT IT.
!!!
AH?!
HUH?
YOU...
WHAT IS WITH YOU?! NORMALLY YOU'RE UNAWARE, AND NOW YOU SUDDENLY...
BUT MY SURPRISE...!
FIDGET
FIDGET
YOU'RE JUST TOO EASY TO READ.
SO THAT'S WHY YOU SUDDENLY GOT A JOB.
...!!
FOUND OUT

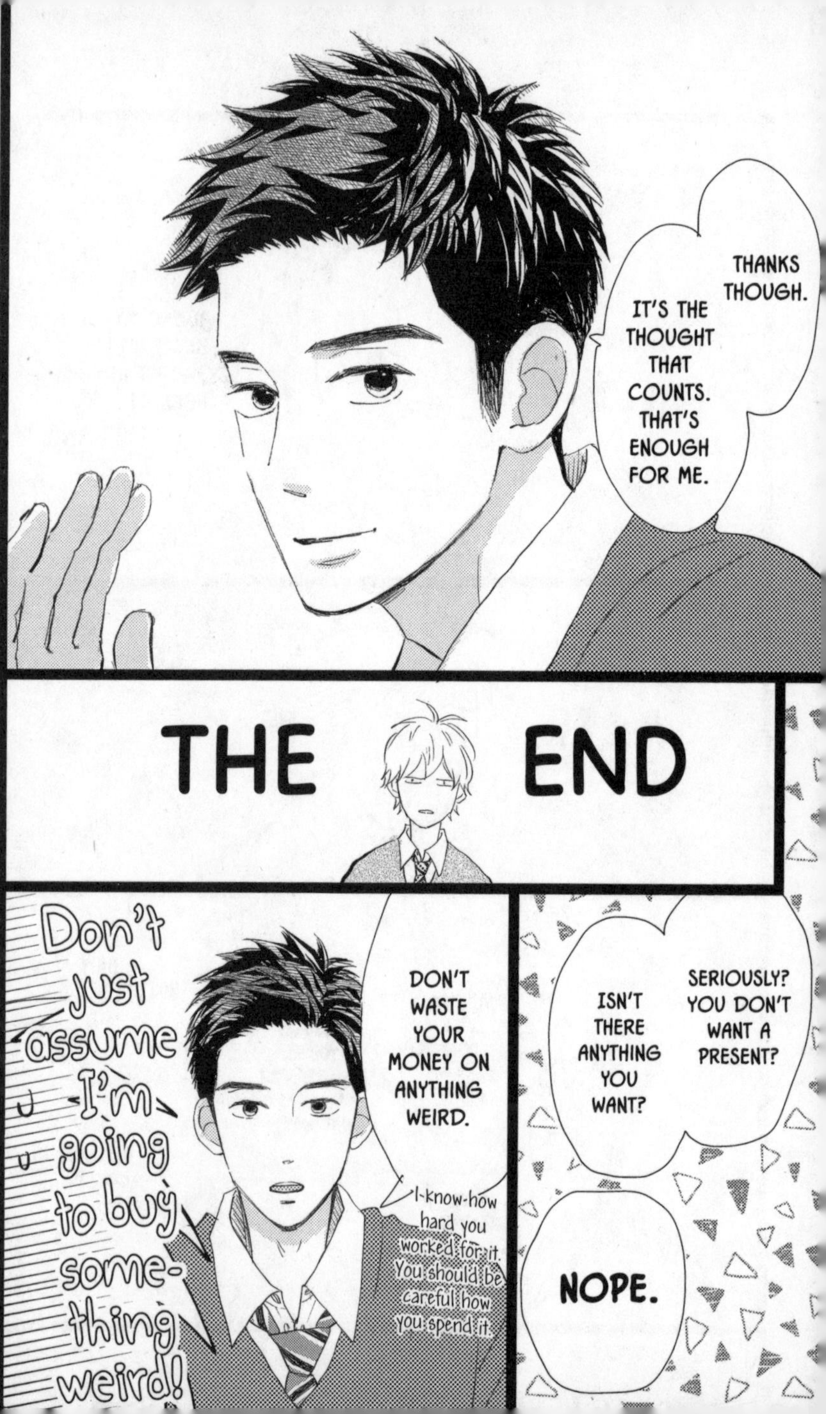
THANKS THOUGH.
IT'S THE THOUGHT THAT COUNTS. THAT'S ENOUGH FOR ME.
THE END
SERIOUSLY? YOU DON'T WANT A PRESENT?
ISN'T THERE ANYTHING YOU WANT?
NOPE.
DON'T WASTE YOUR MONEY ON ANYTHING WEIRD.
I know how hard you worked for it. You should be careful how you spend it.
Don't just assume I'm going to buy something weird!

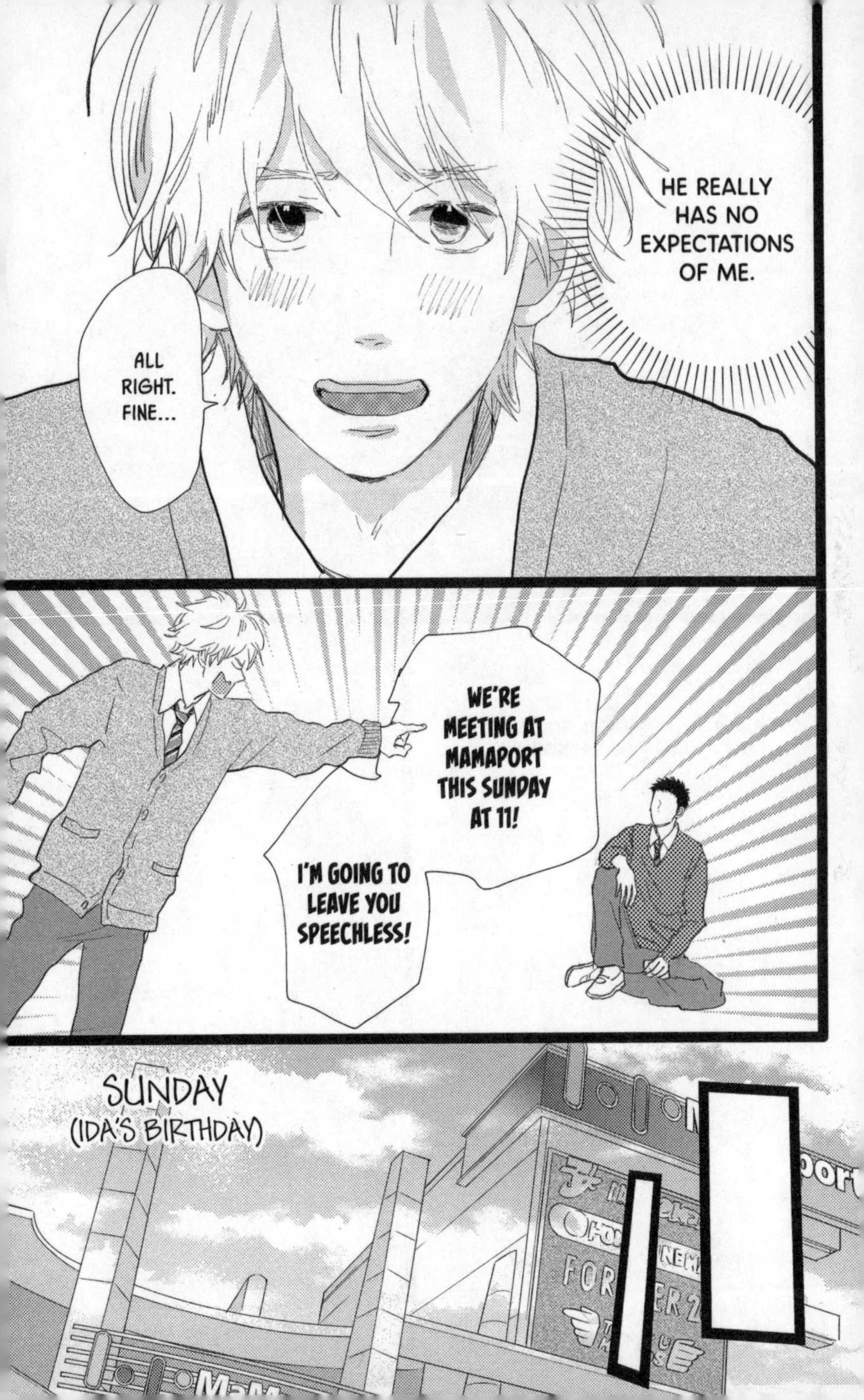
HE REALLY HAS NO EXPECTATIONS OF ME.
ALL RIGHT. FINE...
WE'RE MEETING AT MAMAPORT THIS SUNDAY AT 11!
I'M GOING TO LEAVE YOU SPEECHLESS!
SUNDAY (IDA'S BIRTHDAY)

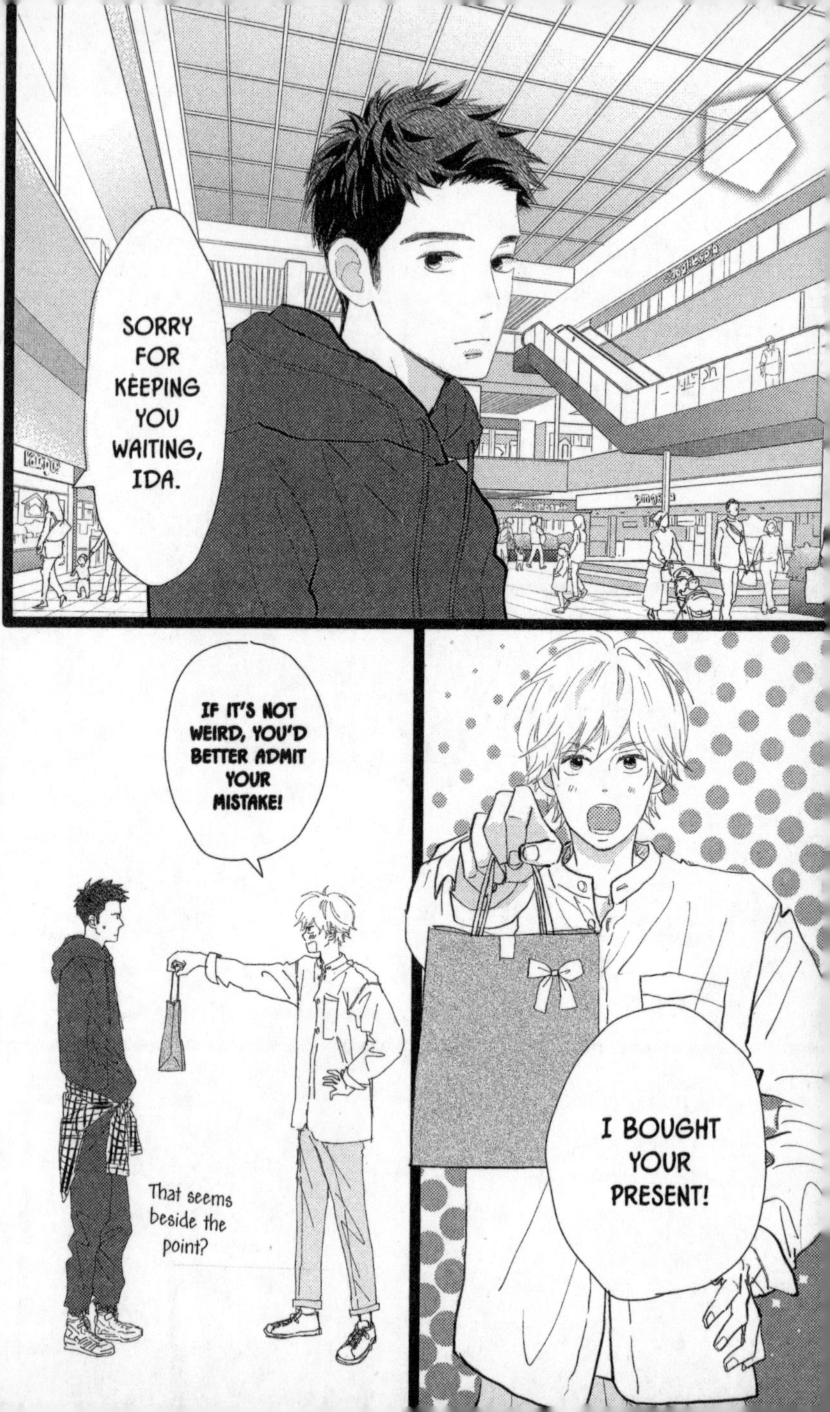
SORRY FOR KEEPING YOU WAITING, IDA.
I BOUGHT YOUR PRESENT!
IF IT'S NOT WEIRD, YOU'D BETTER ADMIT YOUR MISTAKE!
That seems beside the point?

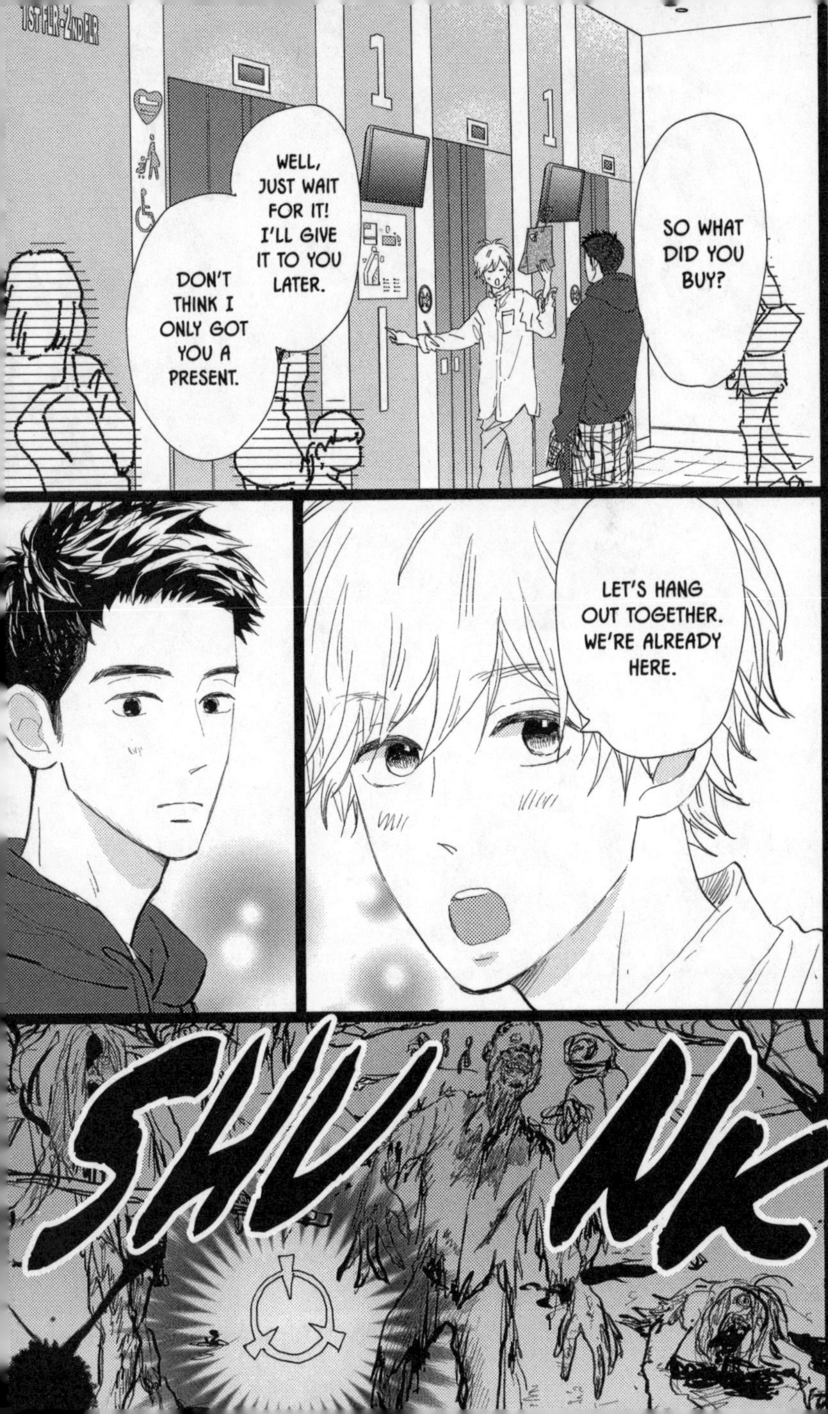
SO WHAT DID YOU BUY?
WELL, JUST WAIT FOR IT! I'LL GIVE IT TO YOU LATER.
DON'T THINK I ONLY GOT YOU A PRESENT.
1ST FLR-2ND FLR
LET'S HANG OUT TOGETHER. WE'RE ALREADY HERE.
SHUNK

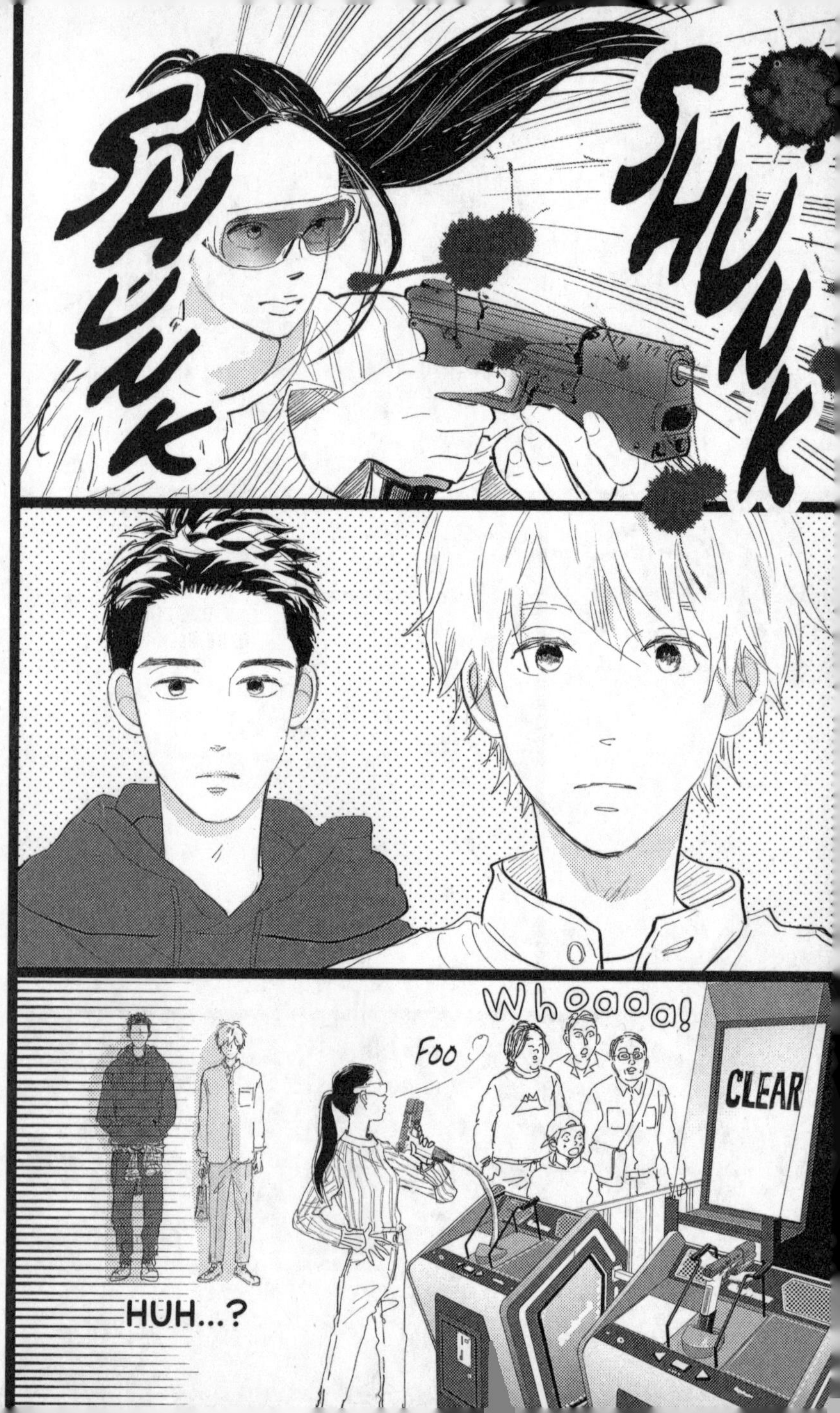
SHUNK
SHUNK
CLEAR
Whoaaa!
Foo
HUH...?

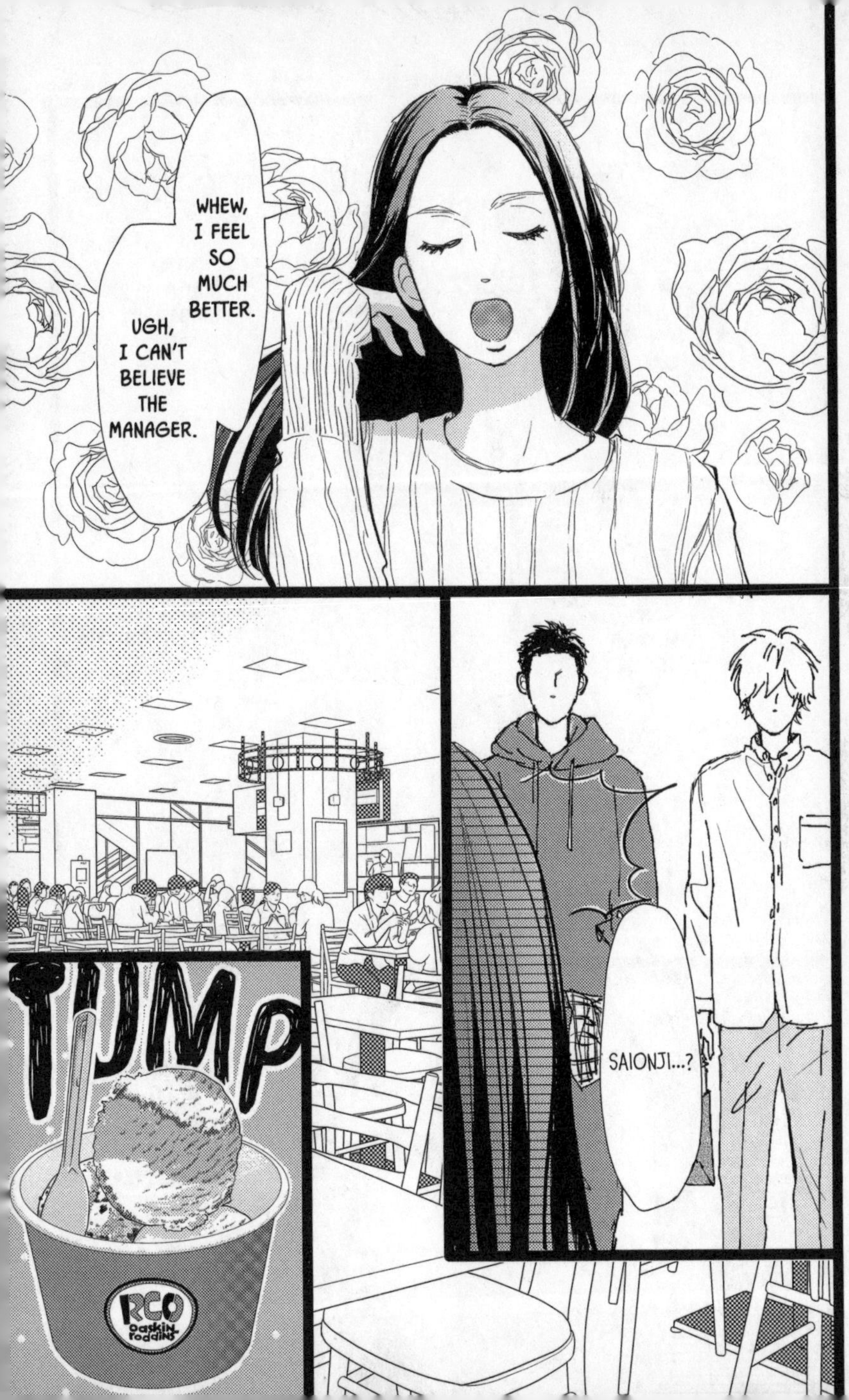
WHEW, I FEEL SO MUCH BETTER.
UGH, I CAN'T BELIEVE THE MANAGER.
SAIONJI...?
TUMP

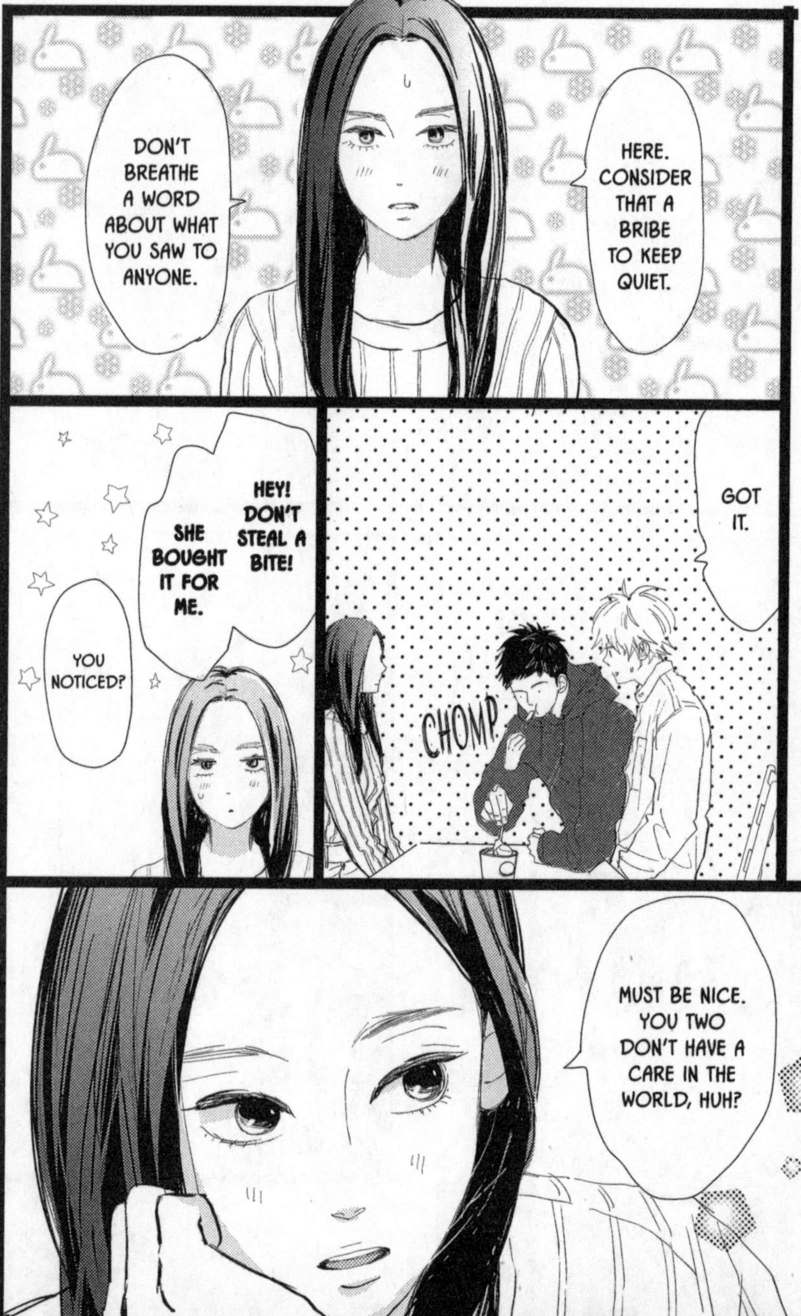
HERE. CONSIDER THAT A BRIBE TO KEEP QUIET.
DON'T BREATHE A WORD ABOUT WHAT YOU SAW TO ANYONE.
GOT IT.
CHOMP
HEY! DON'T STEAL A BITE!
SHE BOUGHT IT FOR ME.
YOU NOTICED?
MUST BE NICE. YOU TWO DON'T HAVE A CARE IN THE WORLD, HUH?

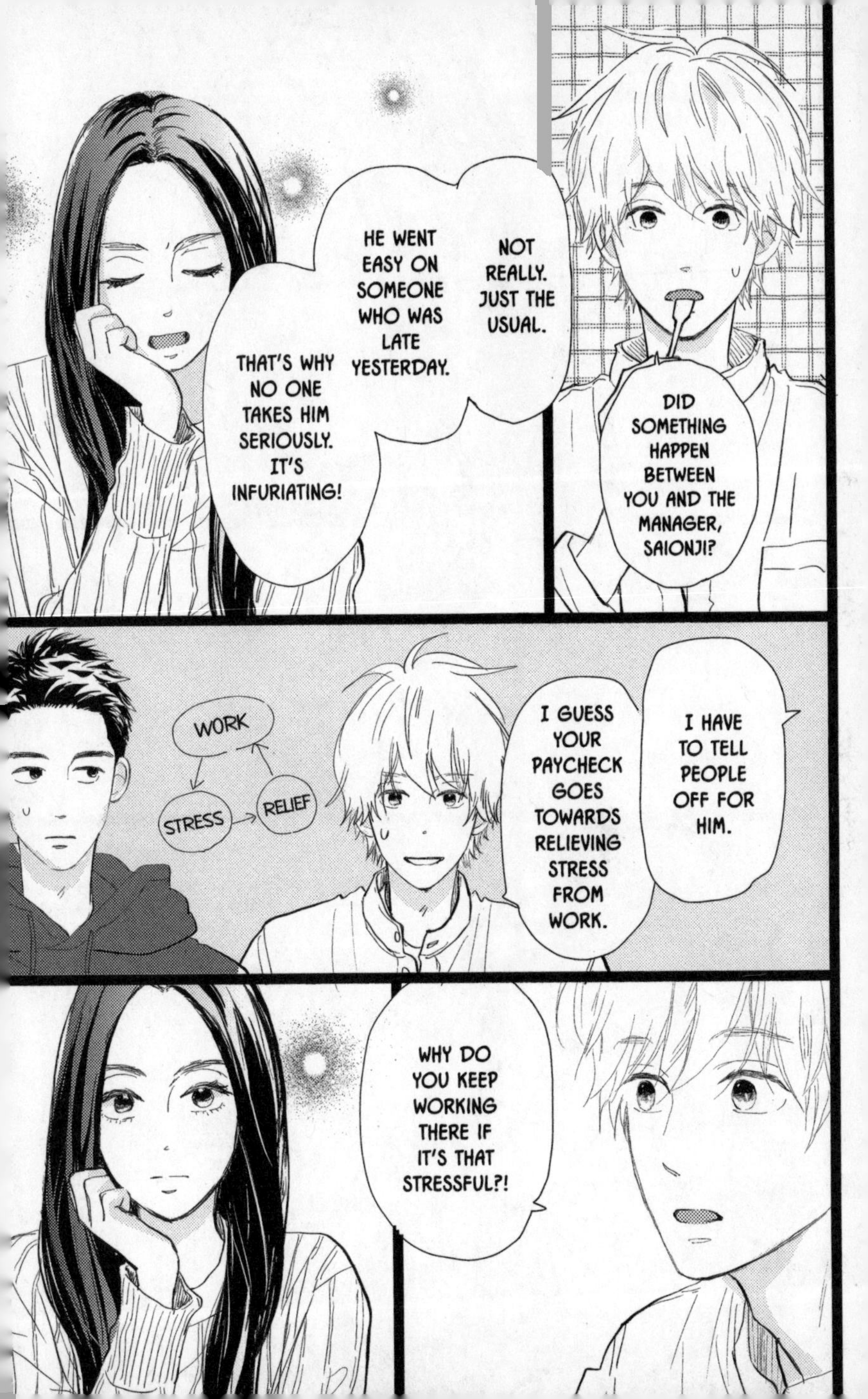
DID SOMETHING HAPPEN BETWEEN YOU AND THE MANAGER, SAIONJI?
NOT REALLY. JUST THE USUAL.
HE WENT EASY ON SOMEONE WHO WAS LATE YESTERDAY.
THAT'S WHY NO ONE TAKES HIM SERIOUSLY. IT'S INFURIATING!
I HAVE TO TELL PEOPLE OFF FOR HIM.
I GUESS YOUR PAYCHECK GOES TOWARDS RELIEVING STRESS FROM WORK.
WORK
STRESS
RELIEF
WHY DO YOU KEEP WORKING THERE IF IT'S THAT STRESSFUL?!

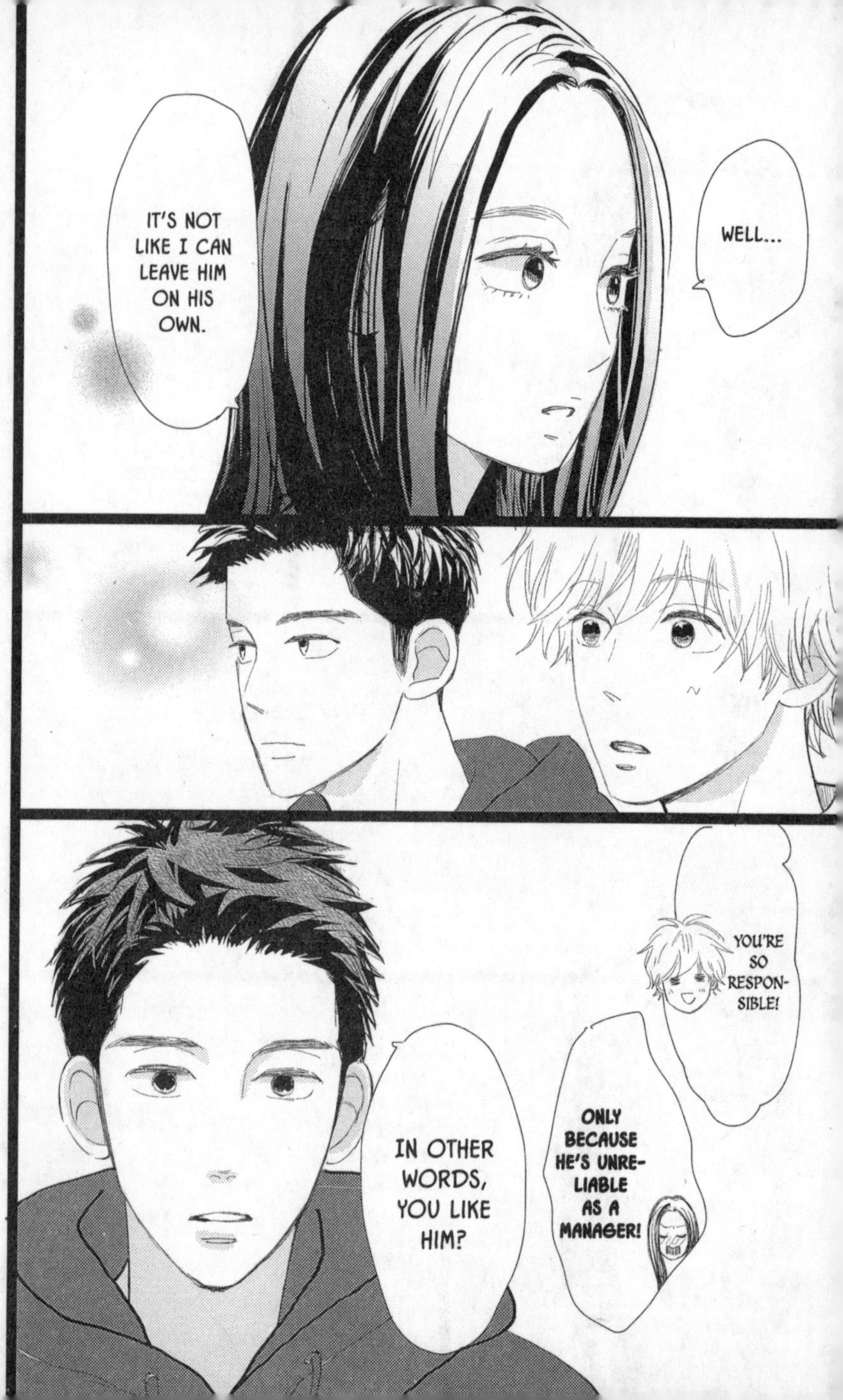
WELL...
IT'S NOT LIKE I CAN LEAVE HIM ON HIS OWN.
YOU'RE SO RESPON-SIBLE!
ONLY BECAUSE HE'S UNRE-LIABLE AS A MANAGER!
IN OTHER WORDS, YOU LIKE HIM?

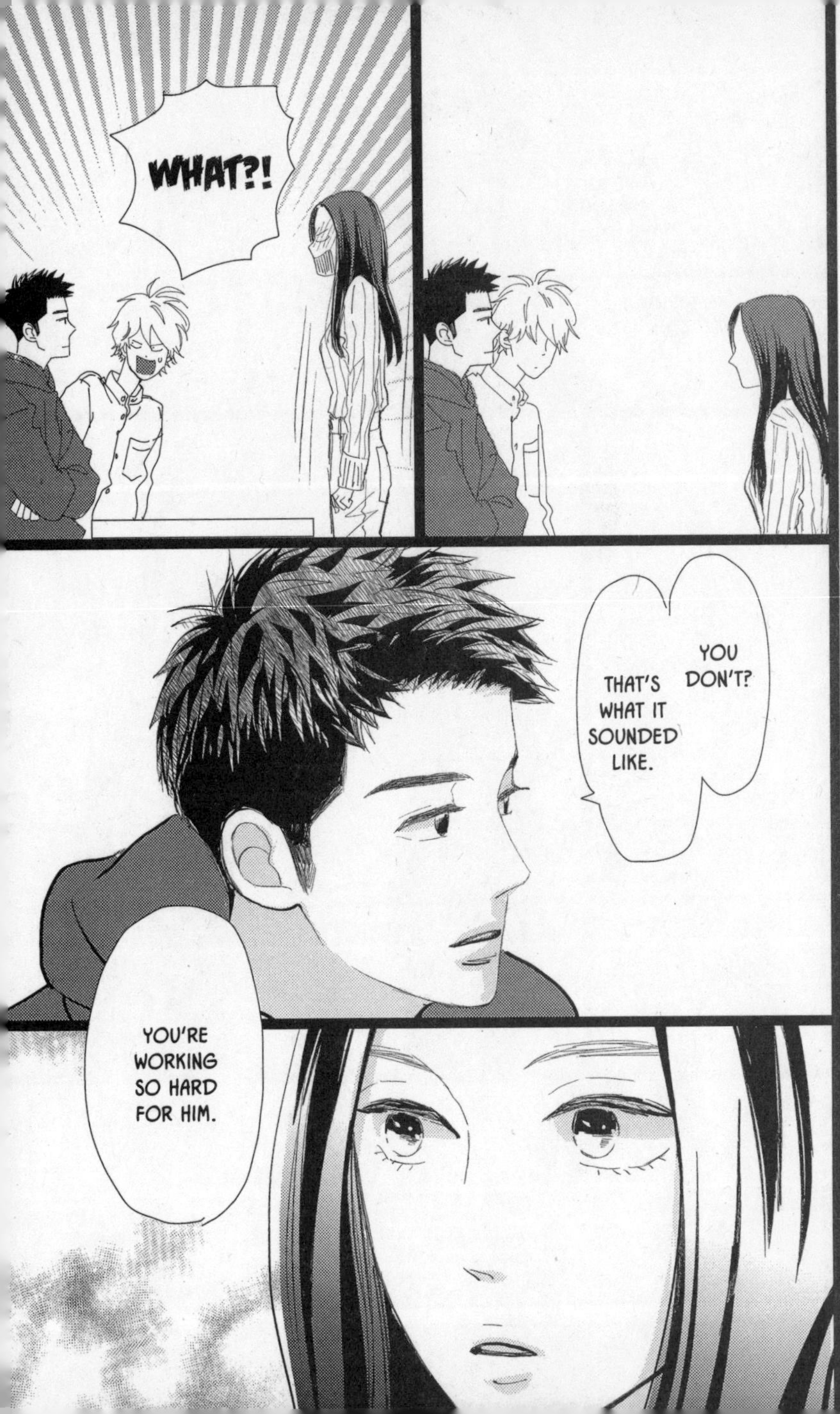
WHAT?!
YOU DON'T?
THAT'S WHAT IT SOUNDED LIKE.
YOU'RE WORKING SO HARD FOR HIM.

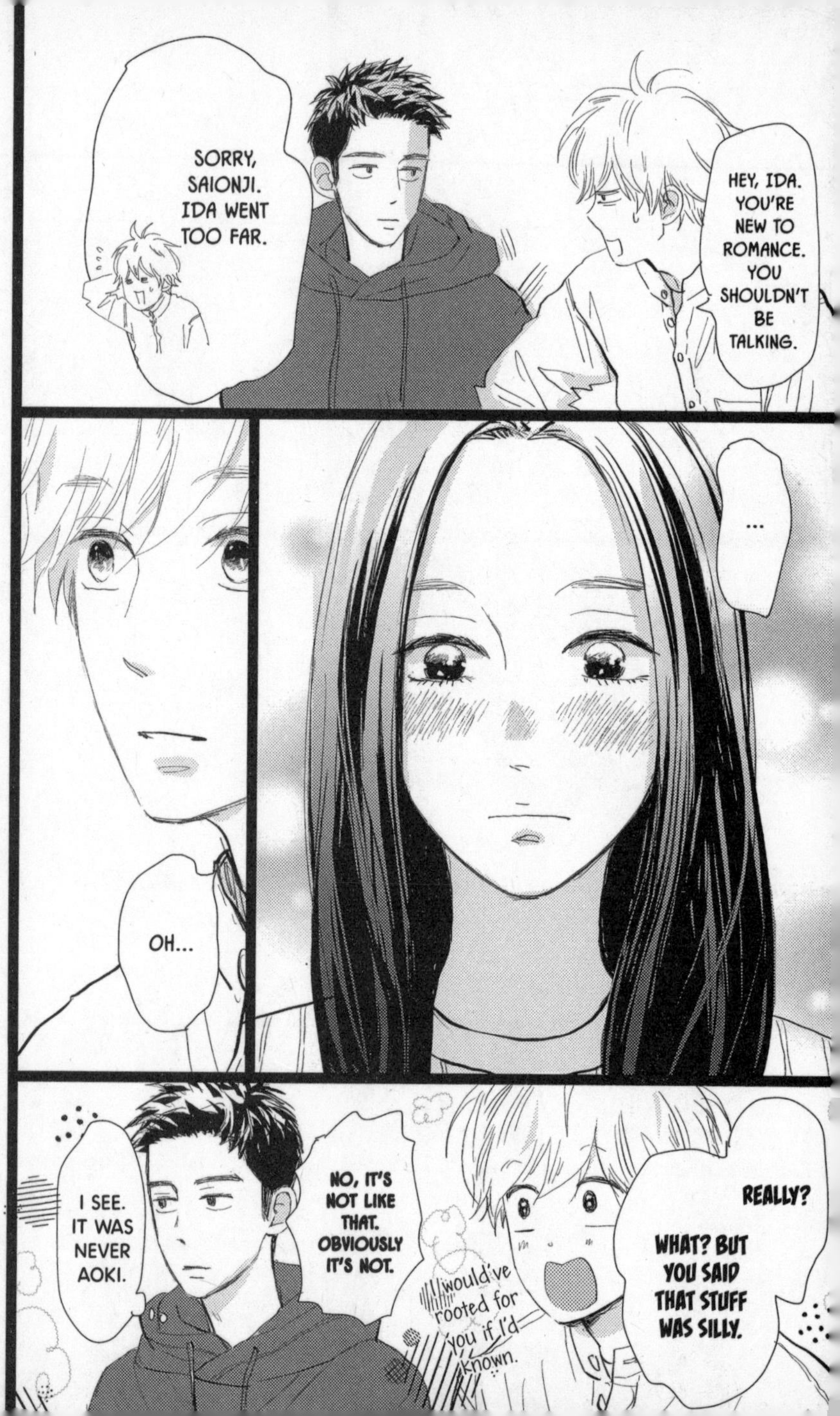
HEY, IDA. YOU'RE NEW TO ROMANCE. YOU SHOULDN'T BE TALKING.
SORRY, SAIONJI. IDA WENT TOO FAR.
...
OH...
REALLY?
WHAT? BUT YOU SAID THAT STUFF WAS SILLY.
would've rooted for you if I'd known.
NO, IT'S NOT LIKE THAT. OBVIOUSLY IT'S NOT.
I SEE. IT WAS NEVER AOKI.

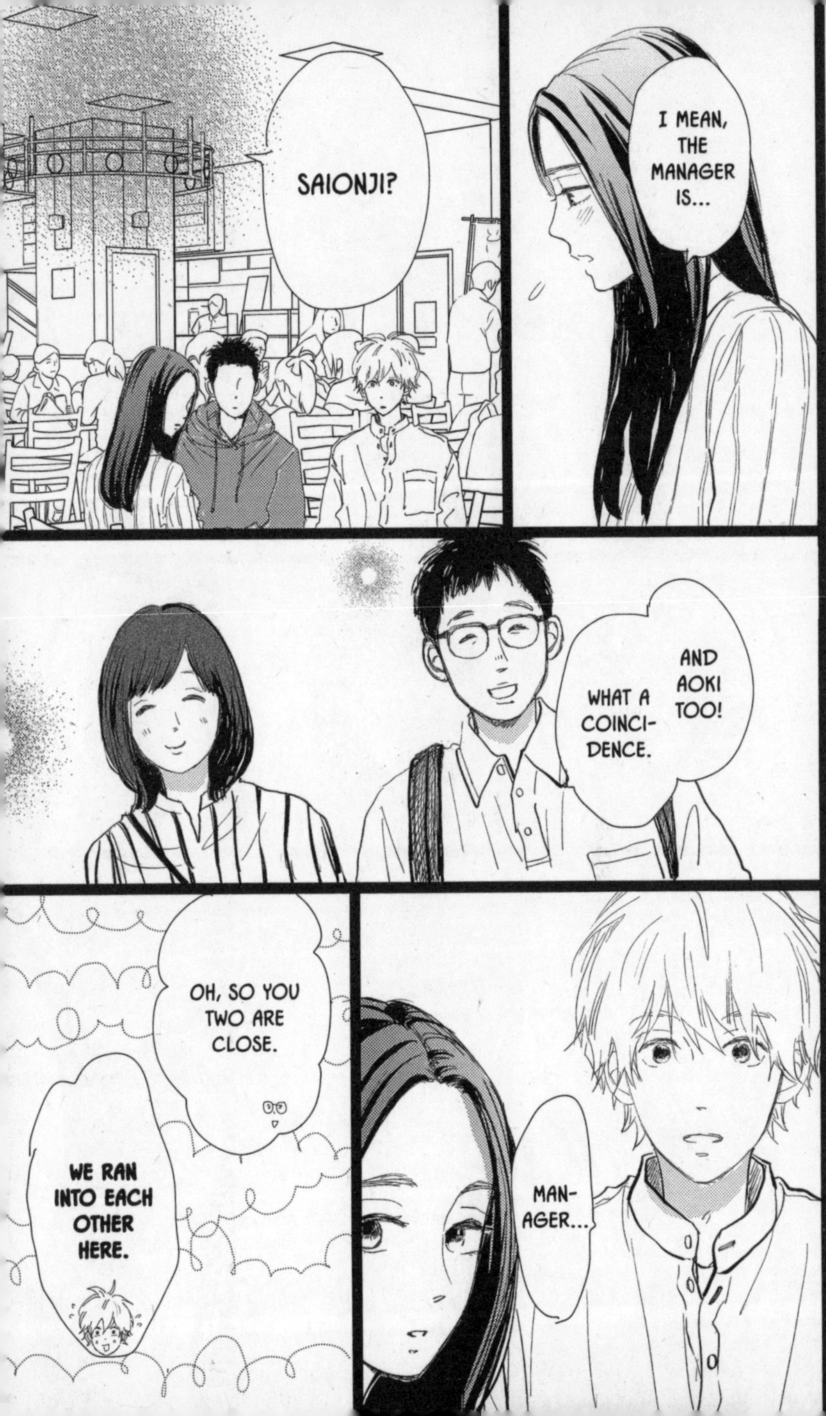
I MEAN, THE MANAGER IS...
SAIONJI?
AND AOKI TOO!
WHAT A COINCI-DENCE.
MAN-AGER...
OH, SO YOU TWO ARE CLOSE.
WE RAN INTO EACH OTHER HERE.

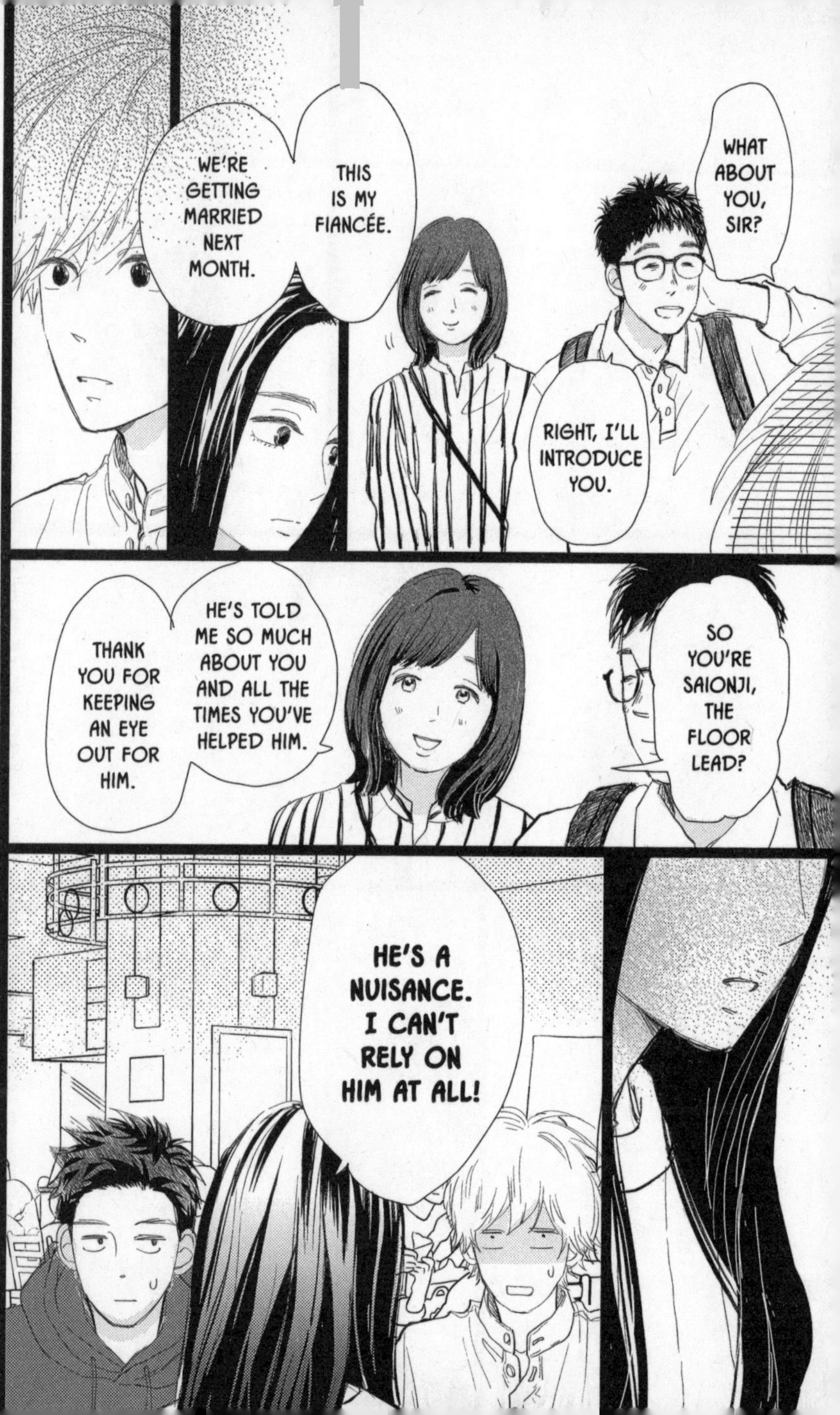
WHAT ABOUT YOU, SIR?
RIGHT, I'LL INTRODUCE YOU.
THIS IS MY FIANCÉE.
WE'RE GETTING MARRIED NEXT MONTH.
SO YOU'RE SAIONJI, THE FLOOR LEAD?
HE'S TOLD ME SO MUCH ABOUT YOU AND ALL THE TIMES YOU'VE HELPED HIM.
THANK YOU FOR KEEPING AN EYE OUT FOR HIM.
HE'S A NUISANCE. I CAN'T RELY ON HIM AT ALL!

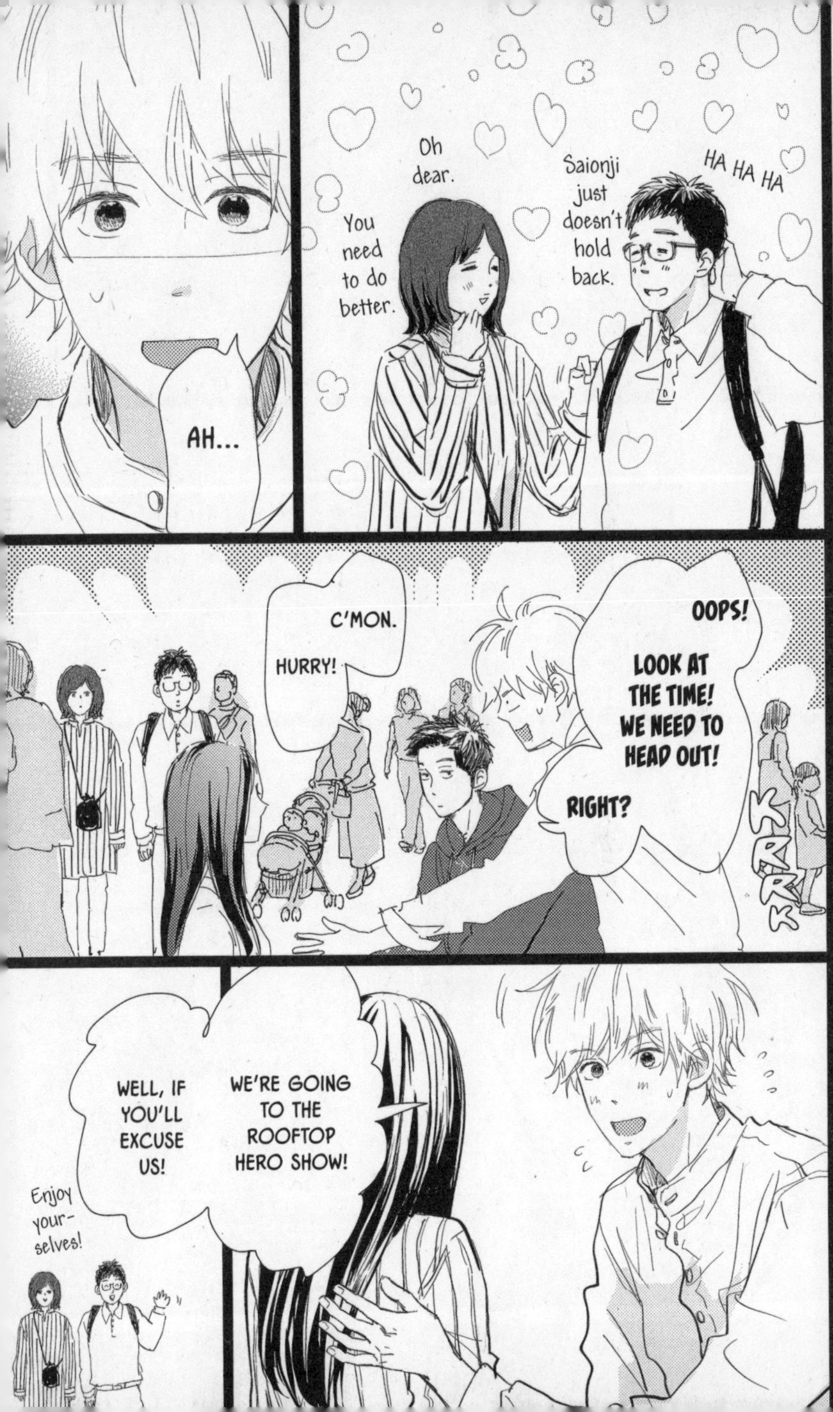

HA HA HA
Saionji just doesn't hold back.
Oh dear.
You need to do better.
AH...
OOPS!
LOOK AT THE TIME! WE NEED TO HEAD OUT!
RIGHT?
KRRK
C'MON.
HURRY!
WE'RE GOING TO THE ROOFTOP HERO SHOW!
WELL, IF YOU'LL EXCUSE US!
Enjoy yourselves!

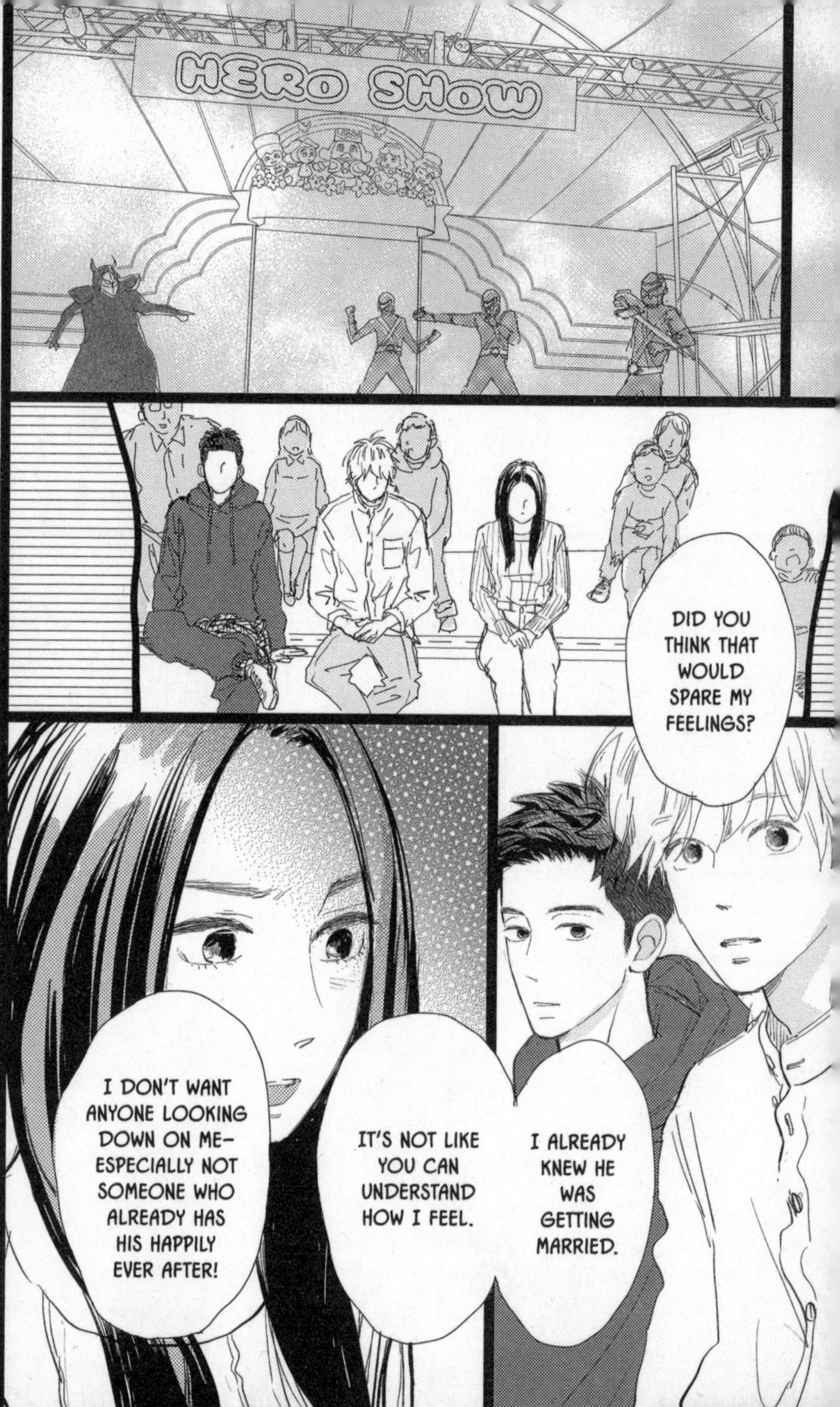
HERO SHOW
DID YOU THINK THAT WOULD SPARE MY FEELINGS?
I ALREADY KNEW HE WAS GETTING MARRIED.
IT'S NOT LIKE YOU CAN UNDERSTAND HOW I FEEL.
I DON'T WANT ANYONE LOOKING DOWN ON ME—ESPECIALLY NOT SOMEONE WHO ALREADY HAS HIS HAPPILY EVER AFTER!

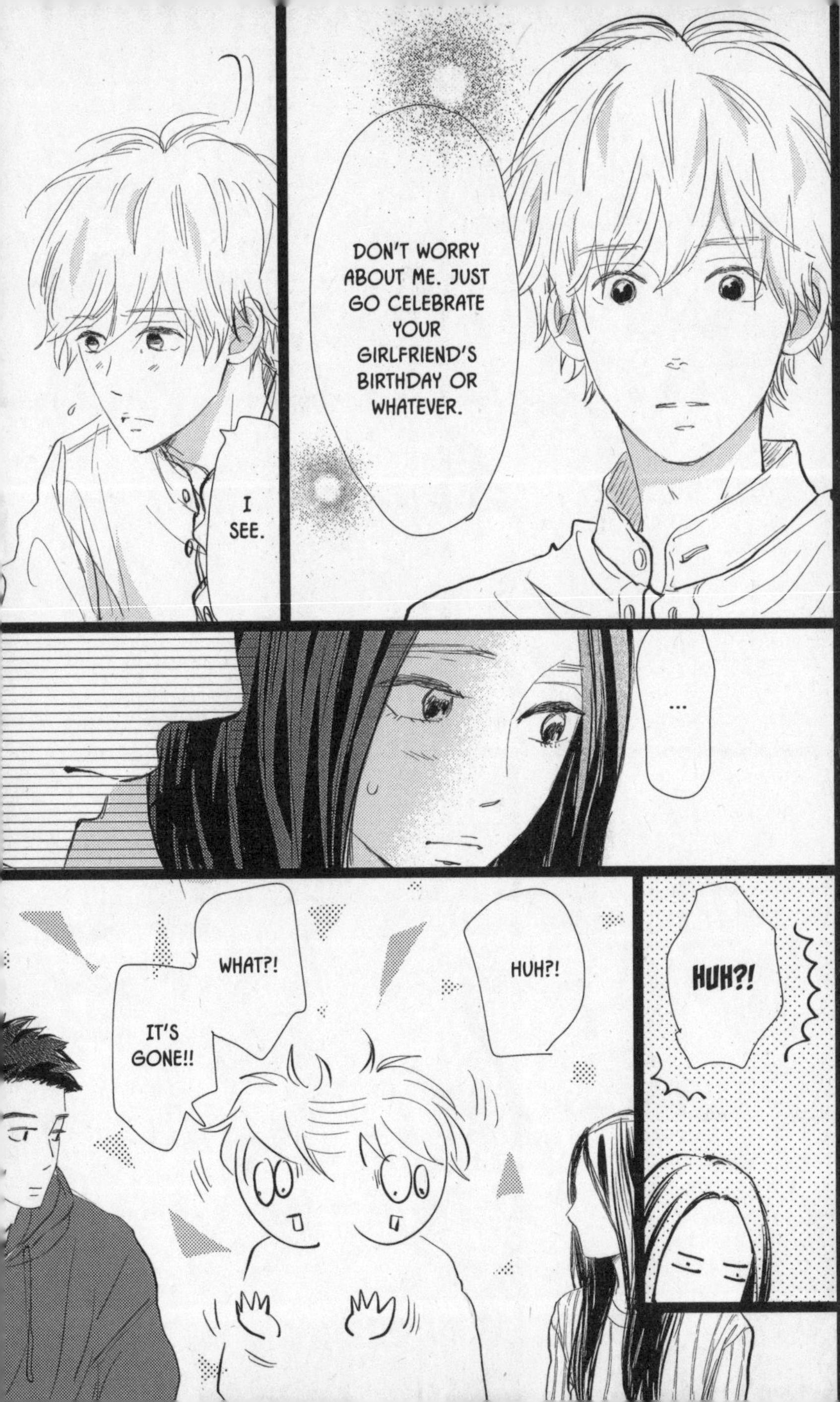
DON'T WORRY ABOUT ME. JUST GO CELEBRATE YOUR GIRLFRIEND'S BIRTHDAY OR WHATEVER.
I SEE.
...
HUH?!
HUH?!
WHAT?!
IT'S GONE!!

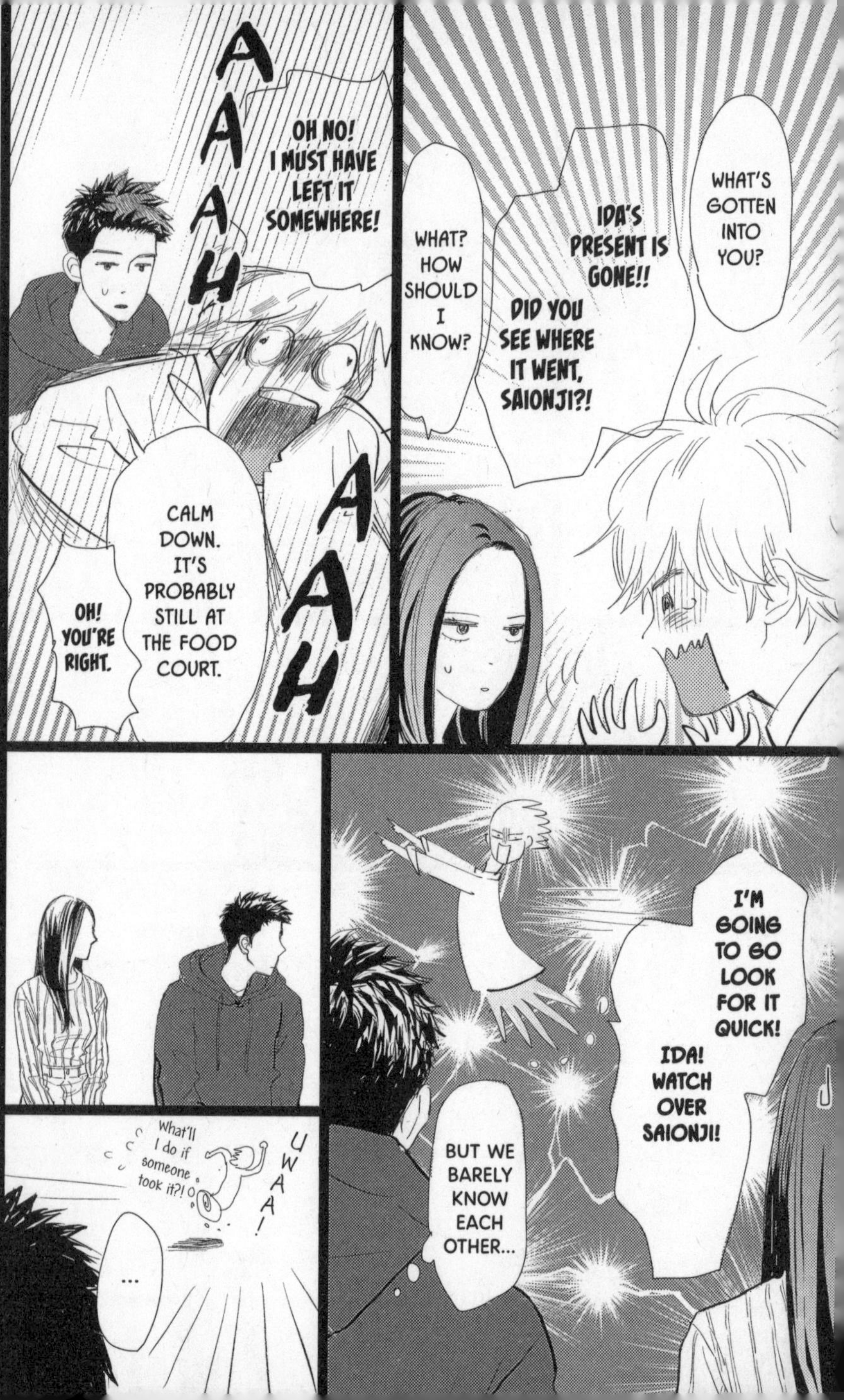
WHAT'S GOTTEN INTO YOU?
IDA'S PRESENT IS GONE!!
DID YOU SEE WHERE IT WENT, SAIONJI?!
WHAT? HOW SHOULD I KNOW?
AAAH
OH NO! I MUST HAVE LEFT IT SOMEWHERE!
AAAH
CALM DOWN. IT'S PROBABLY STILL AT THE FOOD COURT.
OH! YOU'RE RIGHT.
I'M GOING TO GO LOOK FOR IT QUICK!
IDA! WATCH OVER SAIONJI!
BUT WE BARELY KNOW EACH OTHER...
UWAAA!
What'll I do if someone took it?!
...

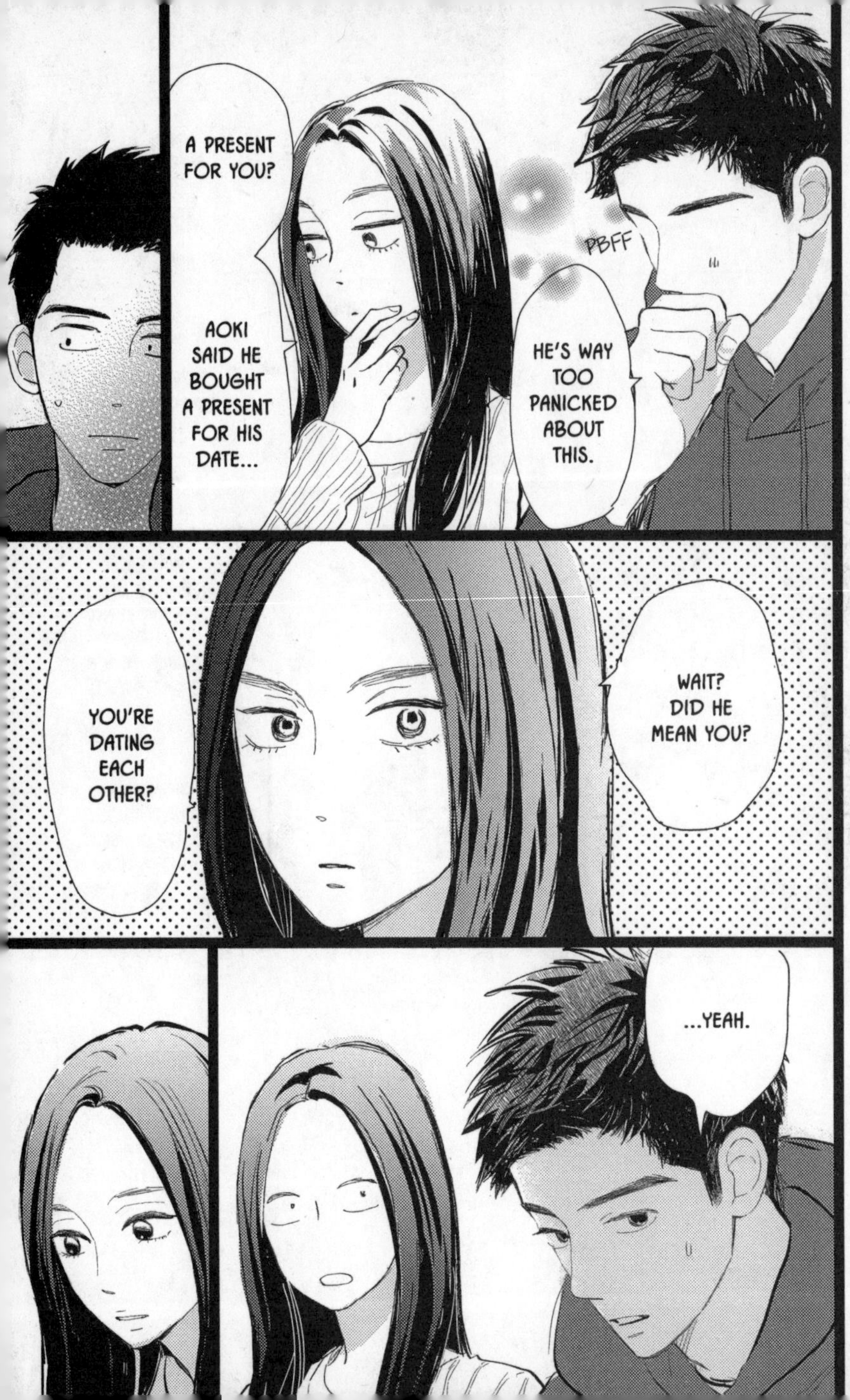
PBFF
HE'S WAY TOO PANICKED ABOUT THIS.
A PRESENT FOR YOU?
AOKI SAID HE BOUGHT A PRESENT FOR HIS DATE...
WAIT? DID HE MEAN YOU?
YOU'RE DATING EACH OTHER?
...YEAH.

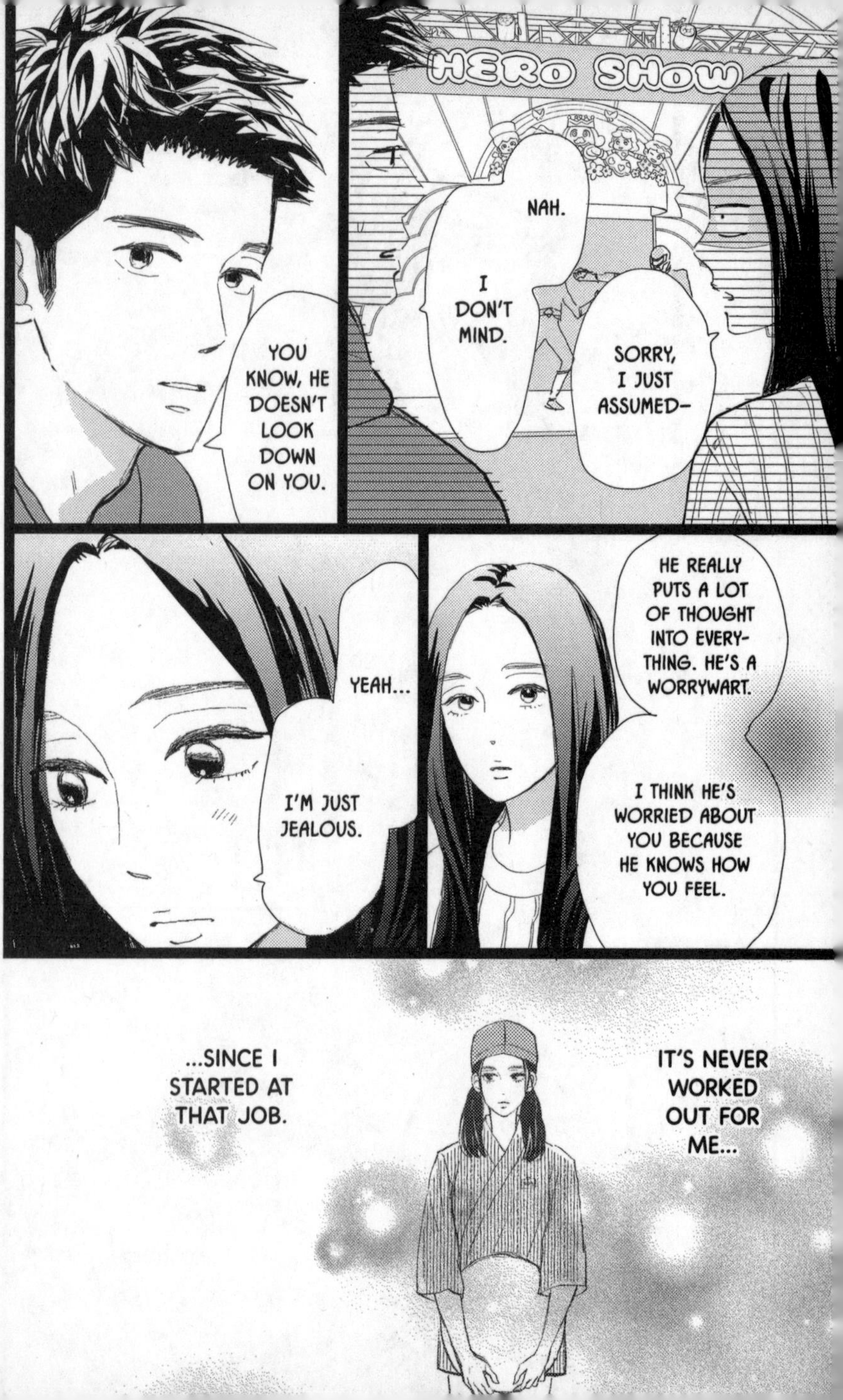
HERO SHOW
SORRY, I JUST ASSUMED—
NAH. I DON'T MIND.
YOU KNOW, HE DOESN'T LOOK DOWN ON YOU.
HE REALLY PUTS A LOT OF THOUGHT INTO EVERY-THING. HE'S A WORRYWART.
I THINK HE'S WORRIED ABOUT YOU BECAUSE HE KNOWS HOW YOU FEEL.
YEAH...
I'M JUST JEALOUS.
IT'S NEVER WORKED OUT FOR ME...
...SINCE I STARTED AT THAT JOB.

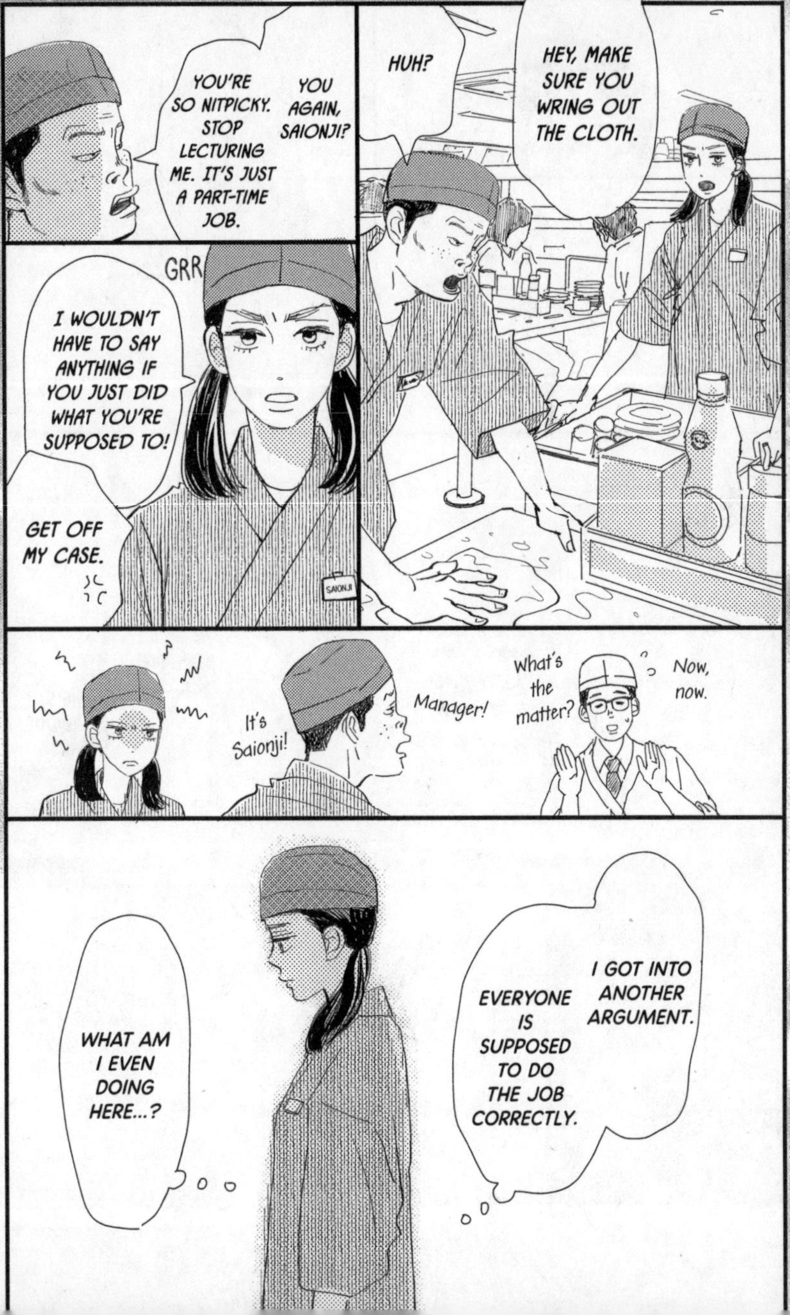
HEY, MAKE SURE YOU WRING OUT THE CLOTH.
HUH?
YOU AGAIN, SAIONJI?
YOU'RE SO NITPICKY. STOP LECTURING ME. IT'S JUST A PART-TIME JOB.
GRR
I WOULDN'T HAVE TO SAY ANYTHING IF YOU JUST DID WHAT YOU'RE SUPPOSED TO!
GET OFF MY CASE.
SAIONJI
Now, now.
What's the matter?
Manager!
It's Saionji!
I GOT INTO ANOTHER ARGUMENT.
EVERYONE IS SUPPOSED TO DO THE JOB CORRECTLY.
WHAT AM I EVEN DOING HERE...?

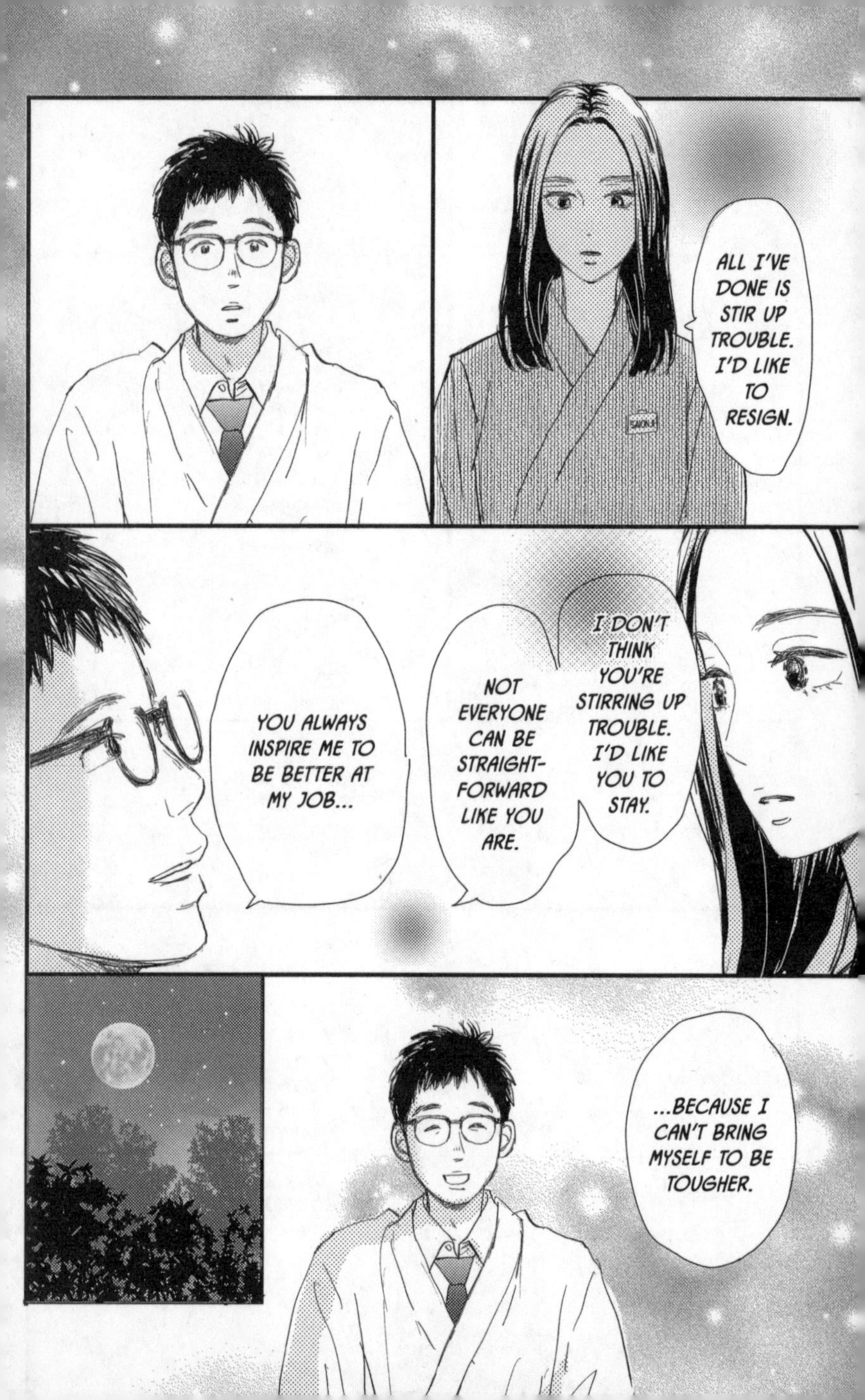
ALL I'VE DONE IS STIR UP TROUBLE. I'D LIKE TO RESIGN.
I DON'T THINK YOU'RE STIRRING UP TROUBLE. I'D LIKE YOU TO STAY.
NOT EVERYONE CAN BE STRAIGHT-FORWARD LIKE YOU ARE.
YOU ALWAYS INSPIRE ME TO BE BETTER AT MY JOB...
...BECAUSE I CAN'T BRING MYSELF TO BE TOUGHER.

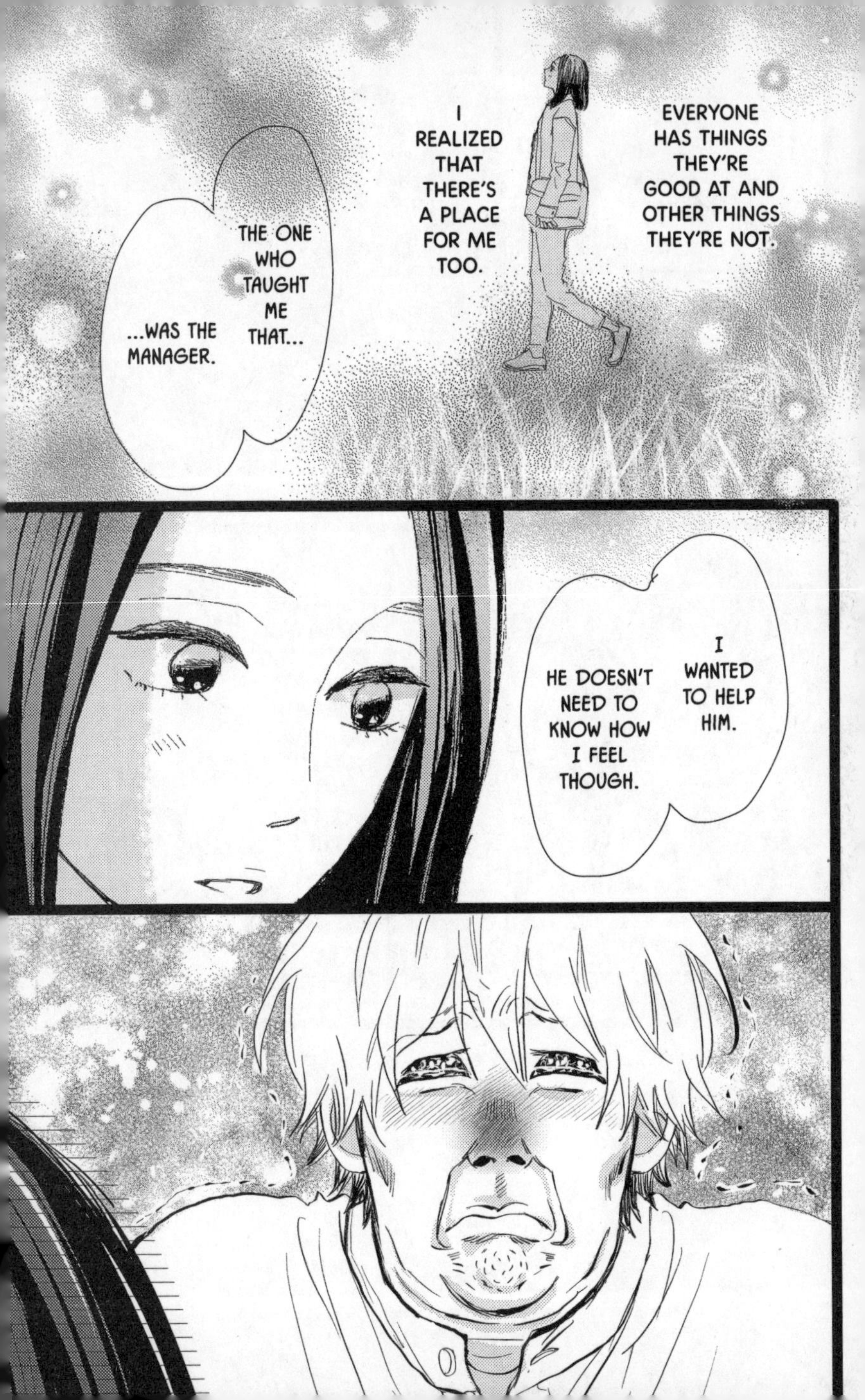
EVERYONE HAS THINGS THEY'RE GOOD AT AND OTHER THINGS THEY'RE NOT.
I REALIZED THAT THERE'S A PLACE FOR ME TOO.
THE ONE WHO TAUGHT ME THAT...
...WAS THE MANAGER.
I WANTED TO HELP HIM.
HE DOESN'T NEED TO KNOW HOW I FEEL THOUGH.

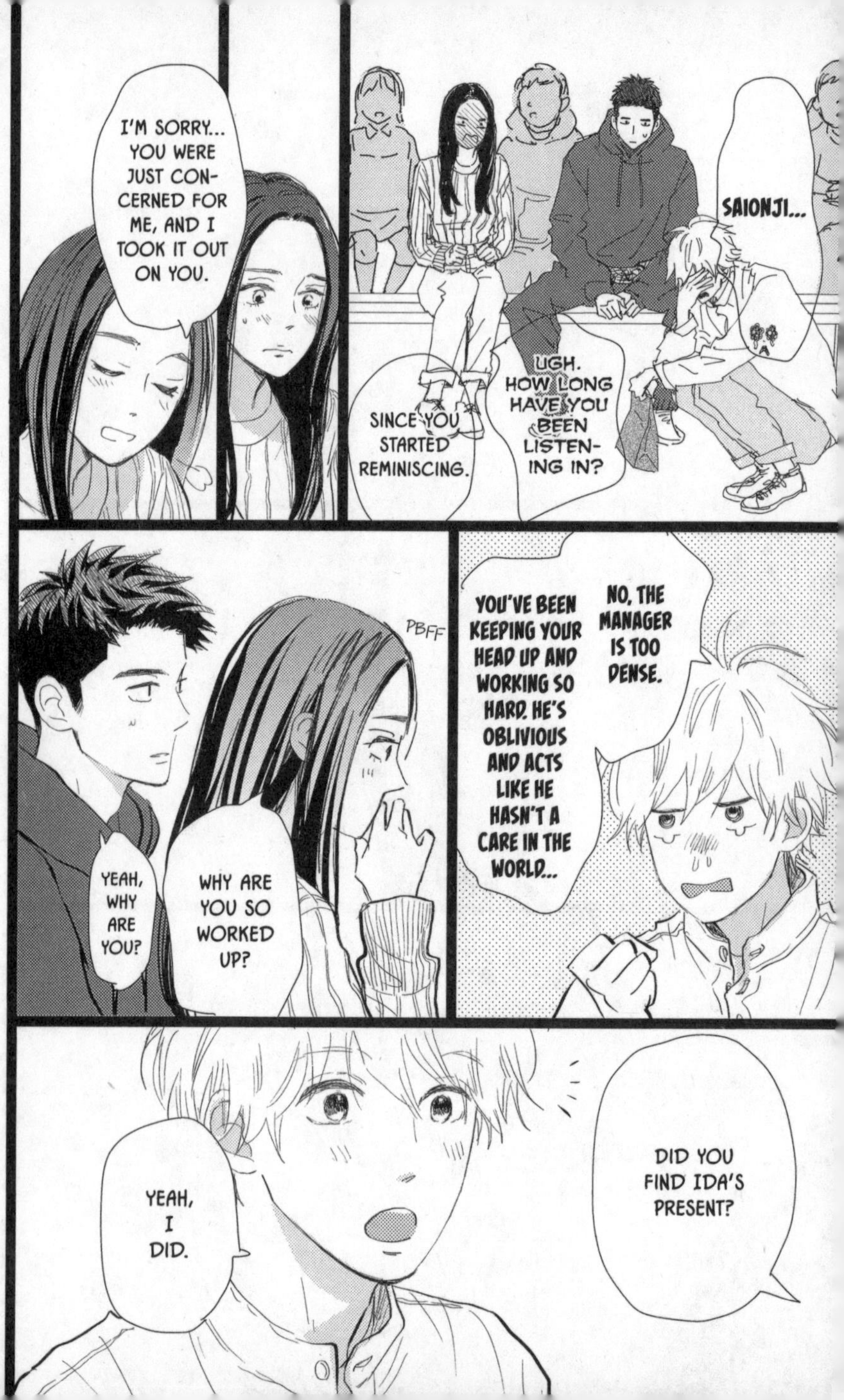
SAIONJI...
UGH. HOW LONG HAVE YOU BEEN LISTENING IN?
SINCE YOU STARTED REMINISCING.
I'M SORRY... YOU WERE JUST CONCERNED FOR ME, AND I TOOK IT OUT ON YOU.
NO, THE MANAGER IS TOO DENSE.
YOU'VE BEEN KEEPING YOUR HEAD UP AND WORKING SO HARD. HE'S OBLIVIOUS AND ACTS LIKE HE HASN'T A CARE IN THE WORLD...
PBFF
WHY ARE YOU SO WORKED UP?
YEAH, WHY ARE YOU?
DID YOU FIND IDA'S PRESENT?
YEAH, I DID.

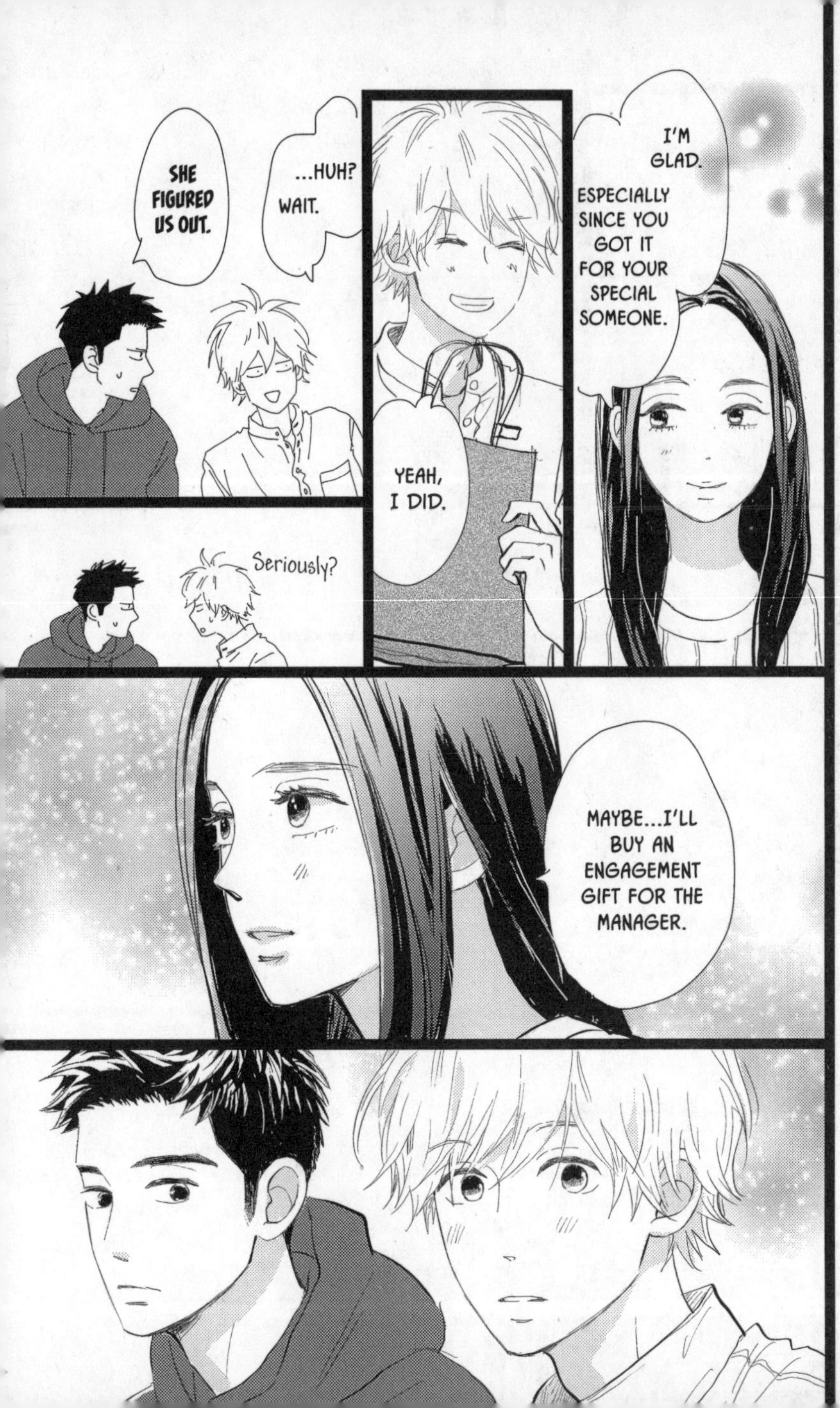
I'M GLAD.
ESPECIALLY SINCE YOU GOT IT FOR YOUR SPECIAL SOMEONE.
YEAH, I DID.
...HUH? WAIT.
SHE FIGURED US OUT.
Seriously?
MAYBE...I'LL BUY AN ENGAGEMENT GIFT FOR THE MANAGER.

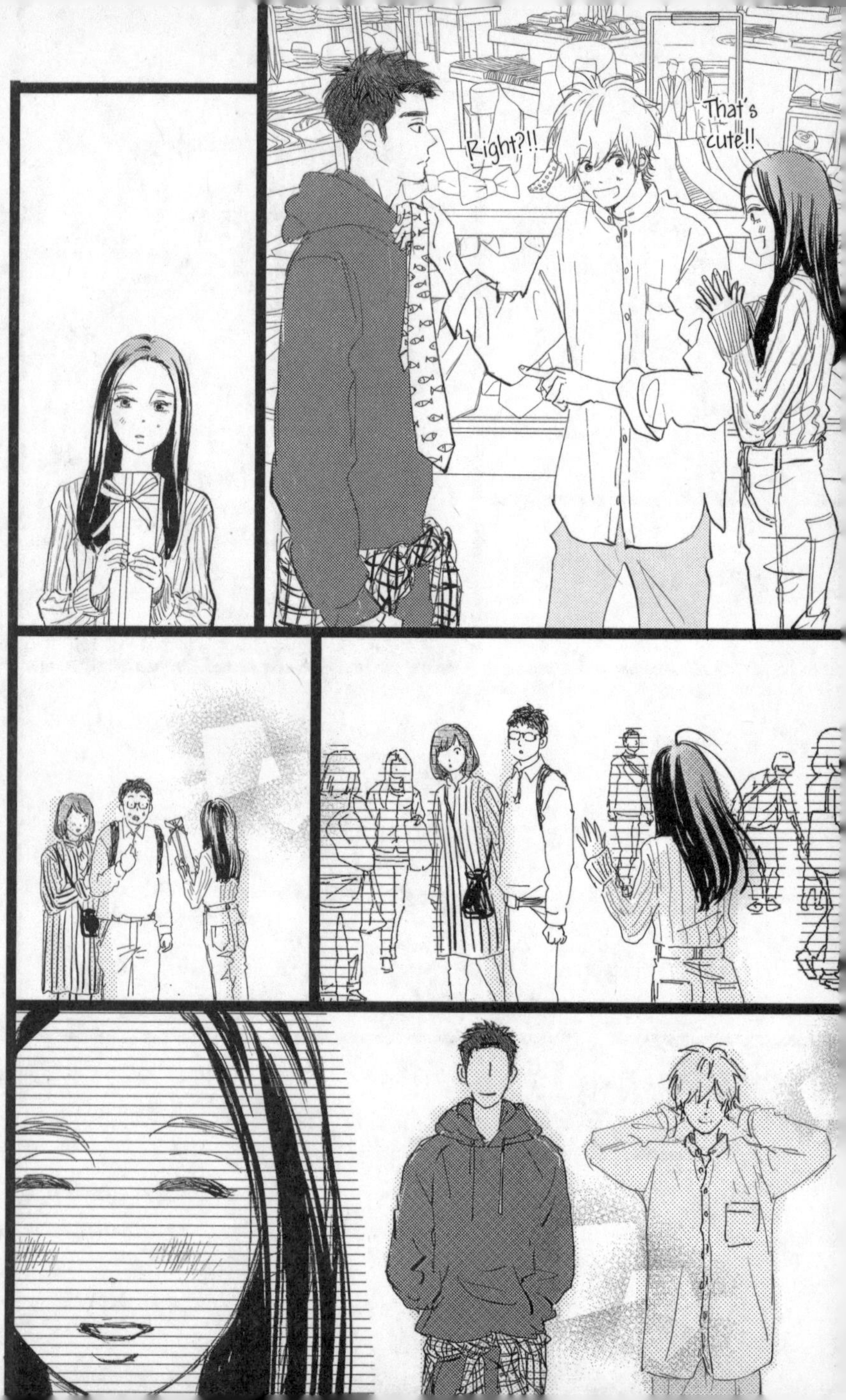
That's cute!!
Right?!!

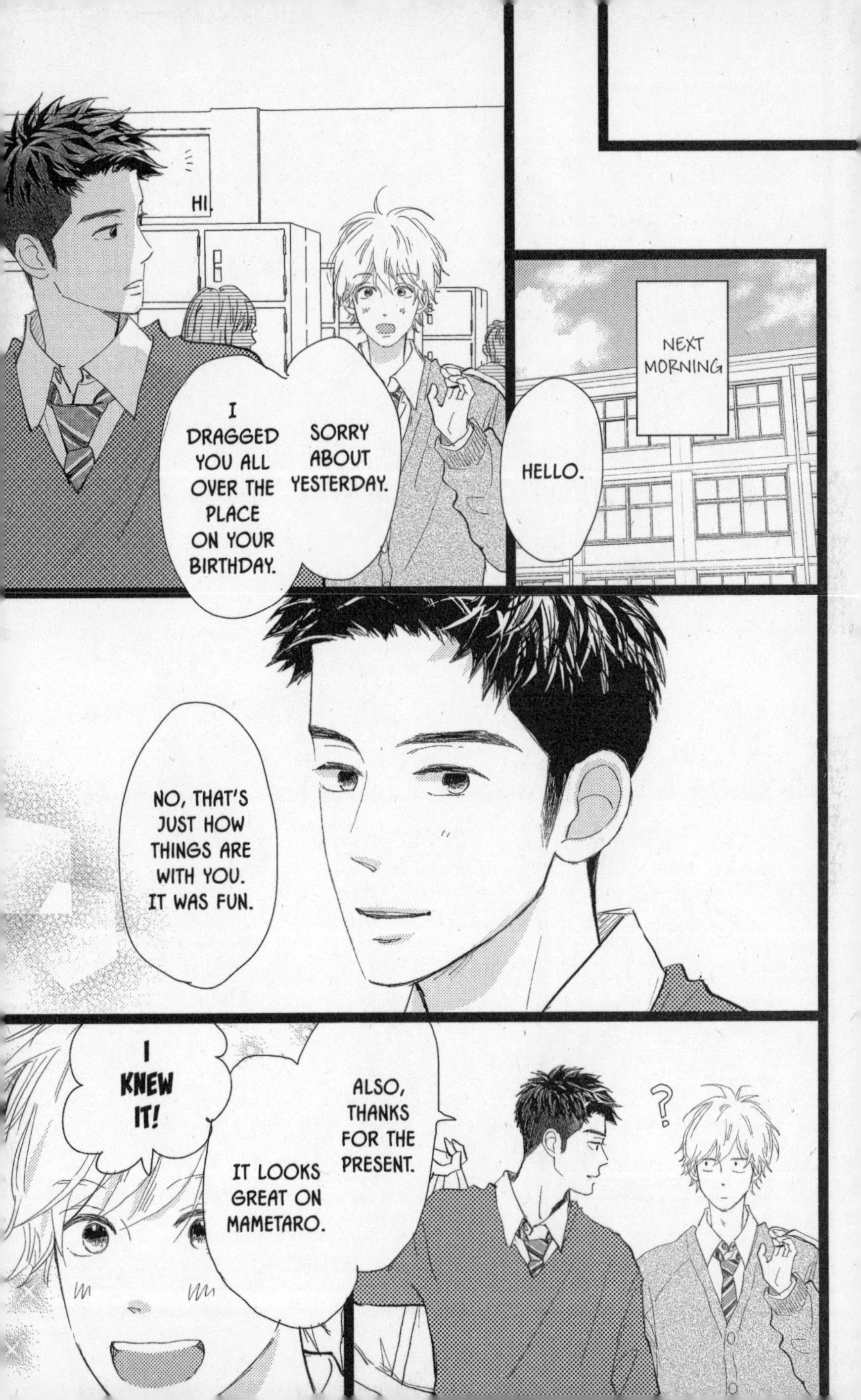
NEXT MORNING
HELLO.
HI.
SORRY ABOUT YESTERDAY.
I DRAGGED YOU ALL OVER THE PLACE ON YOUR BIRTHDAY.
NO, THAT'S JUST HOW THINGS ARE WITH YOU. IT WAS FUN.
ALSO, THANKS FOR THE PRESENT.
IT LOOKS GREAT ON MAMETARO.
I KNEW IT!

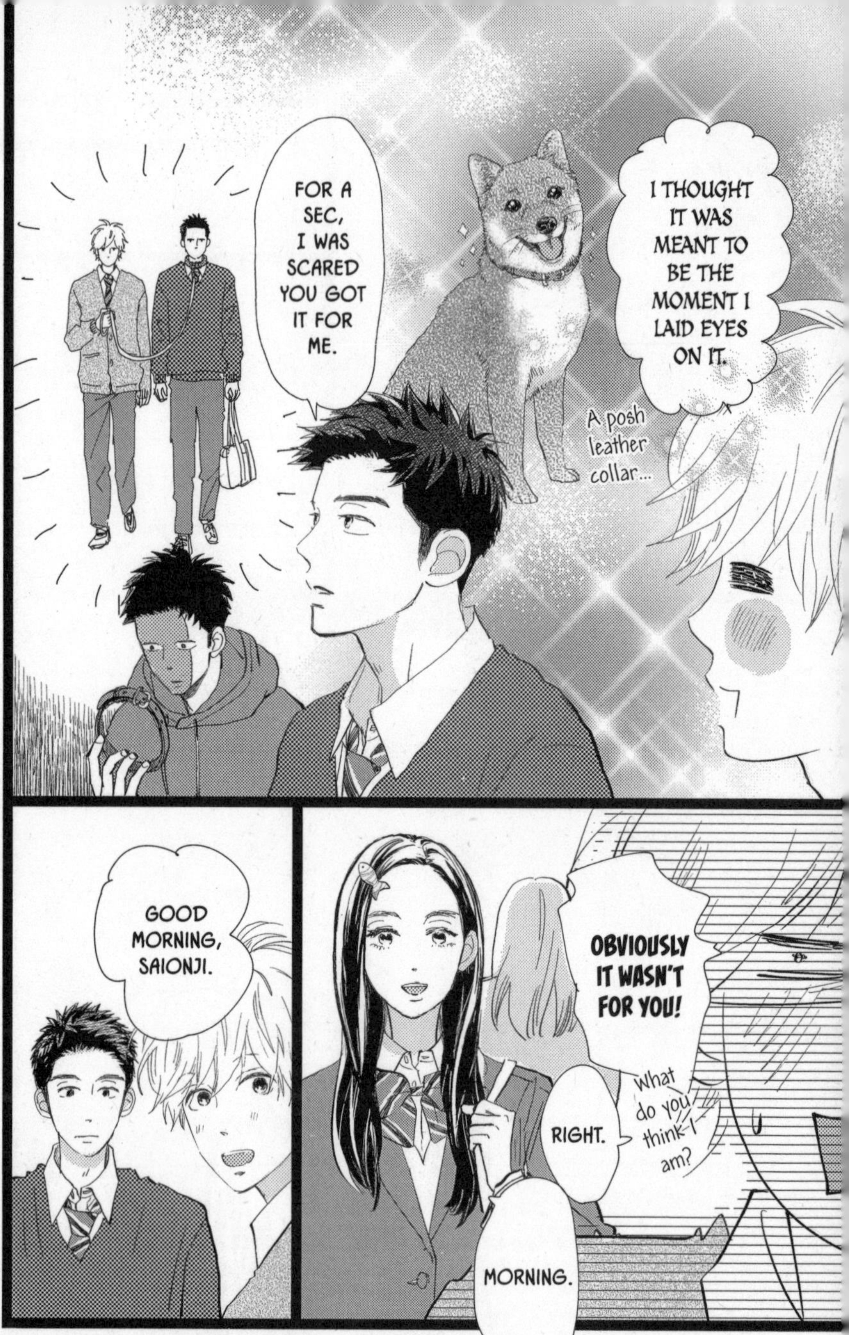
I THOUGHT IT WAS MEANT TO BE THE MOMENT I LAID EYES ON IT.
A posh leather collar...
FOR A SEC, I WAS SCARED YOU GOT IT FOR ME.
OBVIOUSLY IT WASN'T FOR YOU!
What do you think I am?
RIGHT.
MORNING.
GOOD MORNING, SAIONJI.

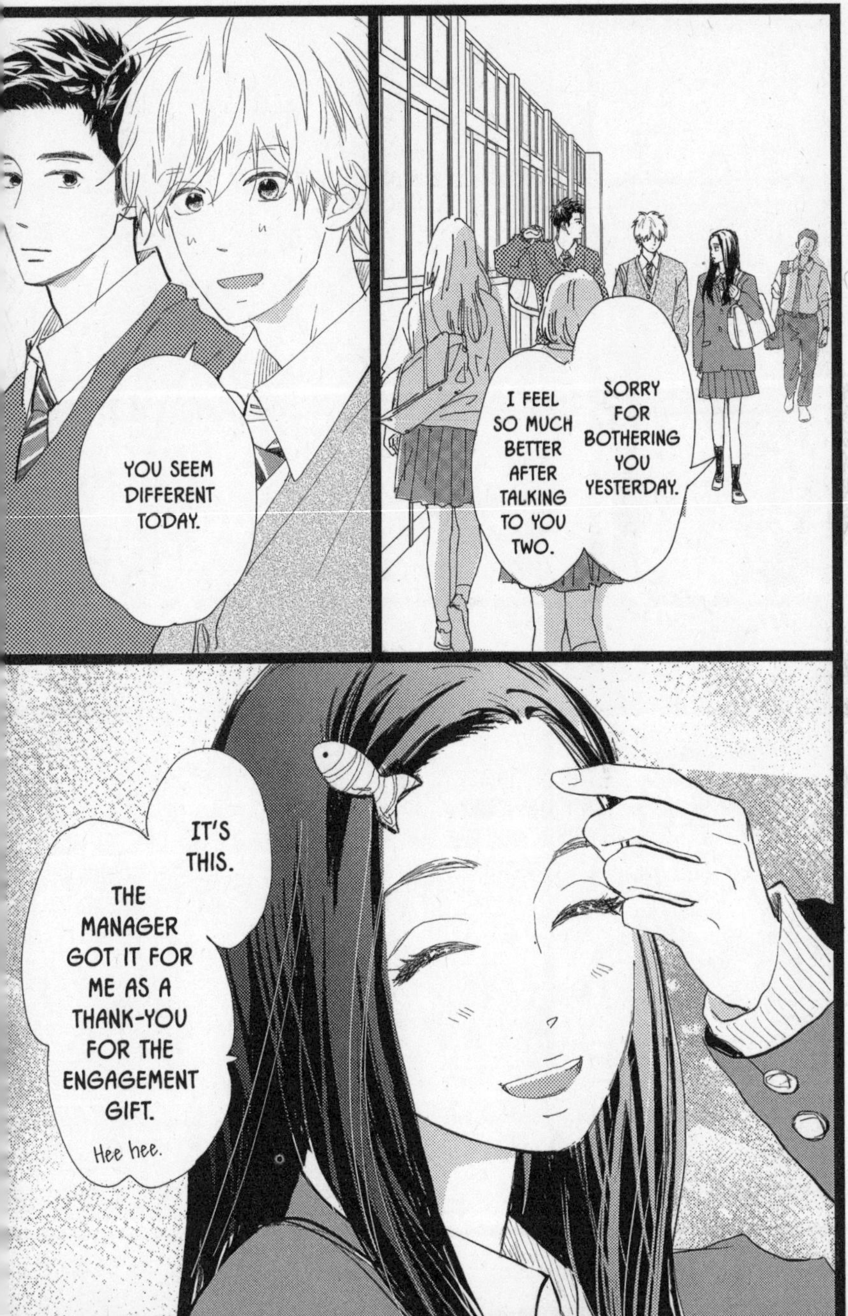
SORRY FOR BOTHERING YOU YESTERDAY.
I FEEL SO MUCH BETTER AFTER TALKING TO YOU TWO.
YOU SEEM DIFFERENT TODAY.
IT'S THIS.
THE MANAGER GOT IT FOR ME AS A THANK-YOU FOR THE ENGAGEMENT GIFT.
Hee hee.

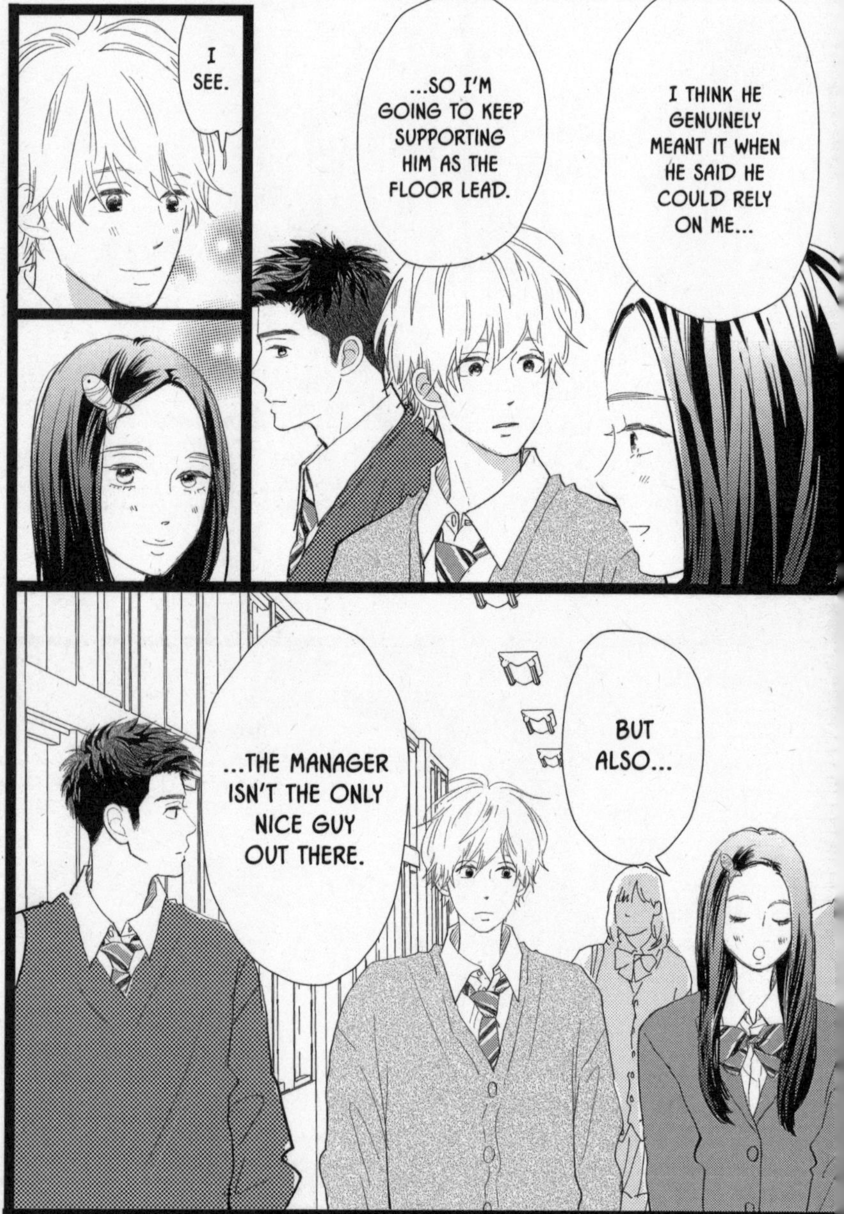
I THINK HE GENUINELY MEANT IT WHEN HE SAID HE COULD RELY ON ME...
...SO I'M GOING TO KEEP SUPPORTING HIM AS THE FLOOR LEAD.
I SEE.
BUT ALSO...
...THE MANAGER ISN'T THE ONLY NICE GUY OUT THERE.

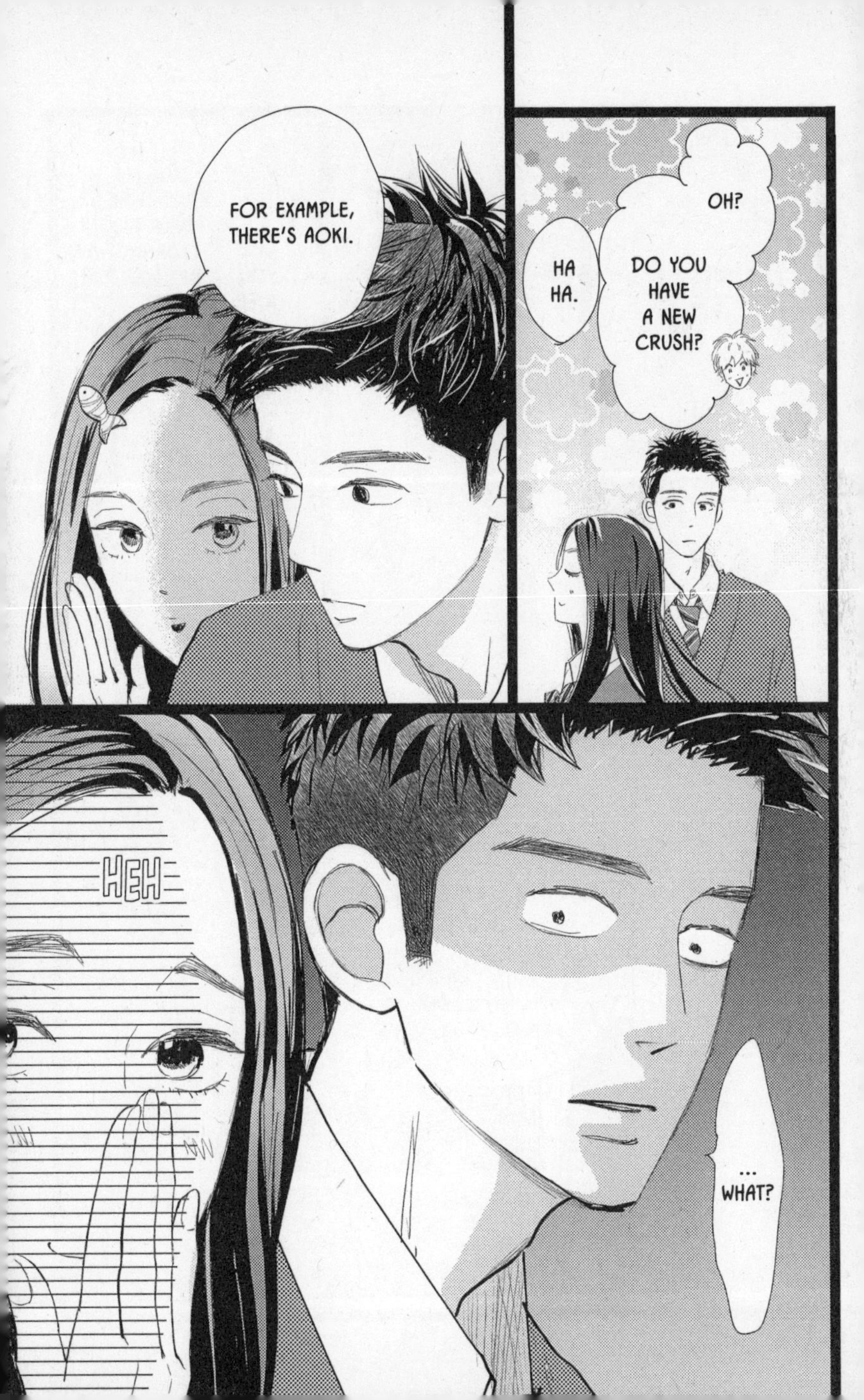
OH? DO YOU HAVE A NEW CRUSH?
HA HA.
FOR EXAMPLE, THERE'S AOKI.
... WHAT?
HEH

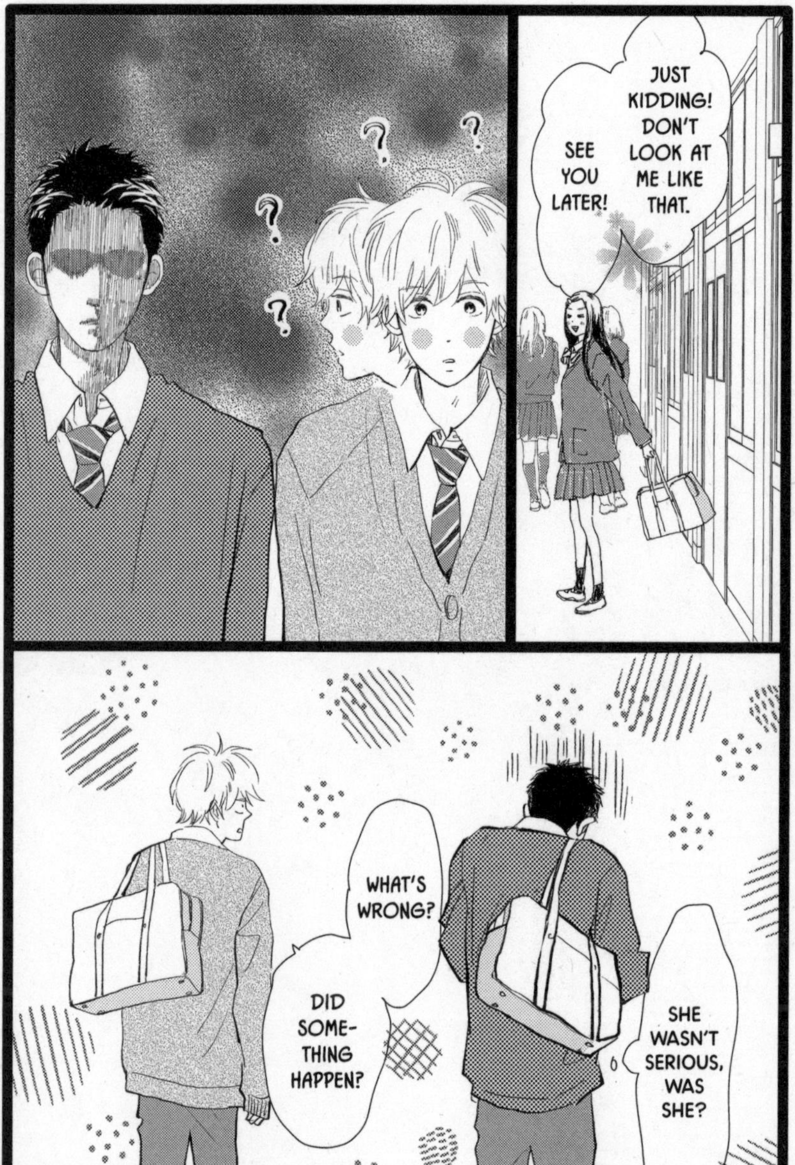
JUST KIDDING! DON'T LOOK AT ME LIKE THAT.
SEE YOU LATER!
SHE WASN'T SERIOUS, WAS SHE?
WHAT'S WRONG?
DID SOME-THING HAPPEN?

Chapter 23

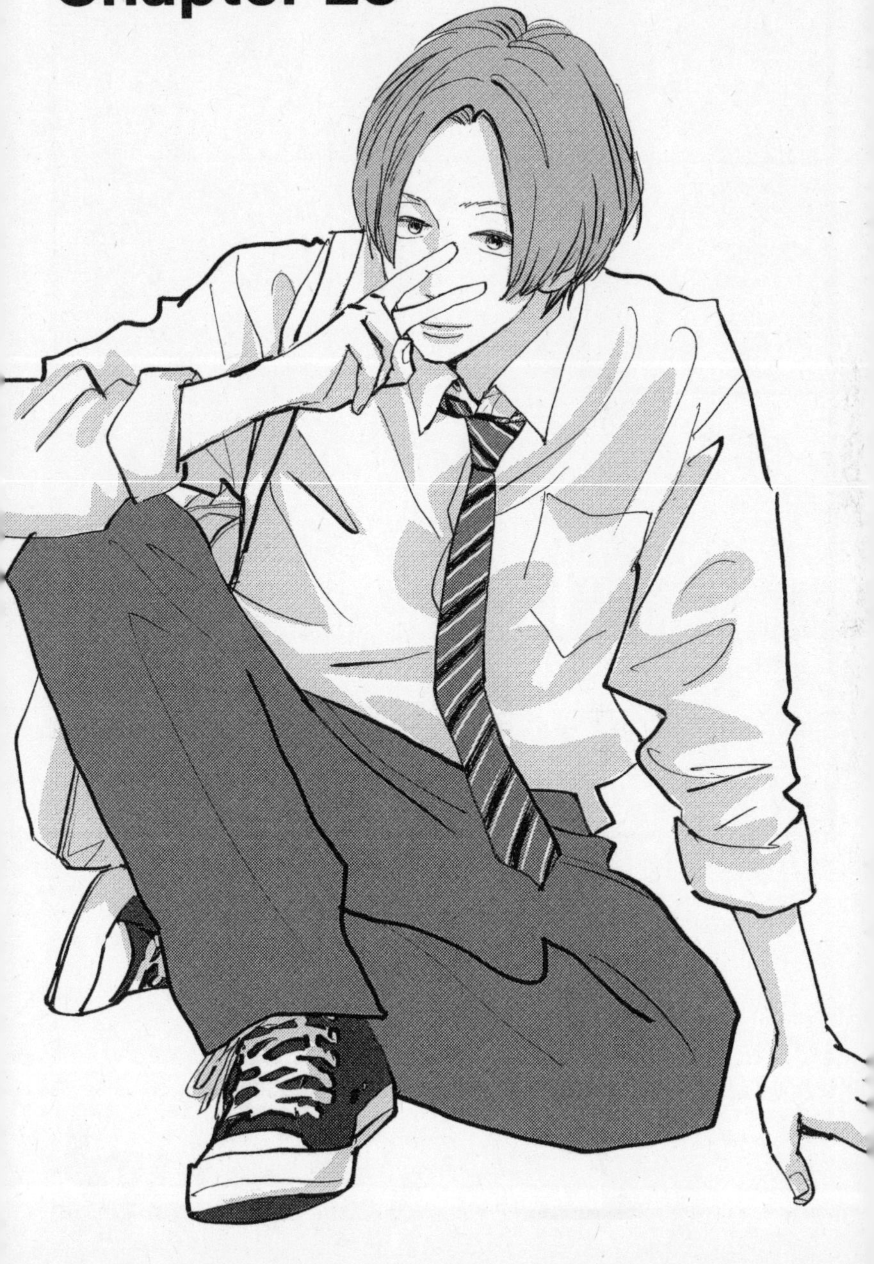

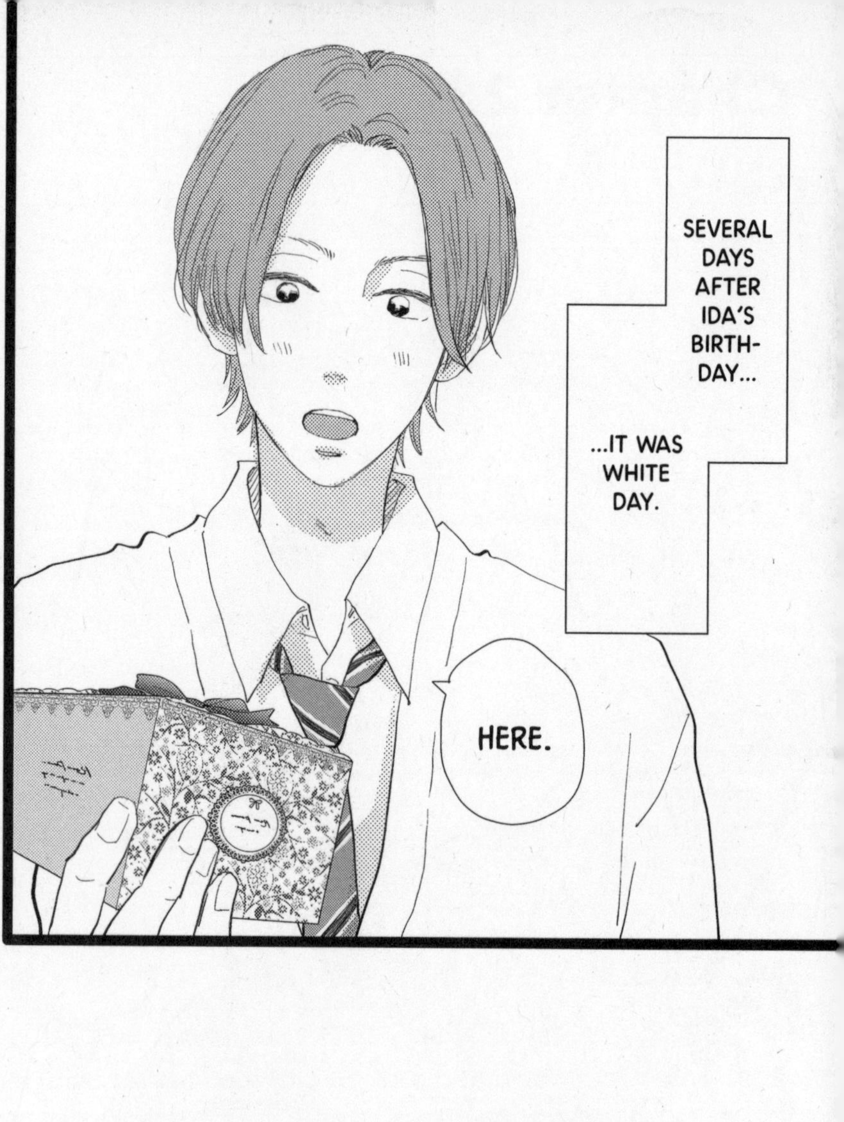
SEVERAL DAYS AFTER IDA'S BIRTH-DAY...
...IT WAS WHITE DAY.
HERE.

My Love Mix-Up!

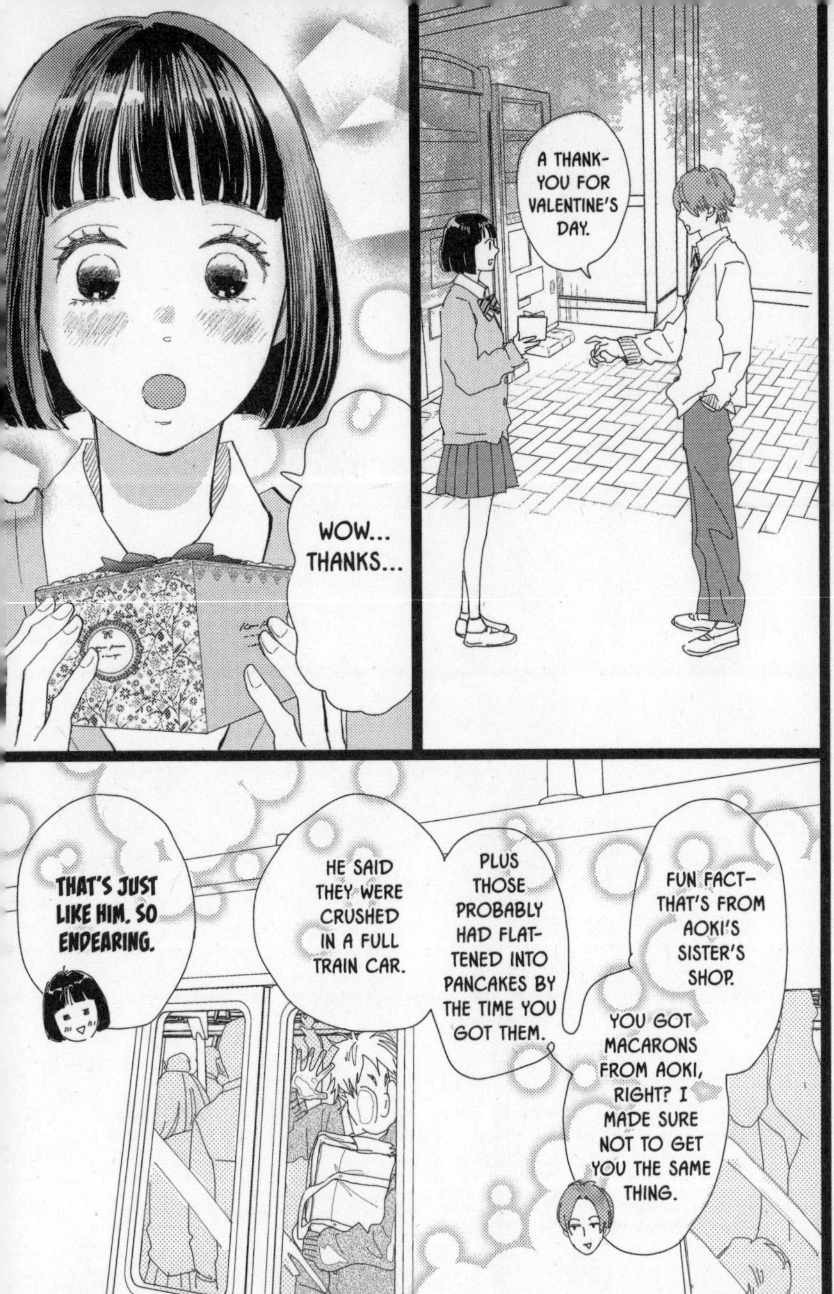
A THANK-YOU FOR VALENTINE'S DAY.
WOW... THANKS...
FUN FACT—THAT'S FROM AOKI'S SISTER'S SHOP.
YOU GOT MACARONS FROM AOKI, RIGHT? I MADE SURE NOT TO GET YOU THE SAME THING.
PLUS THOSE PROBABLY HAD FLATTENED INTO PANCAKES BY THE TIME YOU GOT THEM.
HE SAID THEY WERE CRUSHED IN A FULL TRAIN CAR.
THAT'S JUST LIKE HIM. SO ENDEARING.

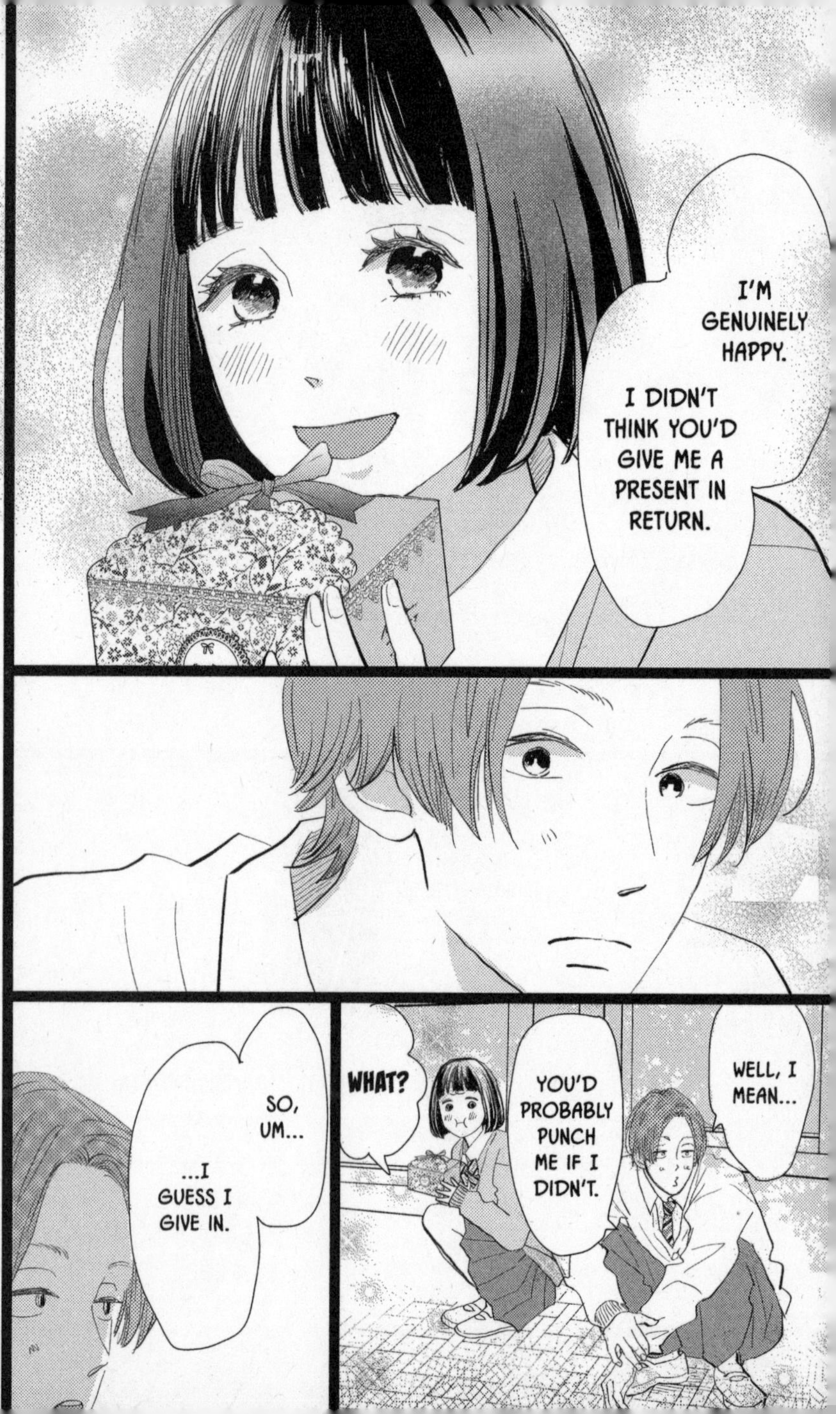
I'M GENUINELY HAPPY.
I DIDN'T THINK YOU'D GIVE ME A PRESENT IN RETURN.
WELL, I MEAN...
YOU'D PROBABLY PUNCH ME IF I DIDN'T.
WHAT?
SO, UM...
...I GUESS I GIVE IN.

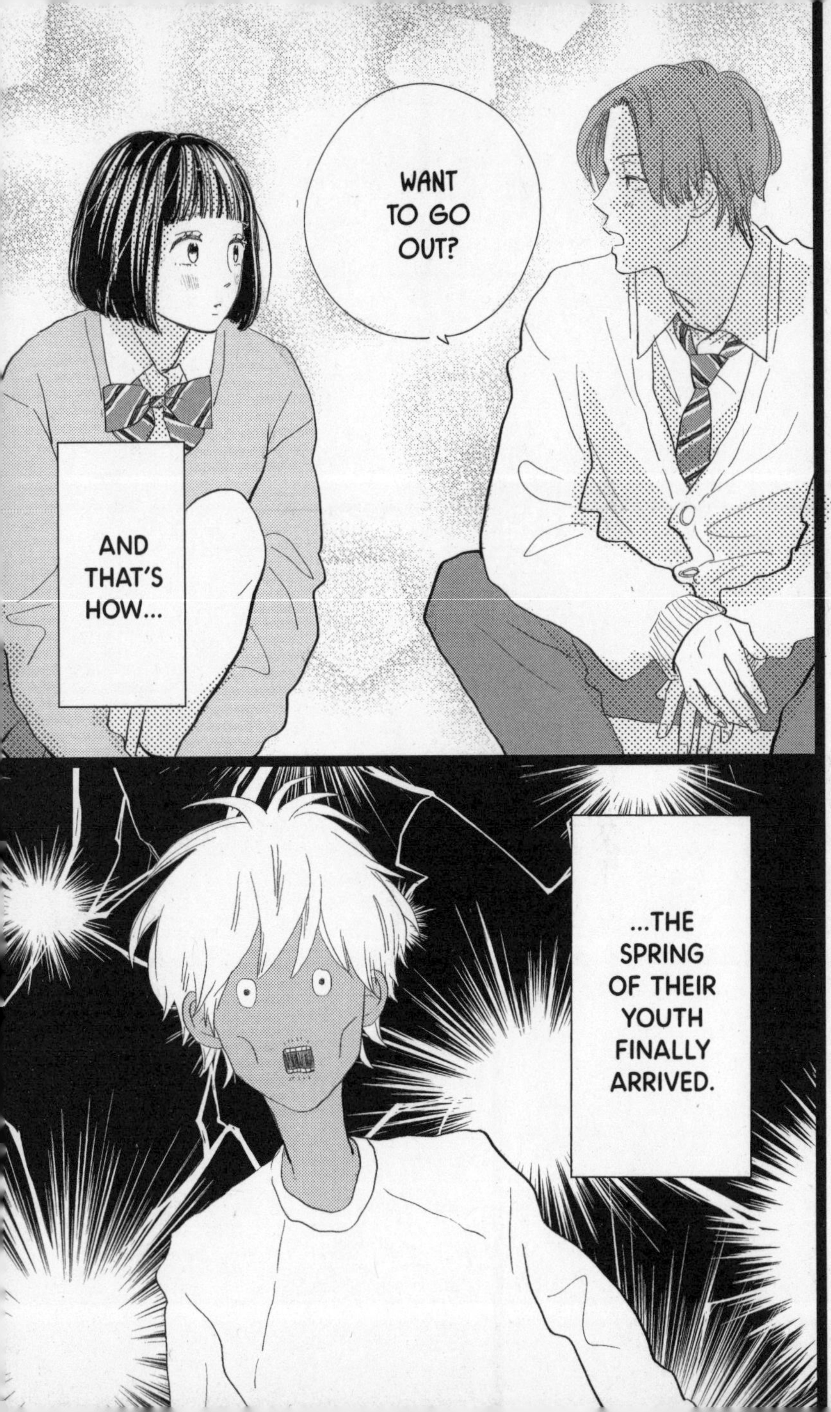
WANT TO GO OUT?
AND THAT'S HOW...
...THE SPRING OF THEIR YOUTH FINALLY ARRIVED.

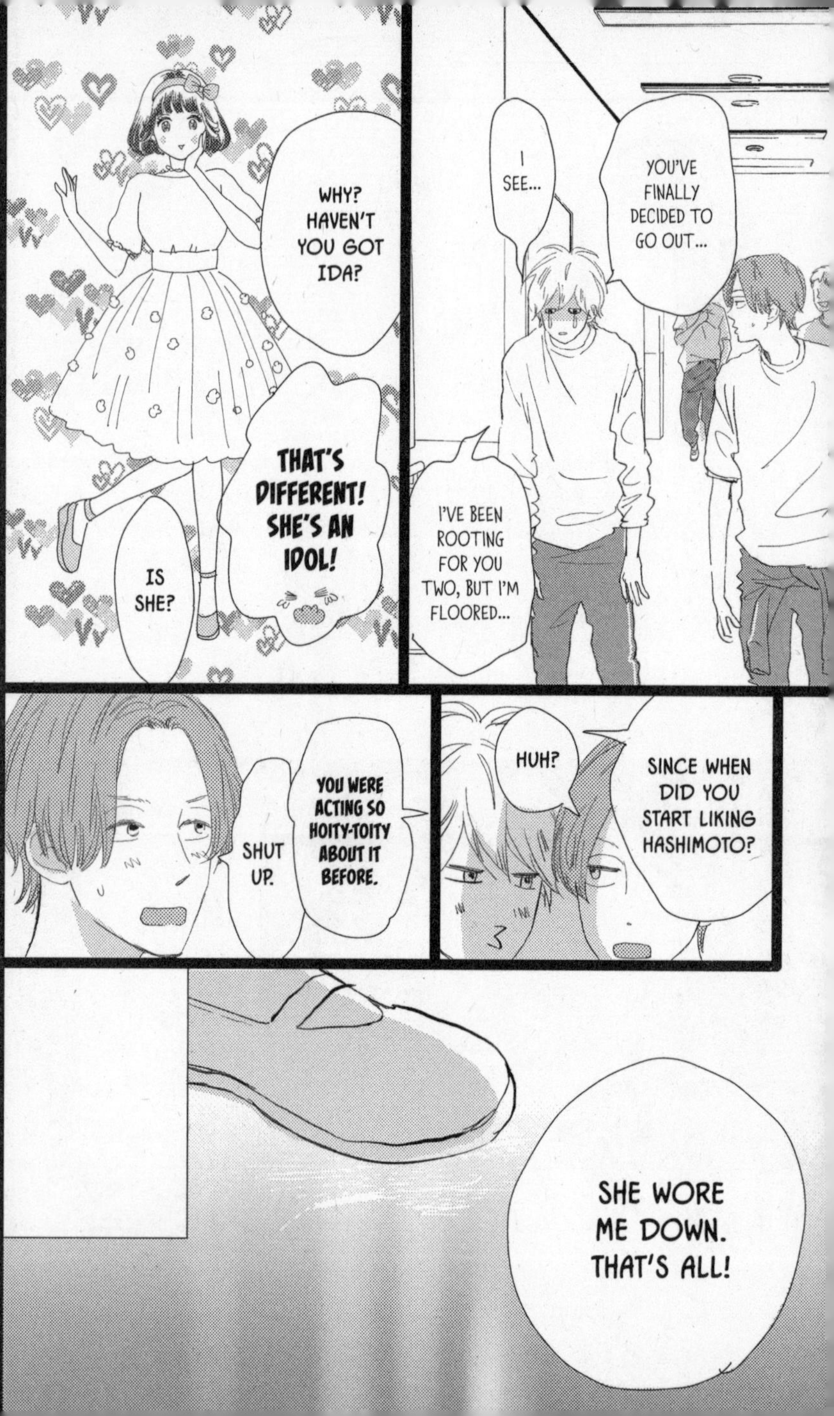
YOU'VE FINALLY DECIDED TO GO OUT...
I SEE...
I'VE BEEN ROOTING FOR YOU TWO, BUT I'M FLOORED...
WHY? HAVEN'T YOU GOT IDA?
THAT'S DIFFERENT! SHE'S AN IDOL!
IS SHE?
SINCE WHEN DID YOU START LIKING HASHIMOTO?
HUH?
YOU WERE ACTING SO HOITY-TOITY ABOUT IT BEFORE.
SHUT UP.
SHE WORE ME DOWN. THAT'S ALL!

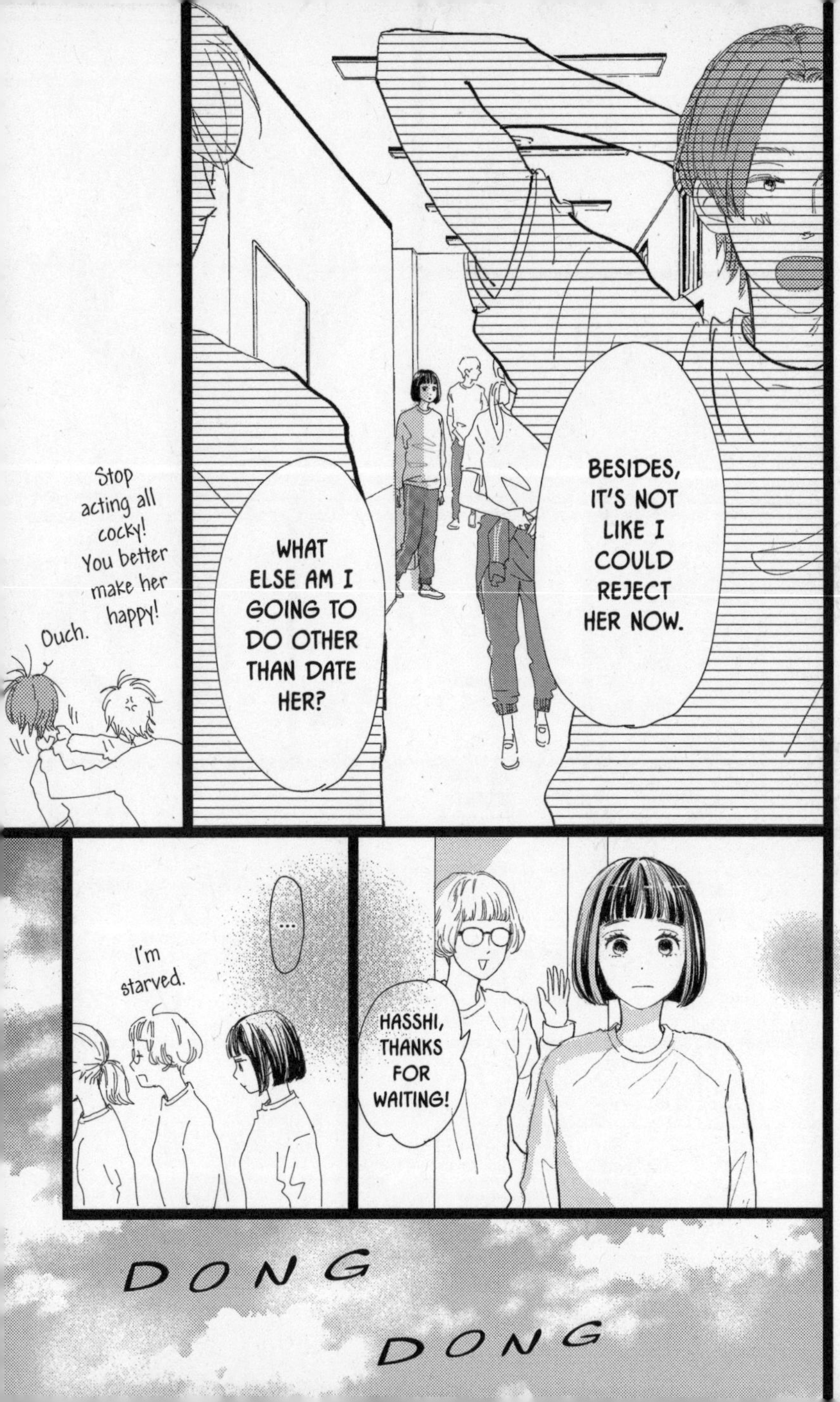
BESIDES, IT'S NOT LIKE I COULD REJECT HER NOW.
WHAT ELSE AM I GOING TO DO OTHER THAN DATE HER?
Stop acting all cocky! You better make her happy!
Ouch.
HASSHI, THANKS FOR WAITING!
...
I'm starved.
DONG
DONG

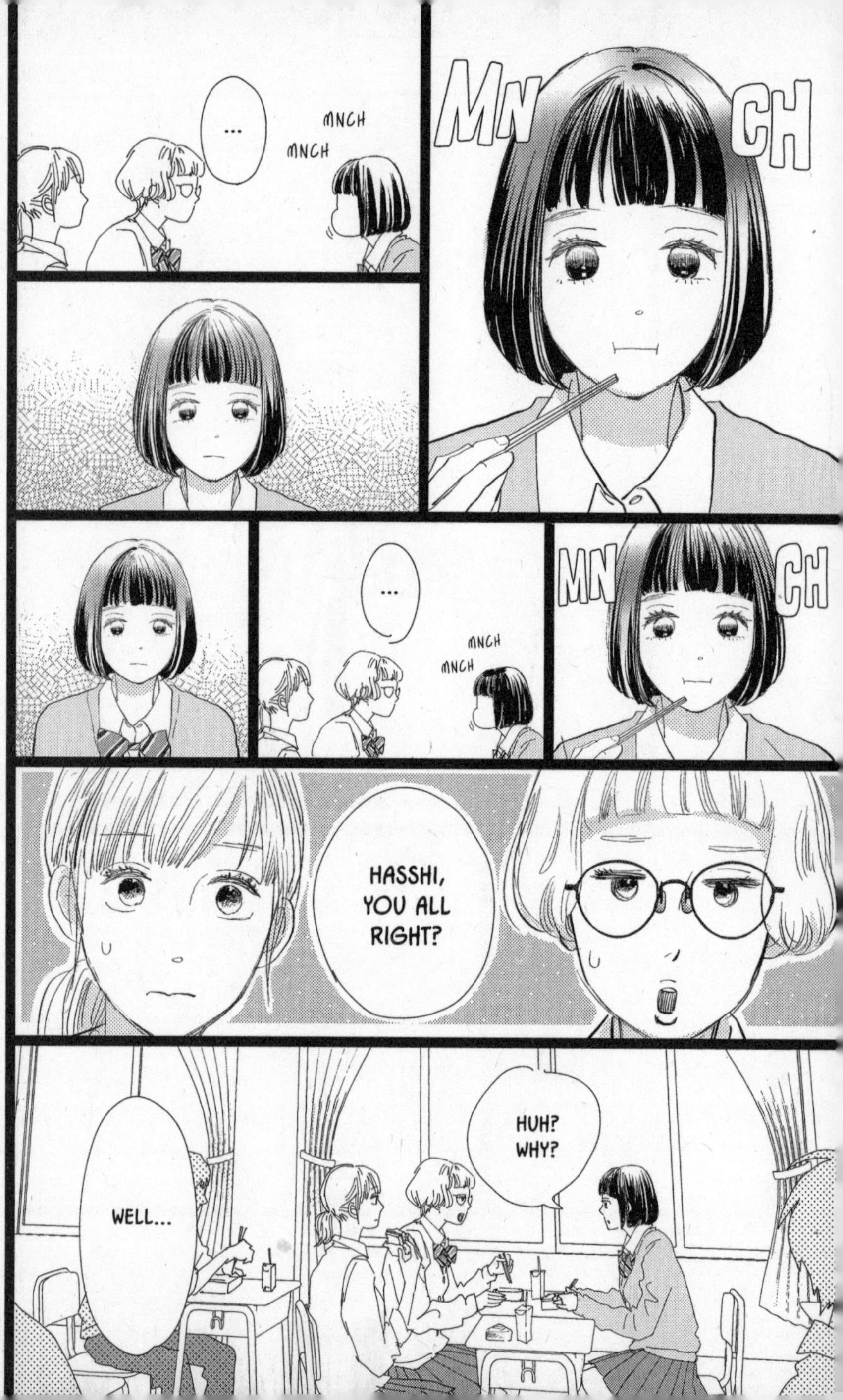
MN CH
...
MNCH
MNCH
MN CH
...
MNCH
MNCH
HASSHI, YOU ALL RIGHT?
HUH? WHY?
WELL...

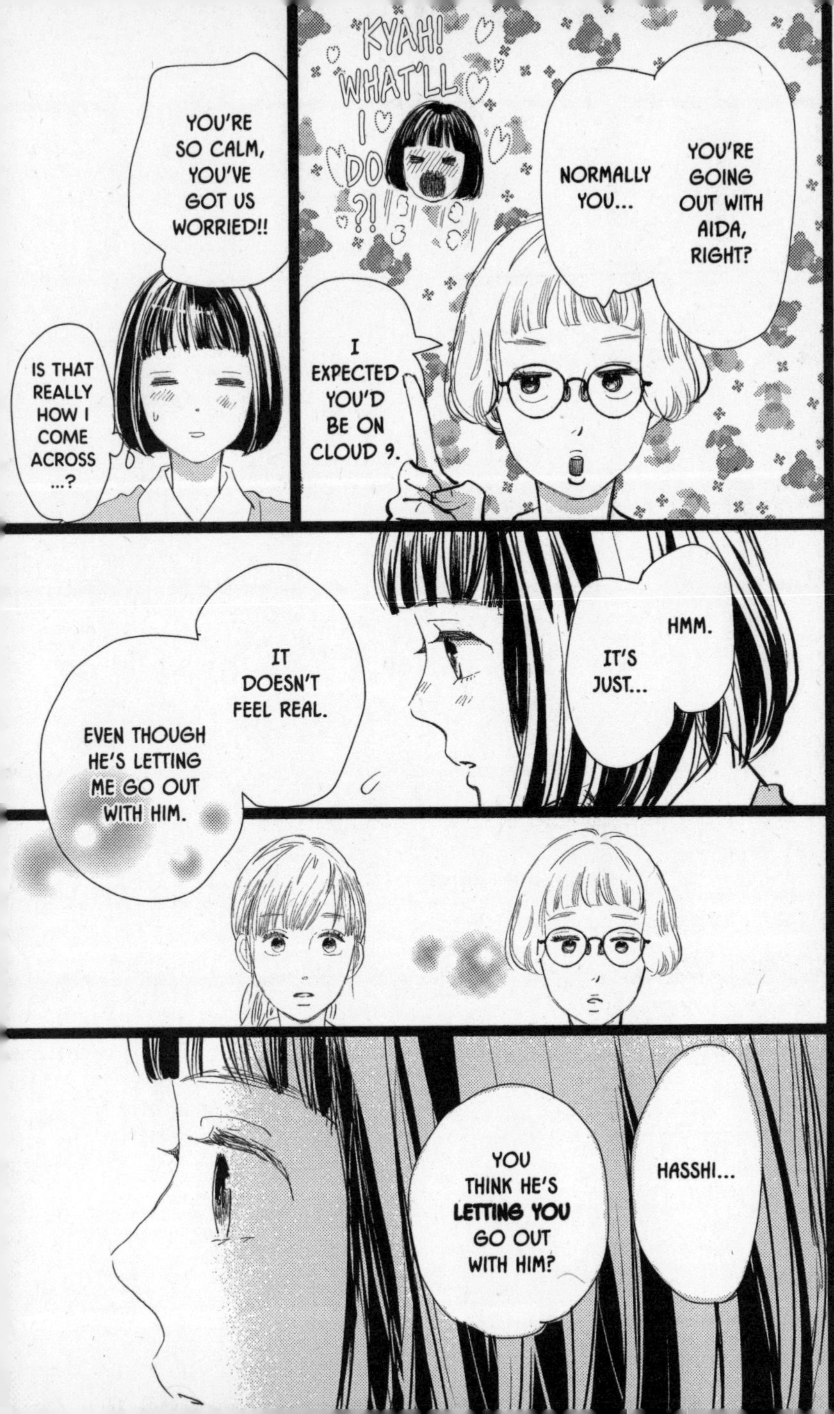
YOU'RE GOING OUT WITH AIDA, RIGHT?
NORMALLY YOU...
KYAH! WHAT'LL I DO?!
I EXPECTED YOU'D BE ON CLOUD 9.
YOU'RE SO CALM, YOU'VE GOT US WORRIED!!
IS THAT REALLY HOW I COME ACROSS...?
HMM.
IT'S JUST...
IT DOESN'T FEEL REAL.
EVEN THOUGH HE'S LETTING ME GO OUT WITH HIM.
HASSHI...
YOU THINK HE'S **LETTING YOU** GO OUT WITH HIM?

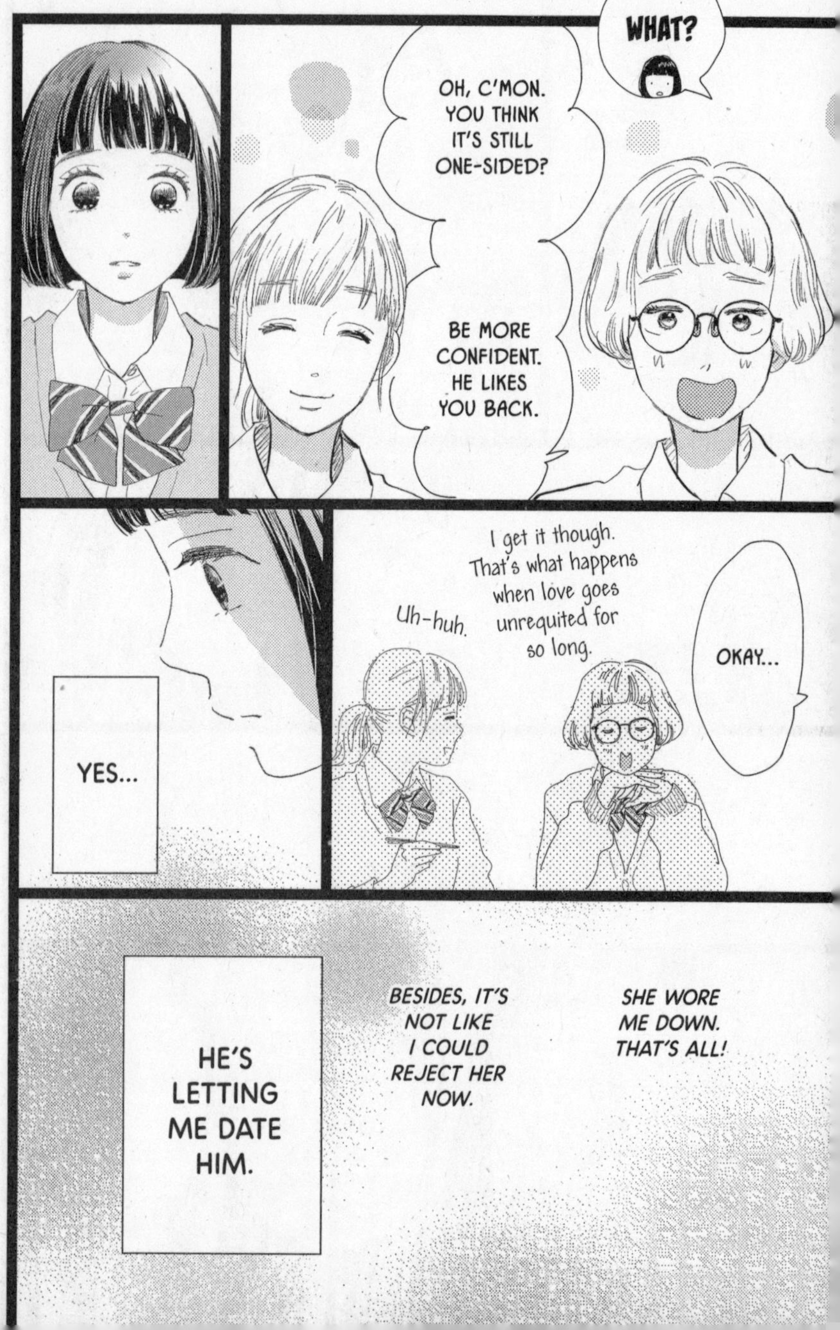
WHAT?
OH, C'MON. YOU THINK IT'S STILL ONE-SIDED?
BE MORE CONFIDENT. HE LIKES YOU BACK.
OKAY...
I get it though. That's what happens when love goes unrequited for so long.
Uh-huh.
YES...
SHE WORE ME DOWN. THAT'S ALL!
BESIDES, IT'S NOT LIKE I COULD REJECT HER NOW.
HE'S LETTING ME DATE HIM.

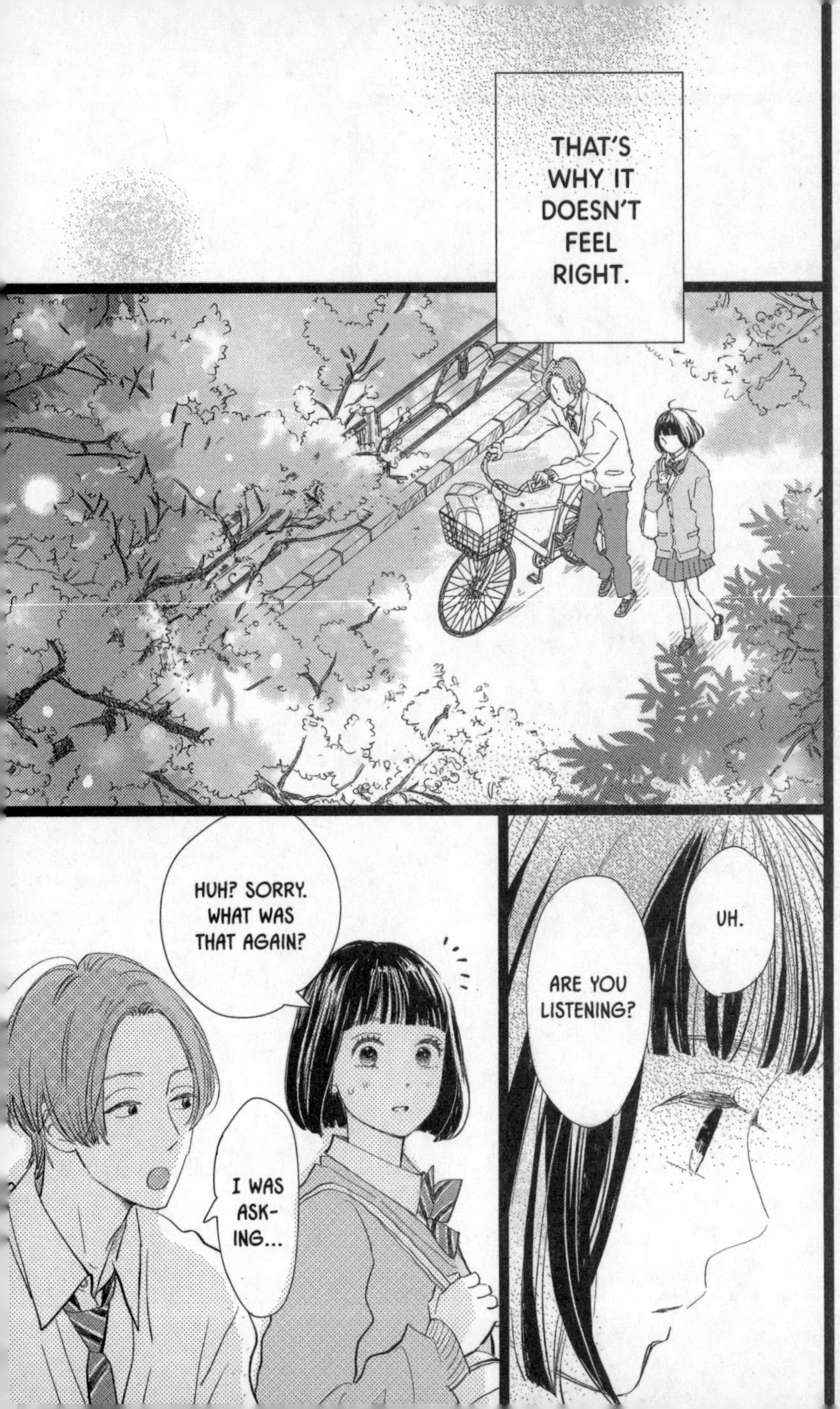
THAT'S WHY IT DOESN'T FEEL RIGHT.
UH.
ARE YOU LISTENING?
HUH? SORRY. WHAT WAS THAT AGAIN?
I WAS ASK-ING...

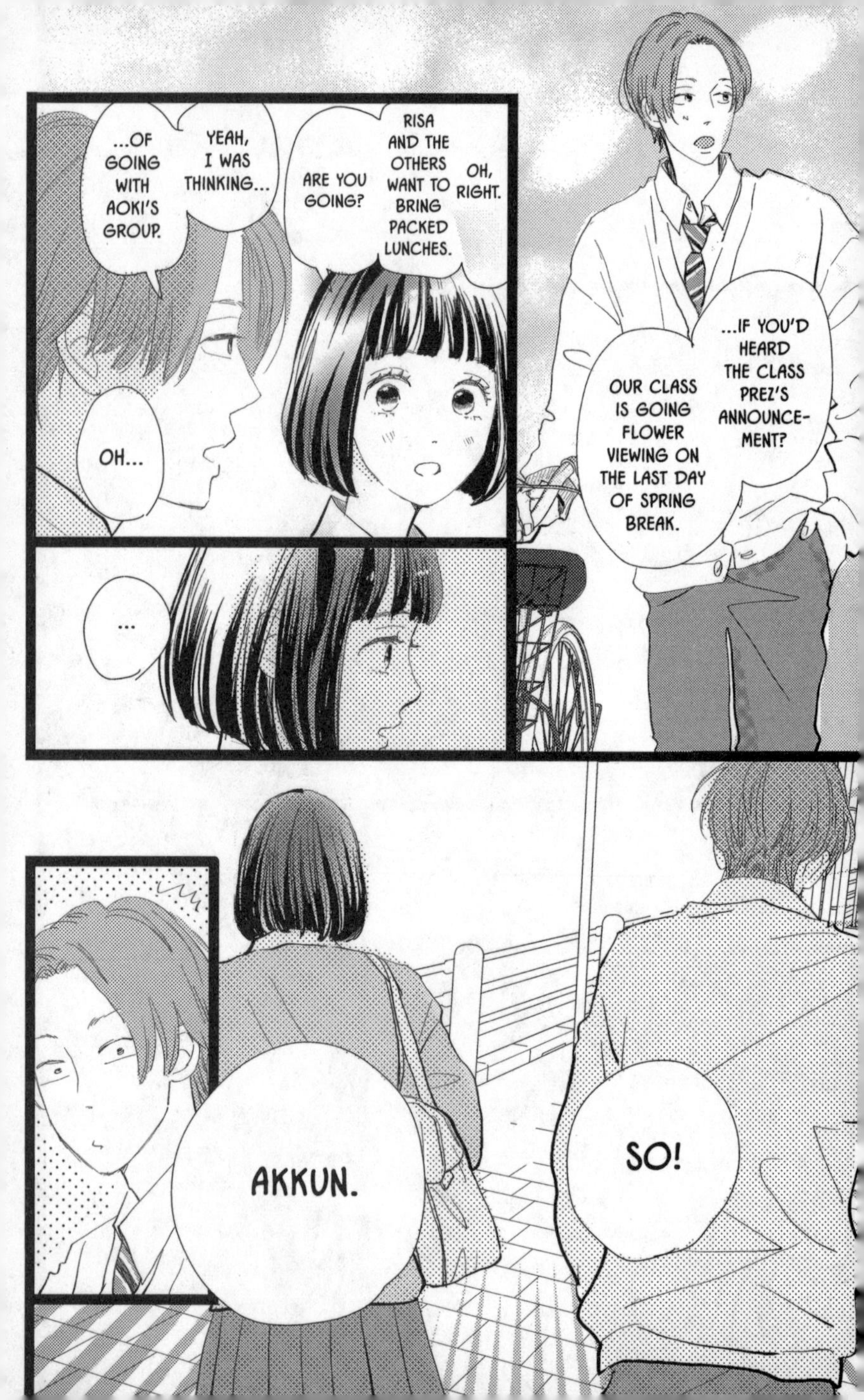
...IF YOU'D HEARD THE CLASS PREZ'S ANNOUNCE-MENT?
OUR CLASS IS GOING FLOWER VIEWING ON THE LAST DAY OF SPRING BREAK.
OH, RIGHT.
RISA AND THE OTHERS WANT TO BRING PACKED LUNCHES.
ARE YOU GOING?
YEAH, I WAS THINKING...
...OF GOING WITH AOKI'S GROUP.
OH...
...
SO!
AKKUN.

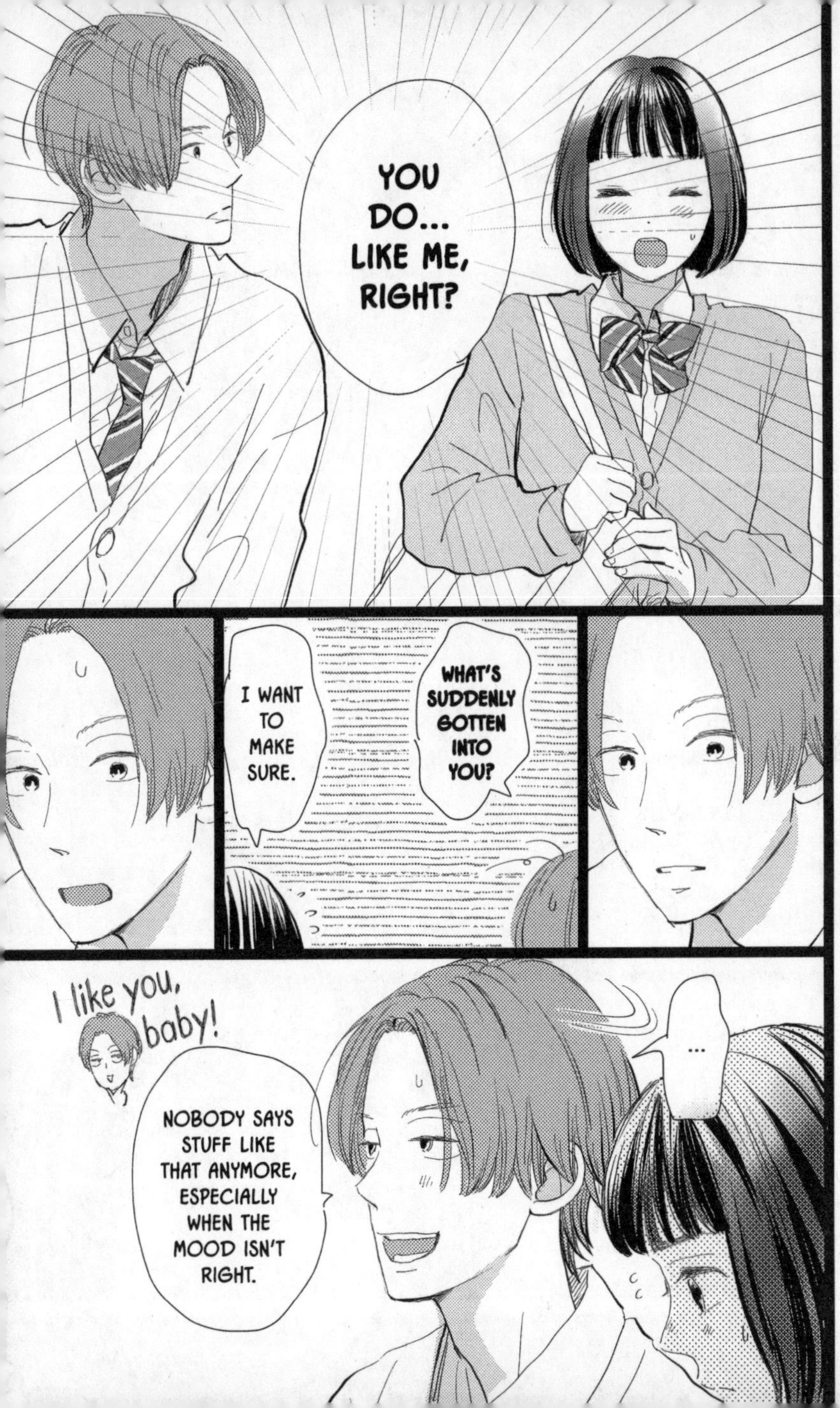
YOU DO... LIKE ME, RIGHT?
WHAT'S SUDDENLY GOTTEN INTO YOU?
I WANT TO MAKE SURE.
...
NOBODY SAYS STUFF LIKE THAT ANYMORE, ESPECIALLY WHEN THE MOOD ISN'T RIGHT.
I like you, baby!

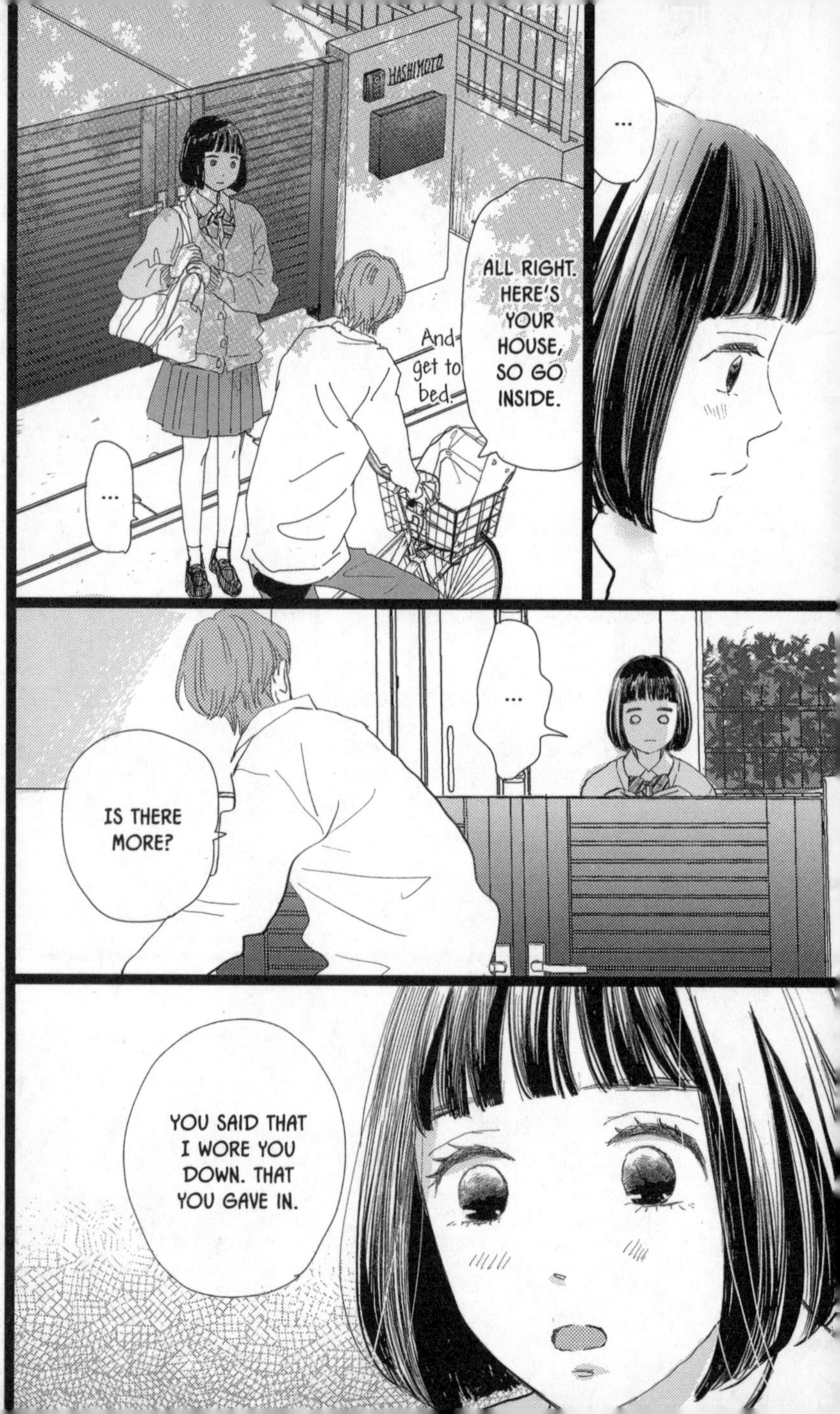
...
ALL RIGHT. HERE'S YOUR HOUSE, SO GO INSIDE.
And— get to bed.
HASHIMOTO
...
...
IS THERE MORE?
YOU SAID THAT I WORE YOU DOWN. THAT YOU GAVE IN.

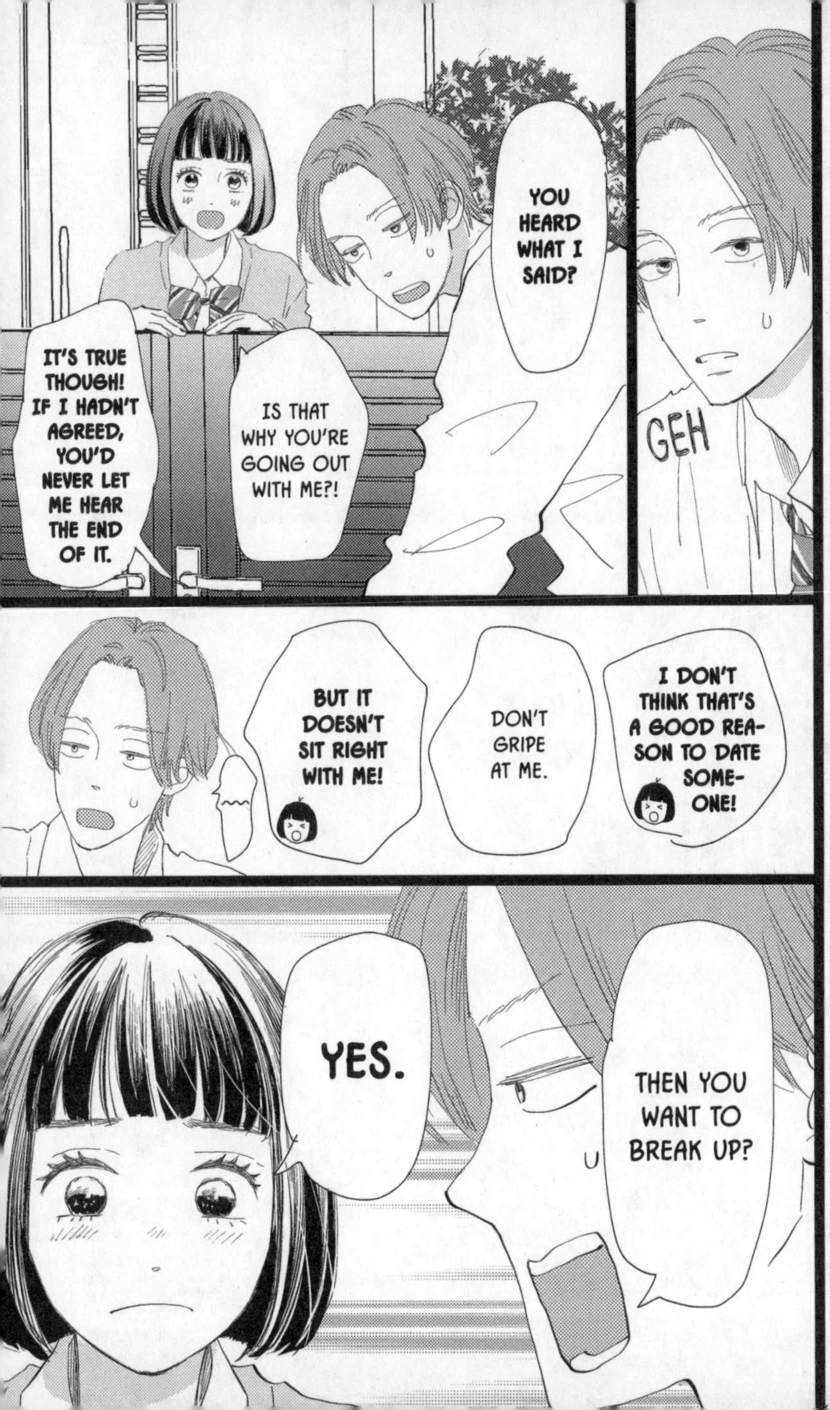
GEH
YOU HEARD WHAT I SAID?
IS THAT WHY YOU'RE GOING OUT WITH ME?!
IT'S TRUE THOUGH! IF I HADN'T AGREED, YOU'D NEVER LET ME HEAR THE END OF IT.
I DON'T THINK THAT'S A GOOD REA-SON TO DATE SOME-ONE!
DON'T GRIPE AT ME.
BUT IT DOESN'T SIT RIGHT WITH ME!
THEN YOU WANT TO BREAK UP?
YES.

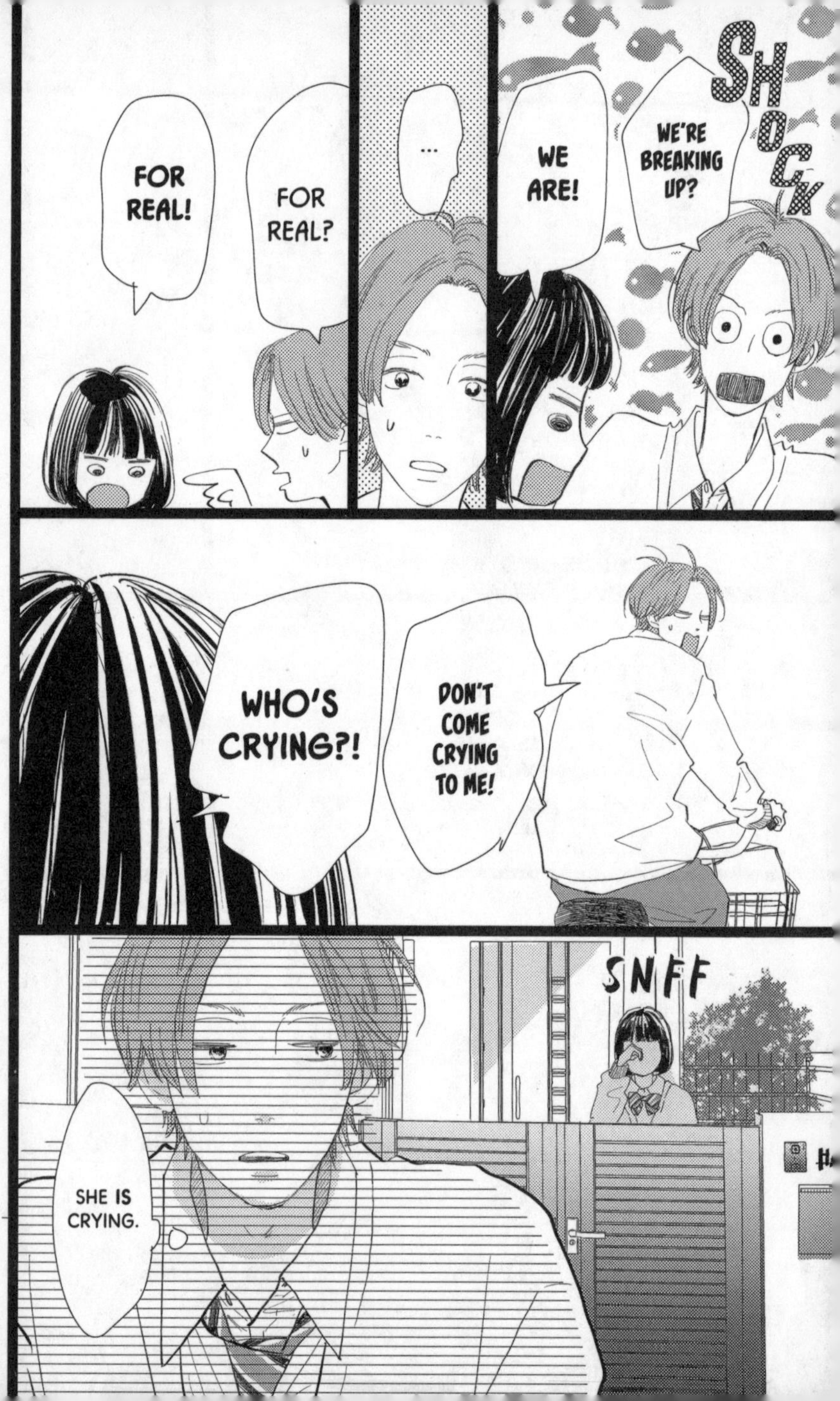
SHOCK
WE'RE BREAKING UP?
WE ARE!
...
FOR REAL?
FOR REAL!
DON'T COME CRYING TO ME!
WHO'S CRYING?!
SNFF
SHE IS CRYING.

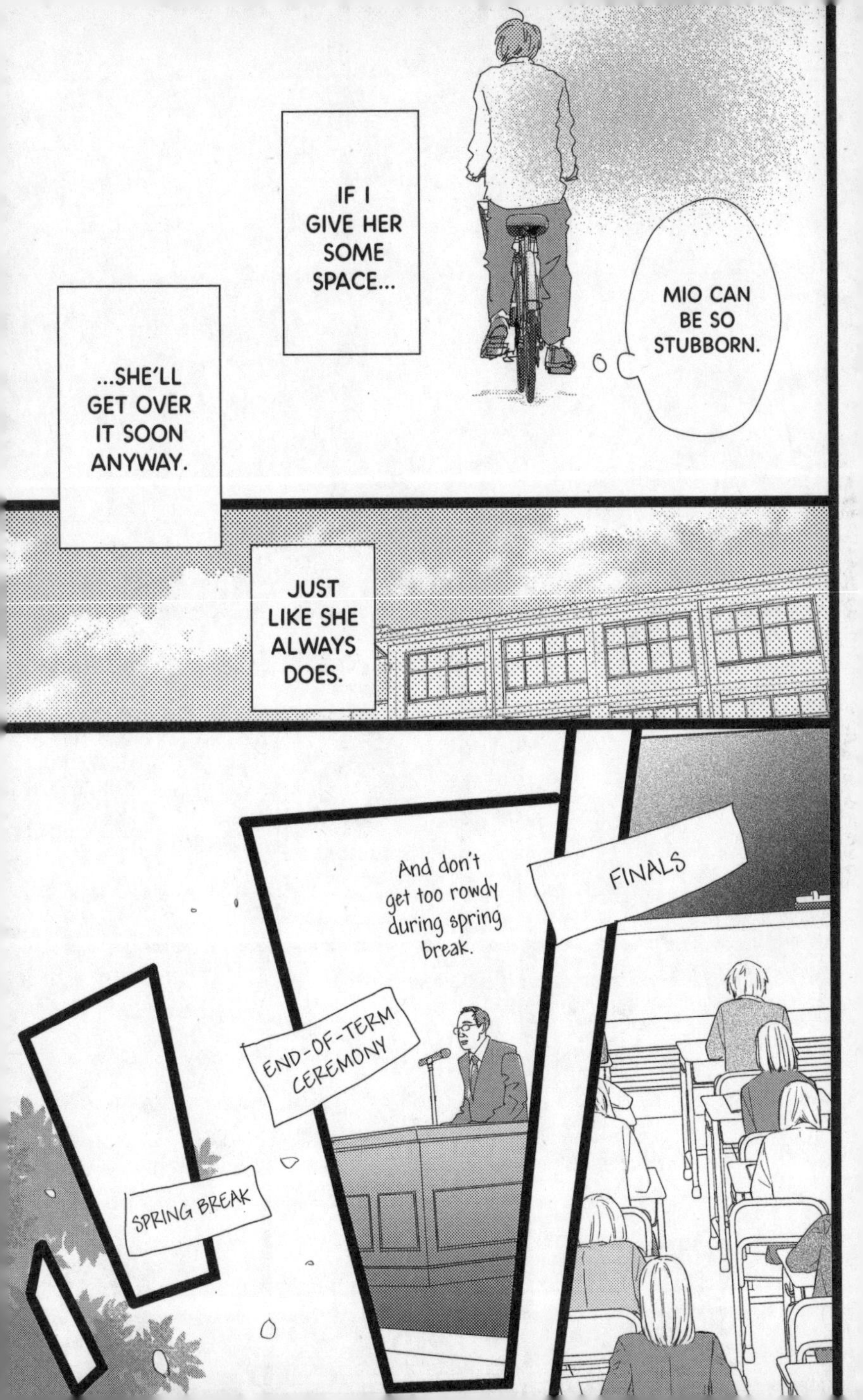
MIO CAN BE SO STUBBORN.
IF I GIVE HER SOME SPACE...
...SHE'LL GET OVER IT SOON ANYWAY.
JUST LIKE SHE ALWAYS DOES.
FINALS
And don't get too rowdy during spring break.
END-OF-TERM CEREMONY
SPRING BREAK

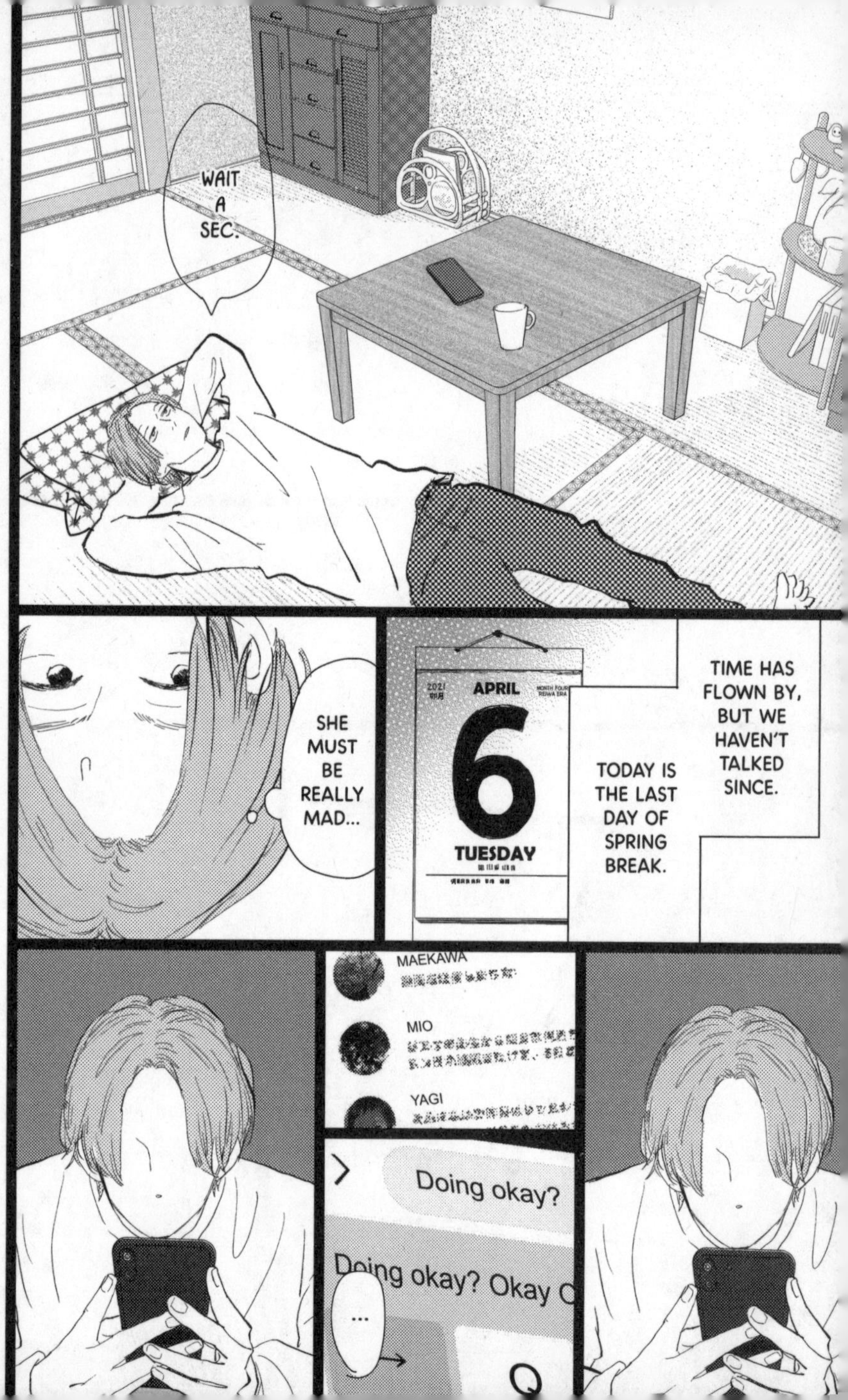
WAIT A SEC.
TIME HAS FLOWN BY, BUT WE HAVEN'T TALKED SINCE.
TODAY IS THE LAST DAY OF SPRING BREAK.
2021
APRIL
MONTH FOUR REIWA ERA
6
TUESDAY
SHE MUST BE REALLY MAD...
MAEKAWA
MIO
YAGI
Doing okay?
Doing okay? Okay C
...

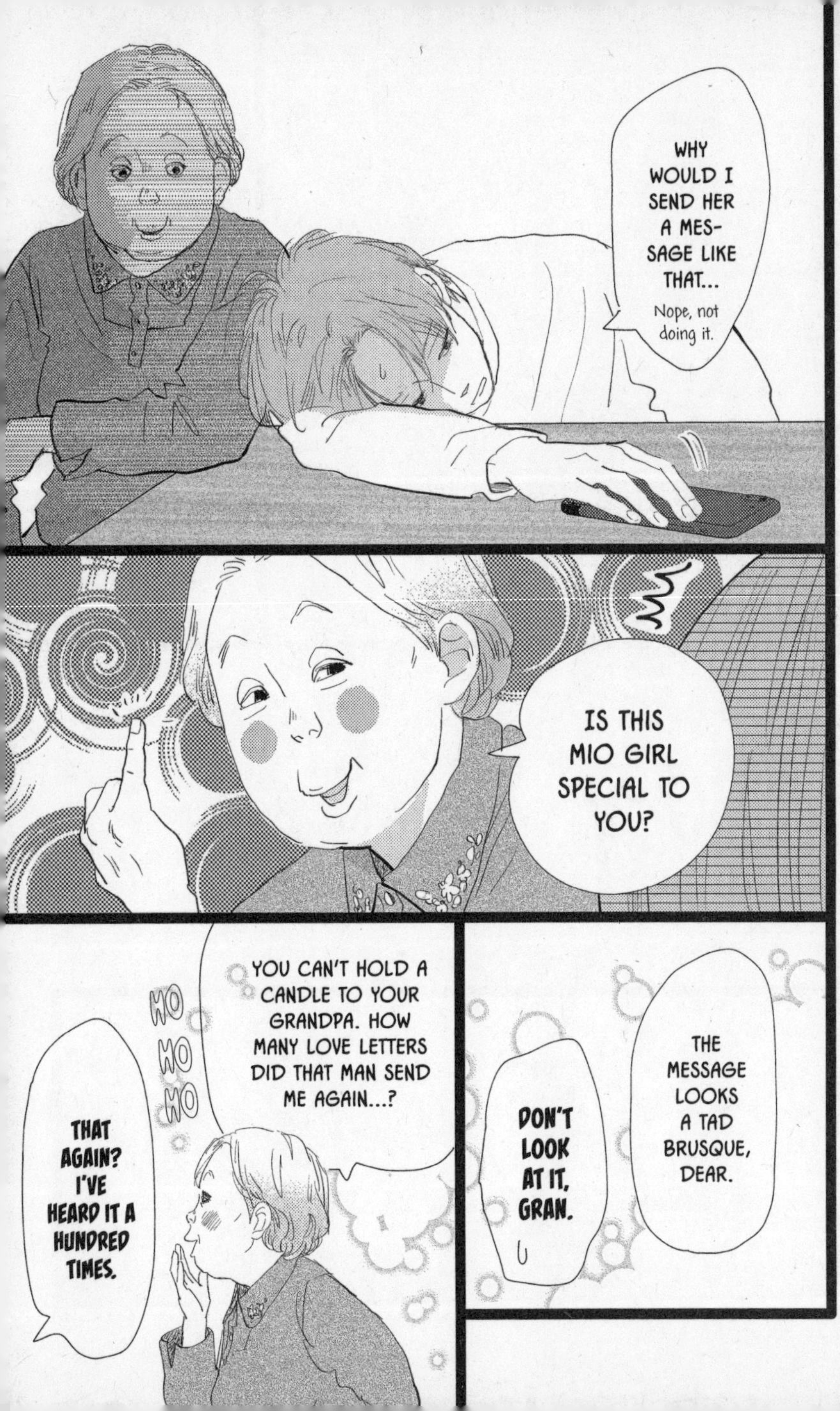
WHY WOULD I SEND HER A MES-SAGE LIKE THAT...
Nope, not doing it.
IS THIS MIO GIRL SPECIAL TO YOU?
THE MESSAGE LOOKS A TAD BRUSQUE, DEAR.
DON'T LOOK AT IT, GRAN.
YOU CAN'T HOLD A CANDLE TO YOUR GRANDPA. HOW MANY LOVE LETTERS DID THAT MAN SEND ME AGAIN...?
HO HO HO
THAT AGAIN? I'VE HEARD IT A HUNDRED TIMES.

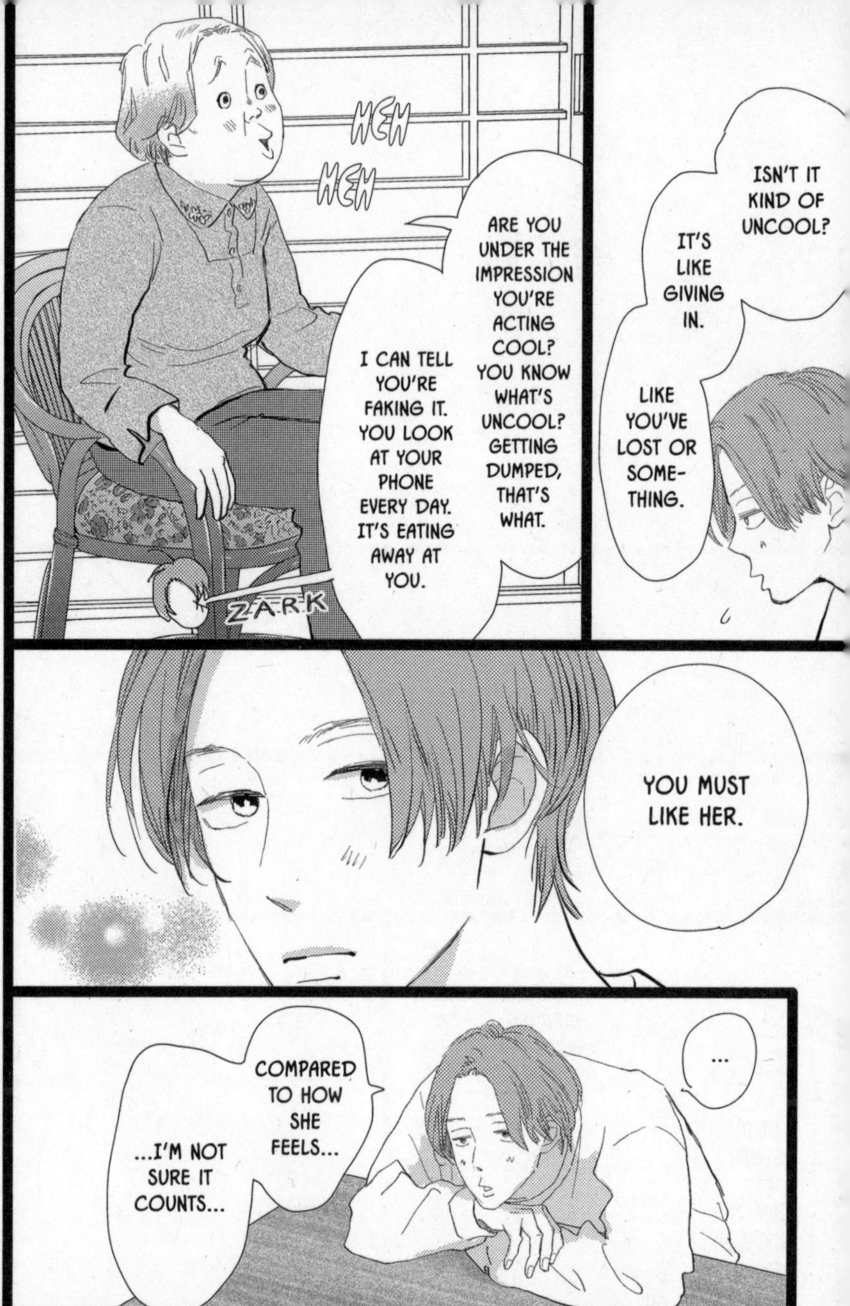
ISN'T IT KIND OF UNCOOL?
IT'S LIKE GIVING IN.
LIKE YOU'VE LOST OR SOME-THING.
HEH HEH
ARE YOU UNDER THE IMPRESSION YOU'RE ACTING COOL? YOU KNOW WHAT'S UNCOOL? GETTING DUMPED, THAT'S WHAT.
I CAN TELL YOU'RE FAKING IT. YOU LOOK AT YOUR PHONE EVERY DAY. IT'S EATING AWAY AT YOU.
ZARK
YOU MUST LIKE HER.
...
COMPARED TO HOW SHE FEELS...
...I'M NOT SURE IT COUNTS...

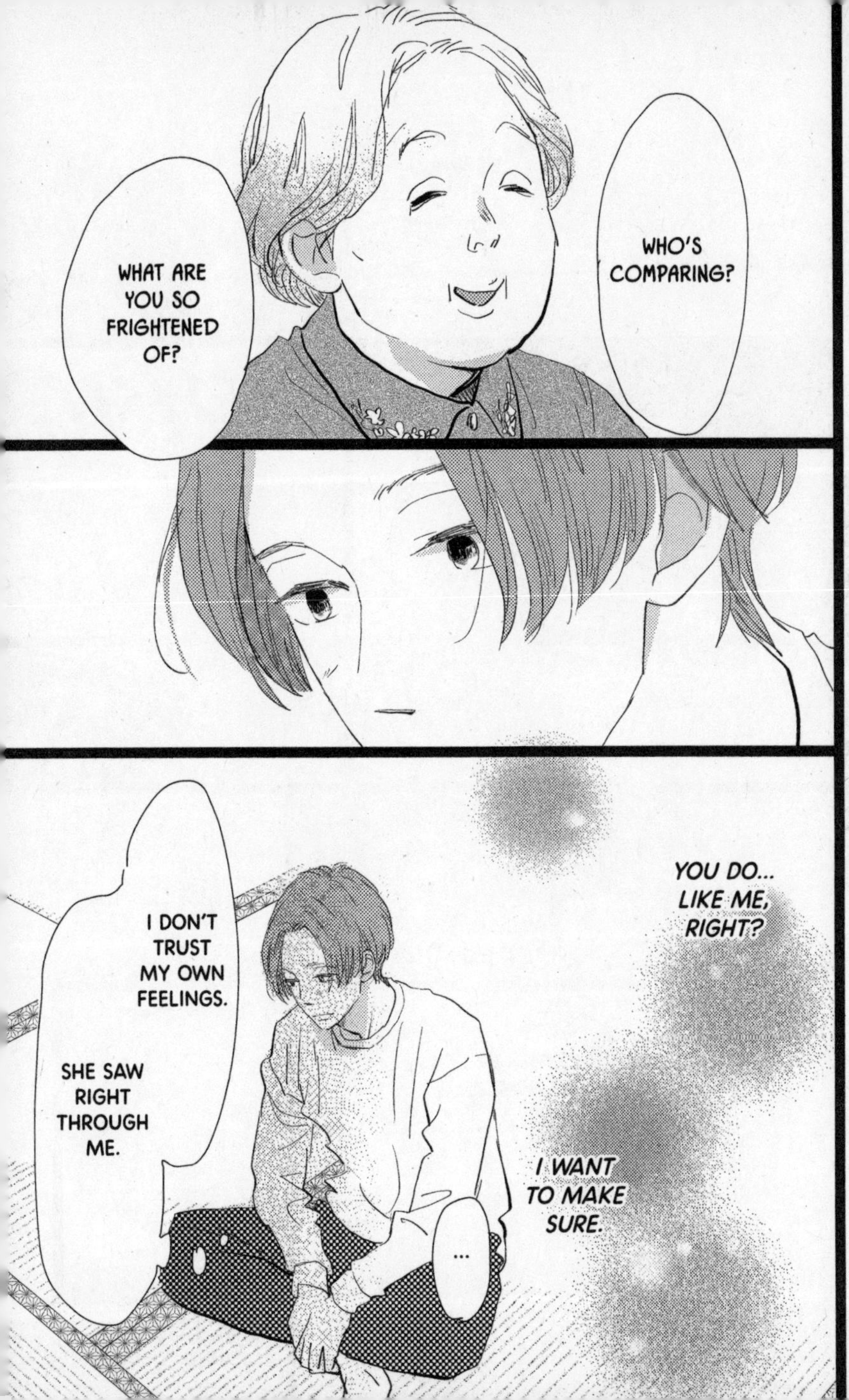
WHO'S COMPARING?
WHAT ARE YOU SO FRIGHTENED OF?
YOU DO... LIKE ME, RIGHT?
I WANT TO MAKE SURE.
...
I DON'T TRUST MY OWN FEELINGS.
SHE SAW RIGHT THROUGH ME.

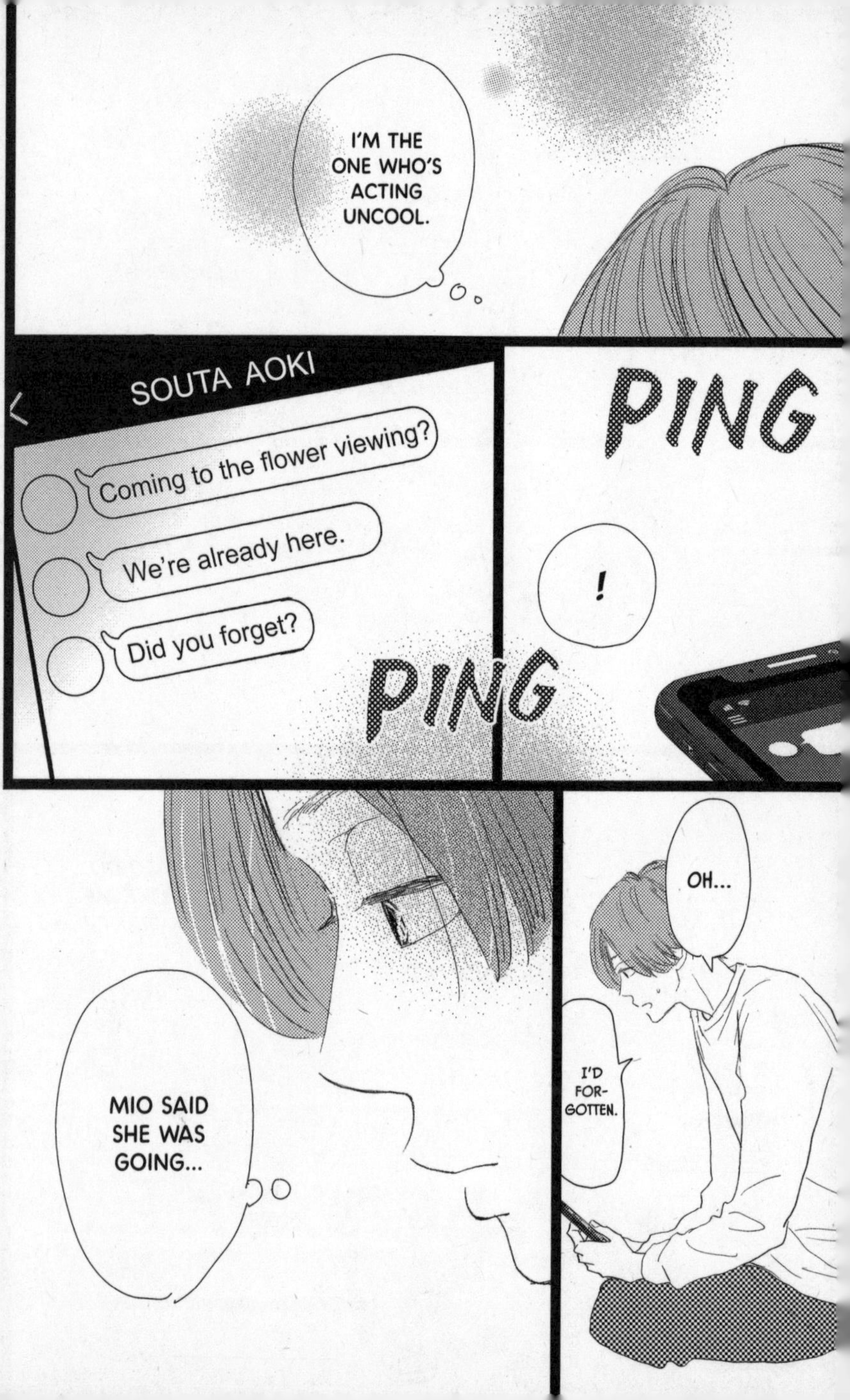
I'M THE ONE WHO'S ACTING UNCOOL.
PING
!
PING
SOUTA AOKI
Coming to the flower viewing?
We're already here.
Did you forget?
OH...
I'D FOR-GOTTEN.
MIO SAID SHE WAS GOING...

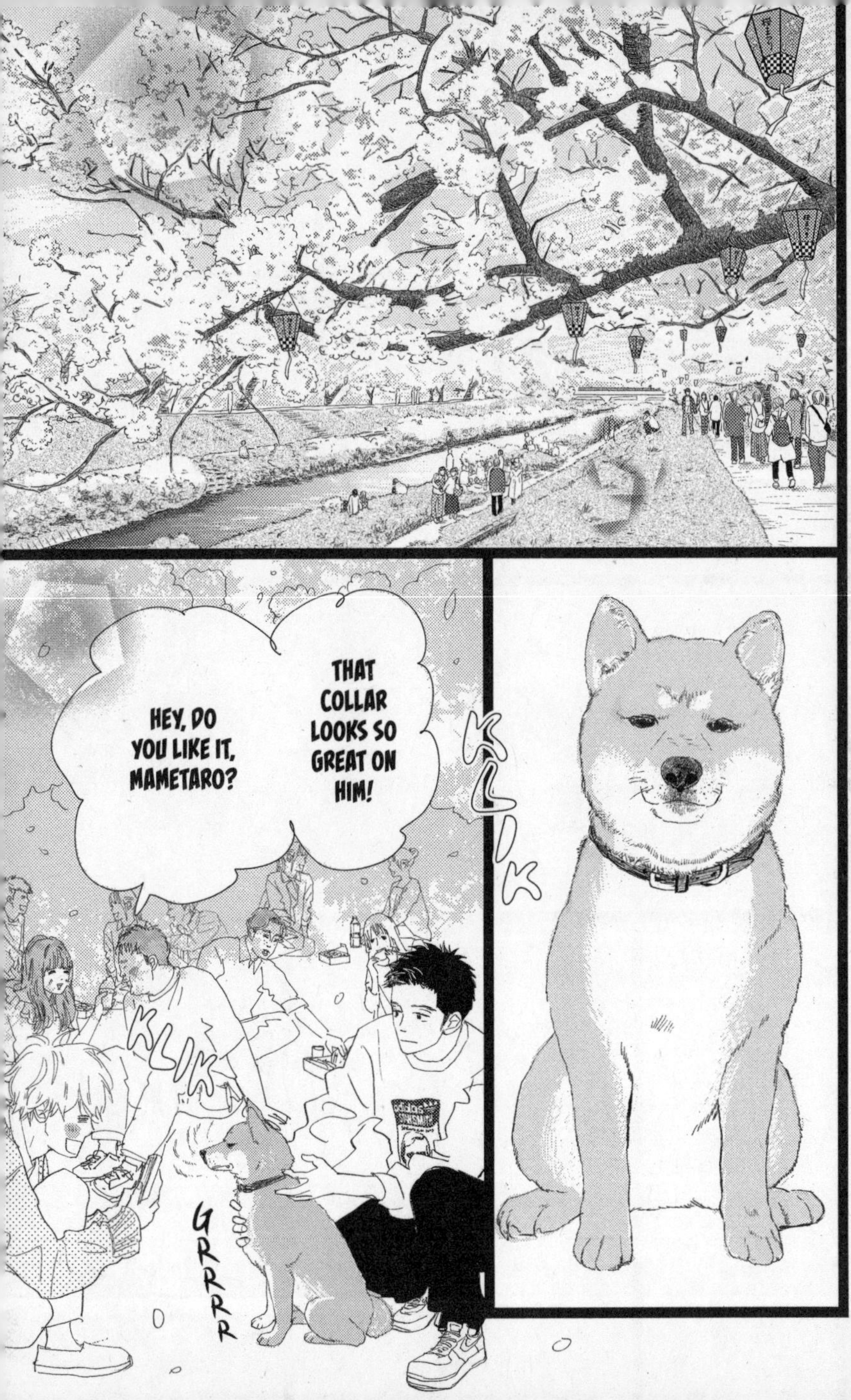
KLIK
THAT COLLAR LOOKS SO GREAT ON HIM!
HEY, DO YOU LIKE IT, MAMETARO?
KLIK
GRRRRR

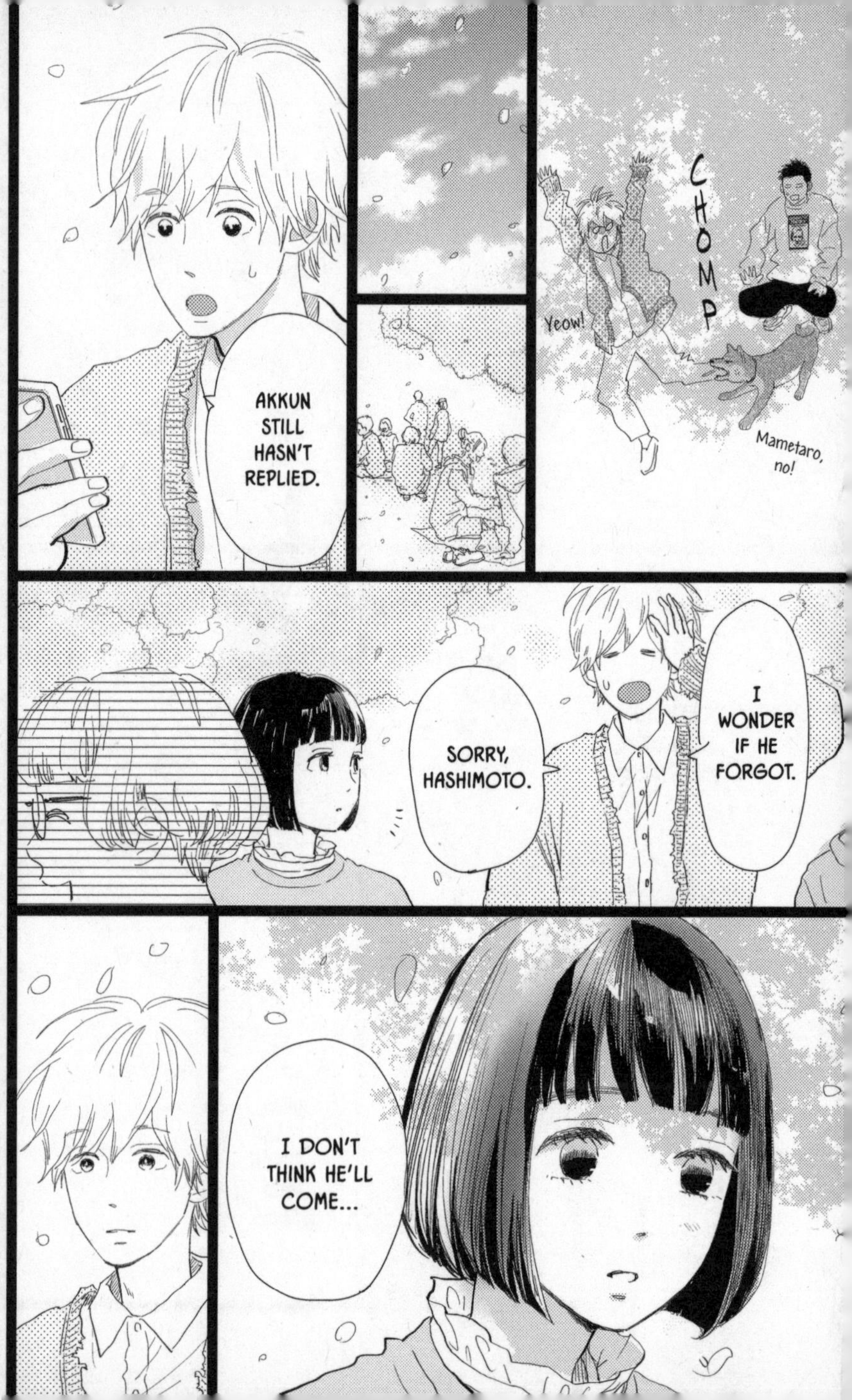
CHOMP
Yeow!
Mametaro, no!
AKKUN STILL HASN'T REPLIED.
I WONDER IF HE FORGOT.
SORRY, HASHIMOTO.
I DON'T THINK HE'LL COME...

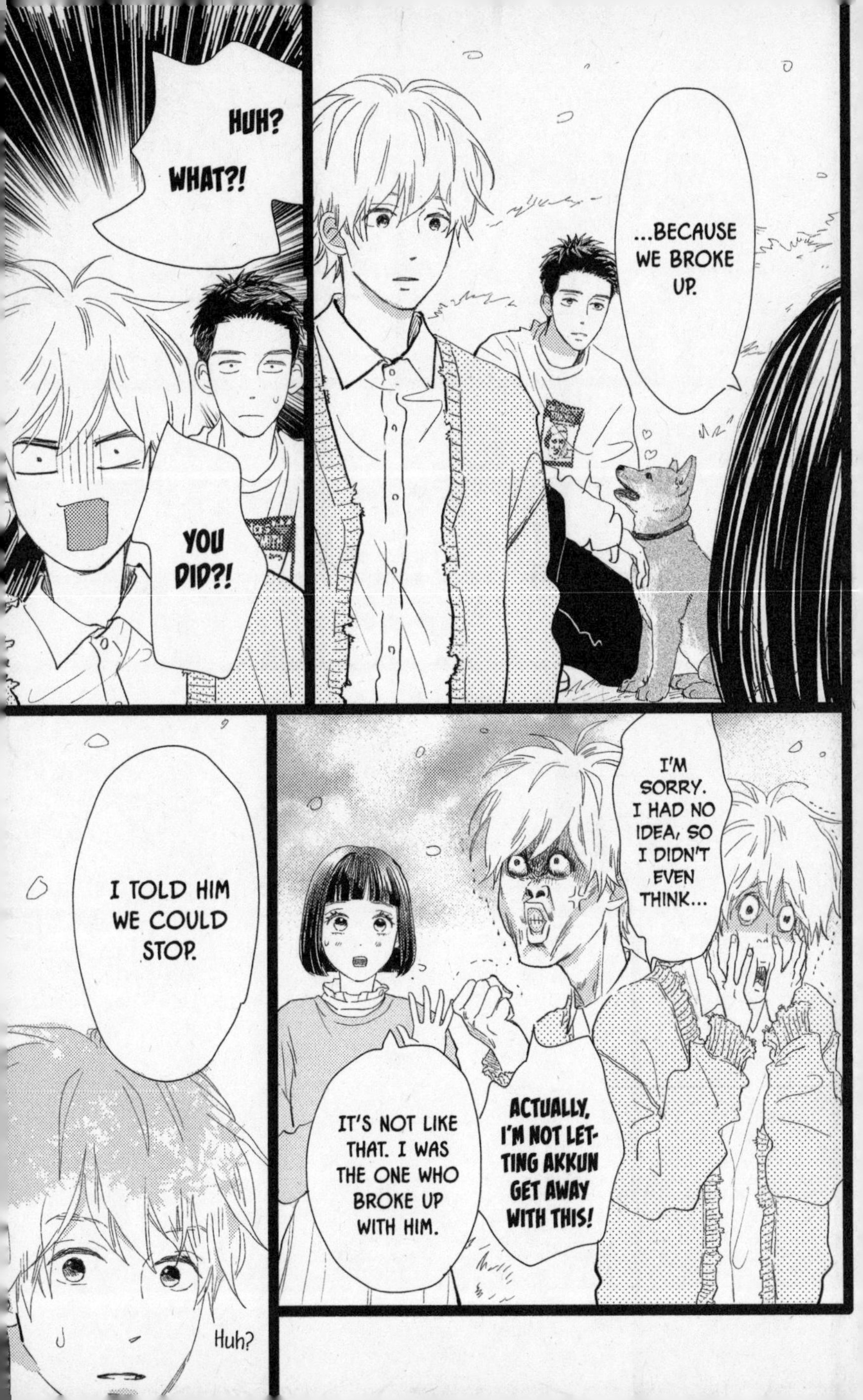
...BECAUSE WE BROKE UP.
HUH?
WHAT?!
YOU DID?!
I'M SORRY. I HAD NO IDEA, SO I DIDN'T EVEN THINK...
ACTUALLY, I'M NOT LET-TING AKKUN GET AWAY WITH THIS!
IT'S NOT LIKE THAT. I WAS THE ONE WHO BROKE UP WITH HIM.
I TOLD HIM WE COULD STOP.
Huh?

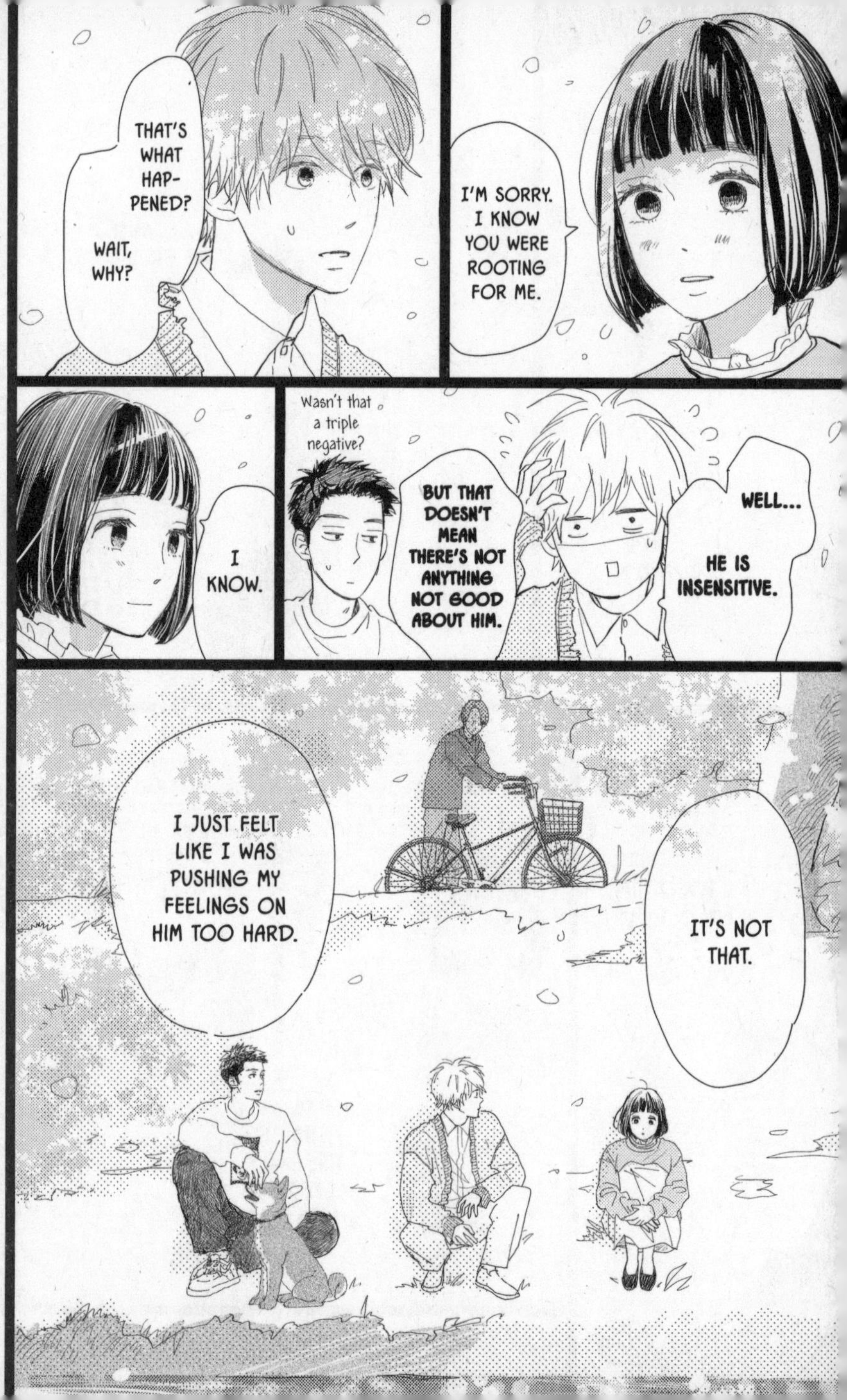
I'M SORRY. I KNOW YOU WERE ROOTING FOR ME.
THAT'S WHAT HAP-PENED?
WAIT, WHY?
WELL...
HE IS INSENSITIVE.
BUT THAT DOESN'T MEAN THERE'S NOT ANYTHING NOT GOOD ABOUT HIM.
Wasn't that a triple negative?
I KNOW.
IT'S NOT THAT.
I JUST FELT LIKE I WAS PUSHING MY FEELINGS ON HIM TOO HARD.

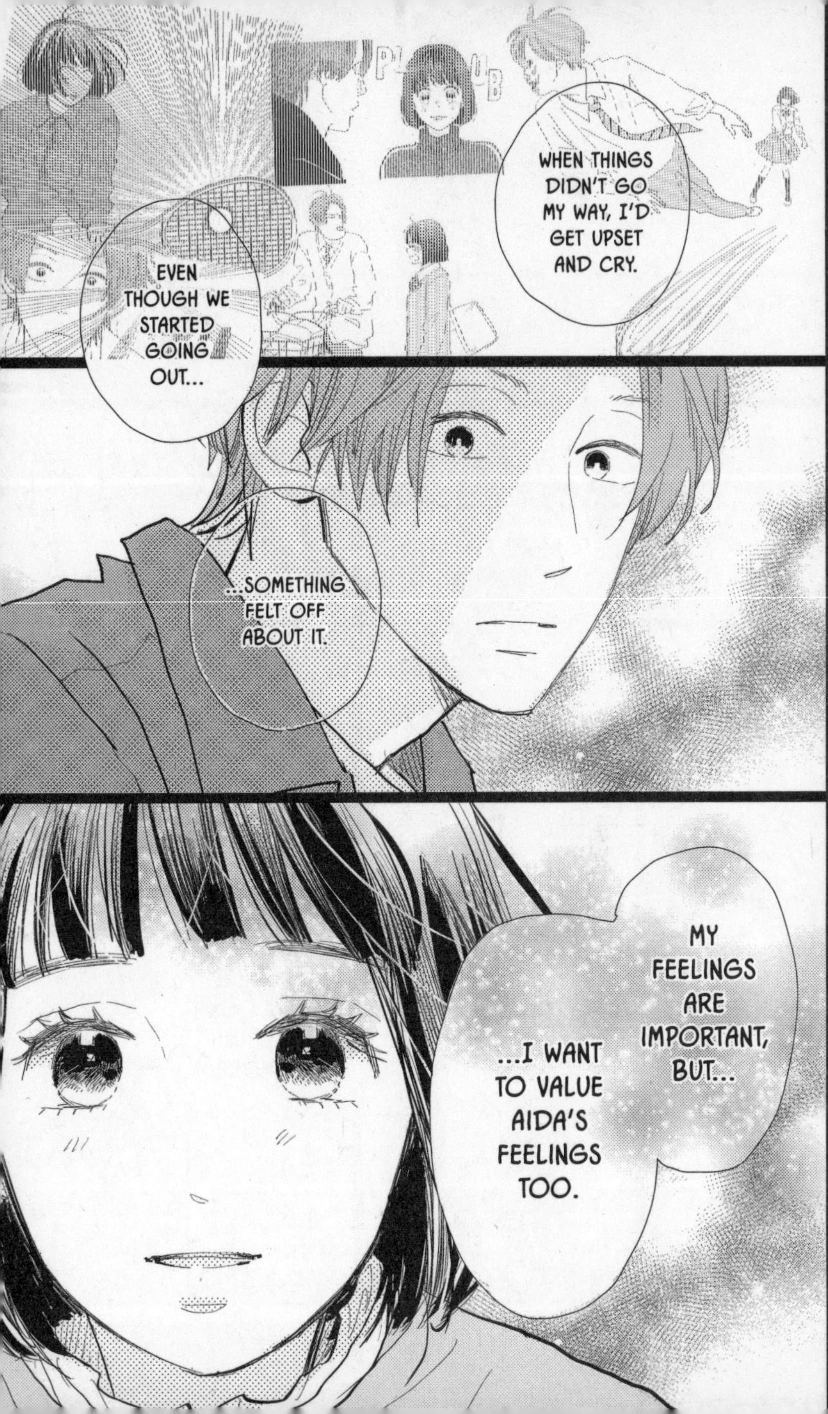
WHEN THINGS DIDN'T GO MY WAY, I'D GET UPSET AND CRY.
EVEN THOUGH WE STARTED GOING OUT...
...SOMETHING FELT OFF ABOUT IT.
MY FEELINGS ARE IMPORTANT, BUT...
...I WANT TO VALUE AIDA'S FEELINGS TOO.

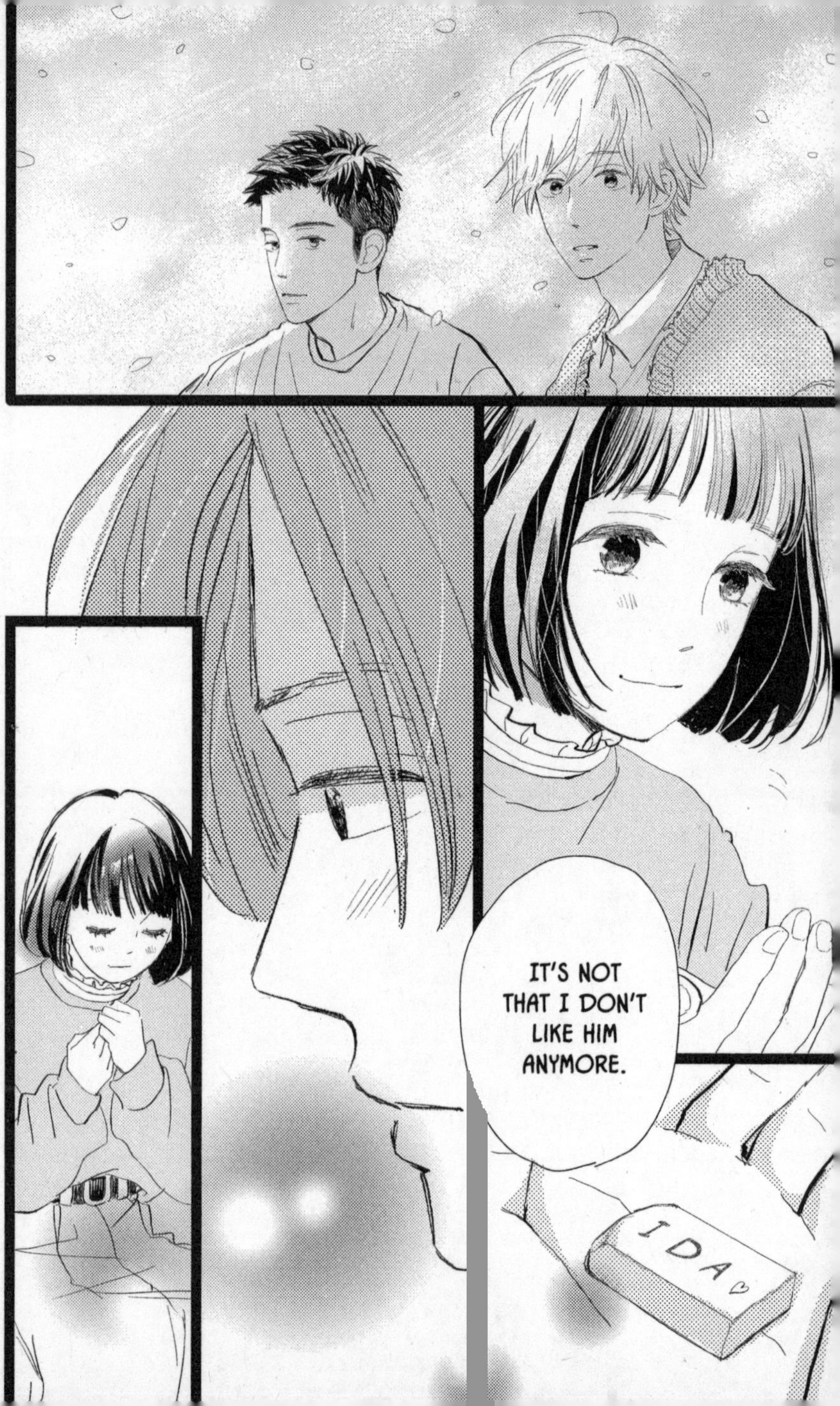
IT'S NOT THAT I DON'T LIKE HIM ANYMORE.
IDA

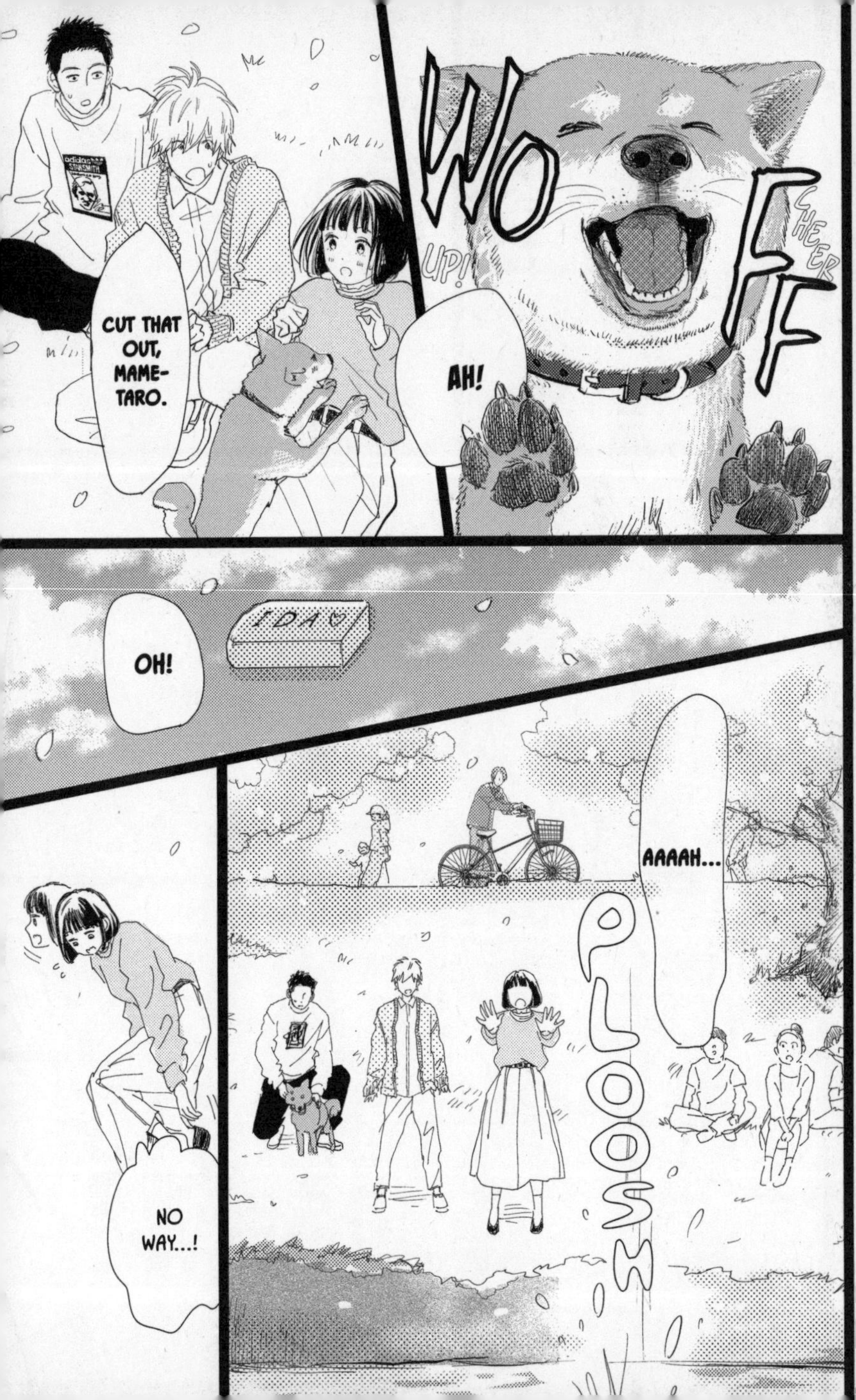
WOOFF
CHEER UP!
AH!
CUT THAT OUT, MAME-TARO.
IDA♡
OH!
AAAAH...
PLOOSH
NO WAY...!

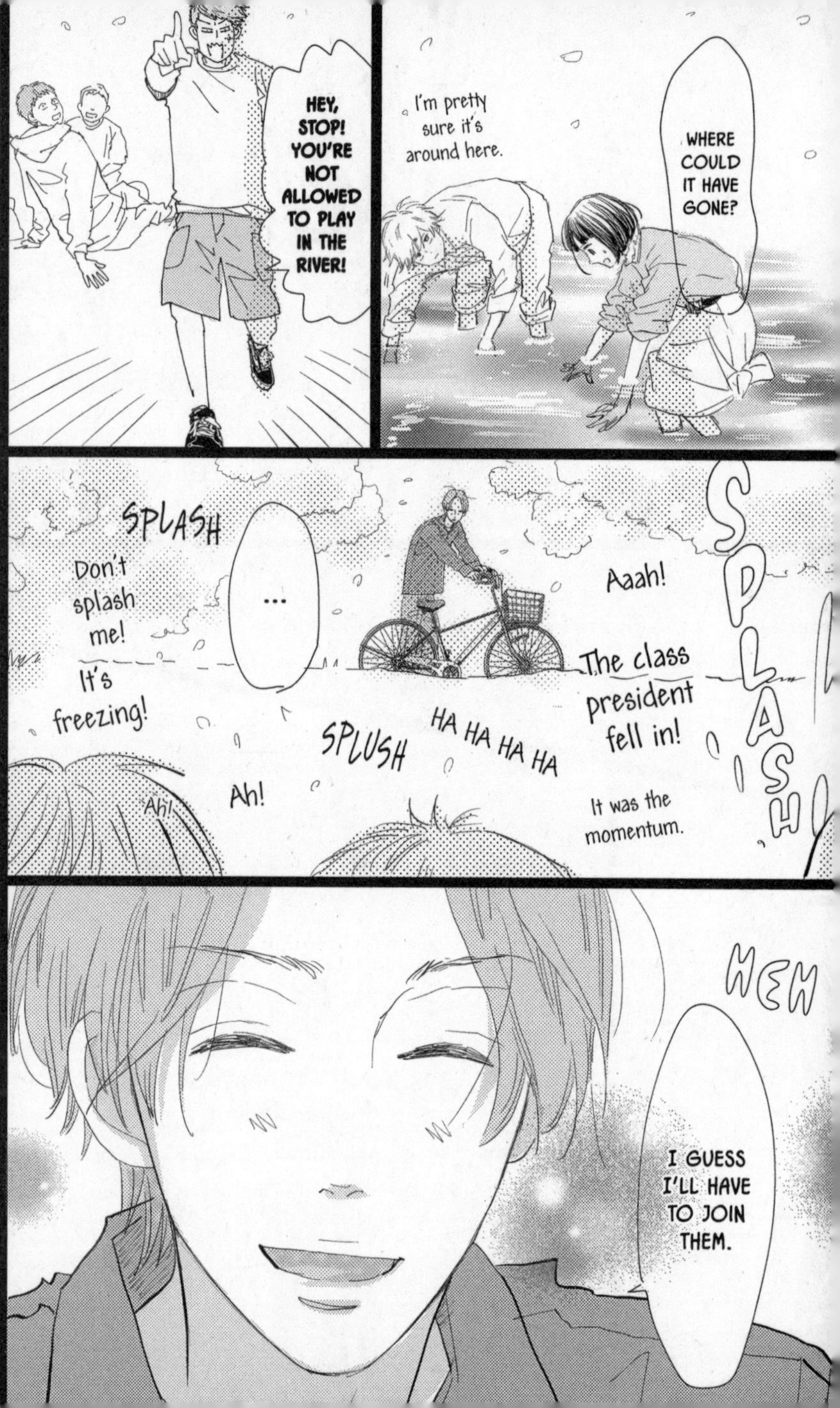
WHERE COULD IT HAVE GONE?
I'm pretty sure it's around here.
HEY, STOP! YOU'RE NOT ALLOWED TO PLAY IN THE RIVER!
SPLASH
Aaah!
The class president fell in!
It was the momentum.
HA HA HA HA
SPLUSH
...
SPLASH
Don't splash me!
It's freezing!
Ah!
Ah!
HEH
I GUESS I'LL HAVE TO JOIN THEM.

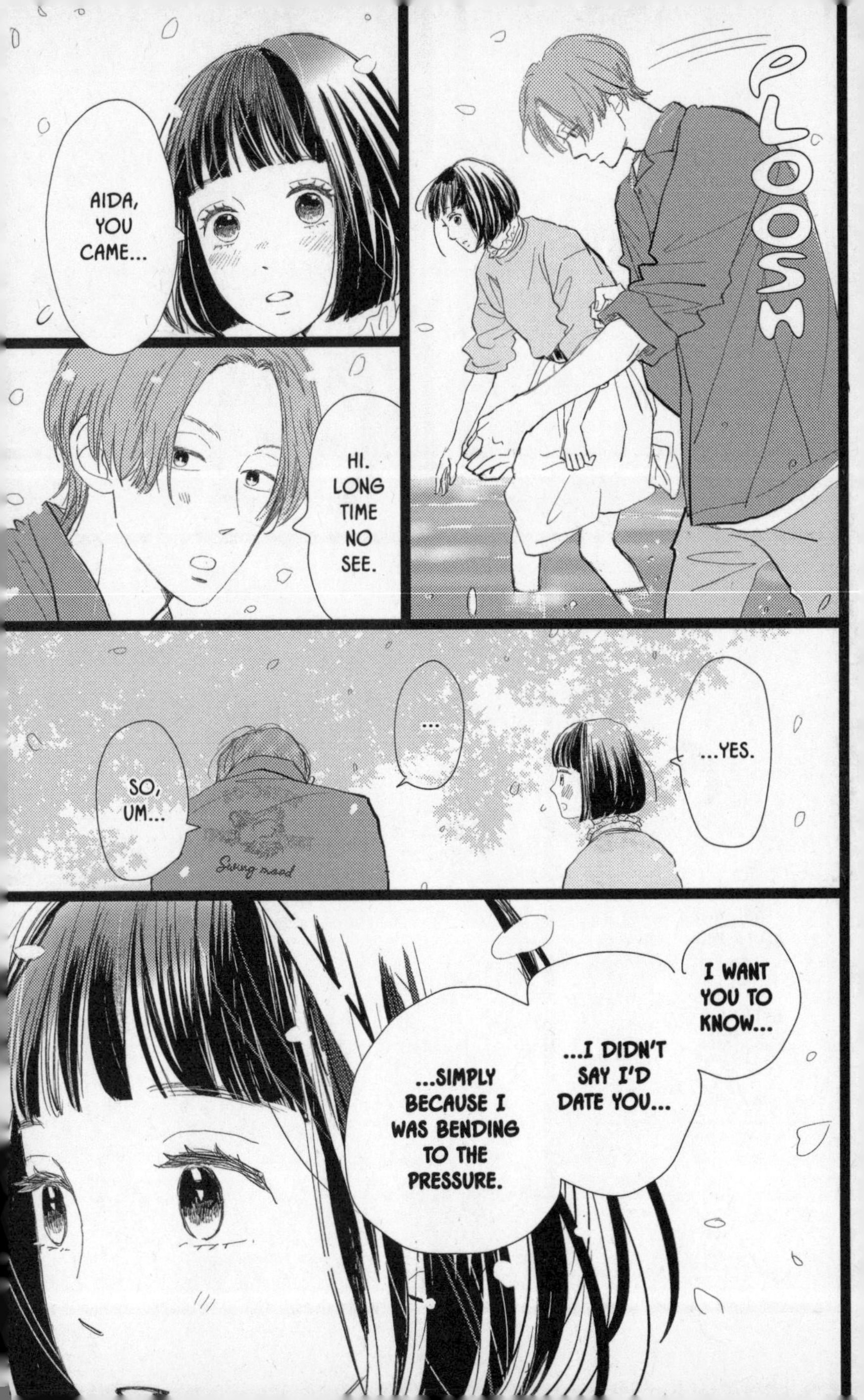
PLOOSH
AIDA, YOU CAME...
HI. LONG TIME NO SEE.
...YES.
...
SO, UM...
I WANT YOU TO KNOW...
...I DIDN'T SAY I'D DATE YOU...
...SIMPLY BECAUSE I WAS BENDING TO THE PRESSURE.

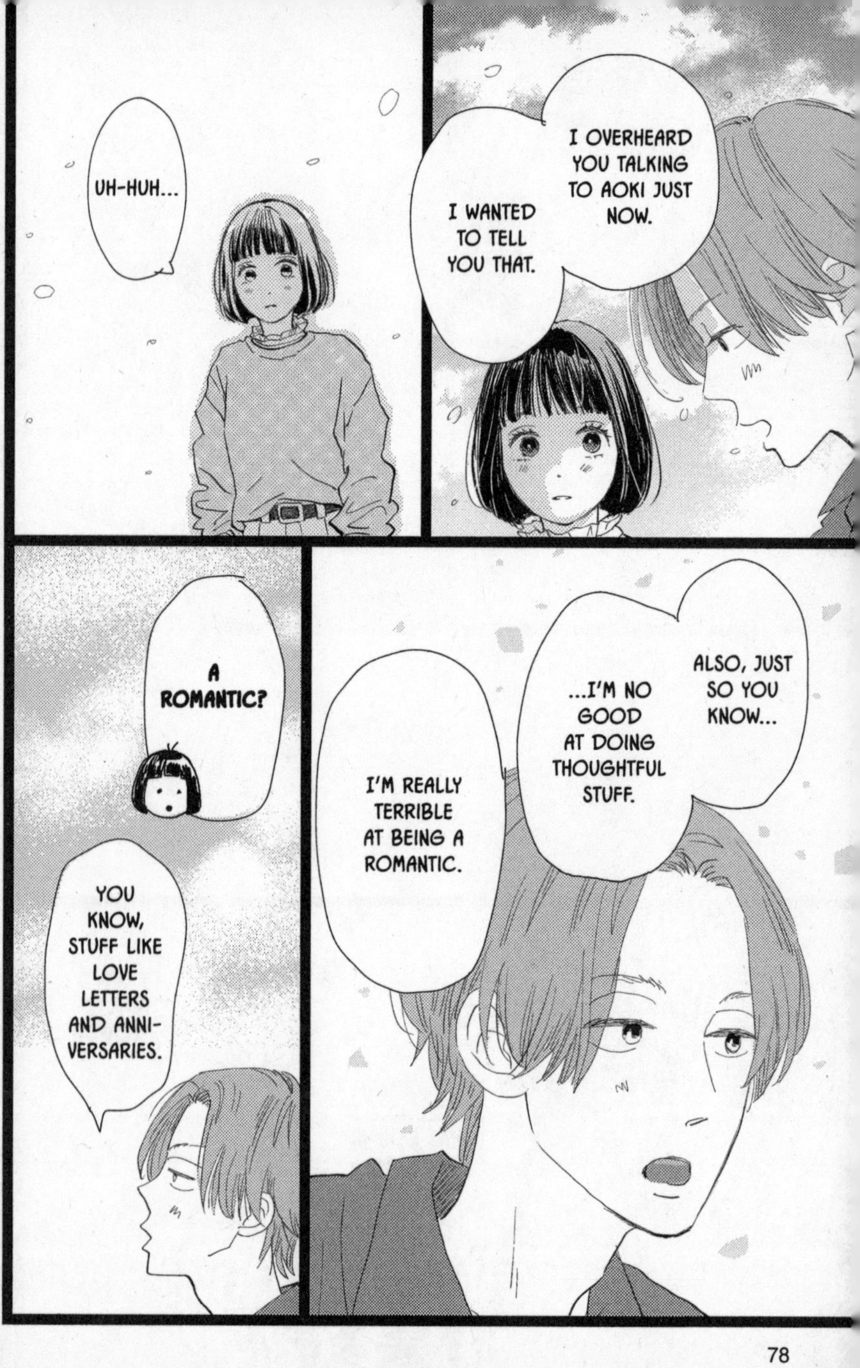
I OVERHEARD YOU TALKING TO AOKI JUST NOW.
I WANTED TO TELL YOU THAT.
UH-HUH...
ALSO, JUST SO YOU KNOW...
...I'M NO GOOD AT DOING THOUGHTFUL STUFF.
I'M REALLY TERRIBLE AT BEING A ROMANTIC.
A ROMANTIC?
YOU KNOW, STUFF LIKE LOVE LETTERS AND ANNI-VERSARIES.

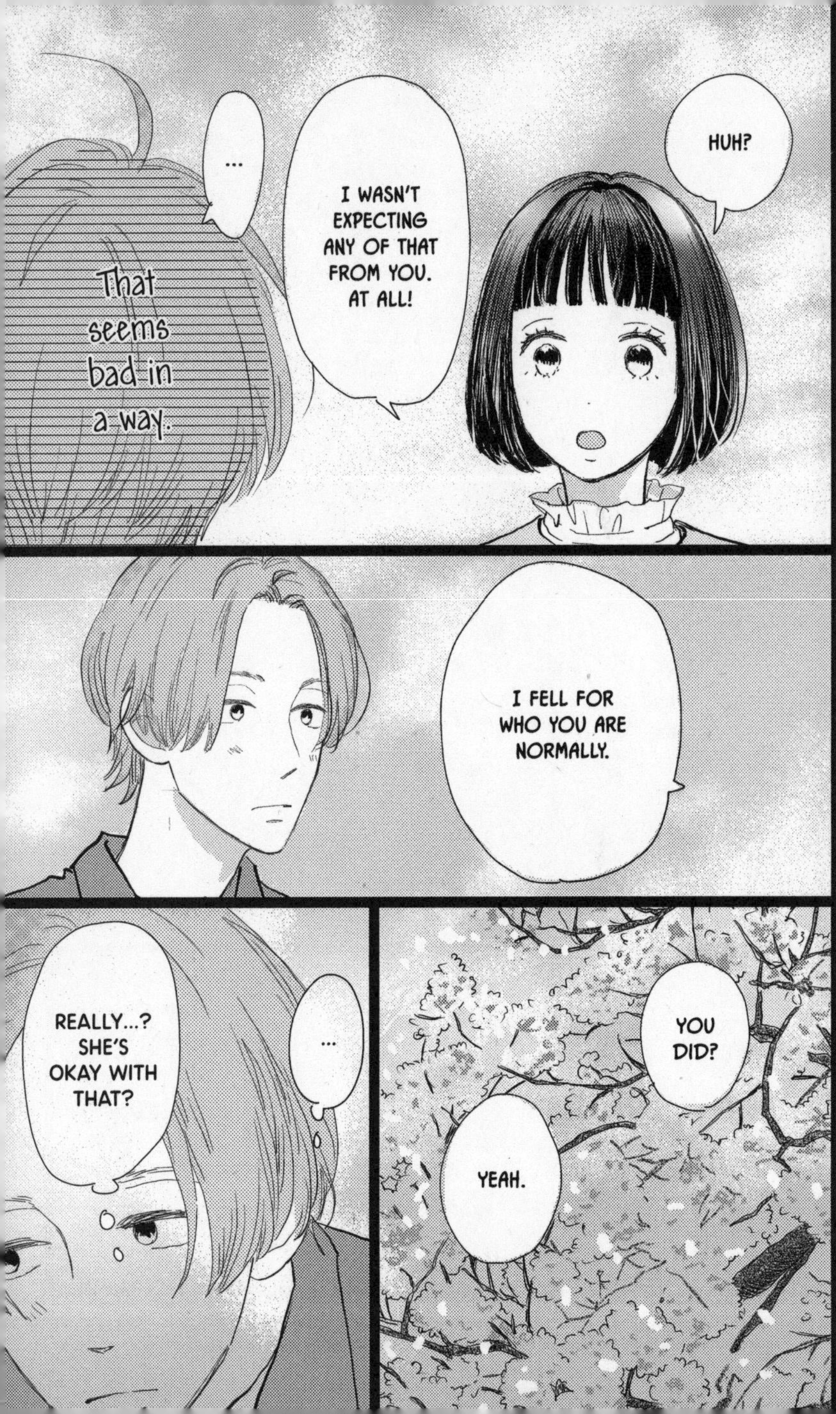
HUH?
I WASN'T EXPECTING ANY OF THAT FROM YOU. AT ALL!
...
That seems bad in a way.
I FELL FOR WHO YOU ARE NORMALLY.
YOU DID?
YEAH.
...
REALLY...? SHE'S OKAY WITH THAT?

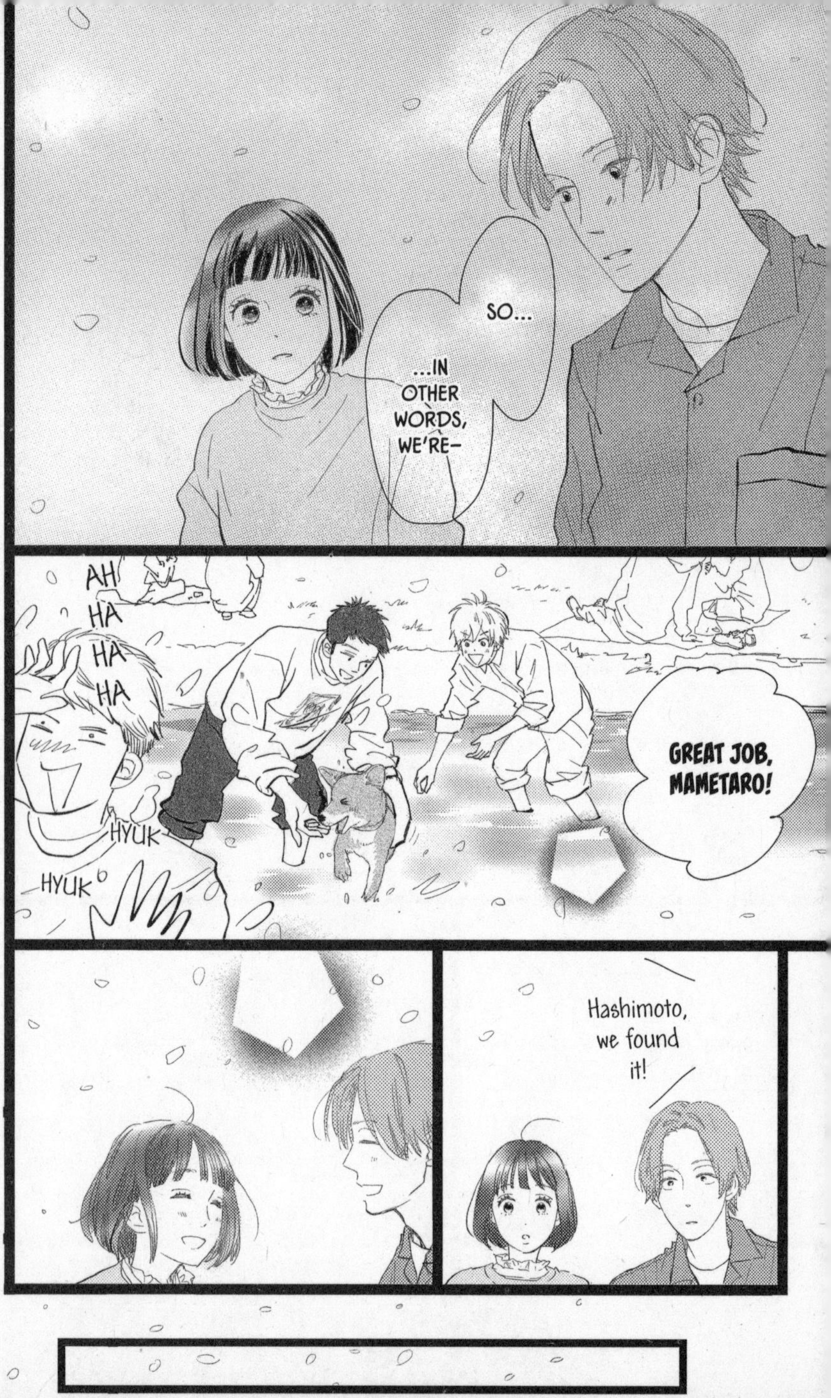
SO...
...IN OTHER WORDS, WE'RE–
GREAT JOB, MAMETARO!
AH HA HA HA
HYUK HYUK
Hashimoto, we found it!

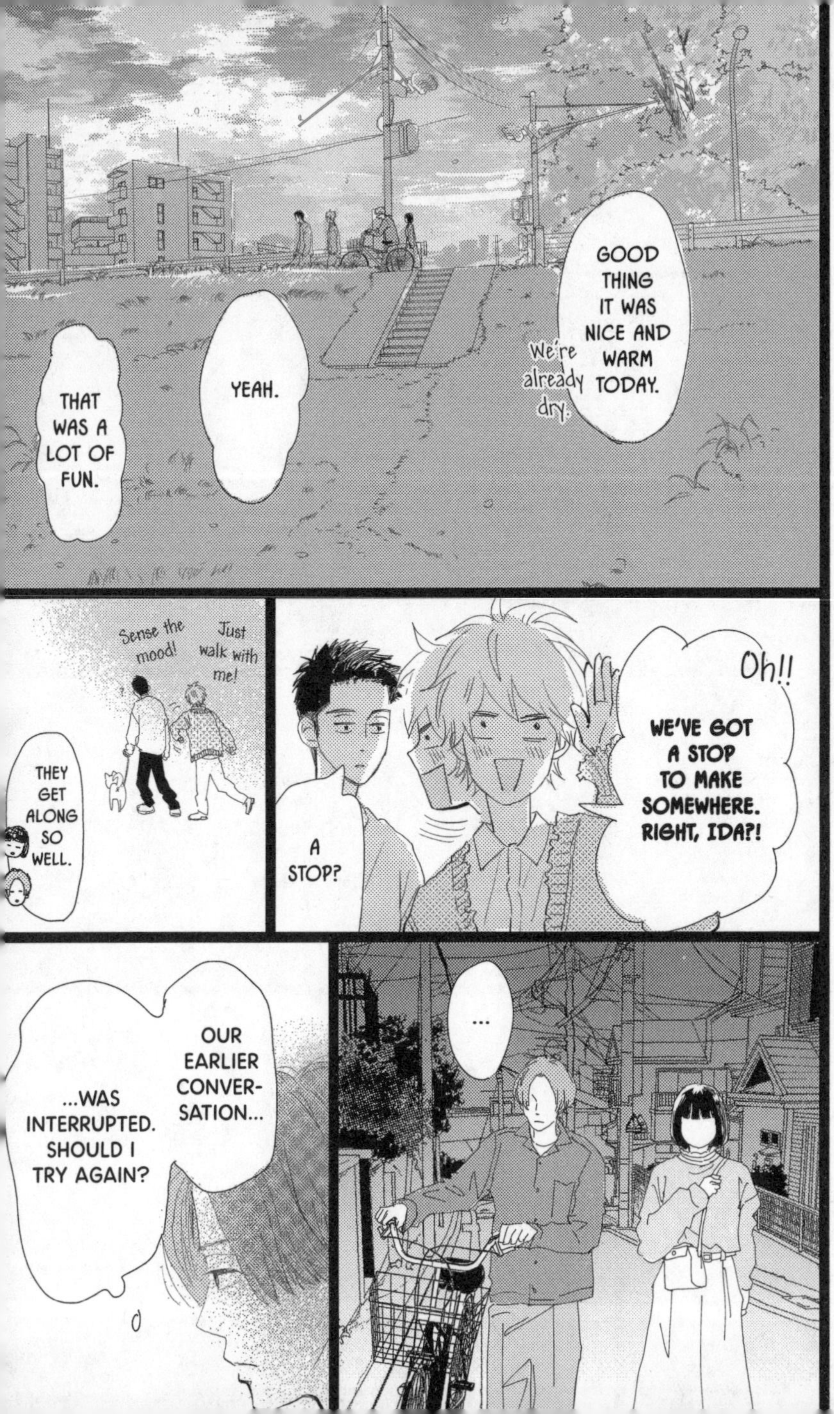
GOOD THING IT WAS NICE AND WARM TODAY.
We're already dry.
YEAH.
THAT WAS A LOT OF FUN.
Oh!!
WE'VE GOT A STOP TO MAKE SOMEWHERE. RIGHT, IDA?!
A STOP?
Just walk with me!
Sense the mood!
THEY GET ALONG SO WELL.
...
OUR EARLIER CONVERSATION...
...WAS INTERRUPTED. SHOULD I TRY AGAIN?

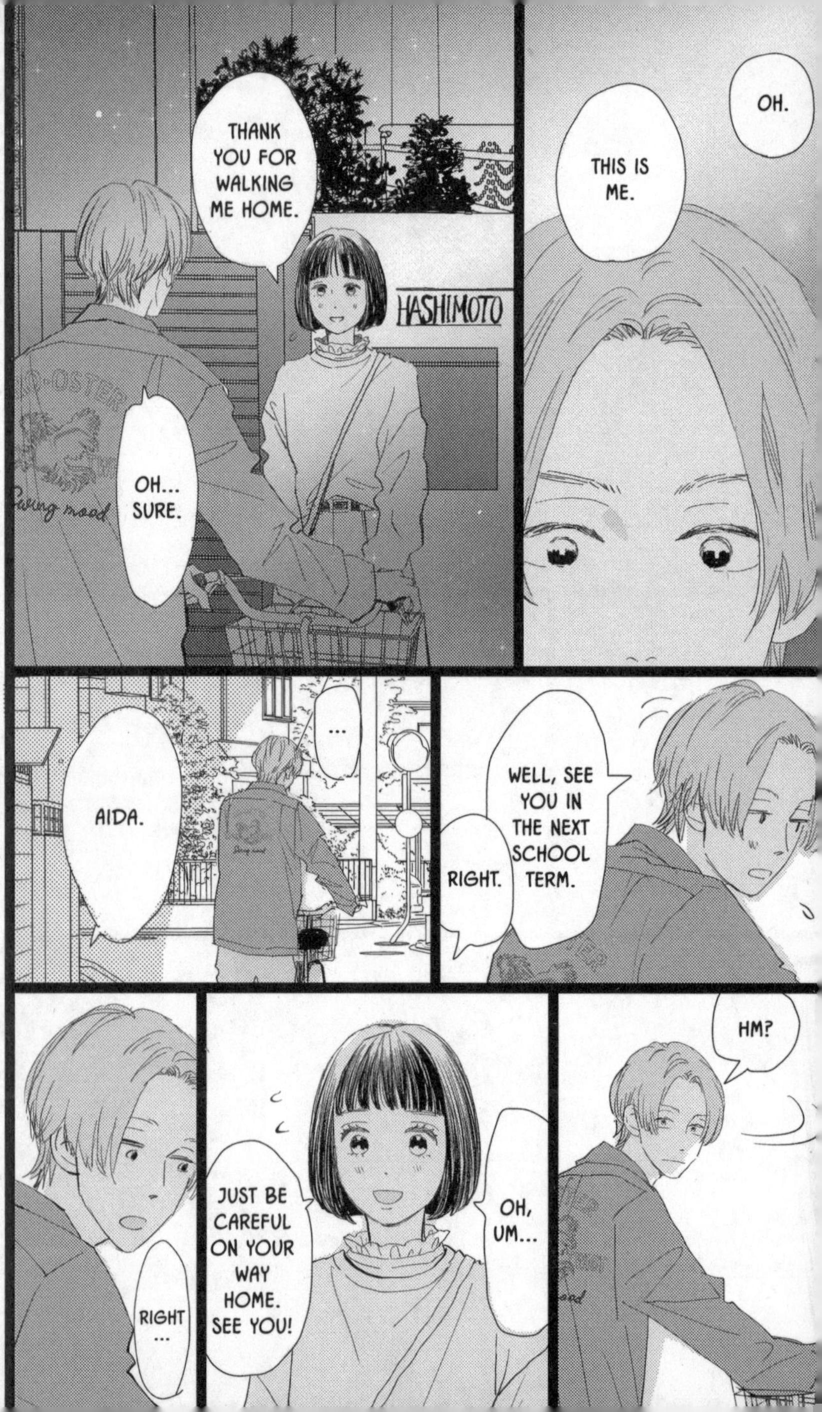
OH.
THIS IS ME.
THANK YOU FOR WALKING ME HOME.
HASHIMOTO
OH... SURE.
WELL, SEE YOU IN THE NEXT SCHOOL TERM.
RIGHT.
...
AIDA.
HM?
OH, UM...
JUST BE CAREFUL ON YOUR WAY HOME. SEE YOU!
RIGHT...

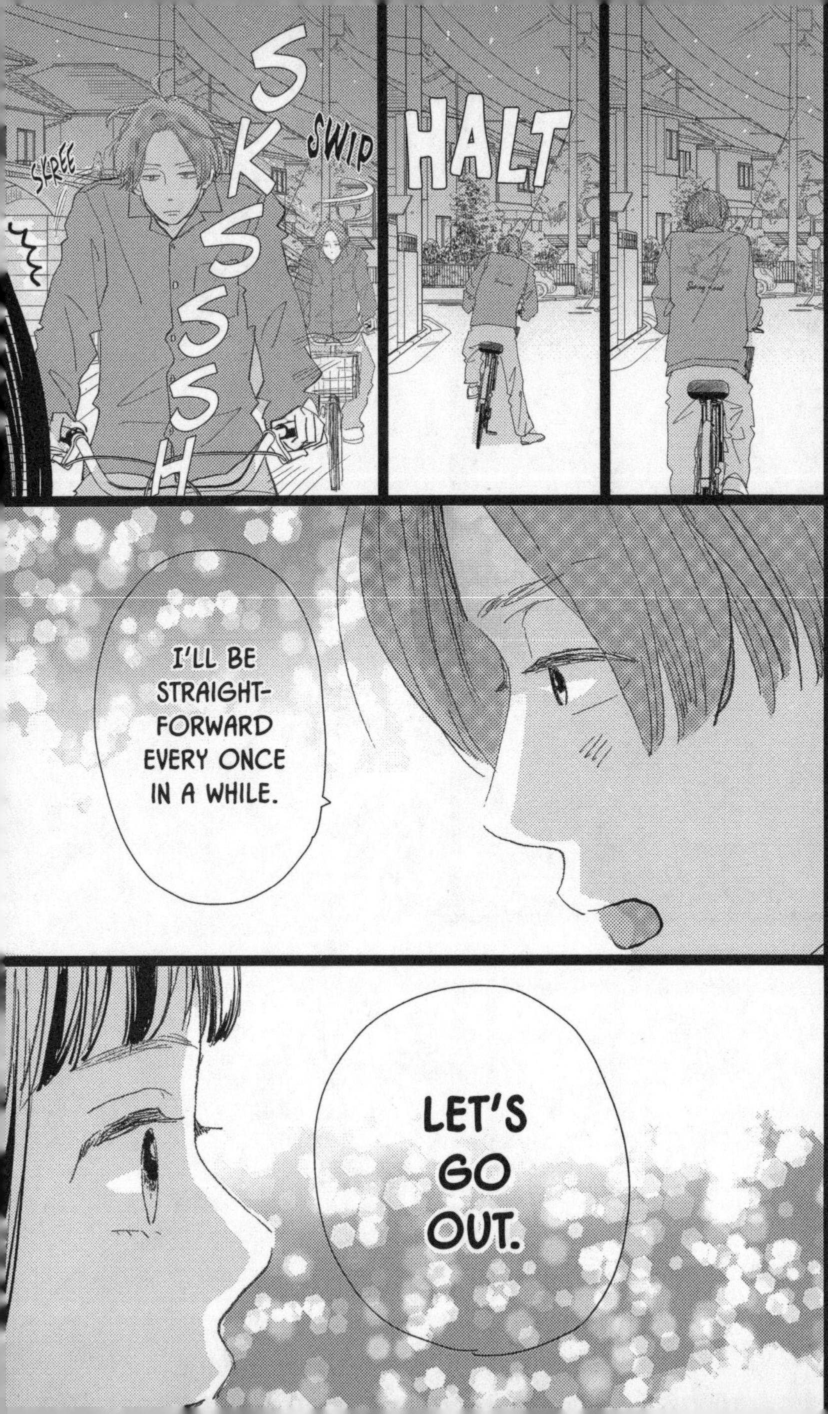
HALT
SWIP
SKSSSH
SKREE
I'LL BE STRAIGHT-FORWARD EVERY ONCE IN A WHILE.
LET'S GO OUT.

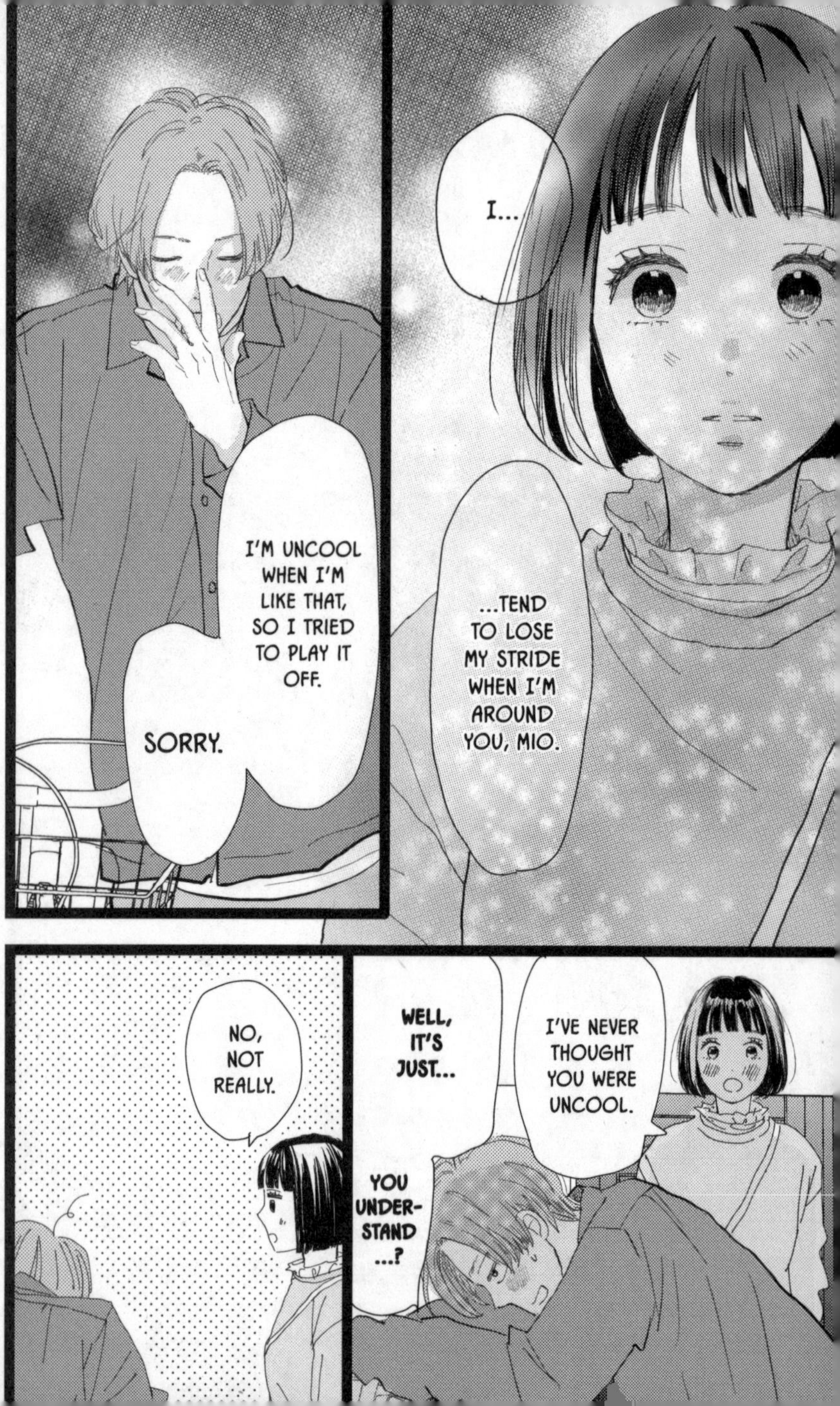
I...
...TEND TO LOSE MY STRIDE WHEN I'M AROUND YOU, MIO.
I'M UNCOOL WHEN I'M LIKE THAT, SO I TRIED TO PLAY IT OFF.
SORRY.
I'VE NEVER THOUGHT YOU WERE UNCOOL.
WELL, IT'S JUST...
YOU UNDERSTAND ...?
NO, NOT REALLY.

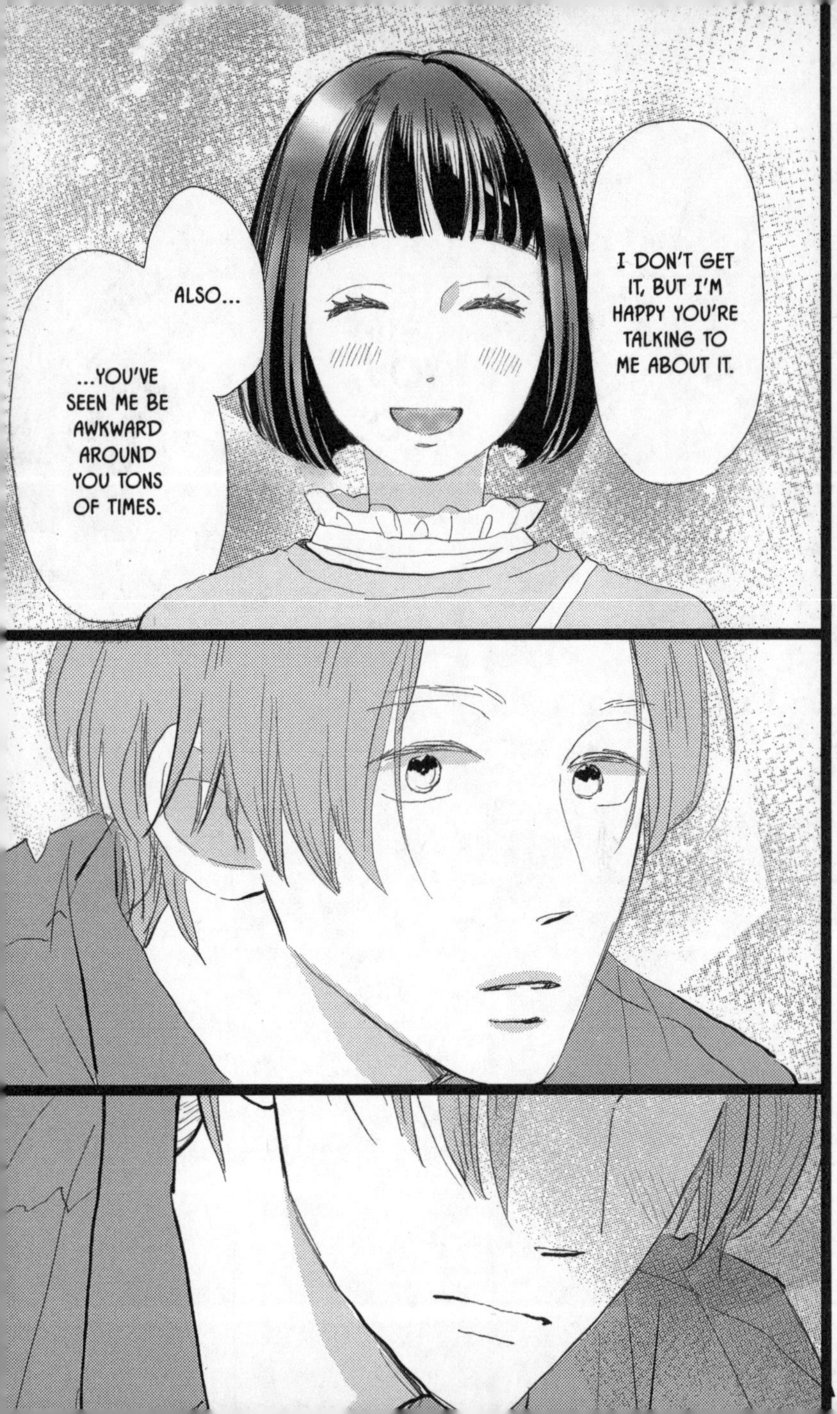
I DON'T GET IT, BUT I'M HAPPY YOU'RE TALKING TO ME ABOUT IT.
ALSO...
...YOU'VE SEEN ME BE AWKWARD AROUND YOU TONS OF TIMES.

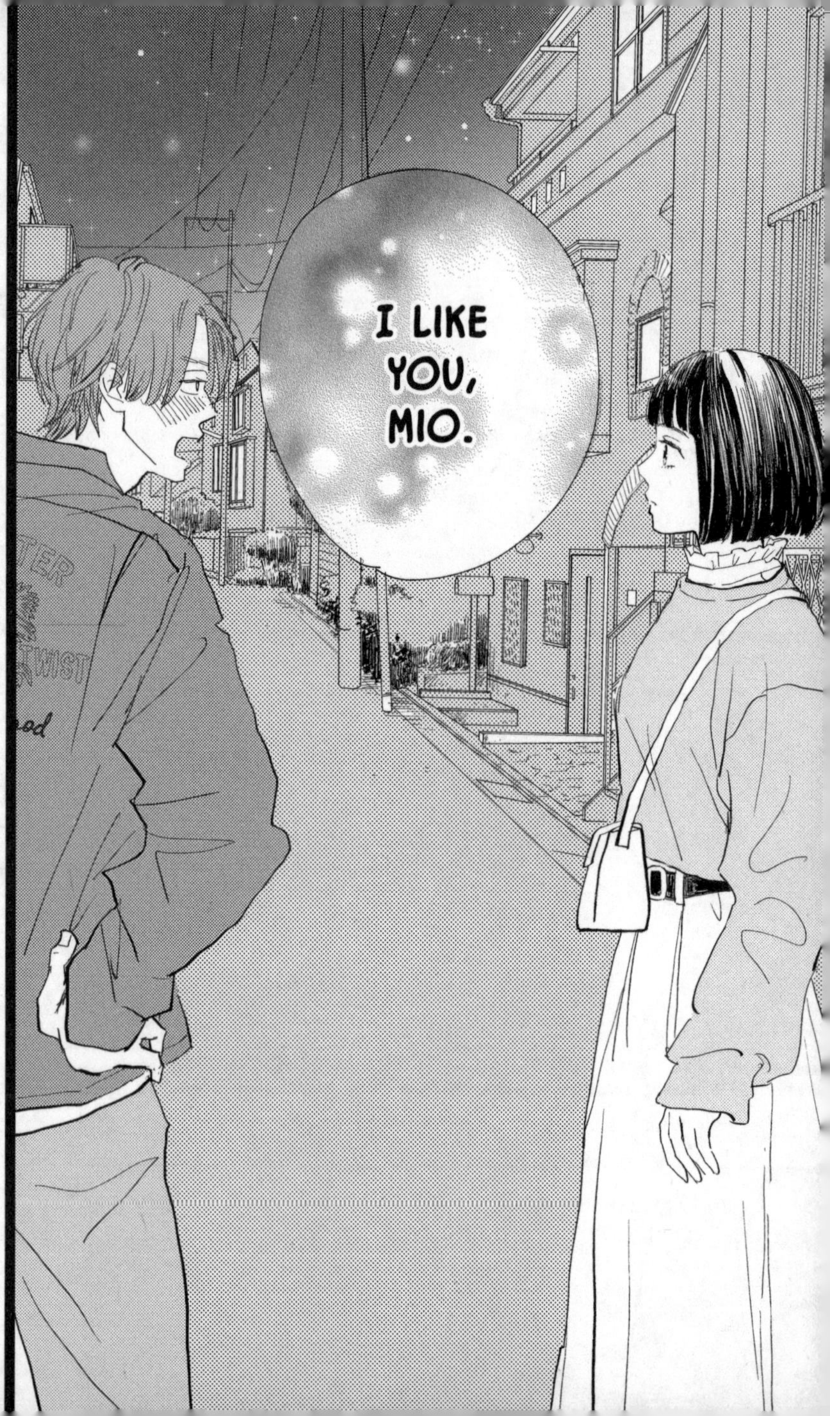
I LIKE YOU, MIO.

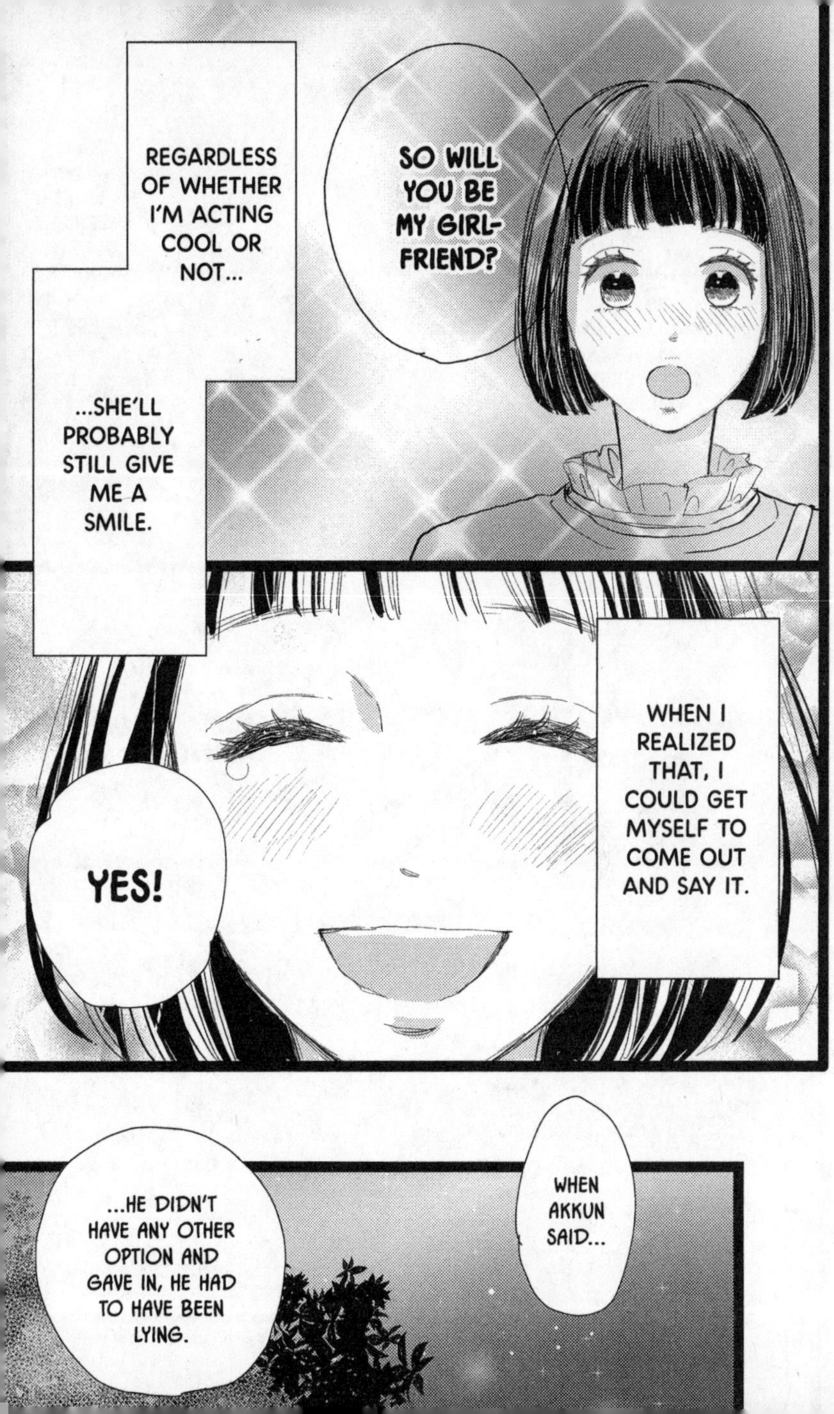
SO WILL YOU BE MY GIRL-FRIEND?
REGARDLESS OF WHETHER I'M ACTING COOL OR NOT...
...SHE'LL PROBABLY STILL GIVE ME A SMILE.
WHEN I REALIZED THAT, I COULD GET MYSELF TO COME OUT AND SAY IT.
YES!
WHEN AKKUN SAID...
...HE DIDN'T HAVE ANY OTHER OPTION AND GAVE IN, HE HAD TO HAVE BEEN LYING.

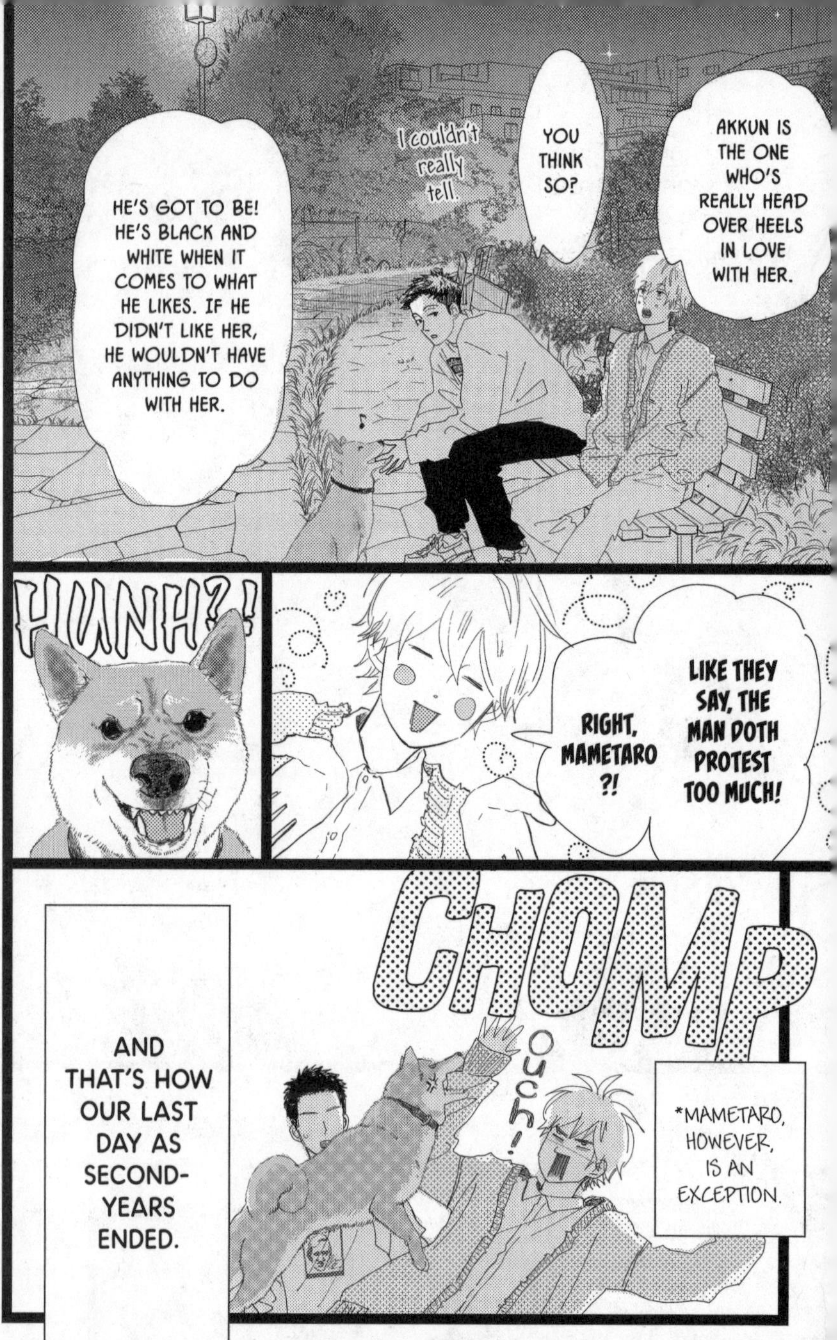
AKKUN IS THE ONE WHO'S REALLY HEAD OVER HEELS IN LOVE WITH HER.
YOU THINK SO?
I couldn't really tell.
HE'S GOT TO BE! HE'S BLACK AND WHITE WHEN IT COMES TO WHAT HE LIKES. IF HE DIDN'T LIKE HER, HE WOULDN'T HAVE ANYTHING TO DO WITH HER.
LIKE THEY SAY, THE MAN DOTH PROTEST TOO MUCH!
RIGHT, MAMETARO?!
HUNH?!
CHOMP
Ouch!
*MAMETARO, HOWEVER, IS AN EXCEPTION.
AND THAT'S HOW OUR LAST DAY AS SECOND-YEARS ENDED.

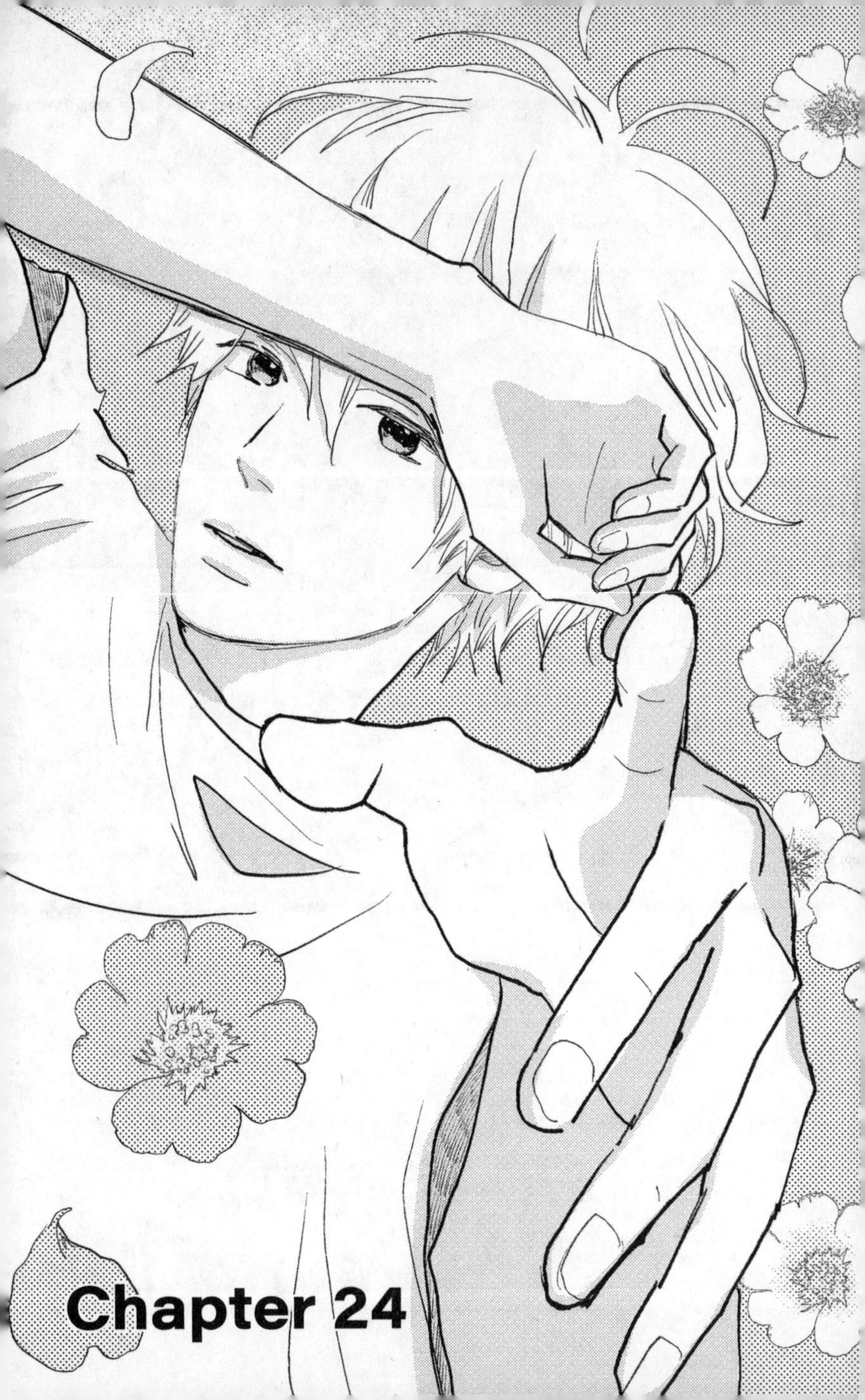
Chapter 24

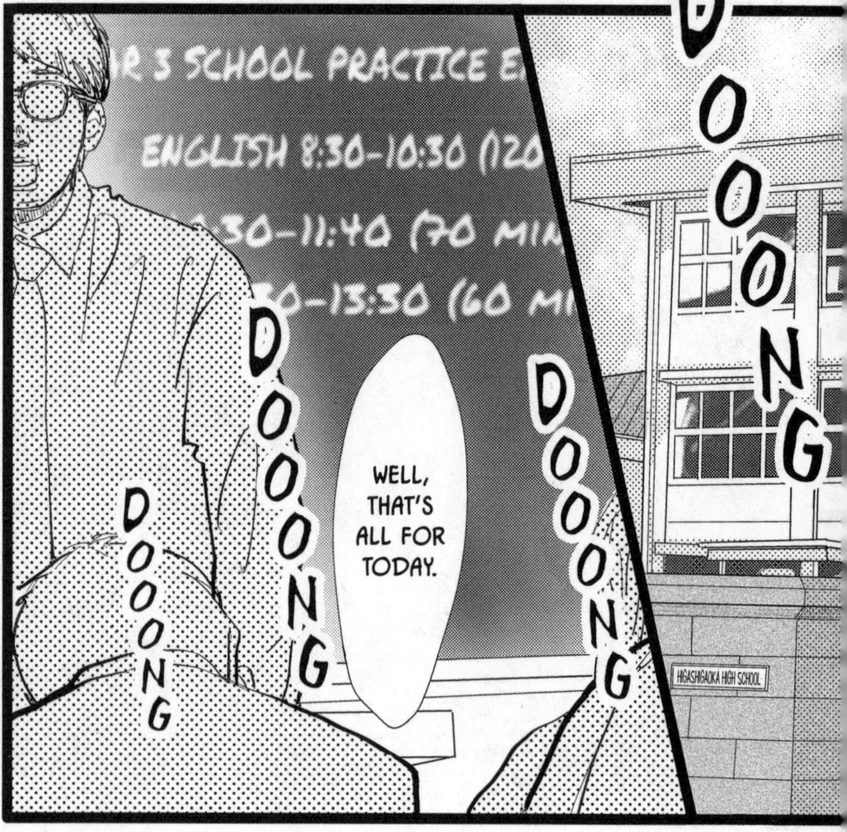
DOOOONG
HIGASHIGAOKA HIGH SCHOOL
ENGLISH 8:30-10:30
DOOOONG
WELL, THAT'S ALL FOR TODAY.
DOOOONG
DOOOONG

My Love Mix-Up!

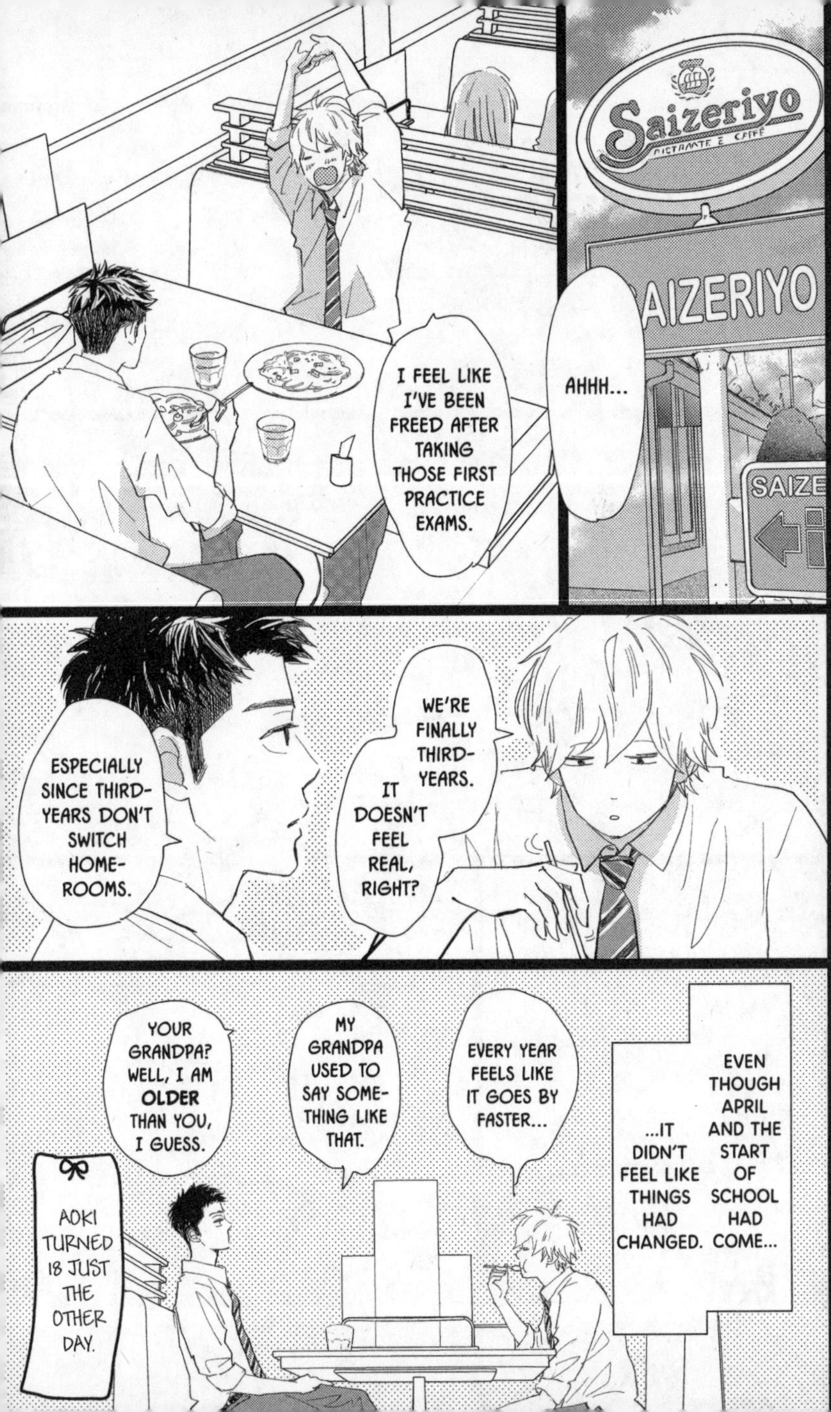
Saizeriyo
SAIZERIYO
SAIZE
AHHH...
I FEEL LIKE I'VE BEEN FREED AFTER TAKING THOSE FIRST PRACTICE EXAMS.
WE'RE FINALLY THIRD-YEARS.
IT DOESN'T FEEL REAL, RIGHT?
ESPECIALLY SINCE THIRD-YEARS DON'T SWITCH HOME-ROOMS.
EVEN THOUGH APRIL AND THE START OF SCHOOL HAD COME...
...IT DIDN'T FEEL LIKE THINGS HAD CHANGED.
EVERY YEAR FEELS LIKE IT GOES BY FASTER...
MY GRANDPA USED TO SAY SOMETHING LIKE THAT.
YOUR GRANDPA? WELL, I AM **OLDER** THAN YOU, I GUESS.
AOKI TURNED 18 JUST THE OTHER DAY.

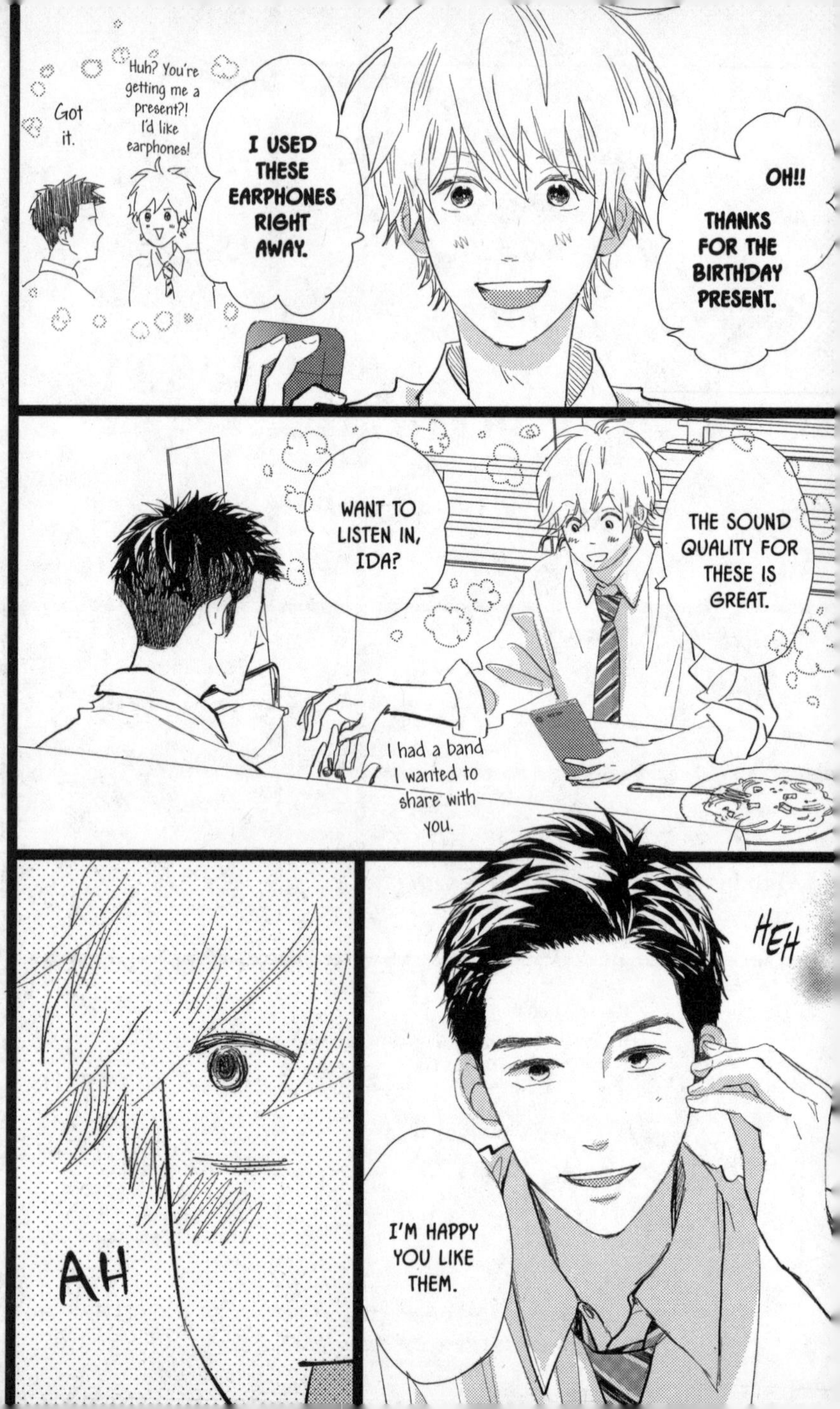
OH!!
THANKS FOR THE BIRTHDAY PRESENT.
I USED THESE EARPHONES RIGHT AWAY.
Huh? You're getting me a present?! I'd like earphones!
Got it.
THE SOUND QUALITY FOR THESE IS GREAT.
WANT TO LISTEN IN, IDA?
I had a band I wanted to share with you.
HEH
I'M HAPPY YOU LIKE THEM.
AH

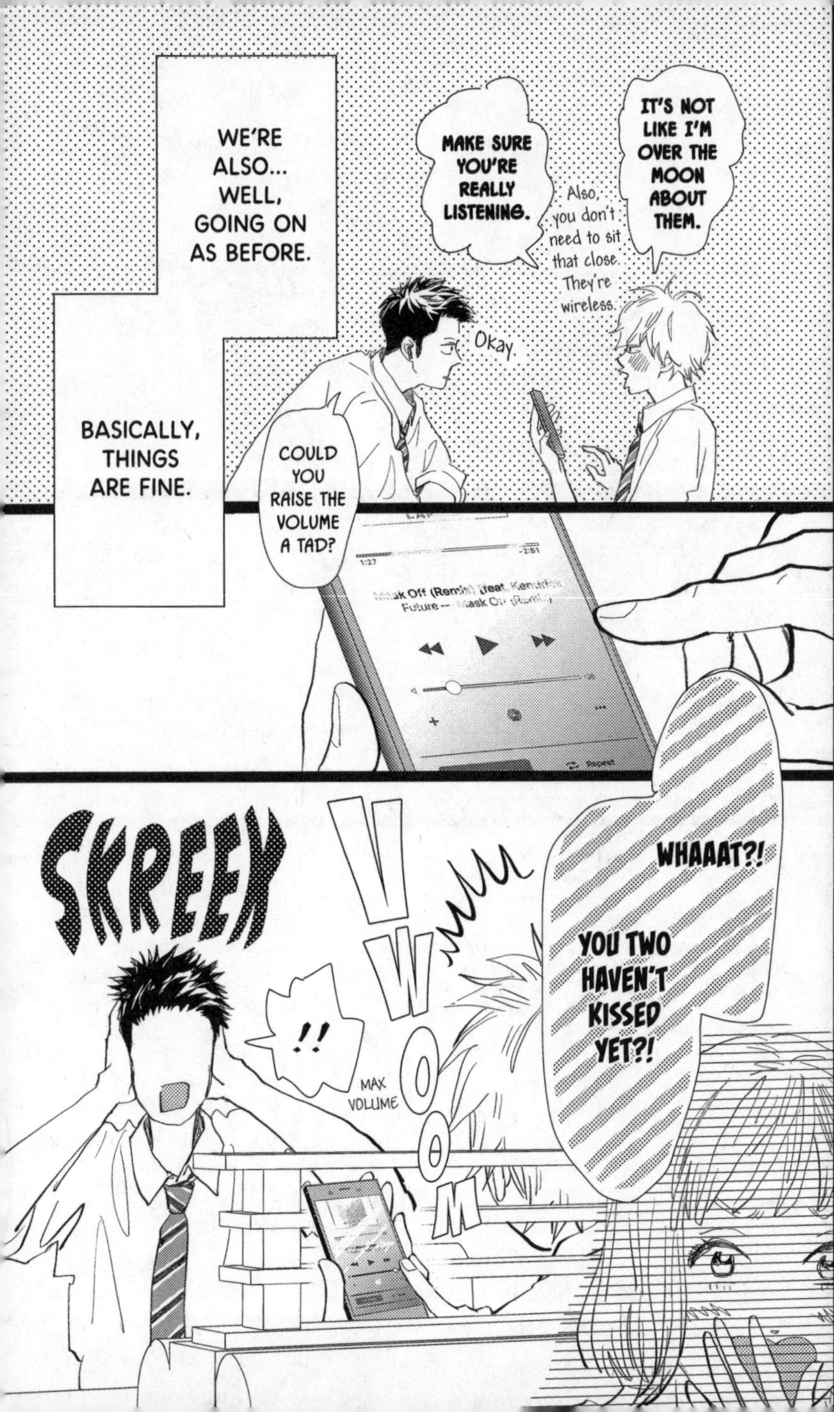
IT'S NOT LIKE I'M OVER THE MOON ABOUT THEM.
Also, you don't need to sit that close. They're wireless.
MAKE SURE YOU'RE REALLY LISTENING.
Okay.
WE'RE ALSO... WELL, GOING ON AS BEFORE.
BASICALLY, THINGS ARE FINE.
COULD YOU RAISE THE VOLUME A TAD?
WHAAAT?!
YOU TWO HAVEN'T KISSED YET?!
VWOOOM
MAX VOLUME
!!
SKREEK

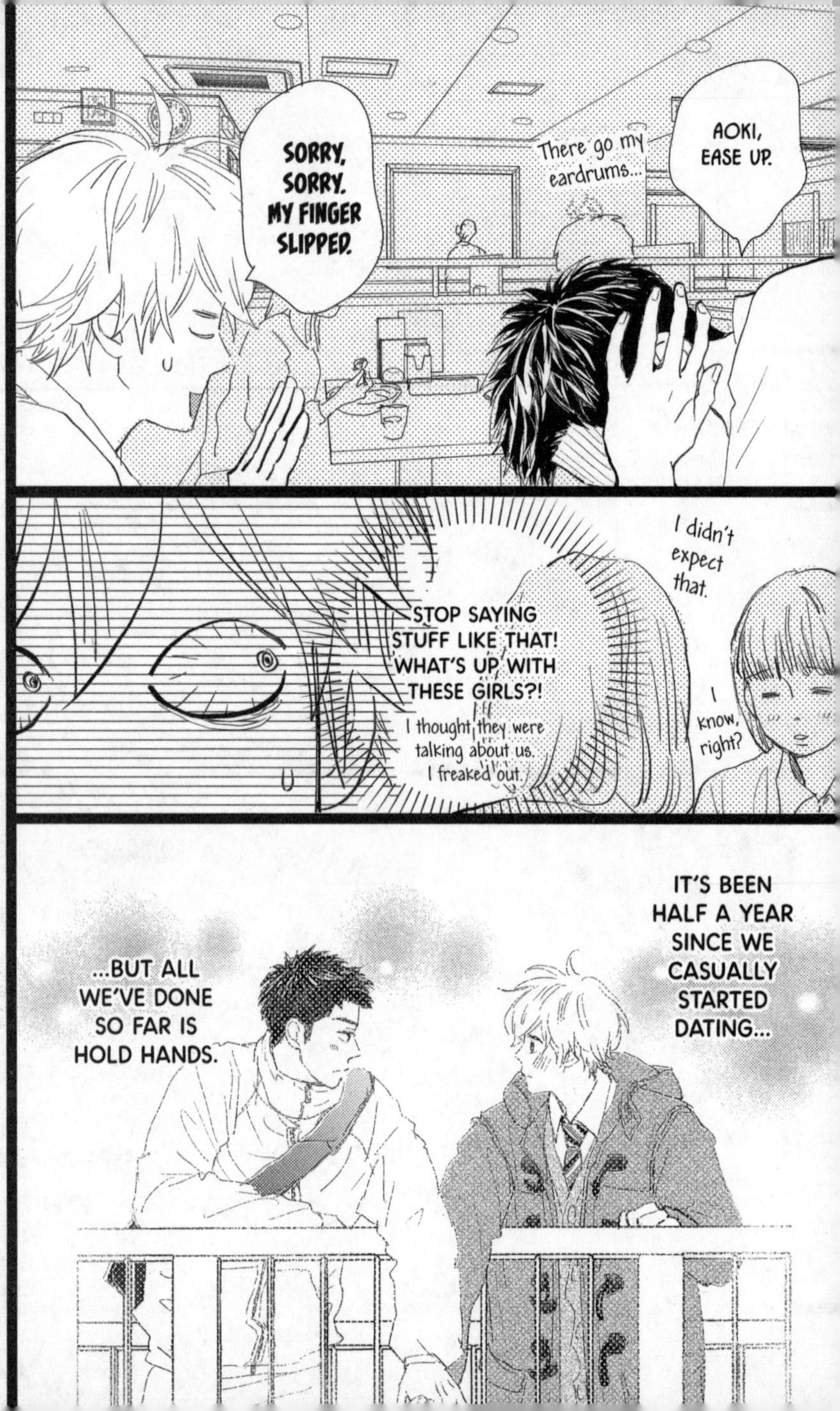
AOKI, EASE UP.
There go my eardrums...
SORRY, SORRY. MY FINGER SLIPPED.
I didn't expect that.
I know, right?
STOP SAYING STUFF LIKE THAT! WHAT'S UP WITH THESE GIRLS?!
I thought they were talking about us. I freaked out.
IT'S BEEN HALF A YEAR SINCE WE CASUALLY STARTED DATING...
...BUT ALL WE'VE DONE SO FAR IS HOLD HANDS.

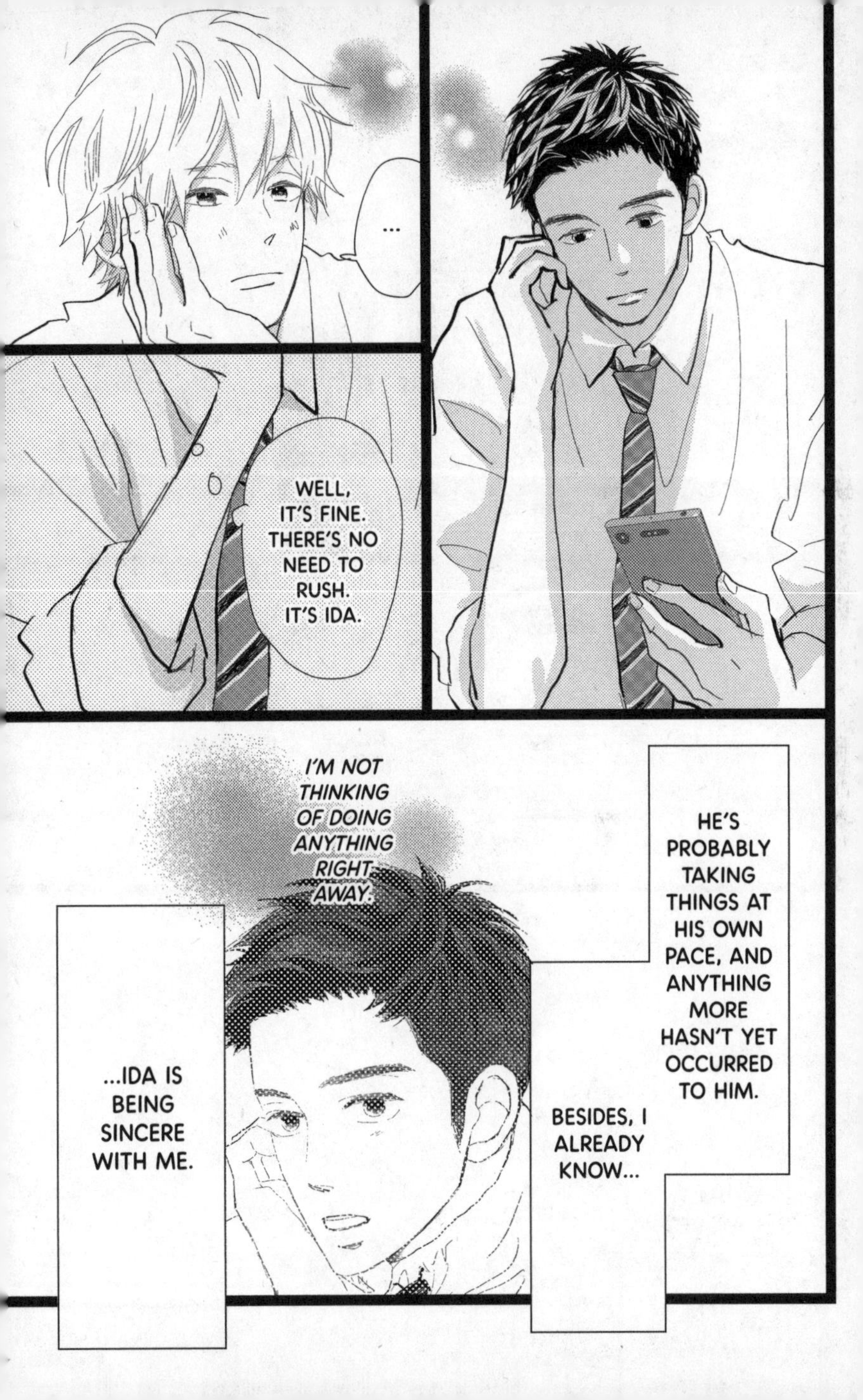
...
WELL, IT'S FINE. THERE'S NO NEED TO RUSH. IT'S IDA.
HE'S PROBABLY TAKING THINGS AT HIS OWN PACE, AND ANYTHING MORE HASN'T YET OCCURRED TO HIM.
I'M NOT THINKING OF DOING ANYTHING RIGHT AWAY.
BESIDES, I ALREADY KNOW...
...IDA IS BEING SINCERE WITH ME.

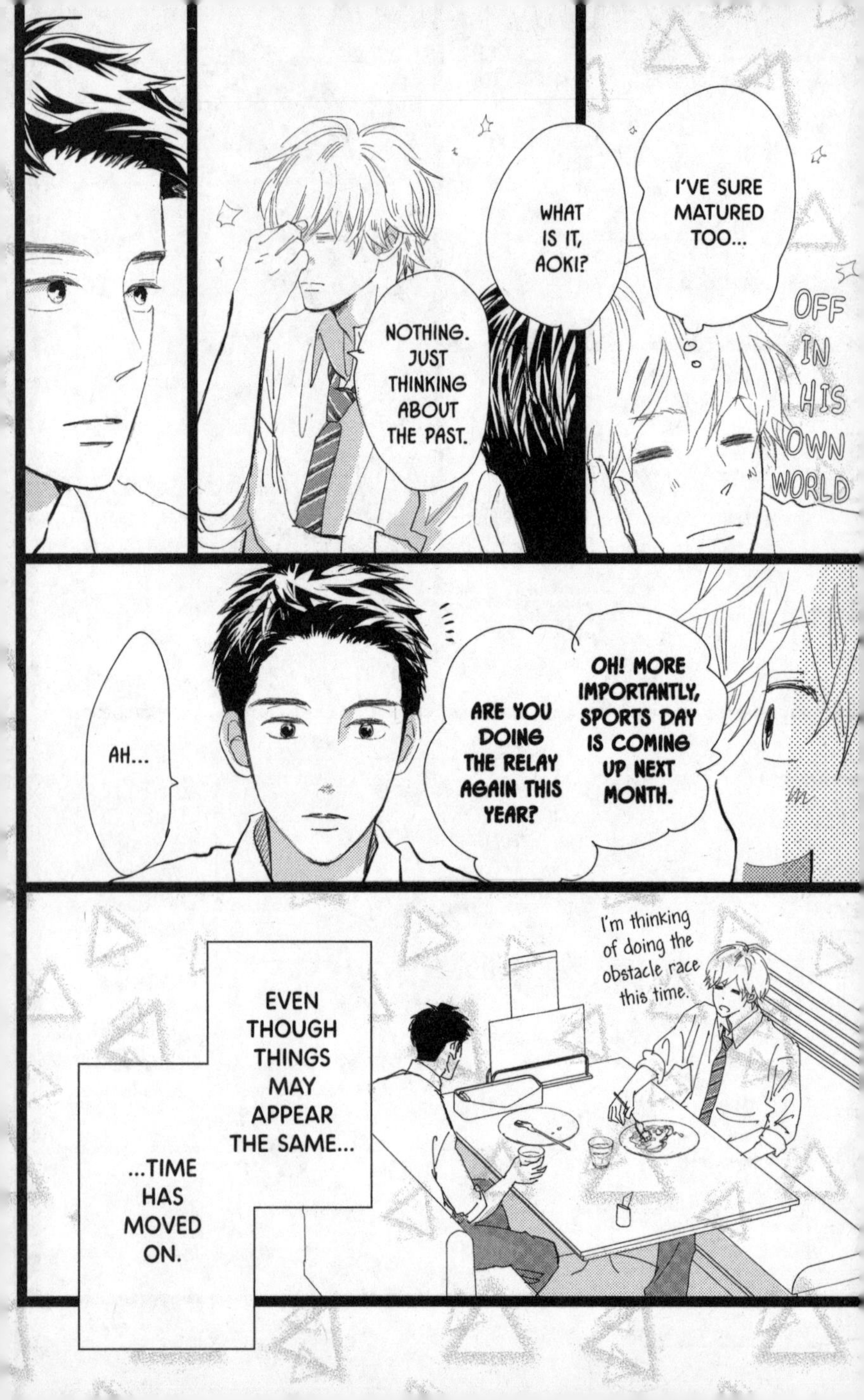
I'VE SURE MATURED TOO...
OFF IN HIS OWN WORLD
WHAT IS IT, AOKI?
NOTHING. JUST THINKING ABOUT THE PAST.
OH! MORE IMPORTANTLY, SPORTS DAY IS COMING UP NEXT MONTH.
ARE YOU DOING THE RELAY AGAIN THIS YEAR?
AH...
I'm thinking of doing the obstacle race this time.
EVEN THOUGH THINGS MAY APPEAR THE SAME...
...TIME HAS MOVED ON.

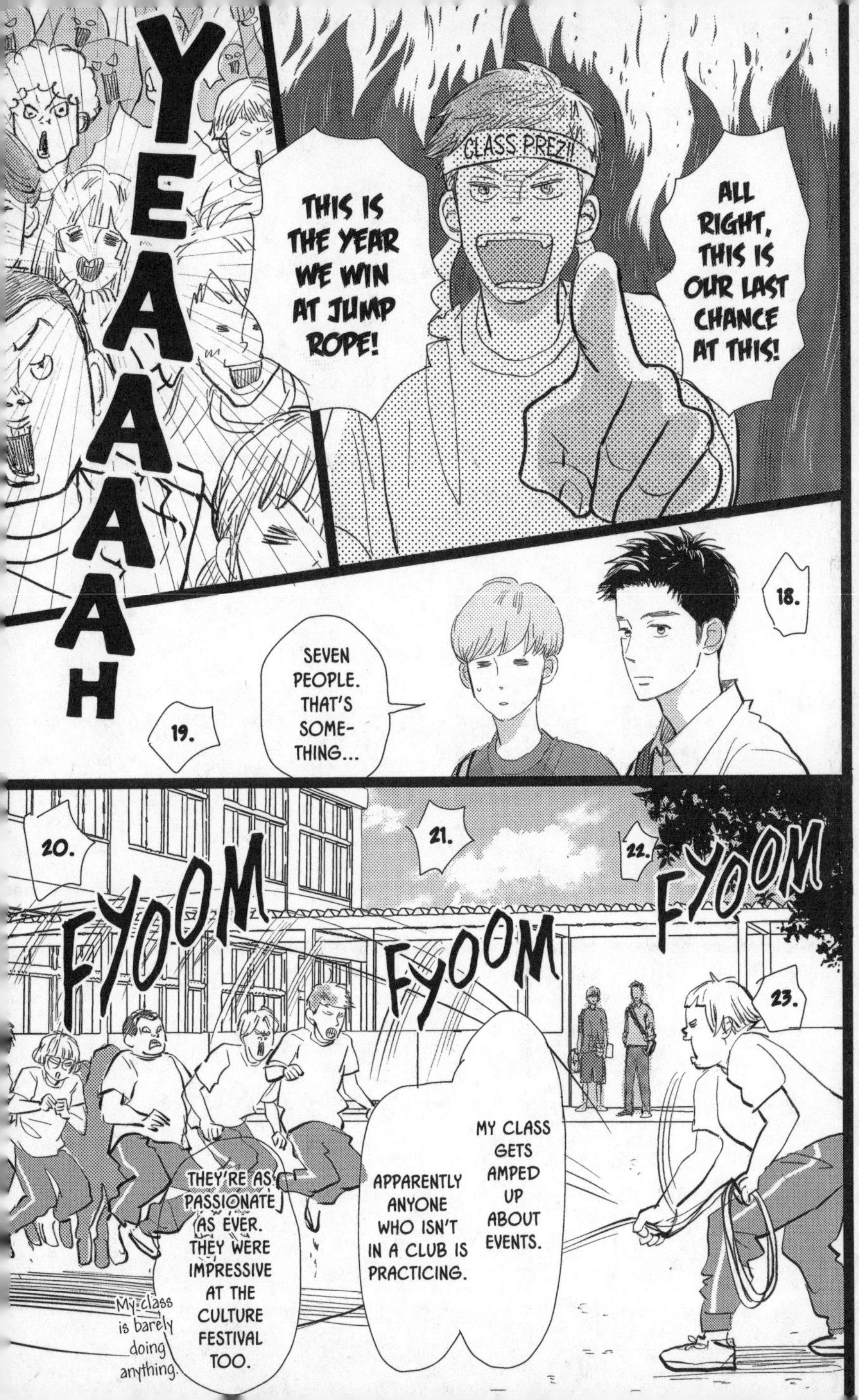
CLASS PREZ!!
ALL RIGHT, THIS IS OUR LAST CHANCE AT THIS!
THIS IS THE YEAR WE WIN AT JUMP ROPE!
YEAAAAAH
18.
SEVEN PEOPLE. THAT'S SOME-THING...
19.
23.
FYOOM
22.
MY CLASS GETS AMPED UP ABOUT EVENTS.
21.
FYOOM
APPARENTLY ANYONE WHO ISN'T IN A CLUB IS PRACTICING.
THEY'RE AS PASSIONATE AS EVER. THEY WERE IMPRESSIVE AT THE CULTURE FESTIVAL TOO.
FYOOM
20.
My class is barely doing anything.

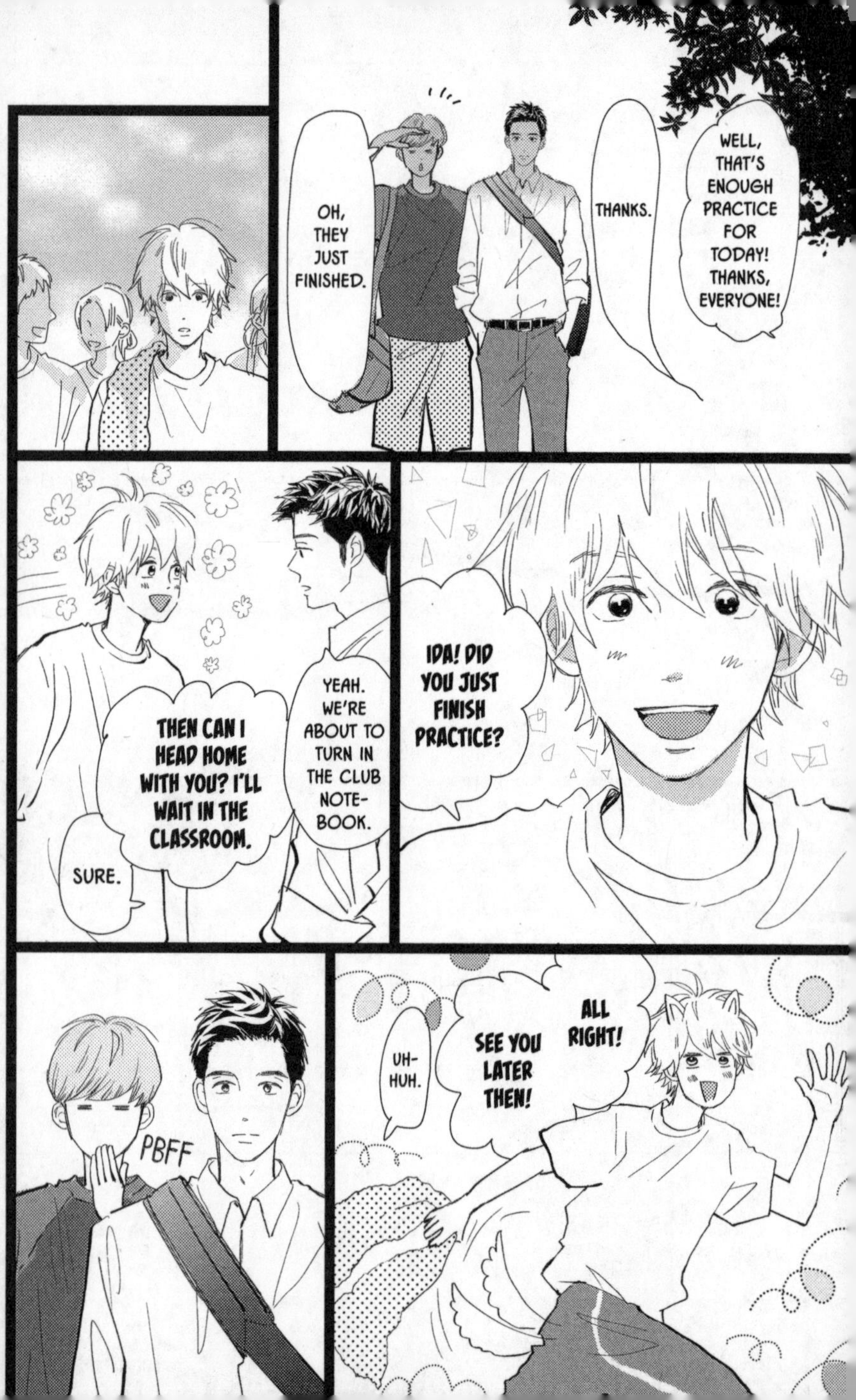
WELL, THAT'S ENOUGH PRACTICE FOR TODAY! THANKS, EVERYONE!
THANKS.
OH, THEY JUST FINISHED.
IDA! DID YOU JUST FINISH PRACTICE?
YEAH. WE'RE ABOUT TO TURN IN THE CLUB NOTE-BOOK.
THEN CAN I HEAD HOME WITH YOU? I'LL WAIT IN THE CLASSROOM.
SURE.
ALL RIGHT!
SEE YOU LATER THEN!
UH-HUH.
PBFF

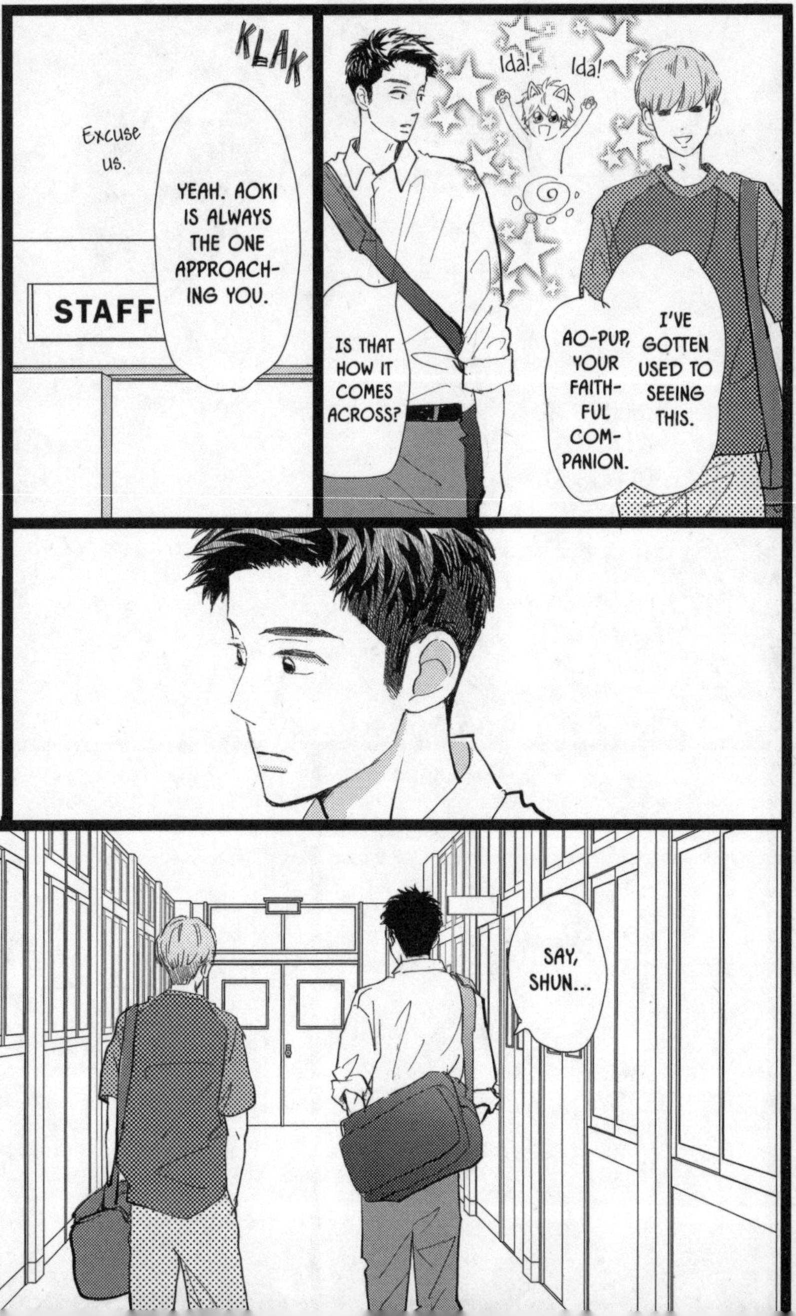
Ida!
Ida!
I'VE GOTTEN USED TO SEEING THIS.
AO-PUP, YOUR FAITHFUL COMPANION.
IS THAT HOW IT COMES ACROSS?
KLAK
YEAH. AOKI IS ALWAYS THE ONE APPROACHING YOU.
Excuse us.
STAFF
SAY, SHUN...

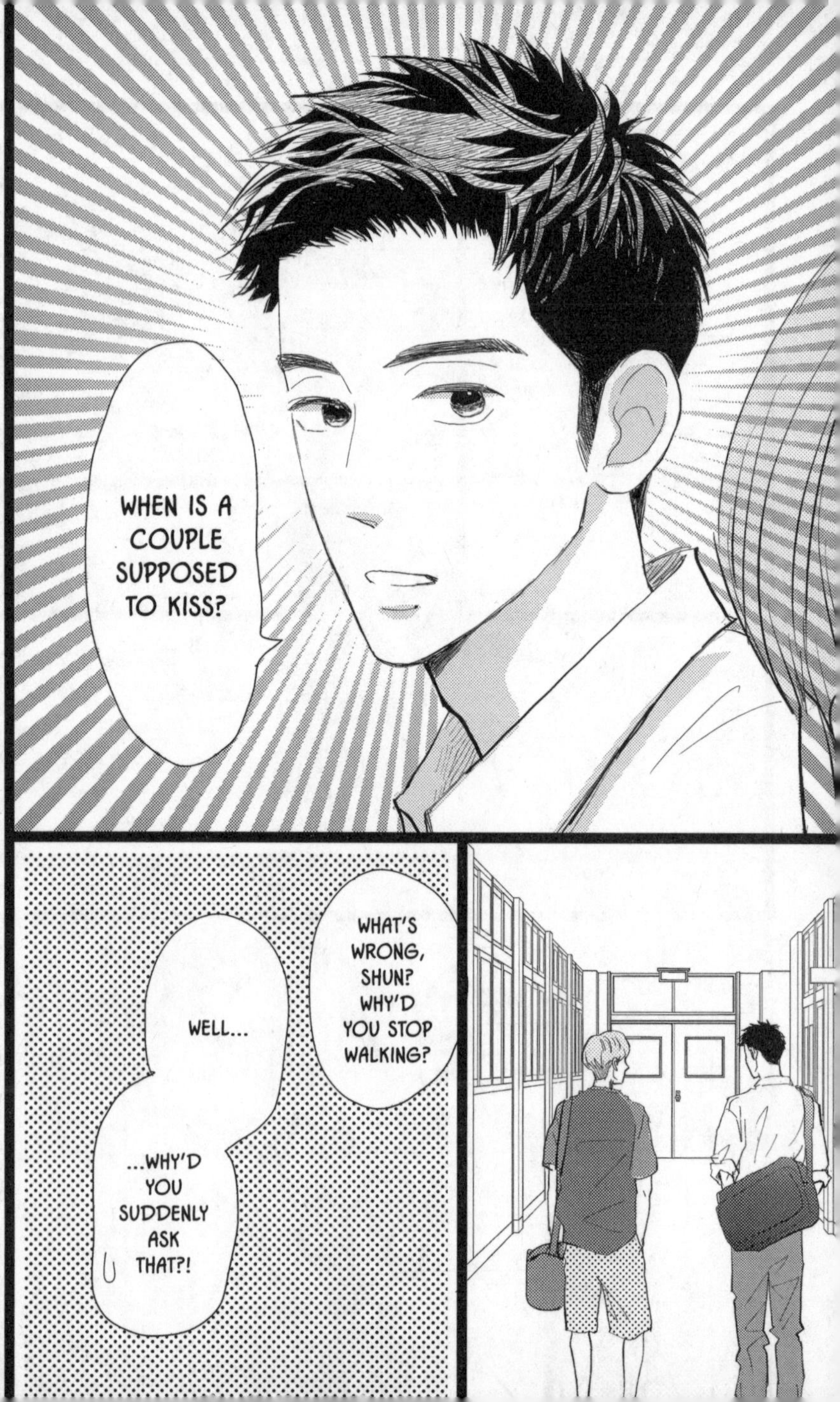
WHEN IS A COUPLE SUPPOSED TO KISS?
WHAT'S WRONG, SHUN? WHY'D YOU STOP WALKING?
WELL...
...WHY'D YOU SUDDENLY ASK THAT?!

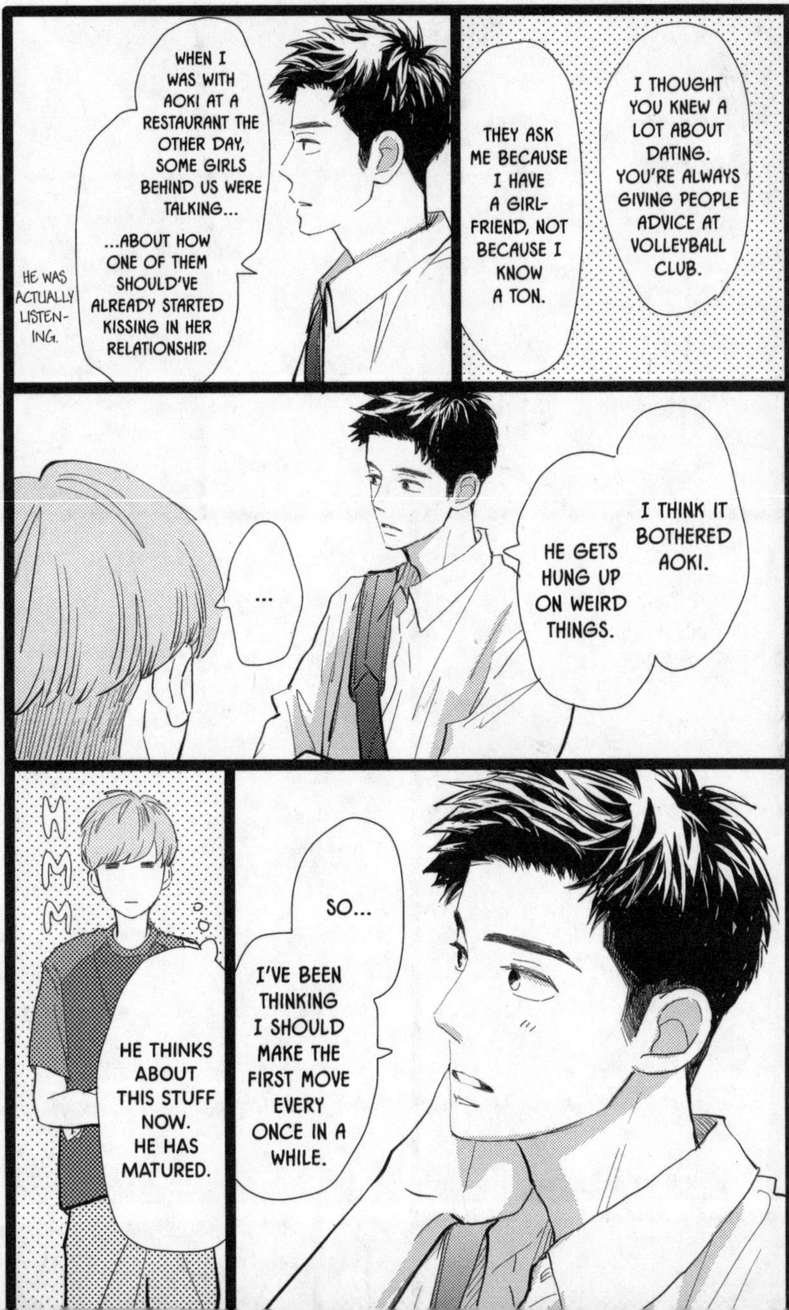
I THOUGHT YOU KNEW A LOT ABOUT DATING. YOU'RE ALWAYS GIVING PEOPLE ADVICE AT VOLLEYBALL CLUB.
THEY ASK ME BECAUSE I HAVE A GIRL-FRIEND, NOT BECAUSE I KNOW A TON.
WHEN I WAS WITH AOKI AT A RESTAURANT THE OTHER DAY, SOME GIRLS BEHIND US WERE TALKING...
...ABOUT HOW ONE OF THEM SHOULD'VE ALREADY STARTED KISSING IN HER RELATIONSHIP.
HE WAS ACTUALLY LISTEN-ING.
I THINK IT BOTHERED AOKI.
HE GETS HUNG UP ON WEIRD THINGS.
...
SO...
I'VE BEEN THINKING I SHOULD MAKE THE FIRST MOVE EVERY ONCE IN A WHILE.
HMMM
HE THINKS ABOUT THIS STUFF NOW. HE HAS MATURED.

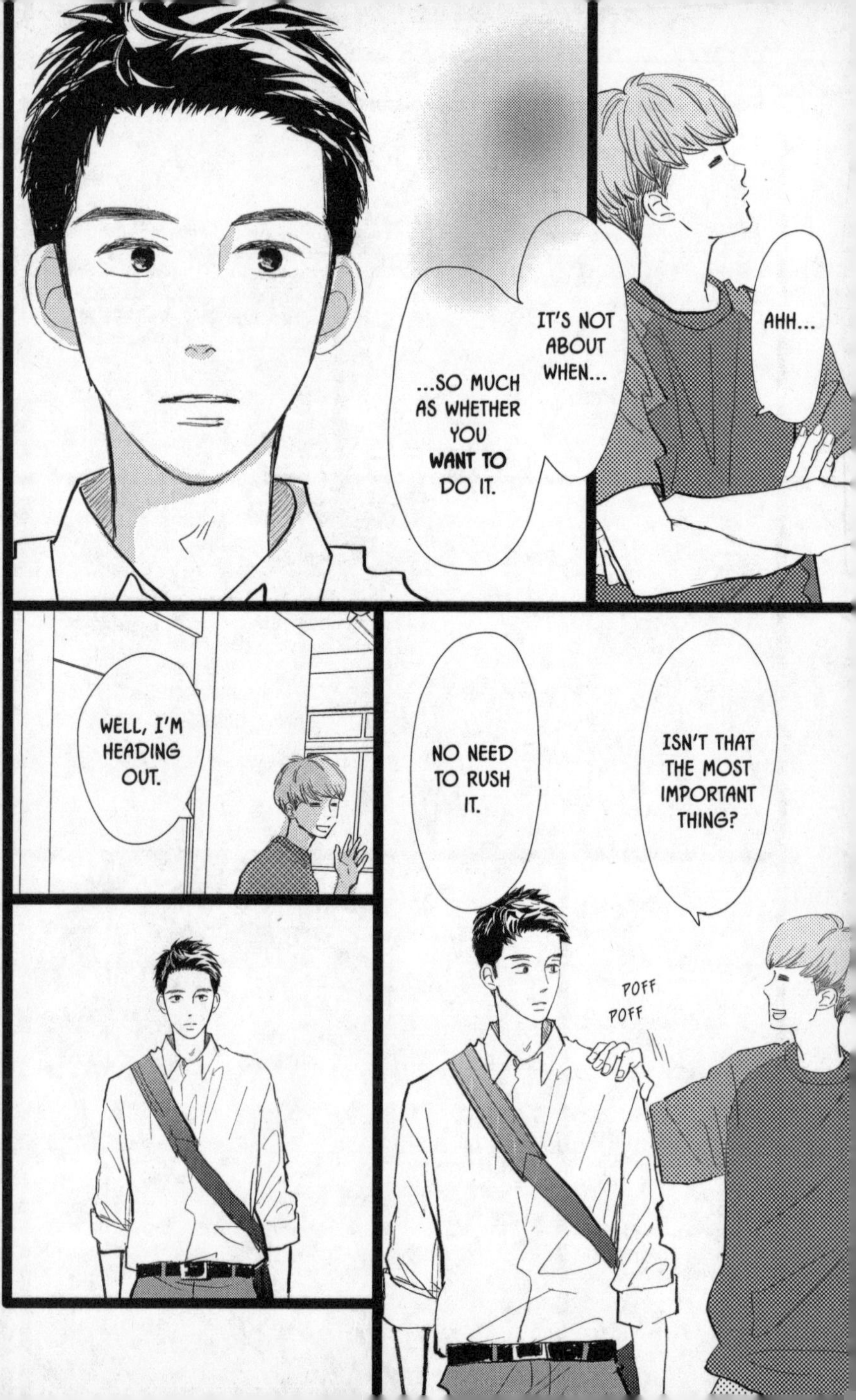
AHH...
IT'S NOT ABOUT WHEN...
...SO MUCH AS WHETHER YOU WANT TO DO IT.
ISN'T THAT THE MOST IMPORTANT THING?
NO NEED TO RUSH IT.
POFF
POFF
WELL, I'M HEADING OUT.

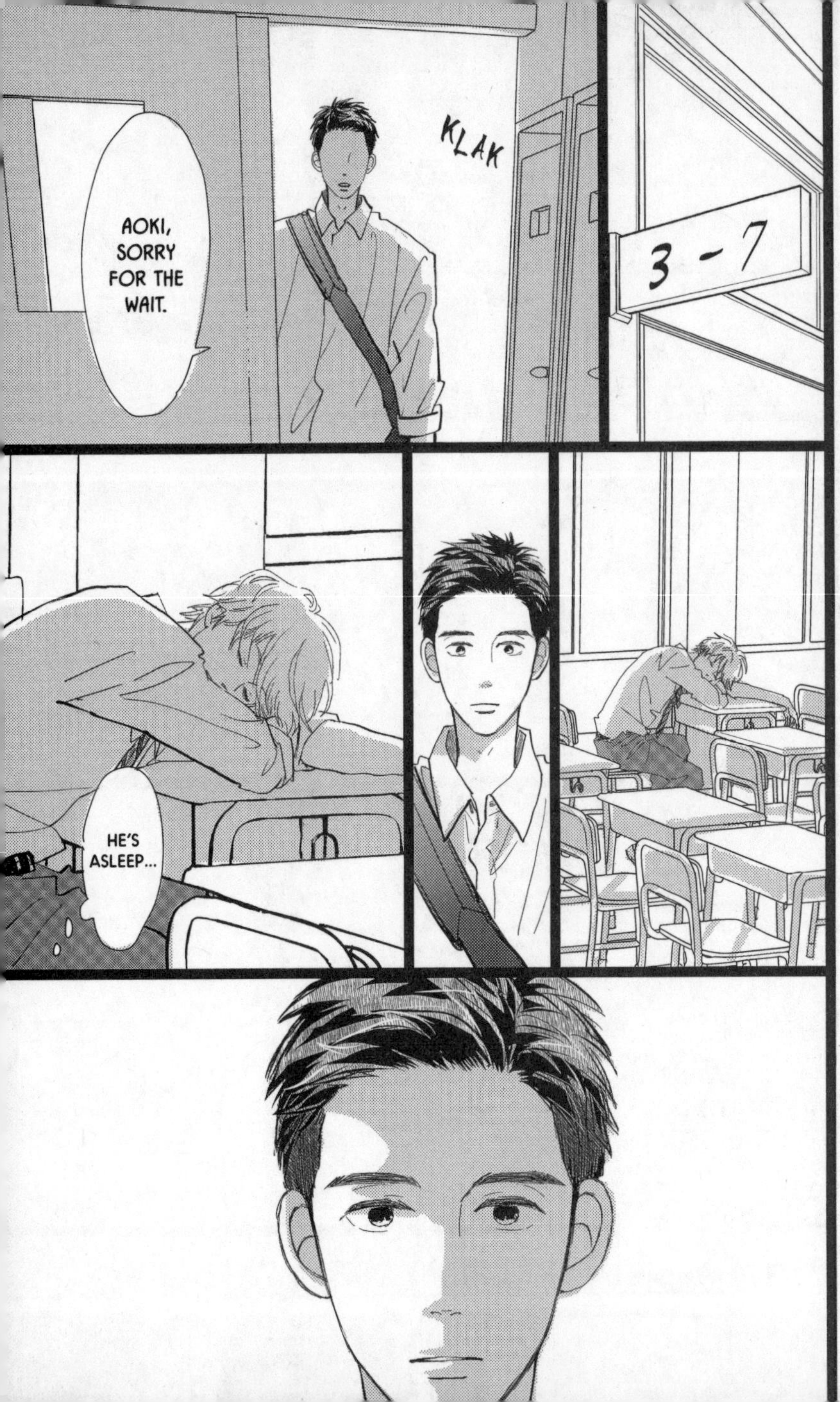
KLAK
AOKI, SORRY FOR THE WAIT.
HE'S ASLEEP...

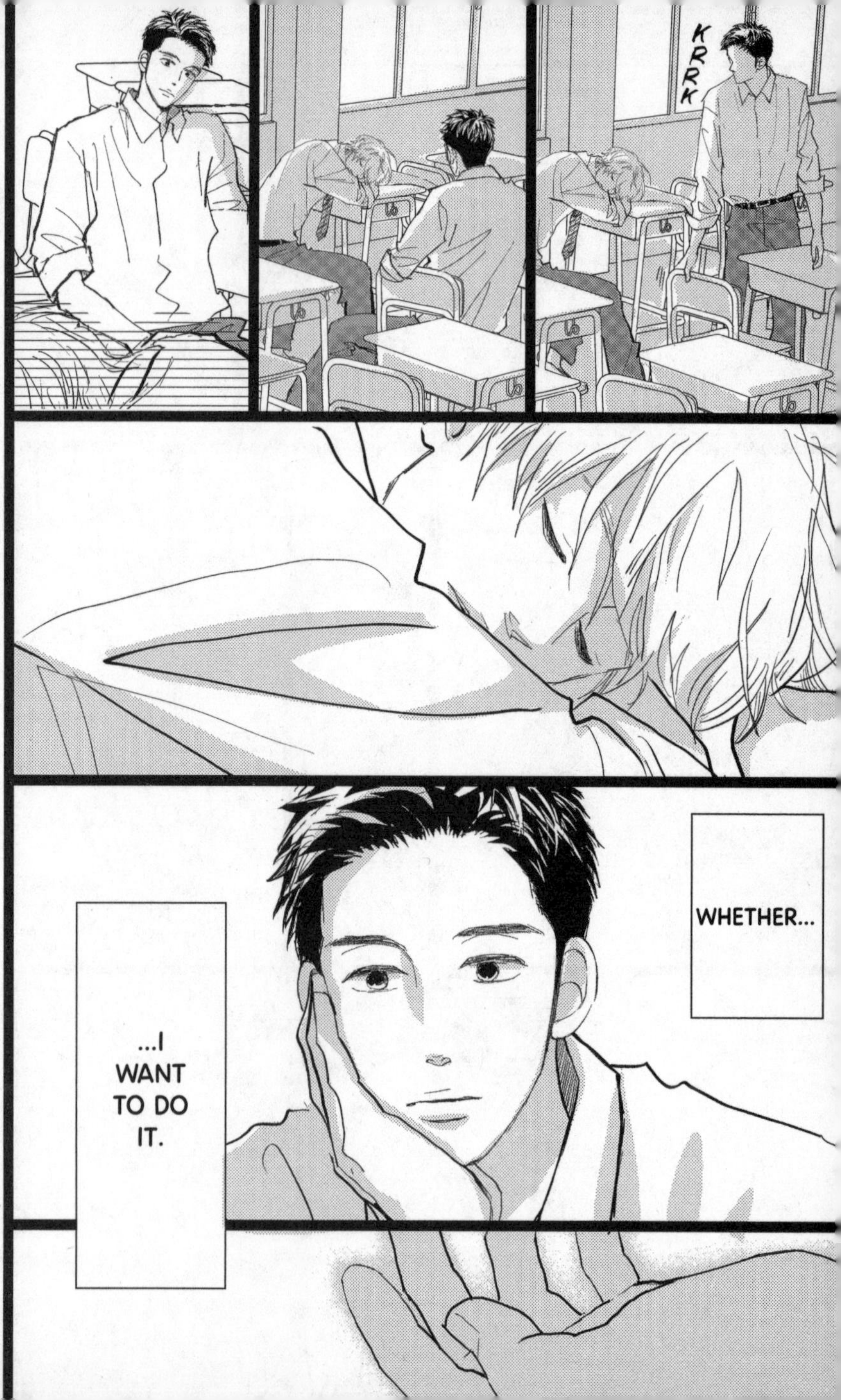
KRRK
WHETHER...
...I WANT TO DO IT.

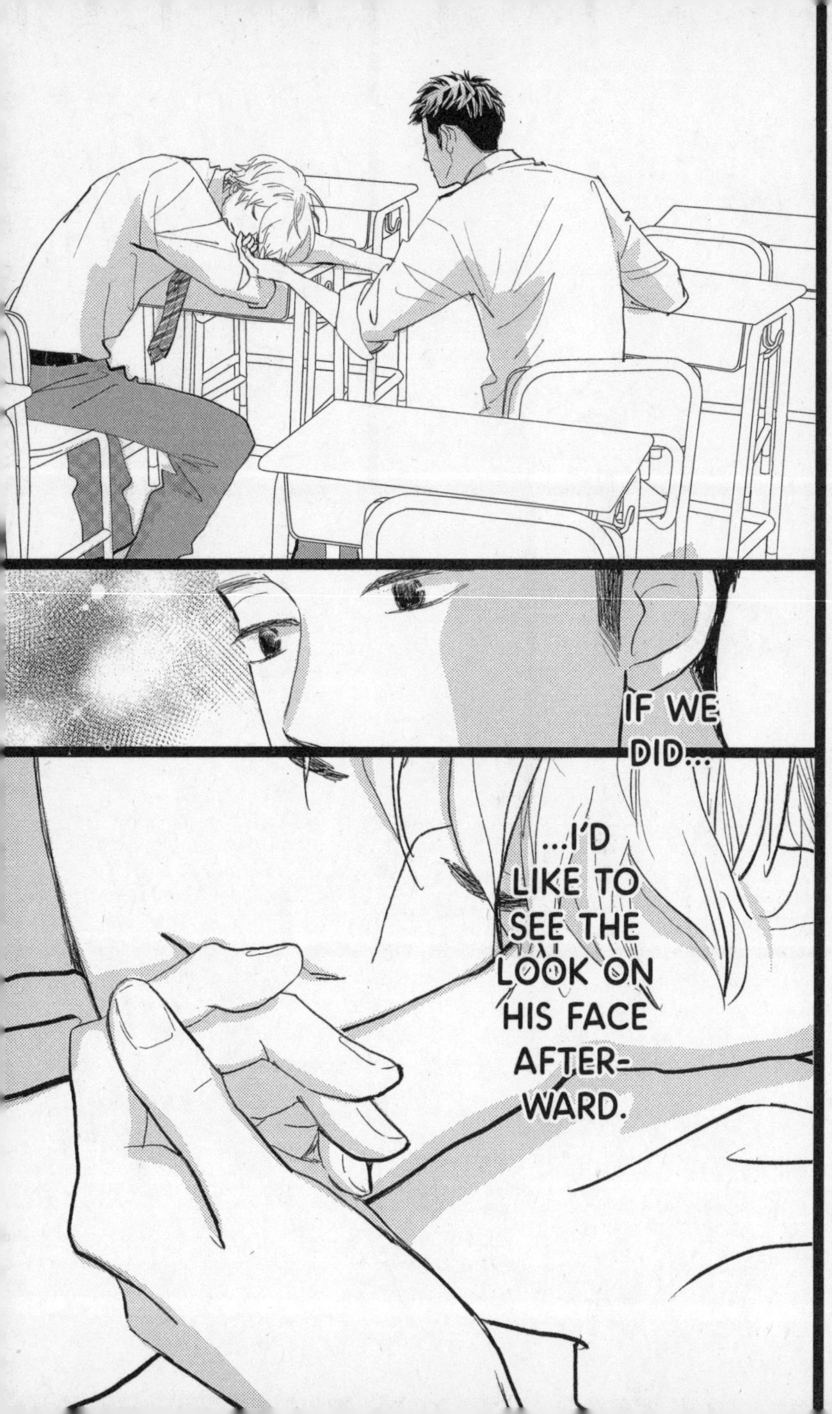
IF WE DID...
...I'D LIKE TO SEE THE LOOK ON HIS FACE AFTER-WARD.

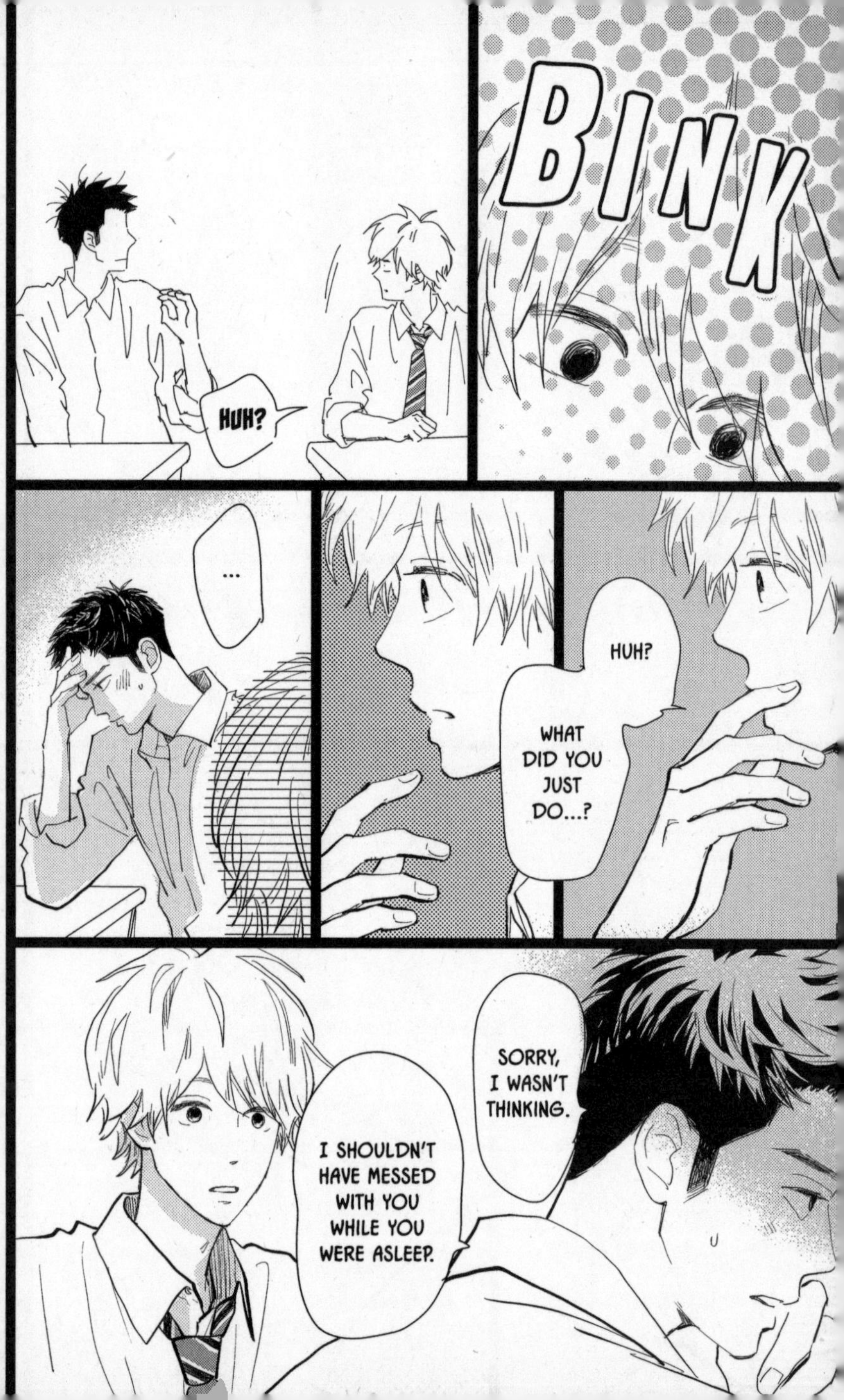
BINK
HUH?
HUH?
WHAT DID YOU JUST DO...?
...
SORRY, I WASN'T THINKING.
I SHOULDN'T HAVE MESSED WITH YOU WHILE YOU WERE ASLEEP.

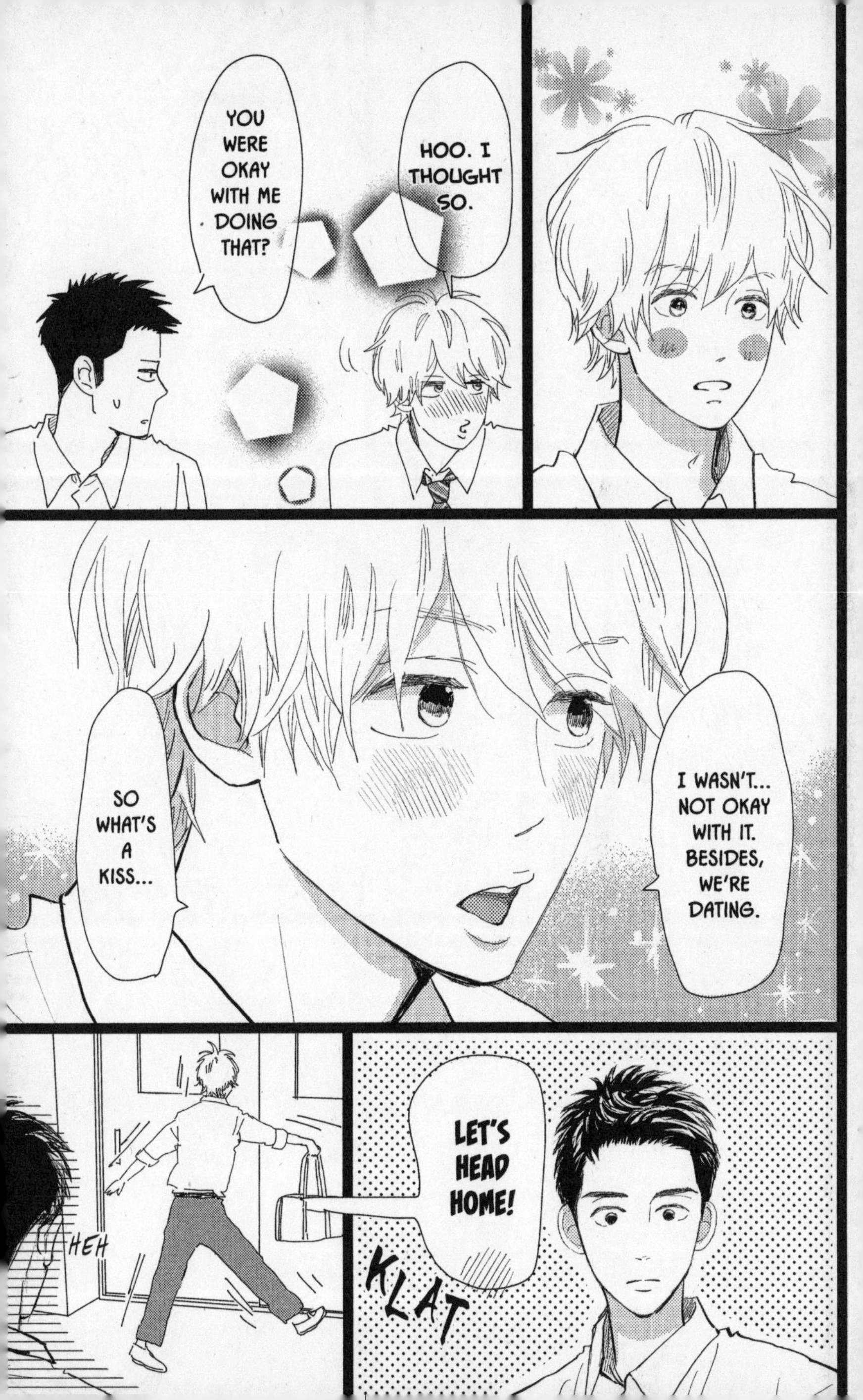
HOO. I THOUGHT SO.
YOU WERE OKAY WITH ME DOING THAT?
I WASN'T... NOT OKAY WITH IT. BESIDES, WE'RE DATING.
SO WHAT'S A KISS...
LET'S HEAD HOME!
KLAT
HEH

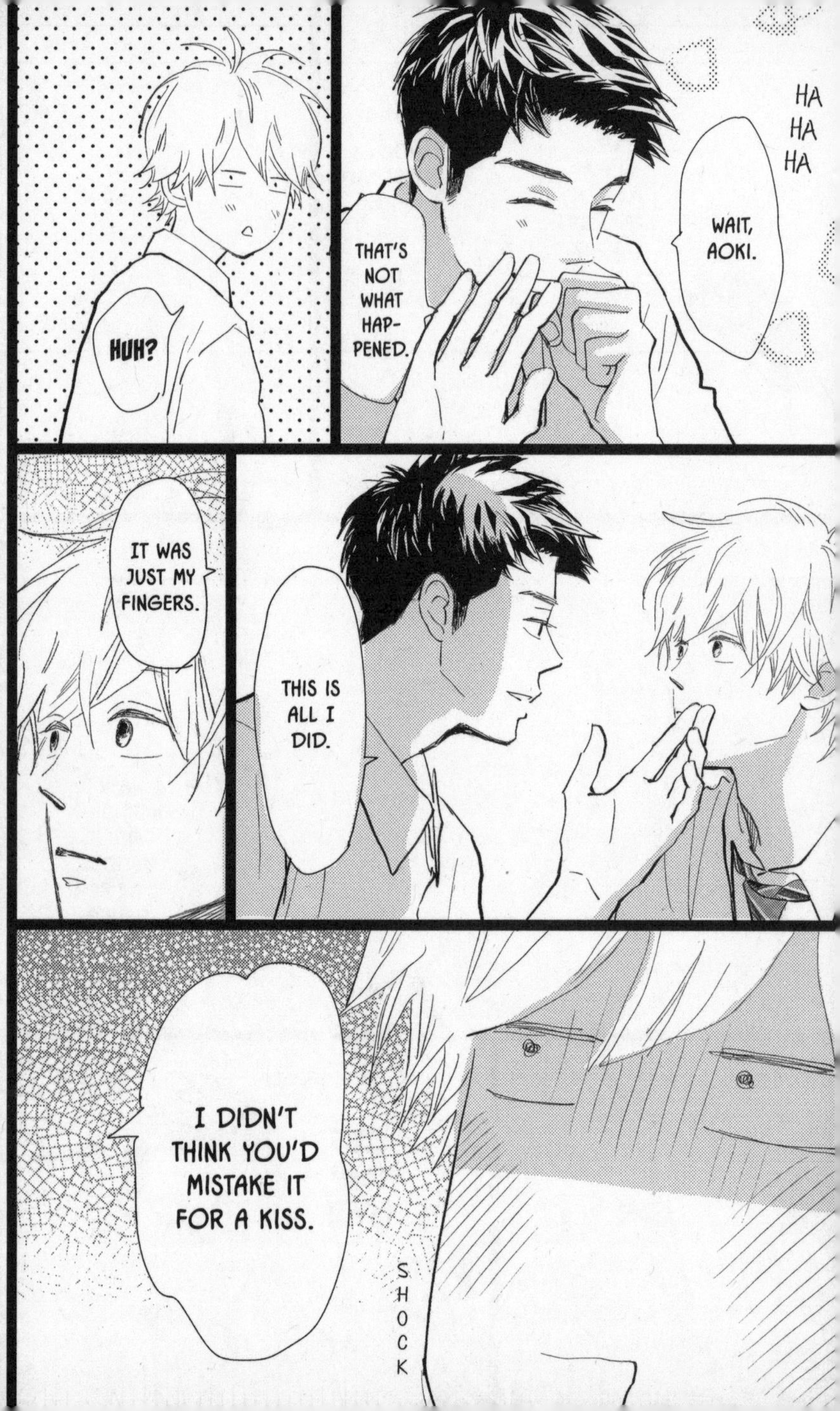
HA HA HA
WAIT, AOKI.
THAT'S NOT WHAT HAP-PENED.
HUH?
THIS IS ALL I DID.
IT WAS JUST MY FINGERS.
I DIDN'T THINK YOU'D MISTAKE IT FOR A KISS.
SHOCK

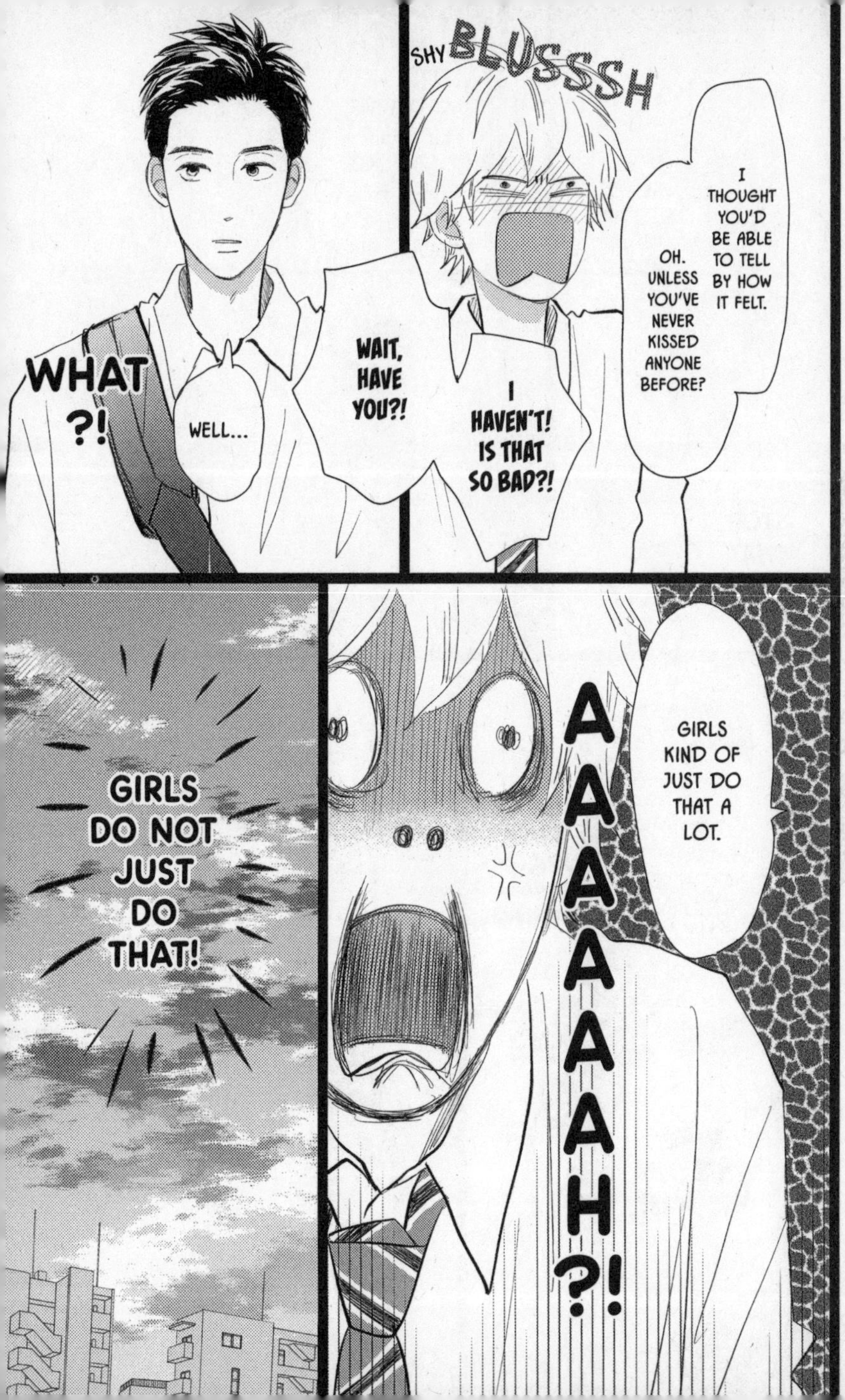
SHY BLUSSSH
I THOUGHT YOU'D BE ABLE TO TELL BY HOW IT FELT.
OH. UNLESS YOU'VE NEVER KISSED ANYONE BEFORE?
I HAVEN'T! IS THAT SO BAD?!
WAIT, HAVE YOU?!
WELL...
WHAT?!
GIRLS KIND OF JUST DO THAT A LOT.
AAAAAAH?!
GIRLS DO NOT JUST DO THAT!

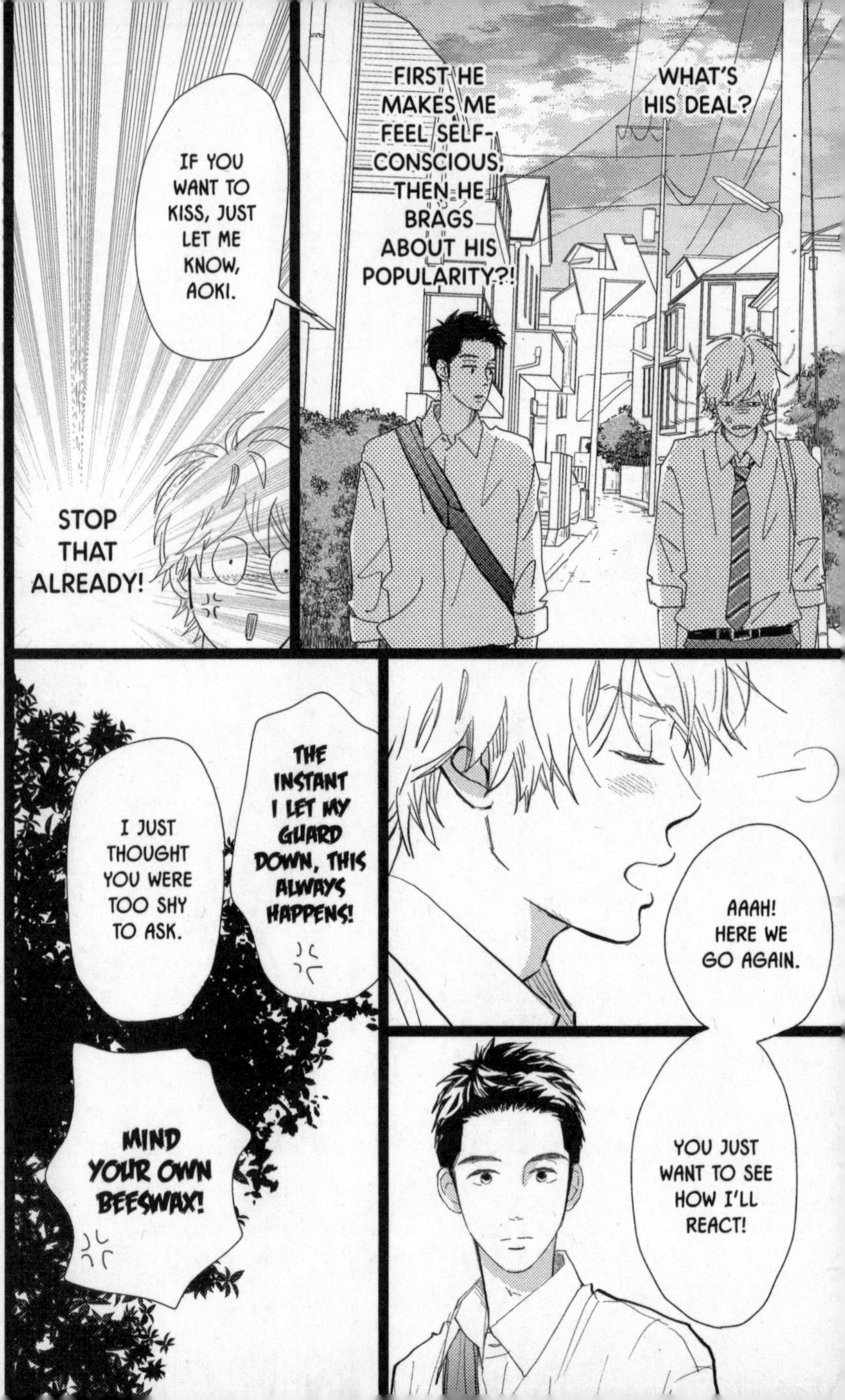
WHAT'S HIS DEAL?
FIRST HE MAKES ME FEEL SELF-CONSCIOUS, THEN HE BRAGS ABOUT HIS POPULARITY?!
IF YOU WANT TO KISS, JUST LET ME KNOW, AOKI.
STOP THAT ALREADY!
AAAH! HERE WE GO AGAIN.
YOU JUST WANT TO SEE HOW I'LL REACT!
THE INSTANT I LET MY GUARD DOWN, THIS ALWAYS HAPPENS!
I JUST THOUGHT YOU WERE TOO SHY TO ASK.
MIND YOUR OWN BEESWAX!

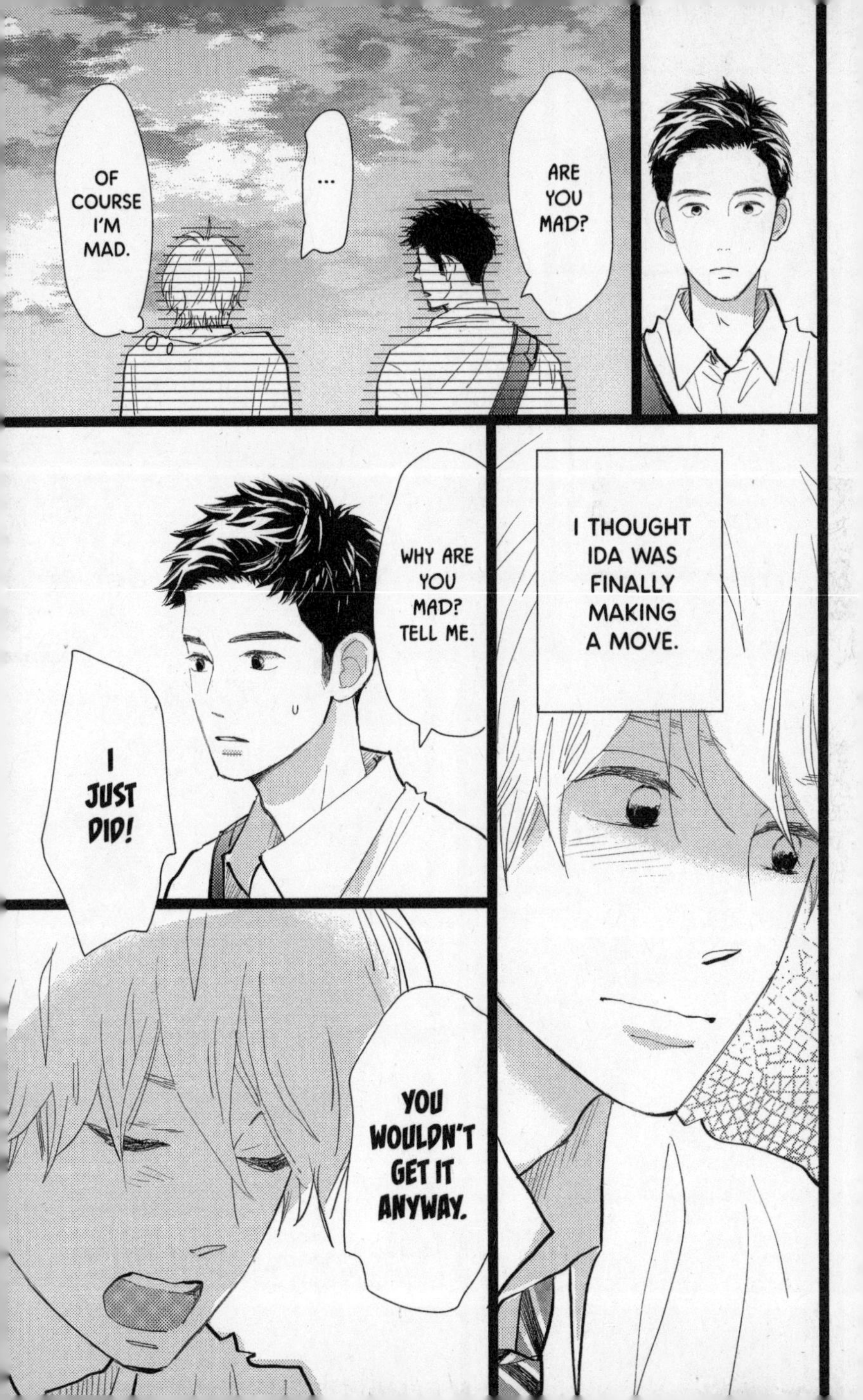
ARE YOU MAD?
...
OF COURSE I'M MAD.
I THOUGHT IDA WAS FINALLY MAKING A MOVE.
WHY ARE YOU MAD? TELL ME.
I JUST DID!
YOU WOULDN'T GET IT ANYWAY.

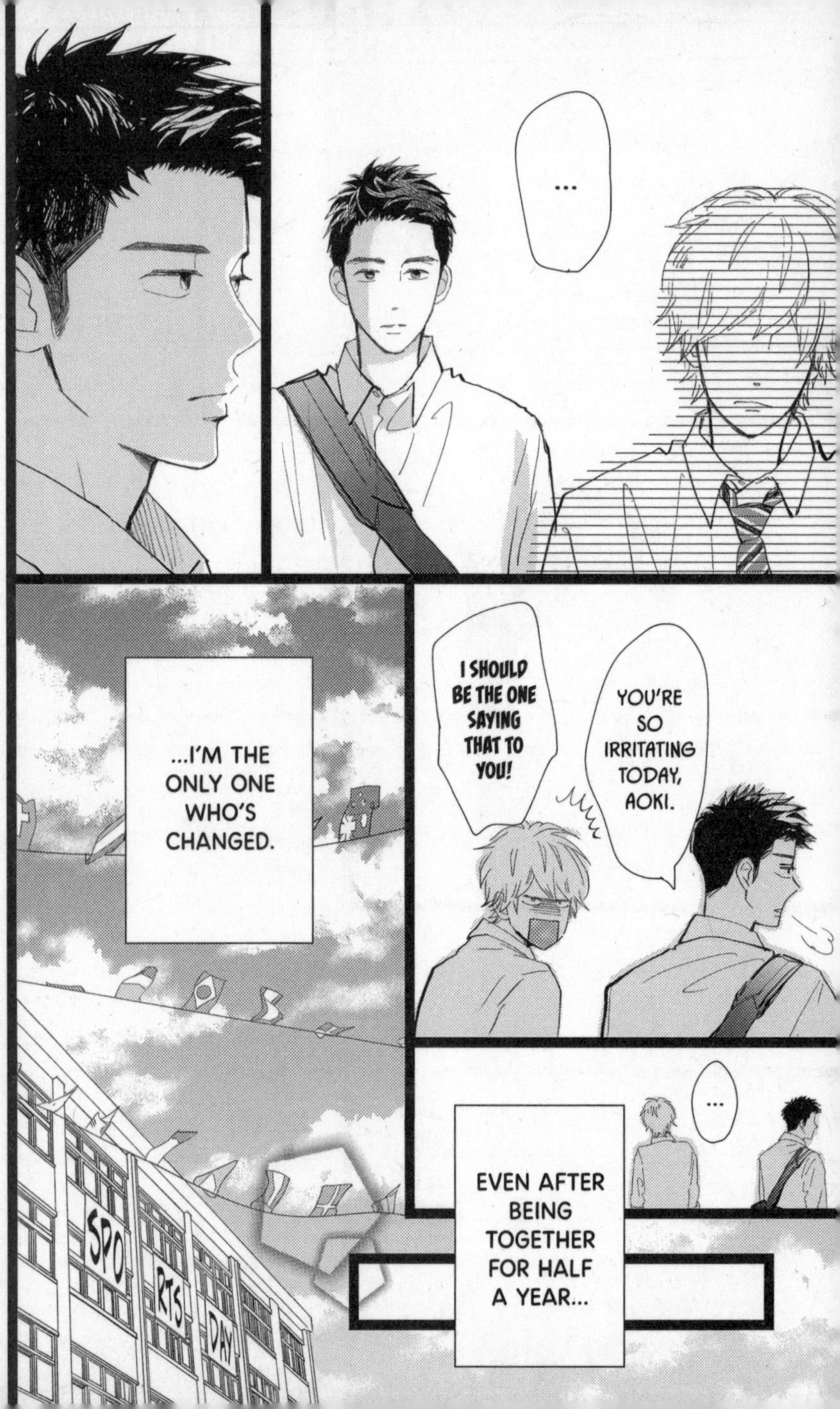
...
YOU'RE SO IRRITATING TODAY, AOKI.
I SHOULD BE THE ONE SAYING THAT TO YOU!
...
EVEN AFTER BEING TOGETHER FOR HALF A YEAR...
...I'M THE ONLY ONE WHO'S CHANGED.
SPORTS DAY

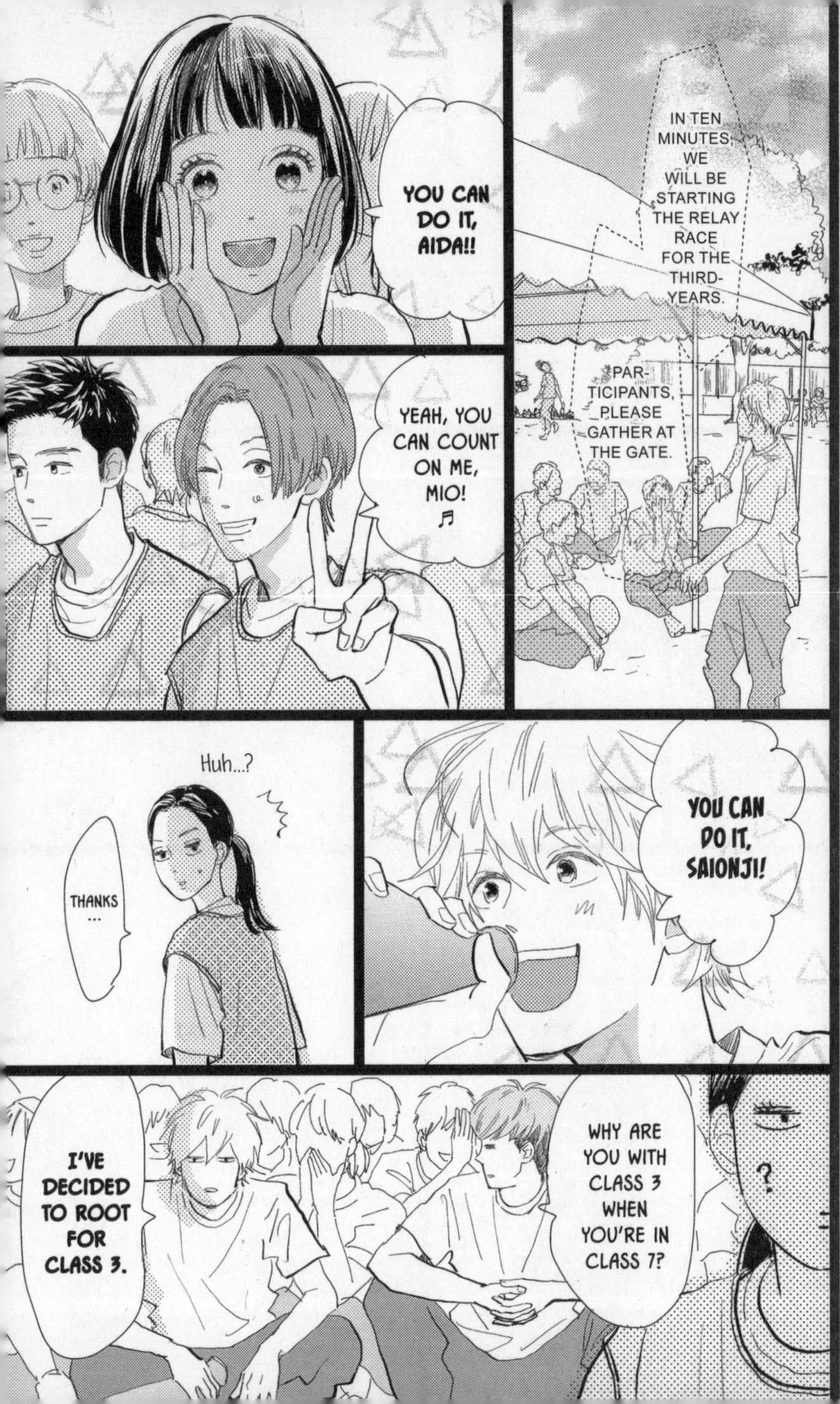
IN TEN MINUTES, WE WILL BE STARTING THE RELAY RACE FOR THE THIRD-YEARS.
PAR-TICIPANTS, PLEASE GATHER AT THE GATE.
YOU CAN DO IT, AIDA!!
YEAH, YOU CAN COUNT ON ME, MIO! ♬
YOU CAN DO IT, SAIONJI!
Huh...?
THANKS...
WHY ARE YOU WITH CLASS 3 WHEN YOU'RE IN CLASS 7?
?
I'VE DECIDED TO ROOT FOR CLASS 3.

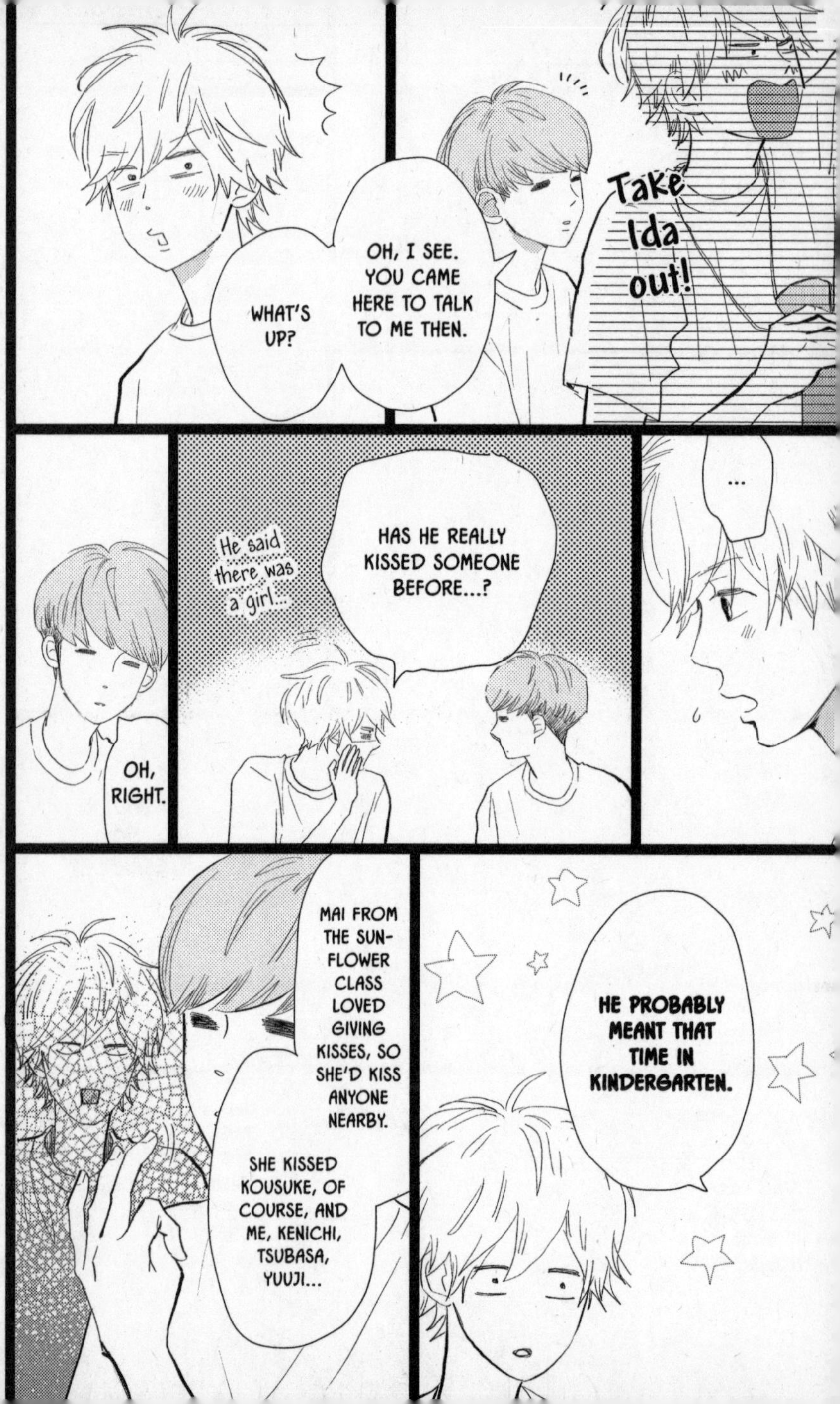
Take Ida out!
OH, I SEE. YOU CAME HERE TO TALK TO ME THEN.
WHAT'S UP?
...
HAS HE REALLY KISSED SOMEONE BEFORE...?
He said there was a girl...
OH, RIGHT.
HE PROBABLY MEANT THAT TIME IN KINDERGARTEN.
MAI FROM THE SUN-FLOWER CLASS LOVED GIVING KISSES, SO SHE'D KISS ANYONE NEARBY.
SHE KISSED KOUSUKE, OF COURSE, AND ME, KENICHI, TSUBASA, YUUJI...

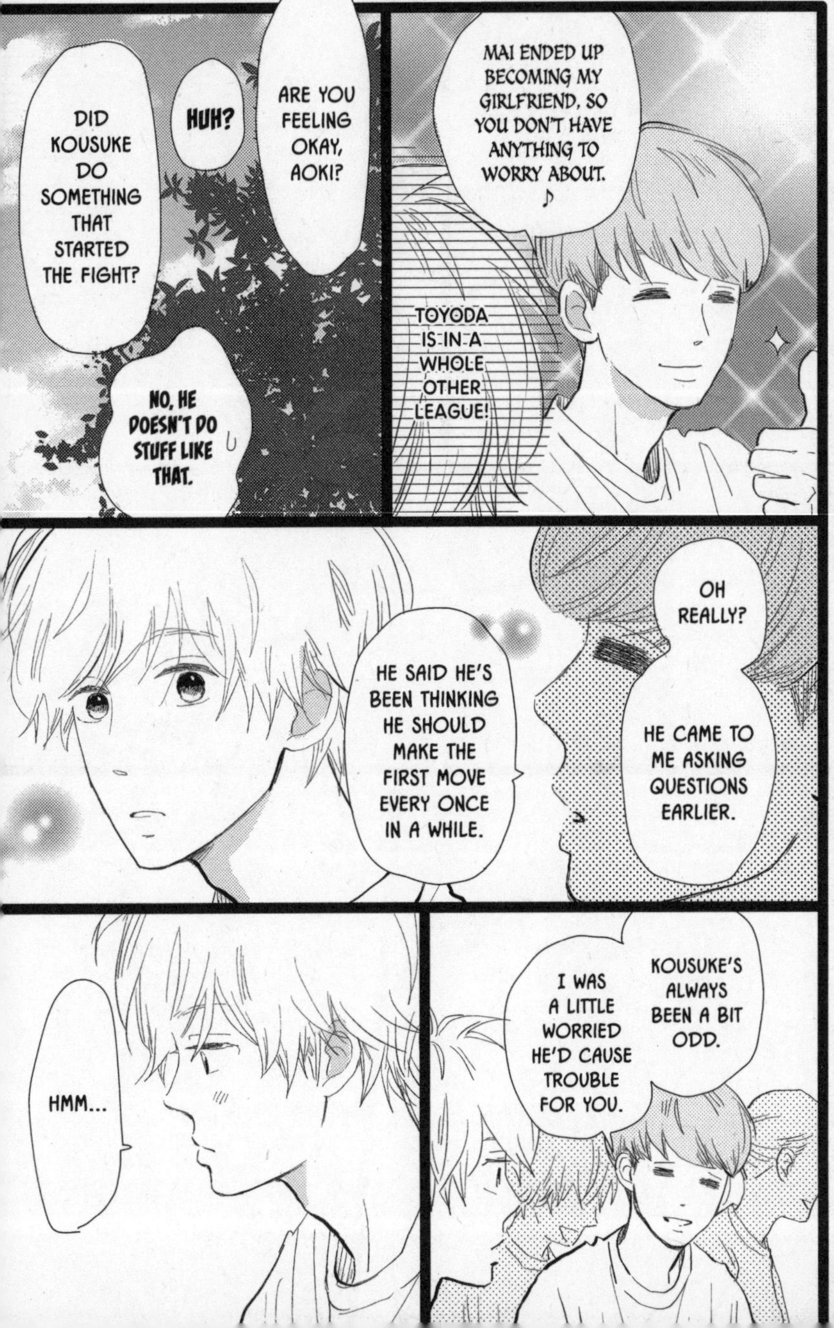
MAI ENDED UP BECOMING MY GIRLFRIEND, SO YOU DON'T HAVE ANYTHING TO WORRY ABOUT. ♪
TOYODA IS IN A WHOLE OTHER LEAGUE!
ARE YOU FEELING OKAY, AOKI?
HUH?
DID KOUSUKE DO SOMETHING THAT STARTED THE FIGHT?
NO, HE DOESN'T DO STUFF LIKE THAT.
OH REALLY?
HE CAME TO ME ASKING QUESTIONS EARLIER.
HE SAID HE'S BEEN THINKING HE SHOULD MAKE THE FIRST MOVE EVERY ONCE IN A WHILE.
KOUSUKE'S ALWAYS BEEN A BIT ODD.
I WAS A LITTLE WORRIED HE'D CAUSE TROUBLE FOR YOU.
HMM...

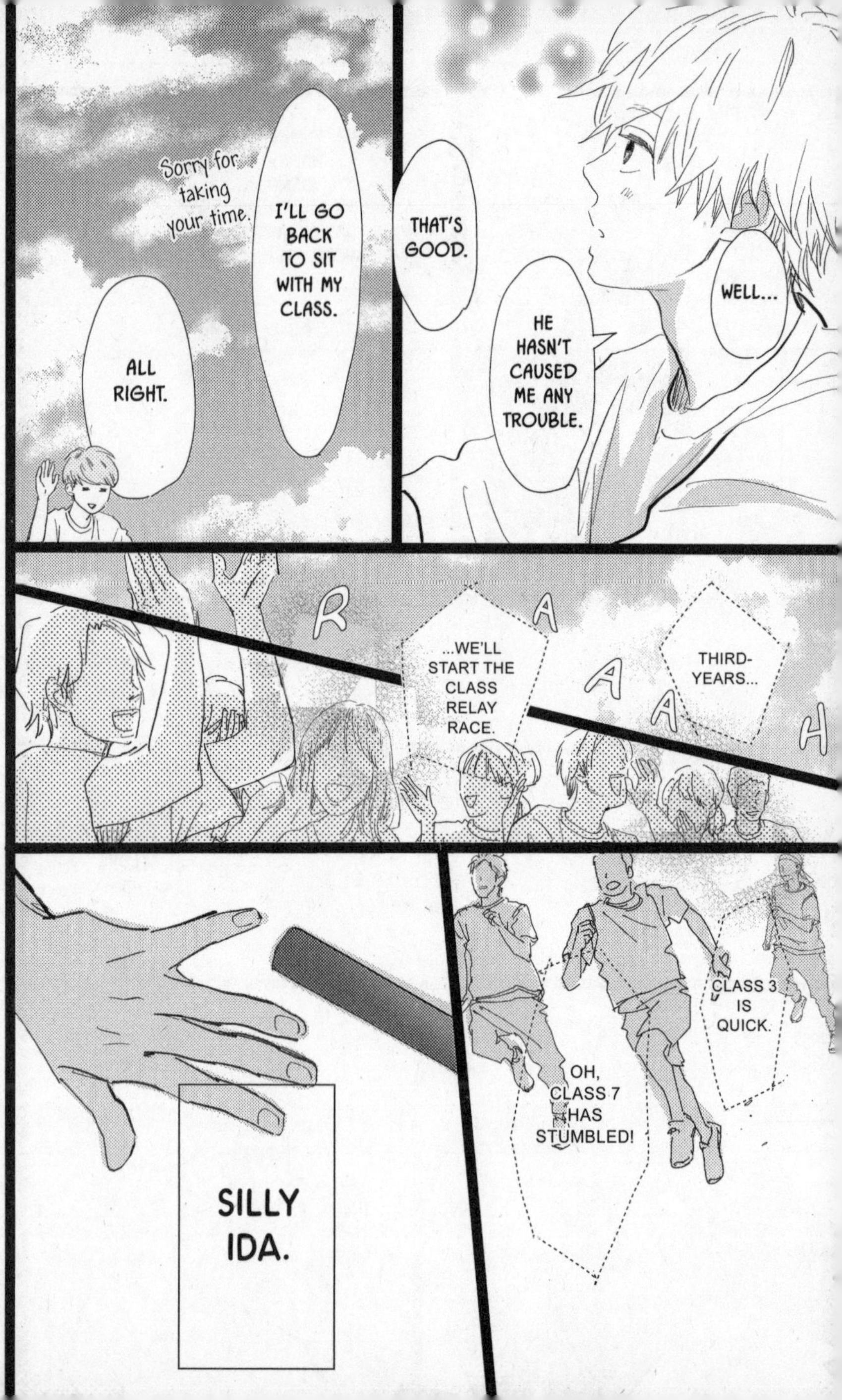
WELL...
HE HASN'T CAUSED ME ANY TROUBLE.
THAT'S GOOD.
I'LL GO BACK TO SIT WITH MY CLASS.
Sorry for taking your time.
ALL RIGHT.
THIRD-YEARS...
...WE'LL START THE CLASS RELAY RACE.
RAAAH
CLASS 3 IS QUICK.
OH, CLASS 7 HAS STUMBLED!
SILLY IDA.

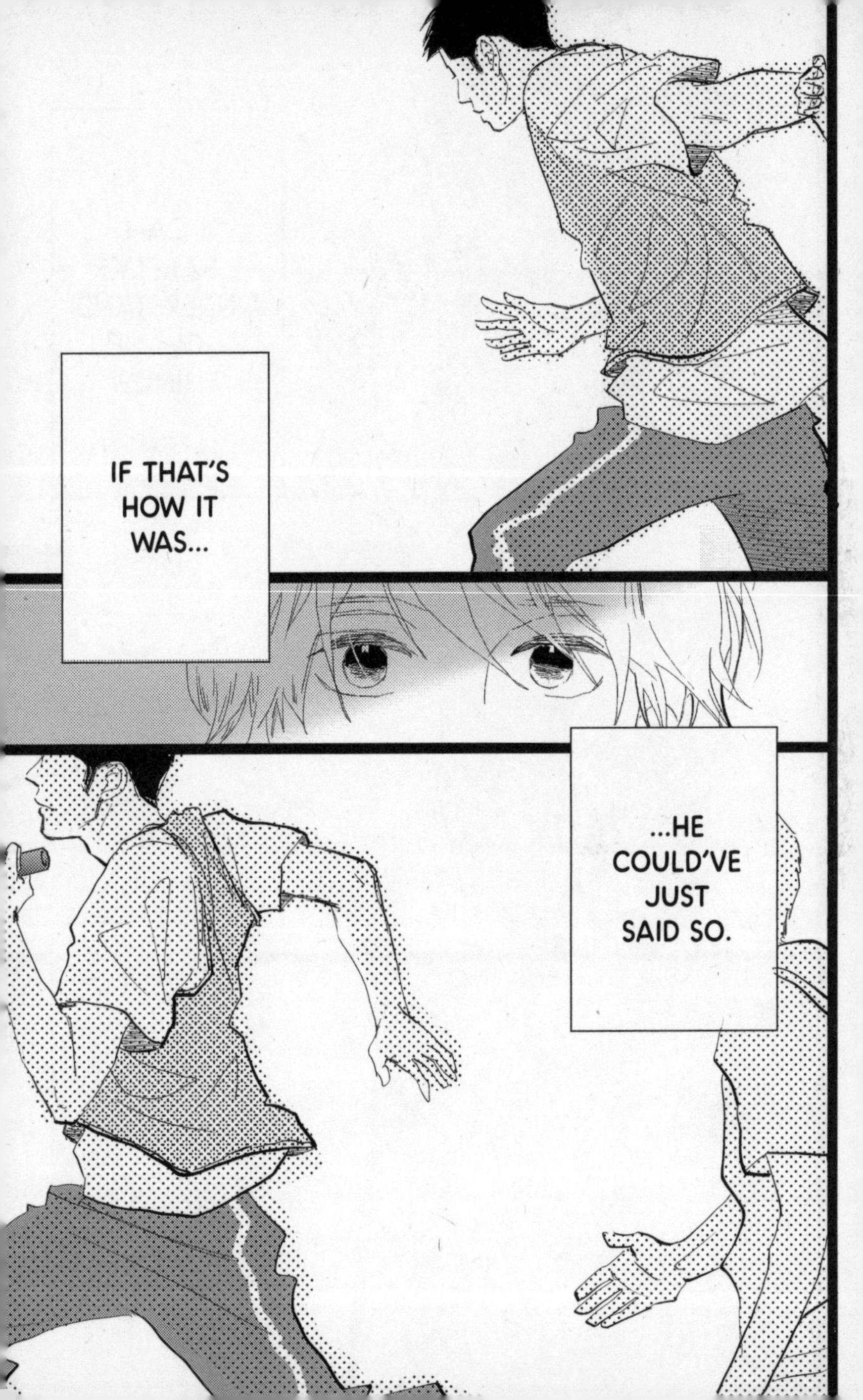
IF THAT'S HOW IT WAS...
...HE COULD'VE JUST SAID SO.

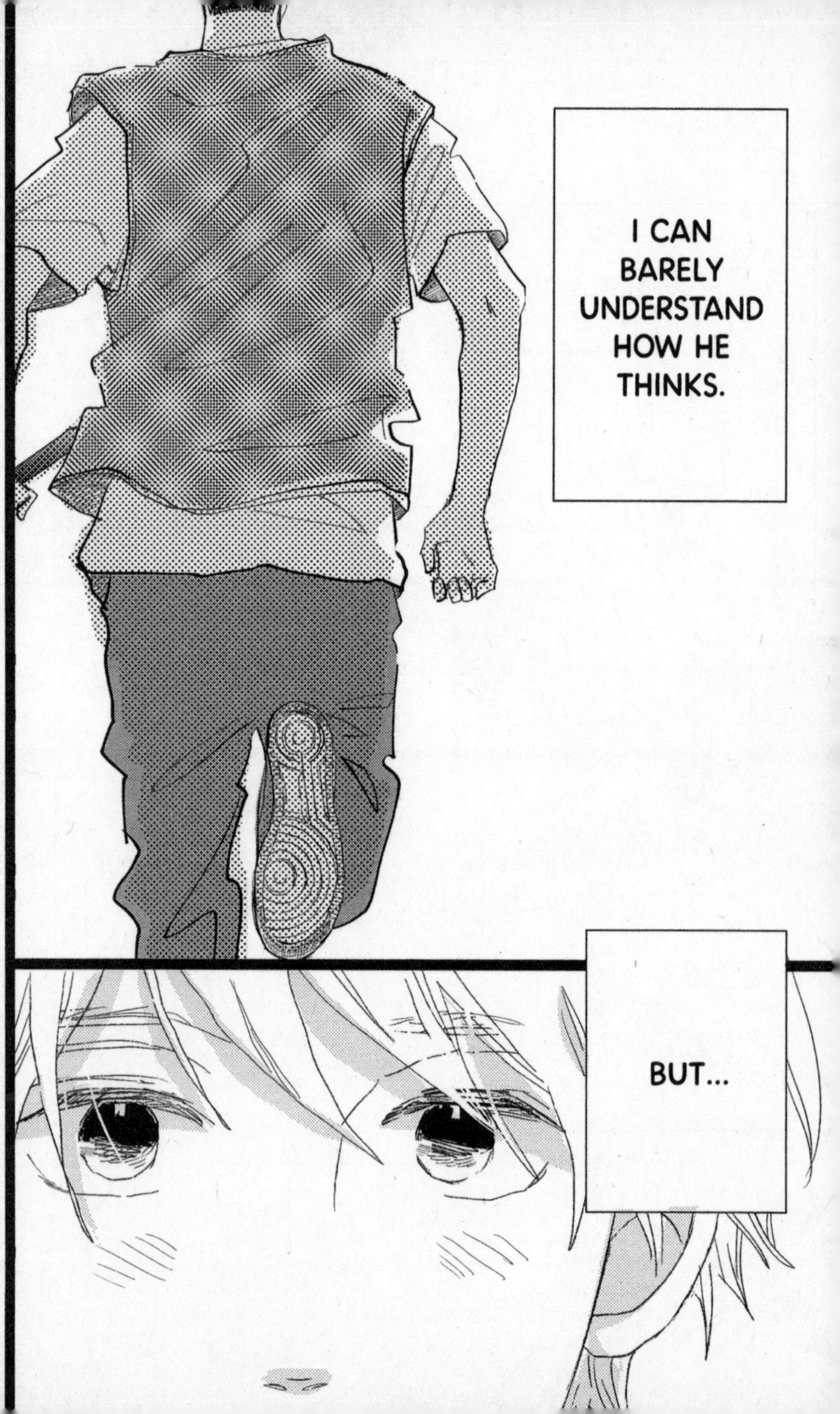
I CAN BARELY UNDERSTAND HOW HE THINKS.
BUT...

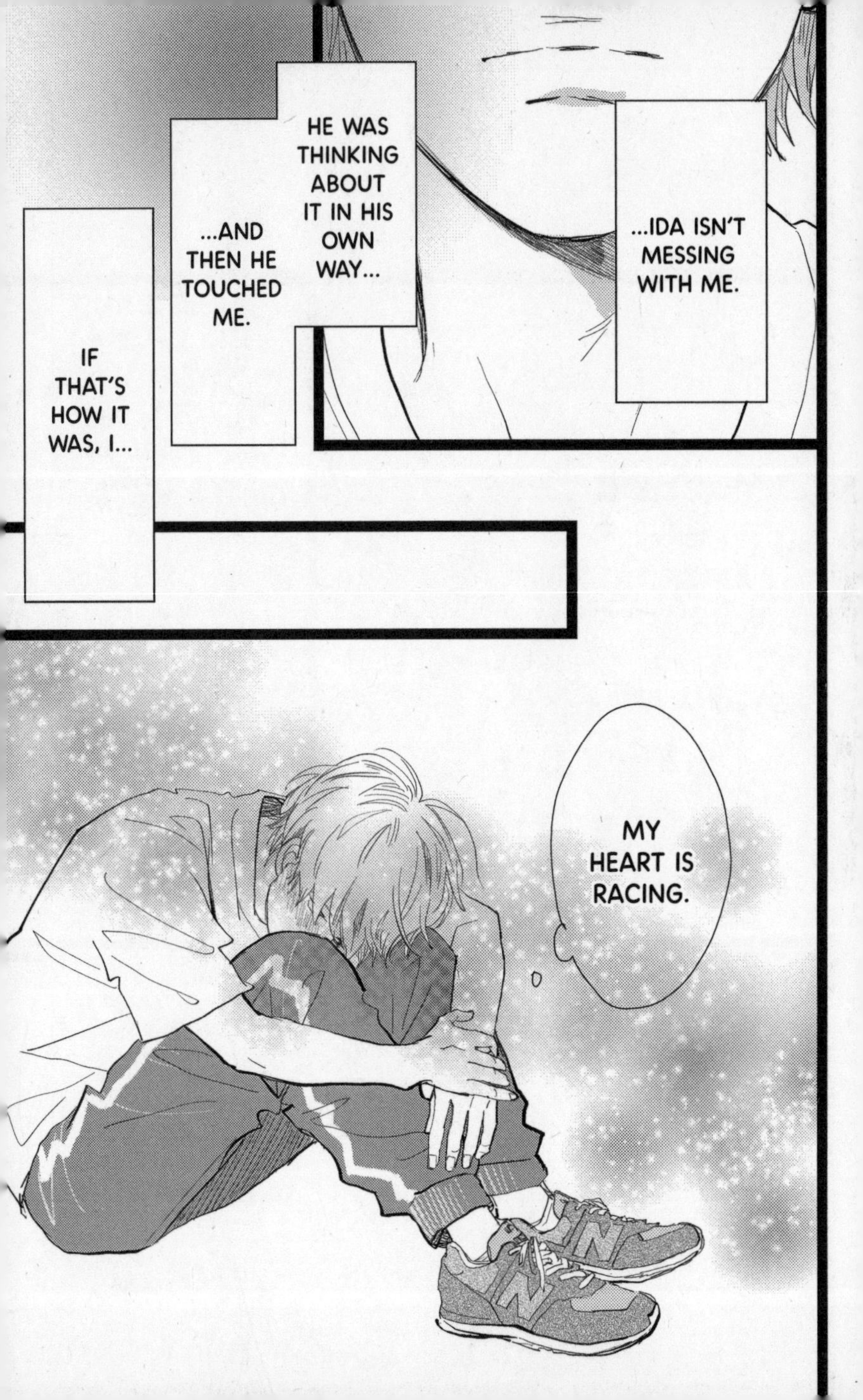
...IDA ISN'T MESSING WITH ME.
HE WAS THINKING ABOUT IT IN HIS OWN WAY...
...AND THEN HE TOUCHED ME.
IF THAT'S HOW IT WAS, I...
MY HEART IS RACING.

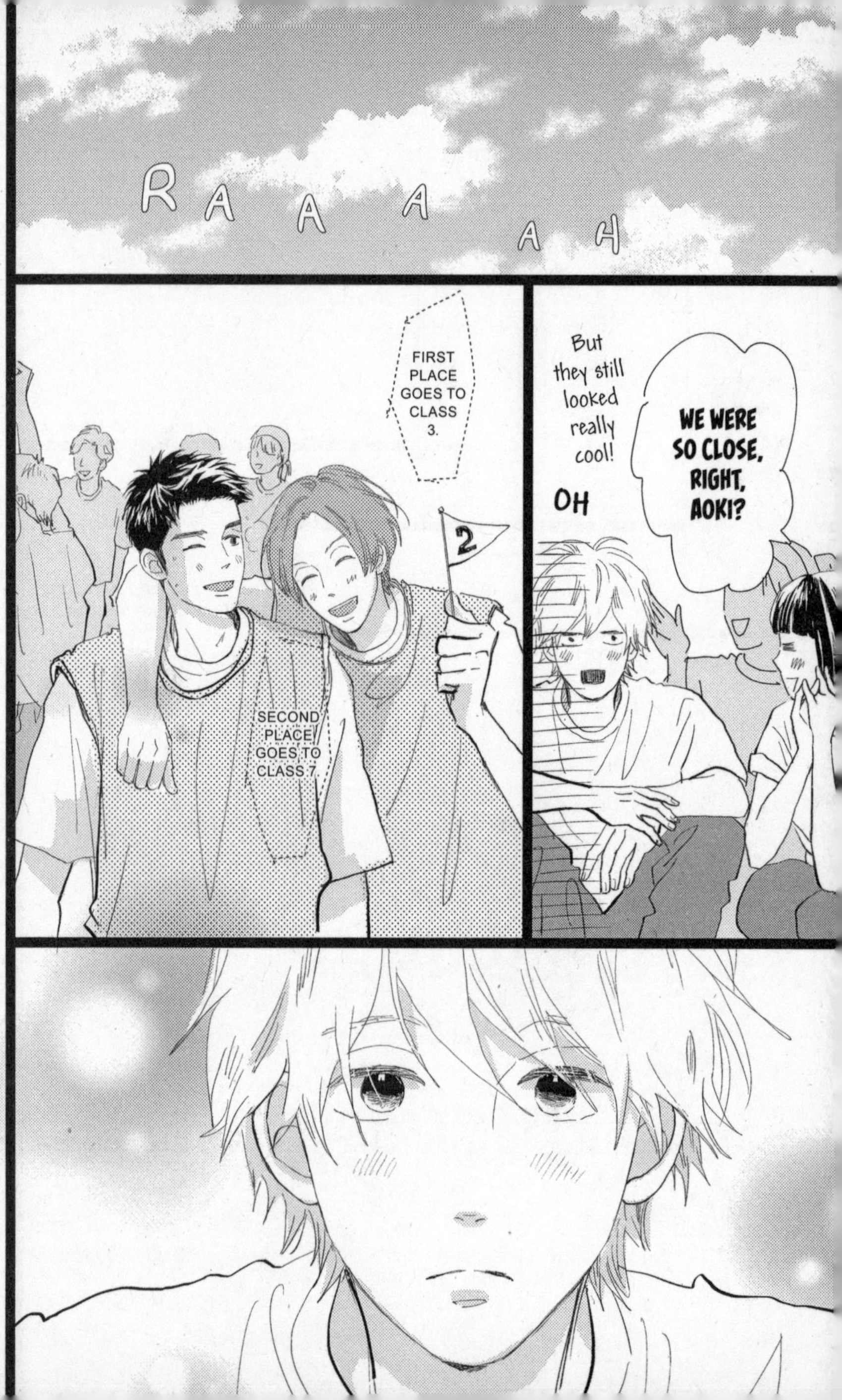
RAAAAH
WE WERE SO CLOSE, RIGHT, AOKI?
But they still looked really cool!
OH
FIRST PLACE GOES TO CLASS 3.
SECOND PLACE GOES TO CLASS 7.

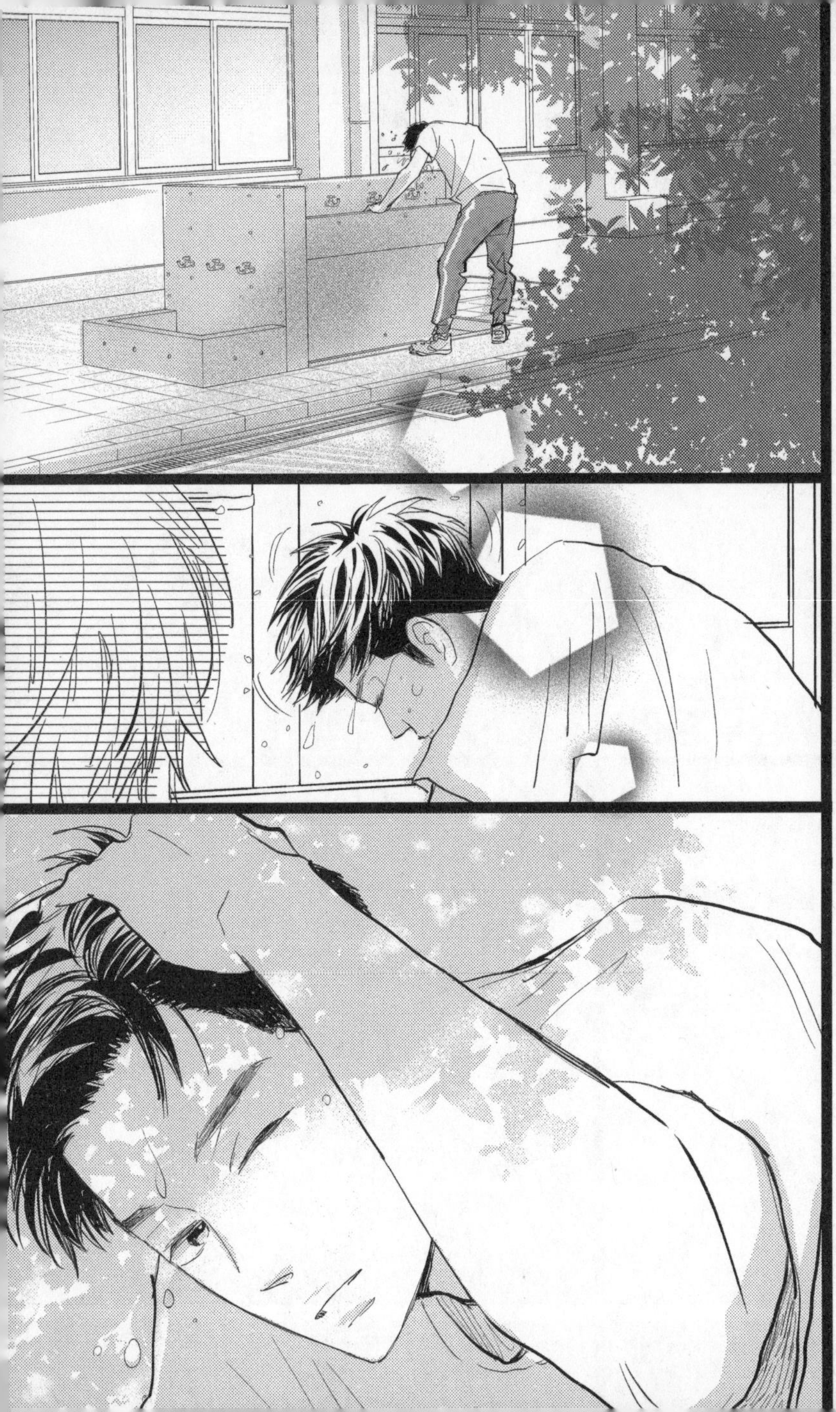

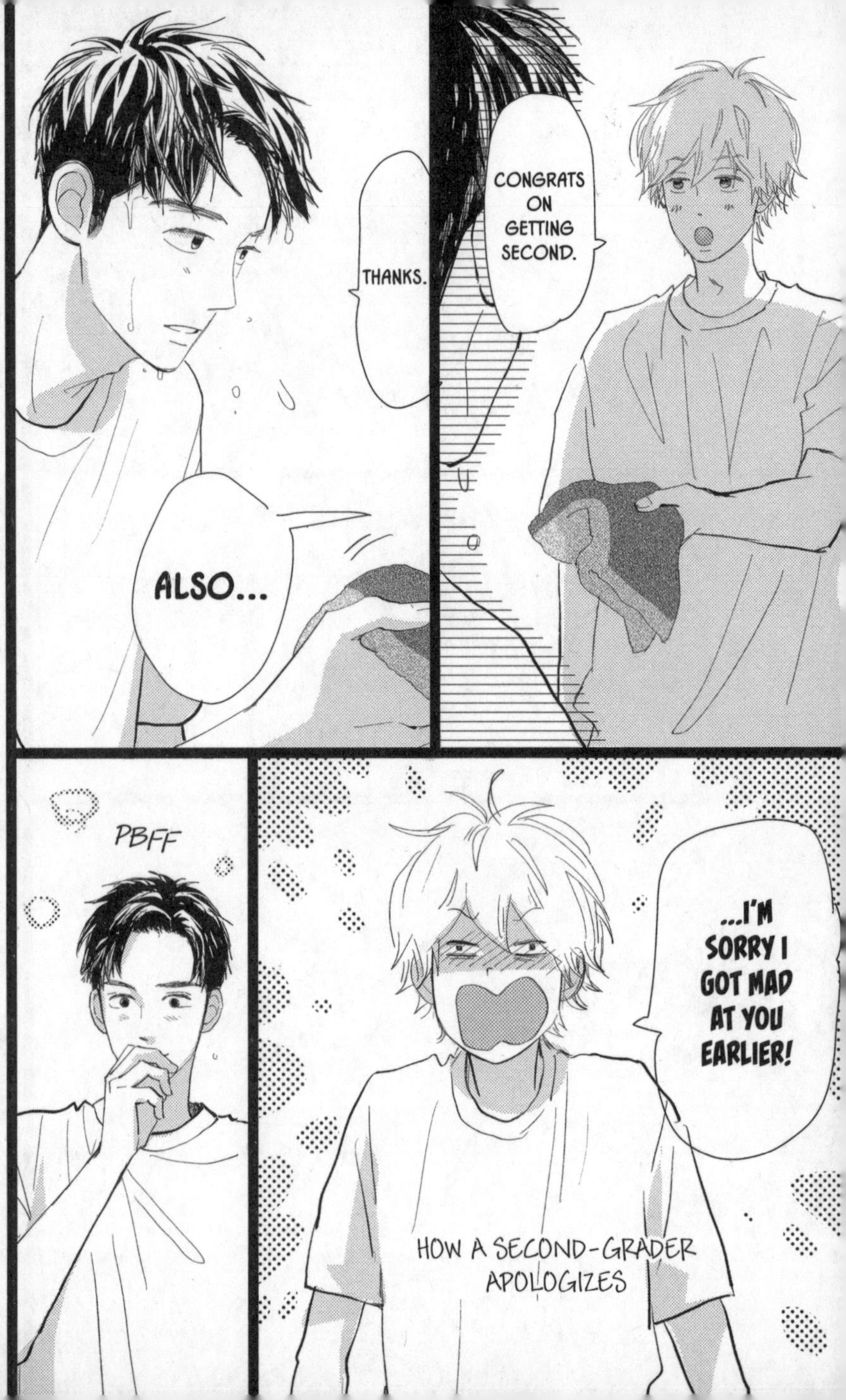
CONGRATS ON GETTING SECOND.
THANKS.
ALSO...
...I'M SORRY I GOT MAD AT YOU EARLIER!
HOW A SECOND-GRADER APOLOGIZES
PBFF

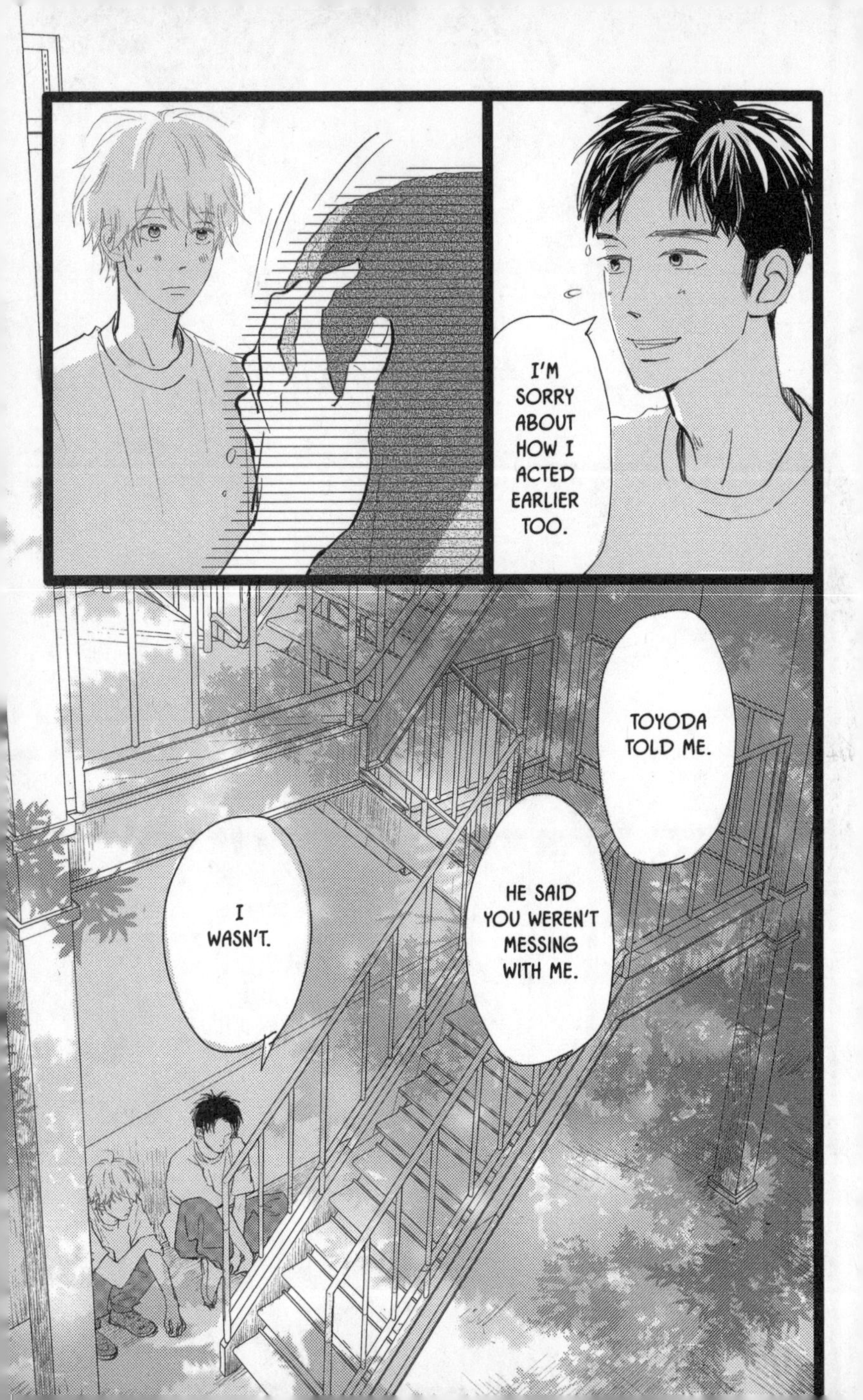
I'M SORRY ABOUT HOW I ACTED EARLIER TOO.
TOYODA TOLD ME.
HE SAID YOU WEREN'T MESSING WITH ME.
I WASN'T.

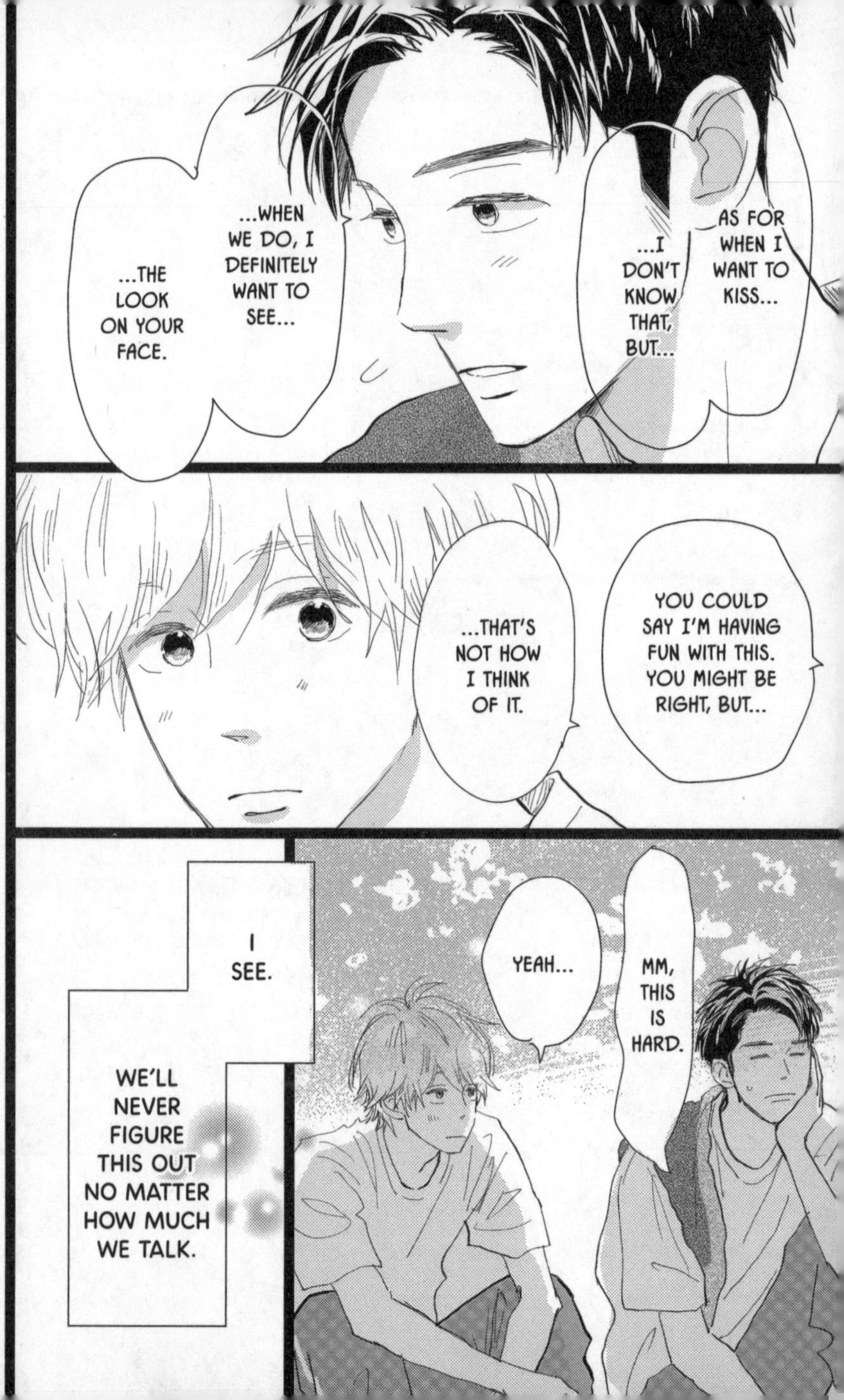
AS FOR WHEN I WANT TO KISS...
...I DON'T KNOW THAT, BUT...
...WHEN WE DO, I DEFINITELY WANT TO SEE...
...THE LOOK ON YOUR FACE.
YOU COULD SAY I'M HAVING FUN WITH THIS. YOU MIGHT BE RIGHT, BUT...
...THAT'S NOT HOW I THINK OF IT.
MM, THIS IS HARD.
YEAH...
I SEE.
WE'LL NEVER FIGURE THIS OUT NO MATTER HOW MUCH WE TALK.

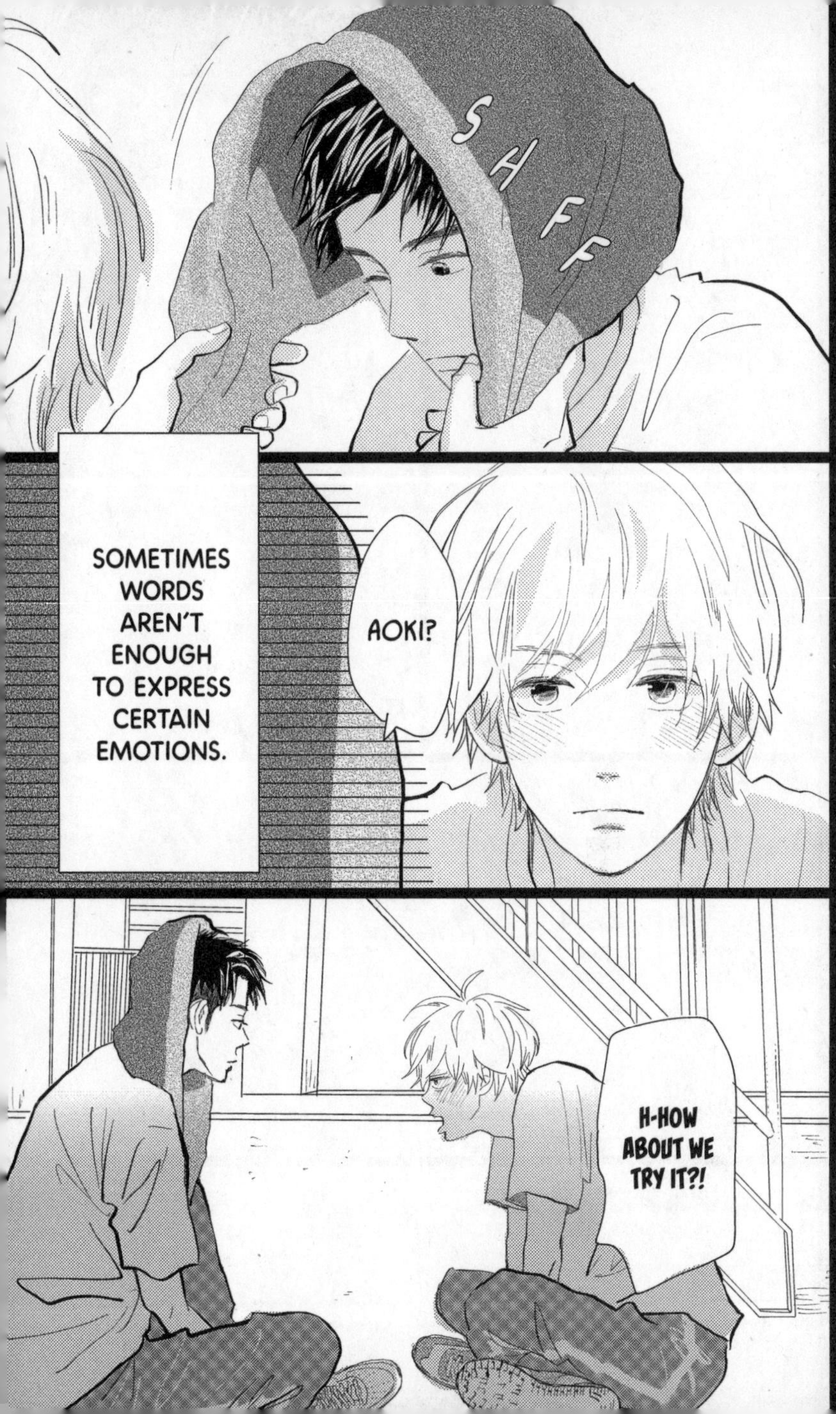
SHFF
AOKI?
SOMETIMES WORDS AREN'T ENOUGH TO EXPRESS CERTAIN EMOTIONS.
H-HOW ABOUT WE TRY IT?!

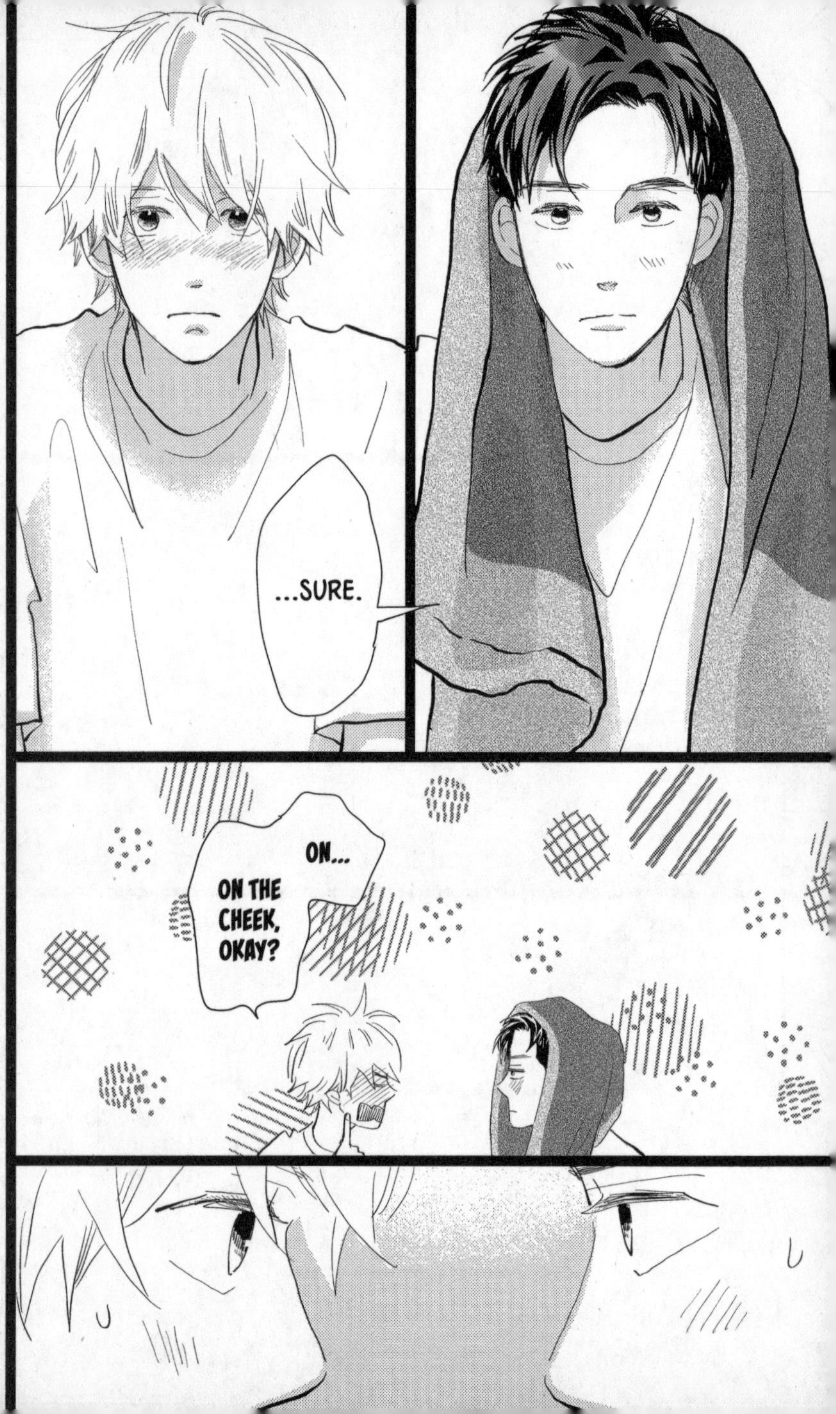
...SURE.
ON...
ON THE CHEEK, OKAY?

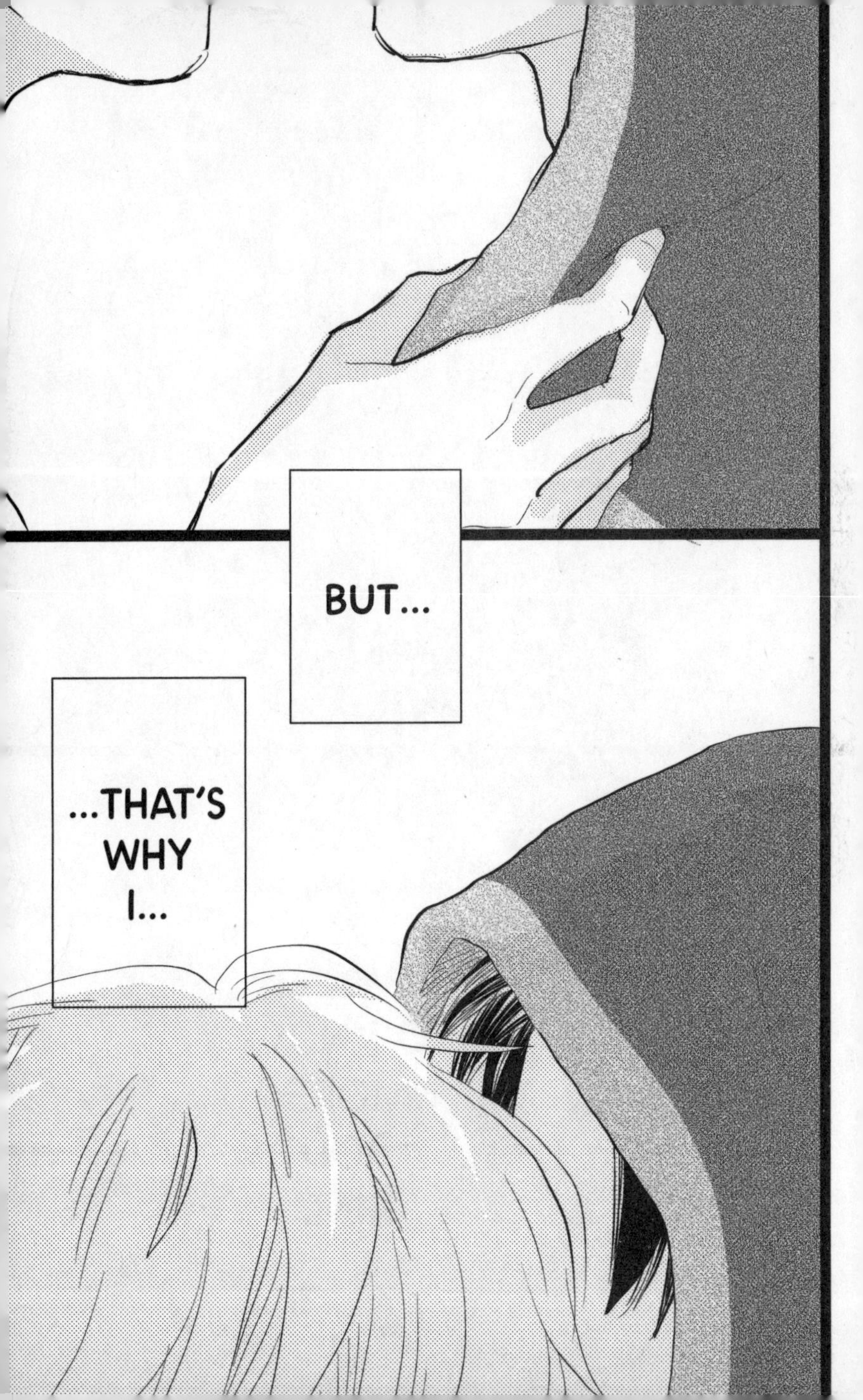
BUT...
...THAT'S WHY I...

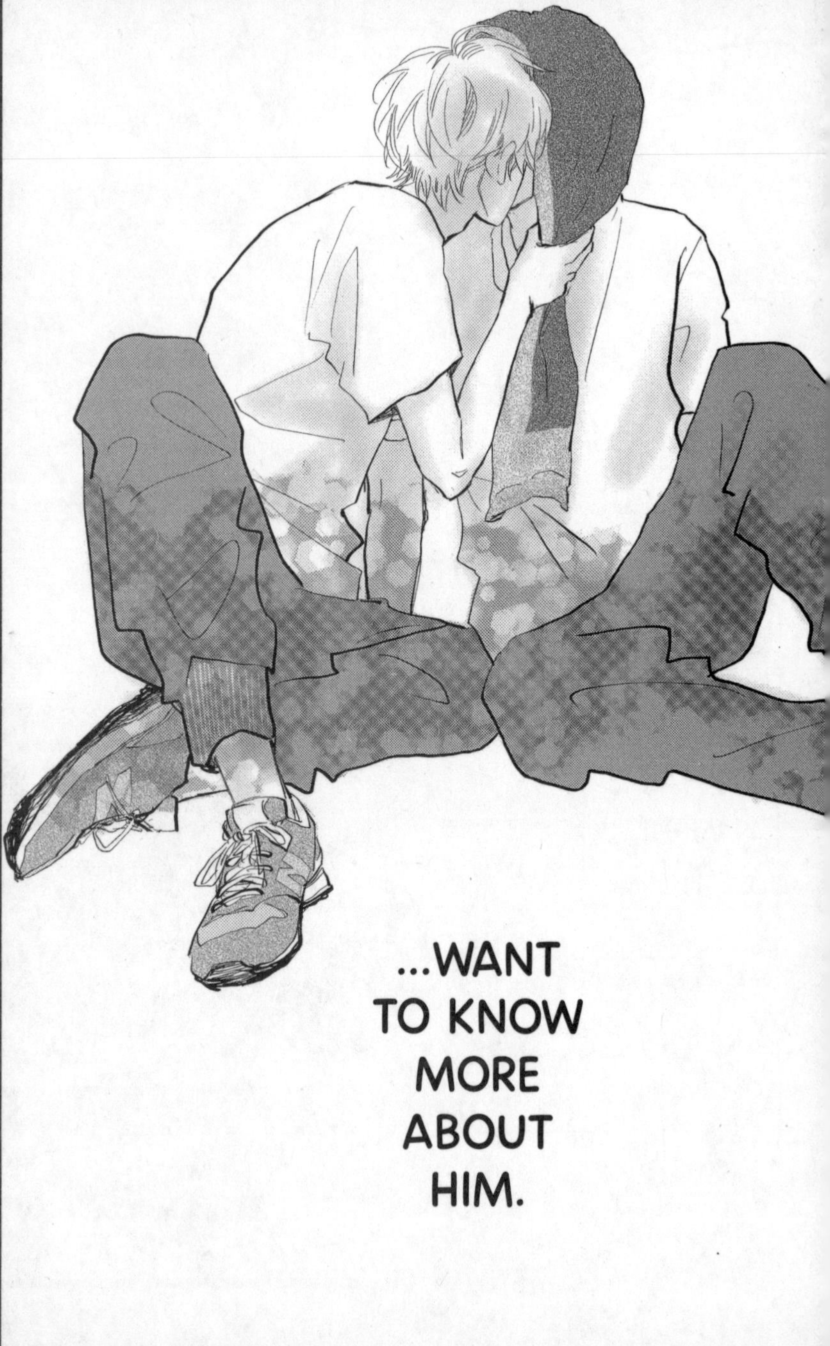
...WANT
TO KNOW
MORE
ABOUT
HIM.

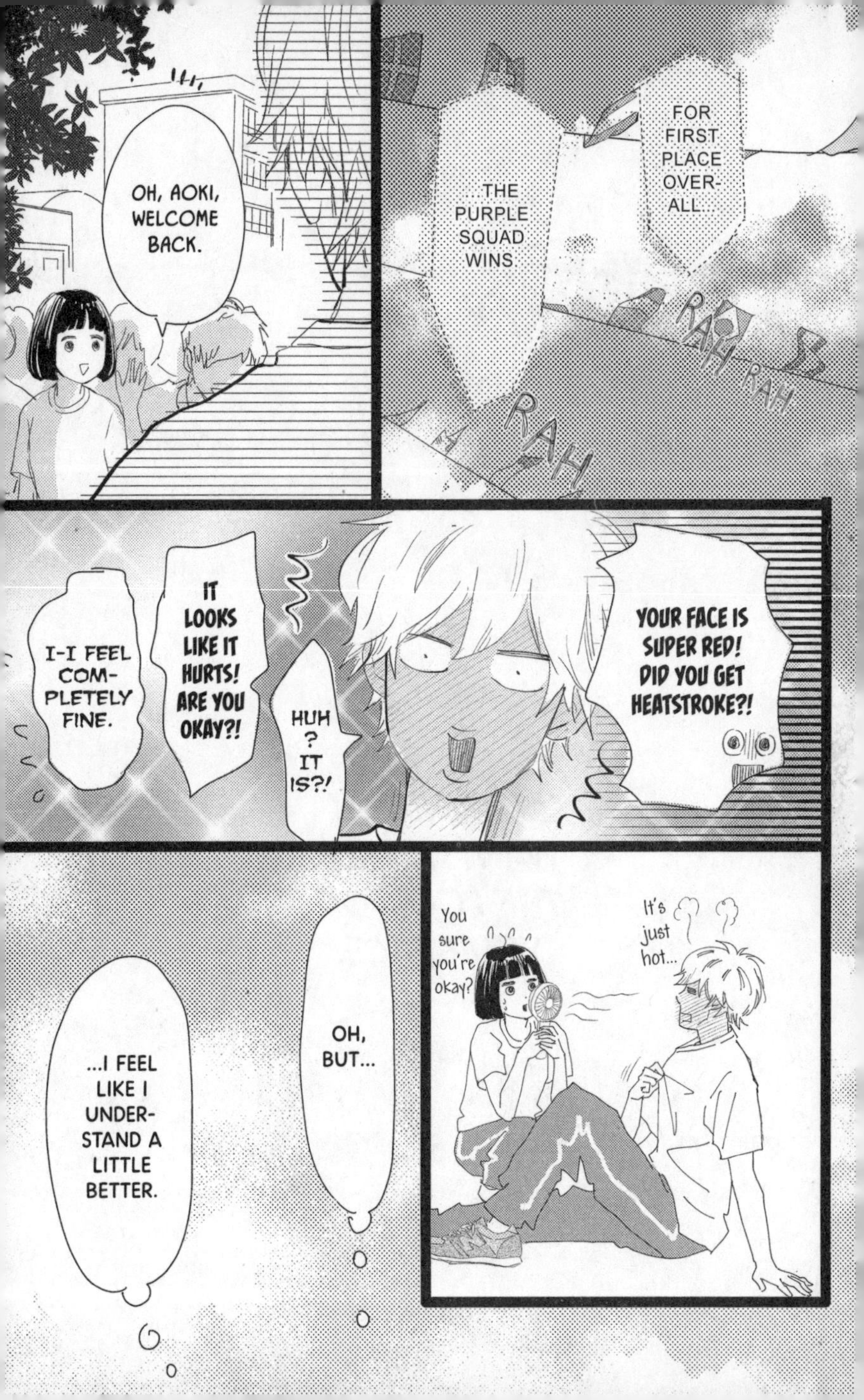
FOR FIRST PLACE OVER-ALL...
...THE PURPLE SQUAD WINS
RAH RAH
RAH
OH, AOKI, WELCOME BACK.
YOUR FACE IS SUPER RED! DID YOU GET HEATSTROKE?!
HUH? IT IS?!
IT LOOKS LIKE IT HURTS! ARE YOU OKAY?!
I-I FEEL COMPLETELY FINE.
It's just hot...
You sure you're okay?
OH, BUT...
...I FEEL LIKE I UNDERSTAND A LITTLE BETTER.

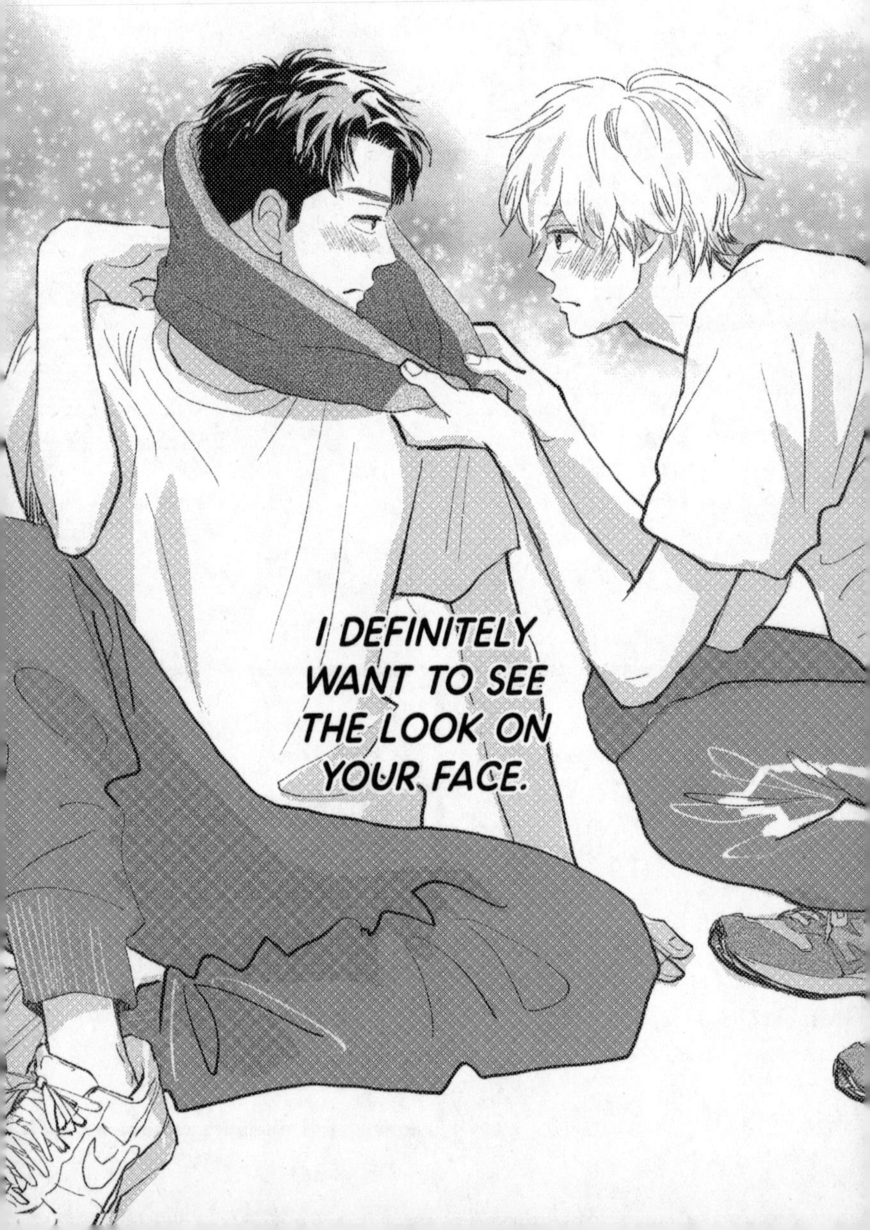
I DEFINITELY WANT TO SEE THE LOOK ON YOUR FACE.

Chapter 25

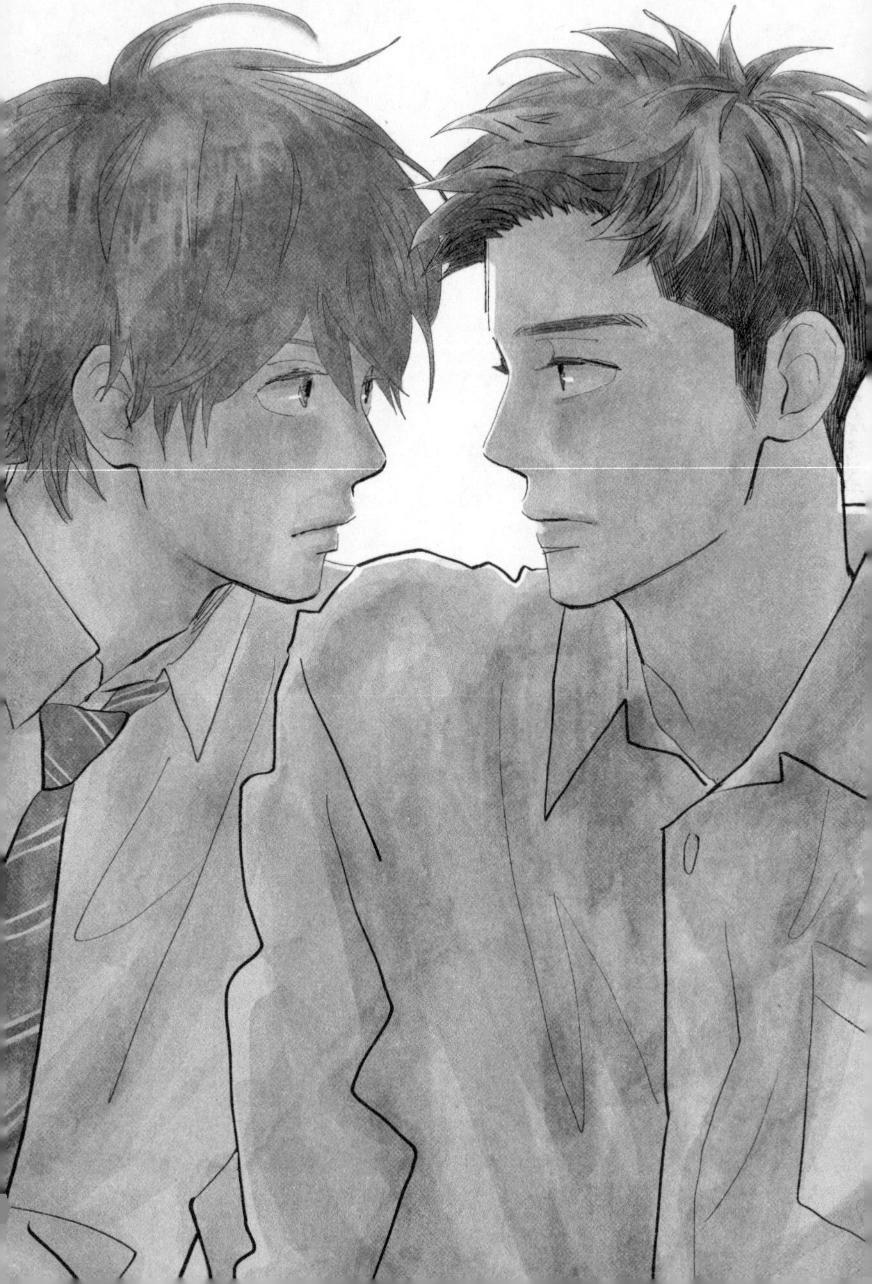

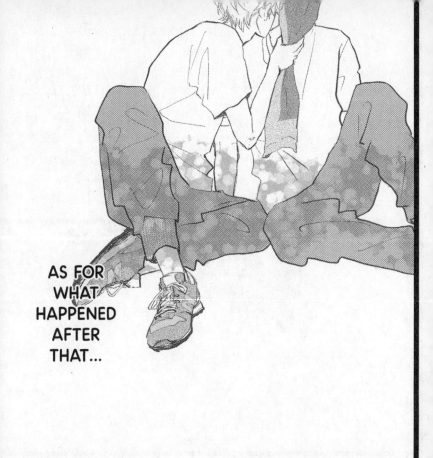

AS FOR
WHAT
HAPPENED
AFTER
THAT...

My Love
Mix-Up!

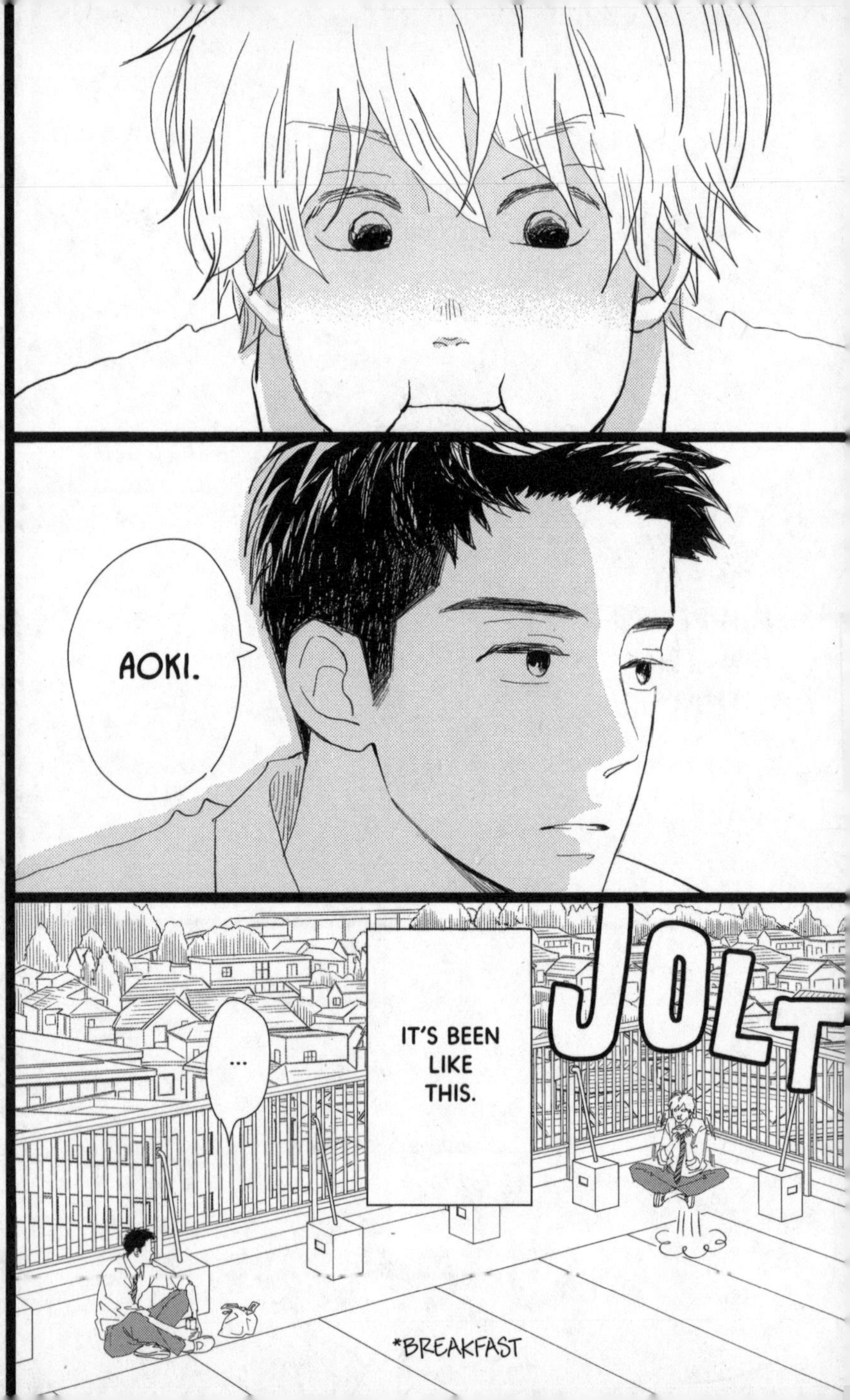
AOKI.
JOLT
IT'S BEEN LIKE THIS.
...
*BREAKFAST

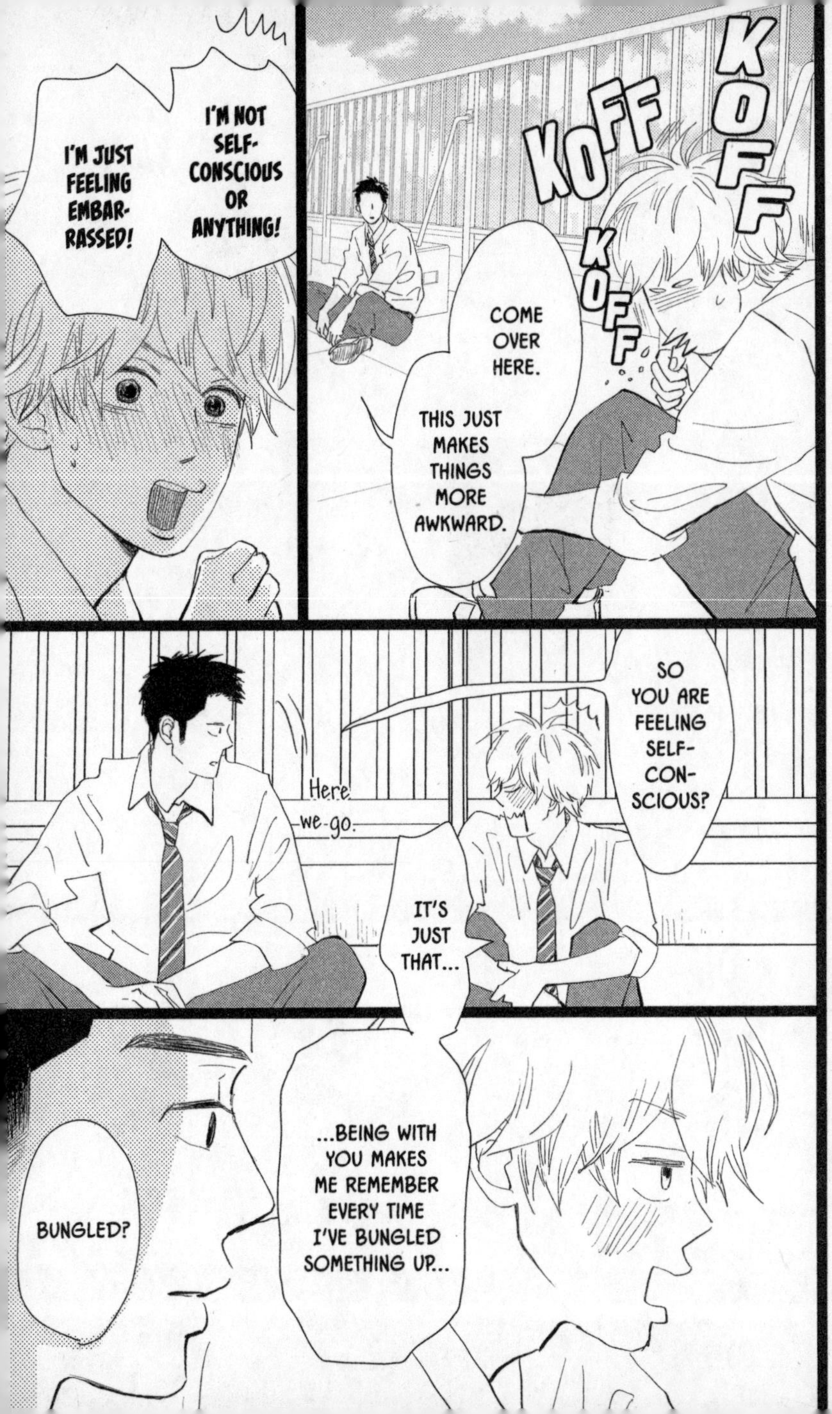
KOFF KOFF
KOFF KOFF
COME OVER HERE.
THIS JUST MAKES THINGS MORE AWKWARD.
I'M NOT SELF-CONSCIOUS OR ANYTHING!
I'M JUST FEELING EMBARRASSED!
SO YOU ARE FEELING SELF-CONSCIOUS?
Here we go.
IT'S JUST THAT...
...BEING WITH YOU MAKES ME REMEMBER EVERY TIME I'VE BUNGLED SOMETHING UP...
BUNGLED?

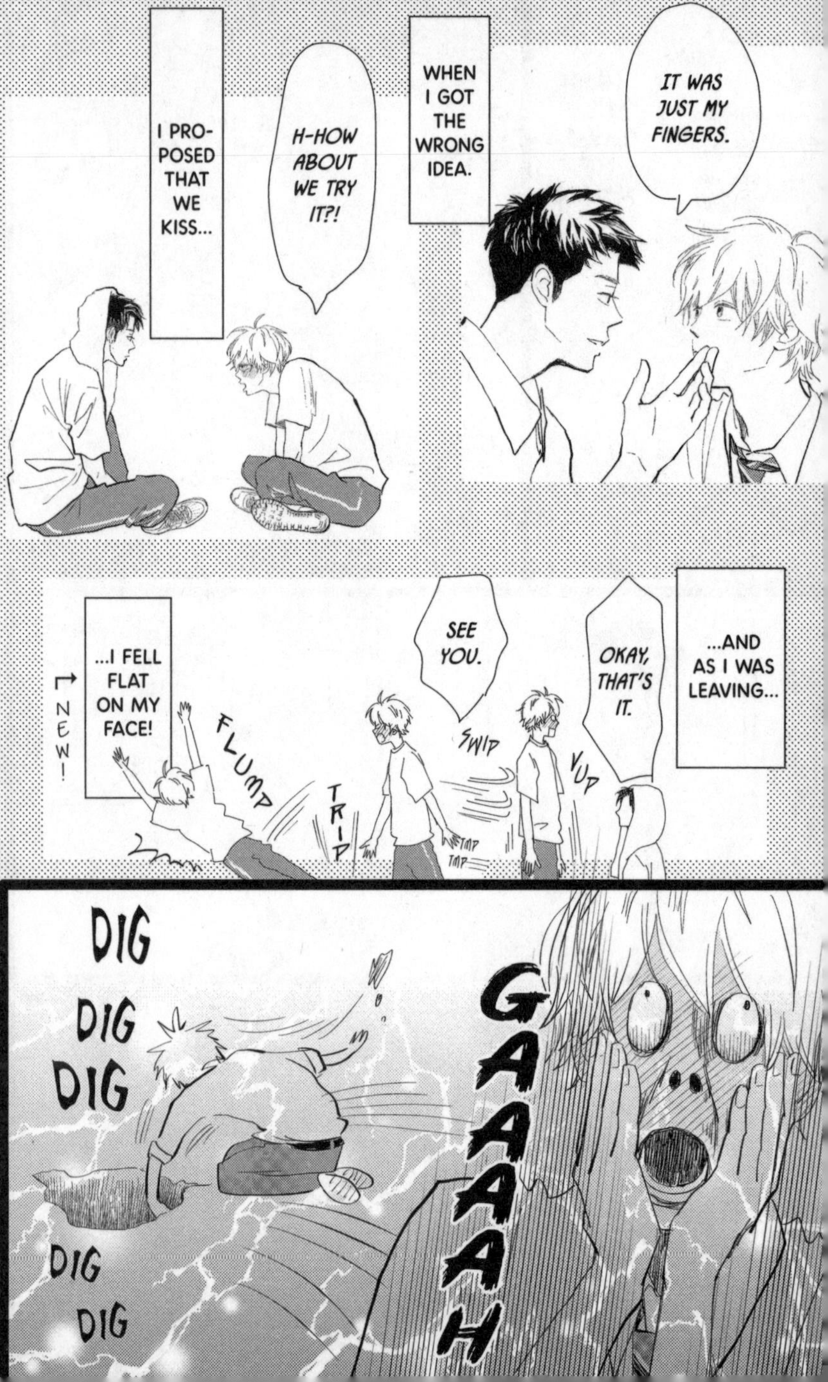
IT WAS JUST MY FINGERS.
WHEN I GOT THE WRONG IDEA.
H-HOW ABOUT WE TRY IT?!
I PRO-POSED THAT WE KISS...
...AND AS I WAS LEAVING...
OKAY, THAT'S IT.
VUP
SEE YOU.
SWIP
TMP TMP
TRIP
FLUMP
...I FELL FLAT ON MY FACE!
NEW!
GAAAAAH
DIG DIG DIG
DIG DIG

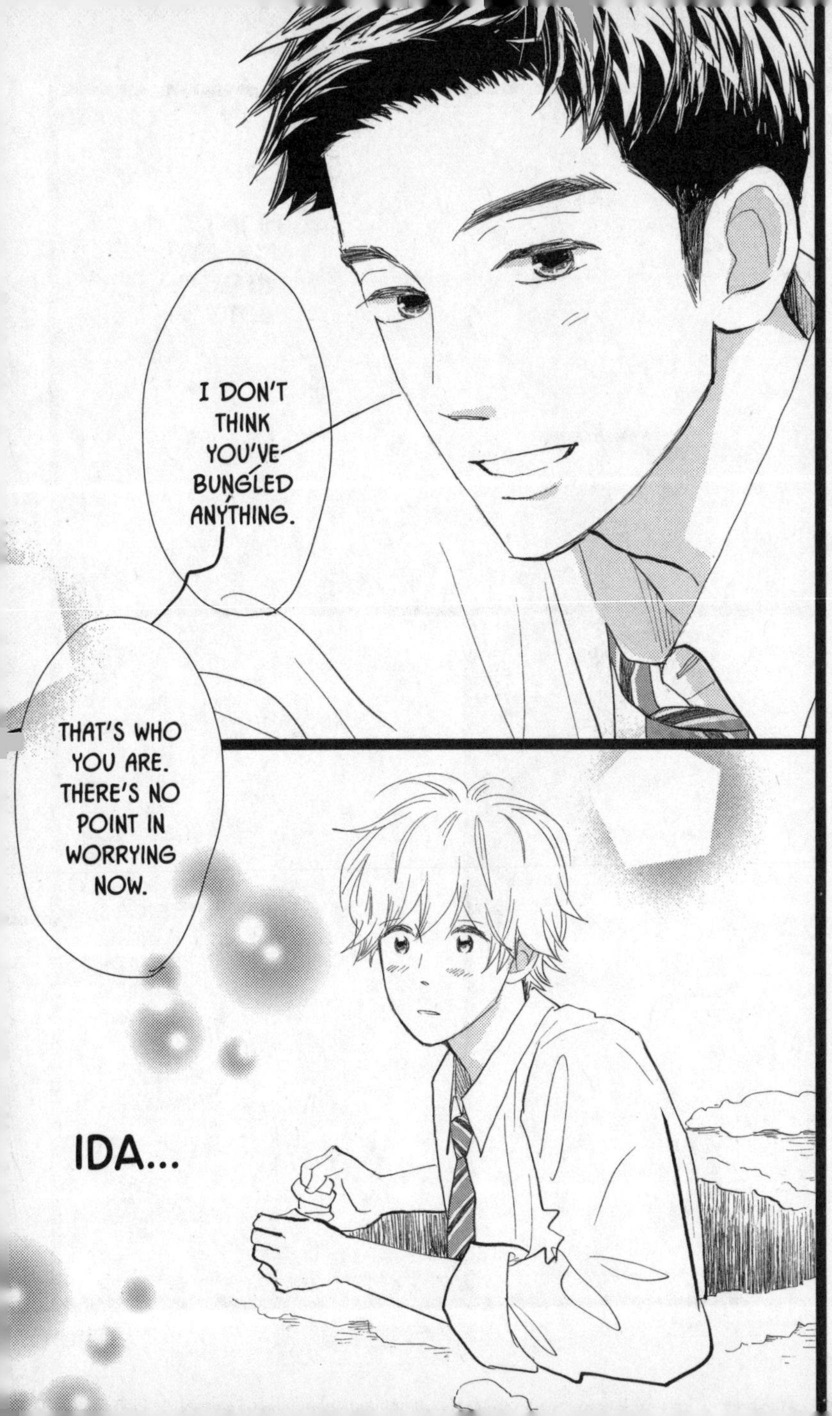
I DON'T THINK YOU'VE BUNGLED ANYTHING.
THAT'S WHO YOU ARE. THERE'S NO POINT IN WORRYING NOW.
IDA...

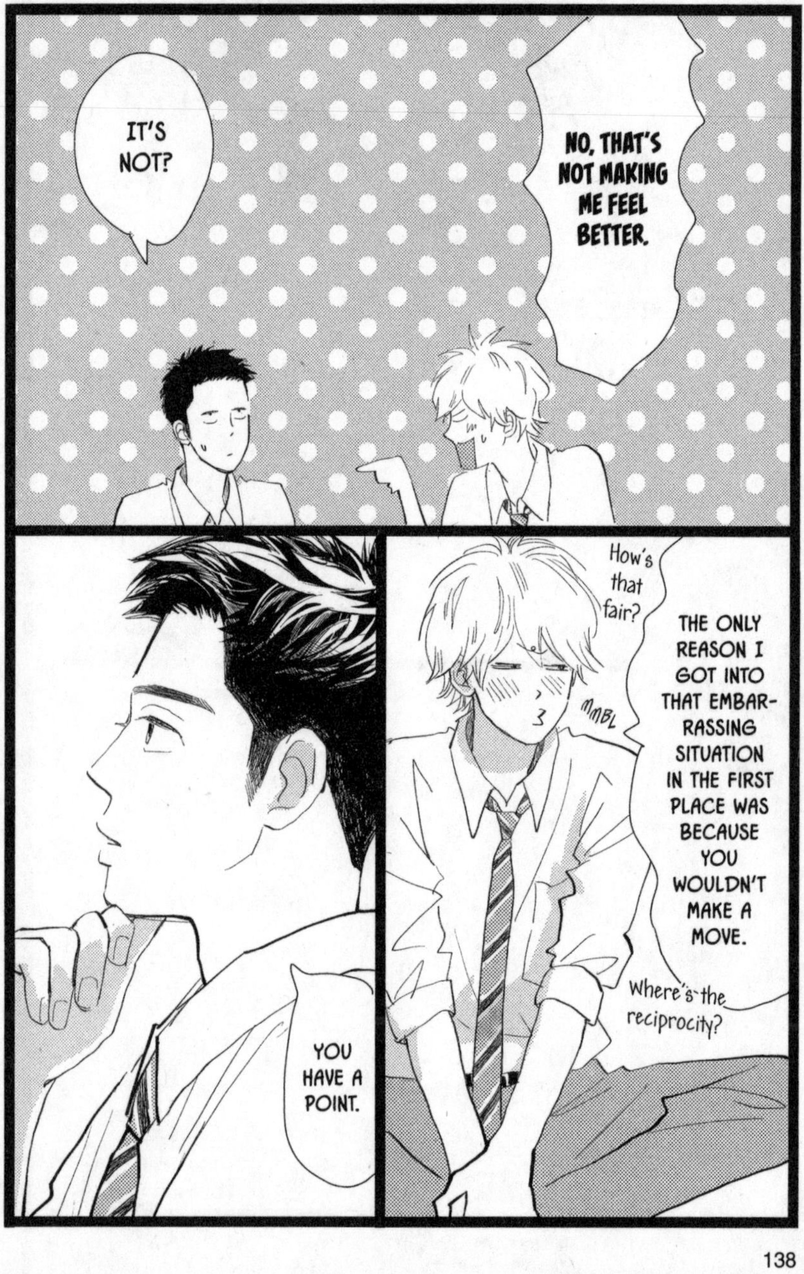
NO, THAT'S NOT MAKING ME FEEL BETTER.
IT'S NOT?
How's that fair?
THE ONLY REASON I GOT INTO THAT EMBAR-RASSING SITUATION IN THE FIRST PLACE WAS BECAUSE YOU WOULDN'T MAKE A MOVE.
MMBL
Where's the reciprocity?
YOU HAVE A POINT.

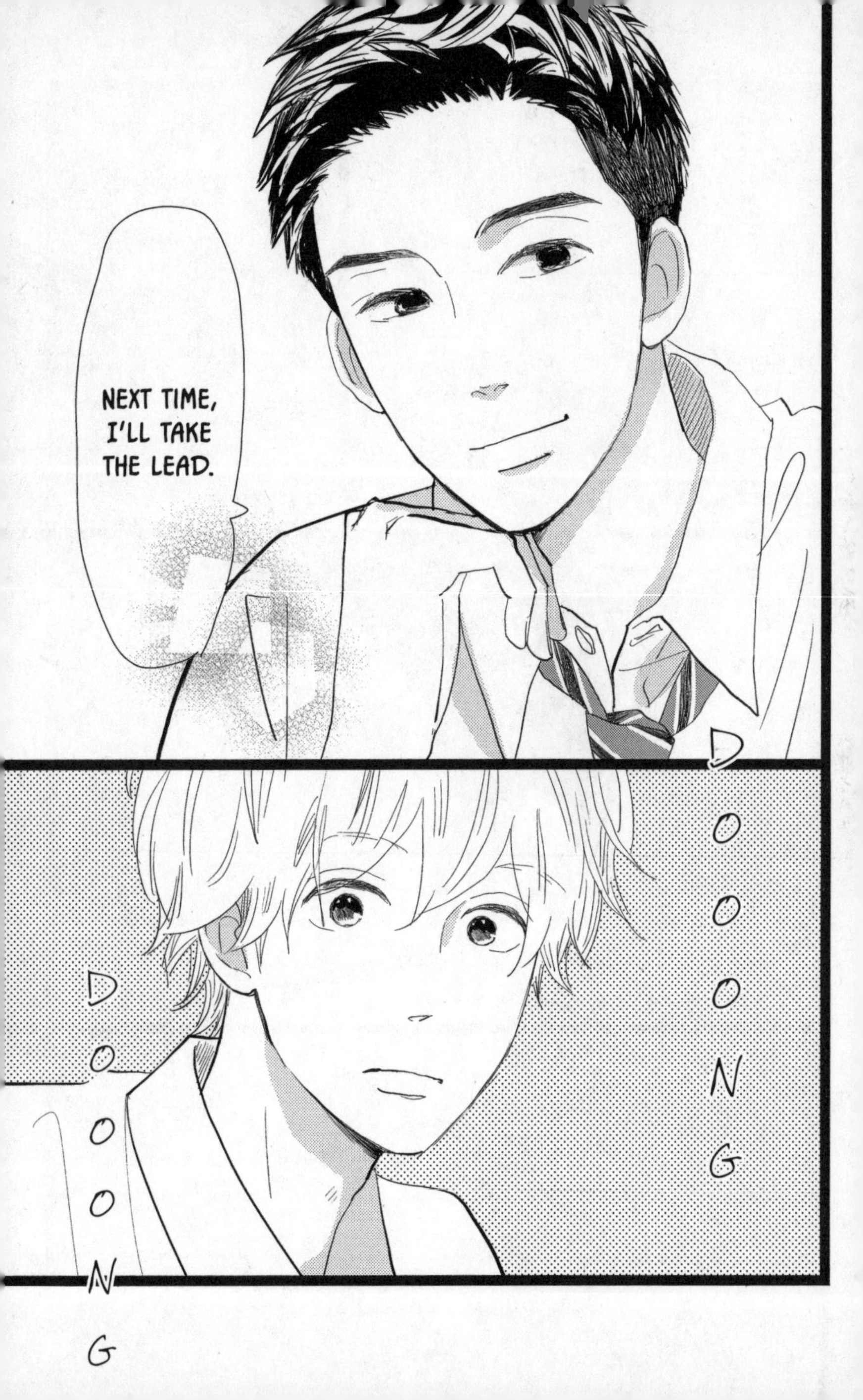
NEXT TIME, I'LL TAKE THE LEAD.
DOOOONG
DOOOONG

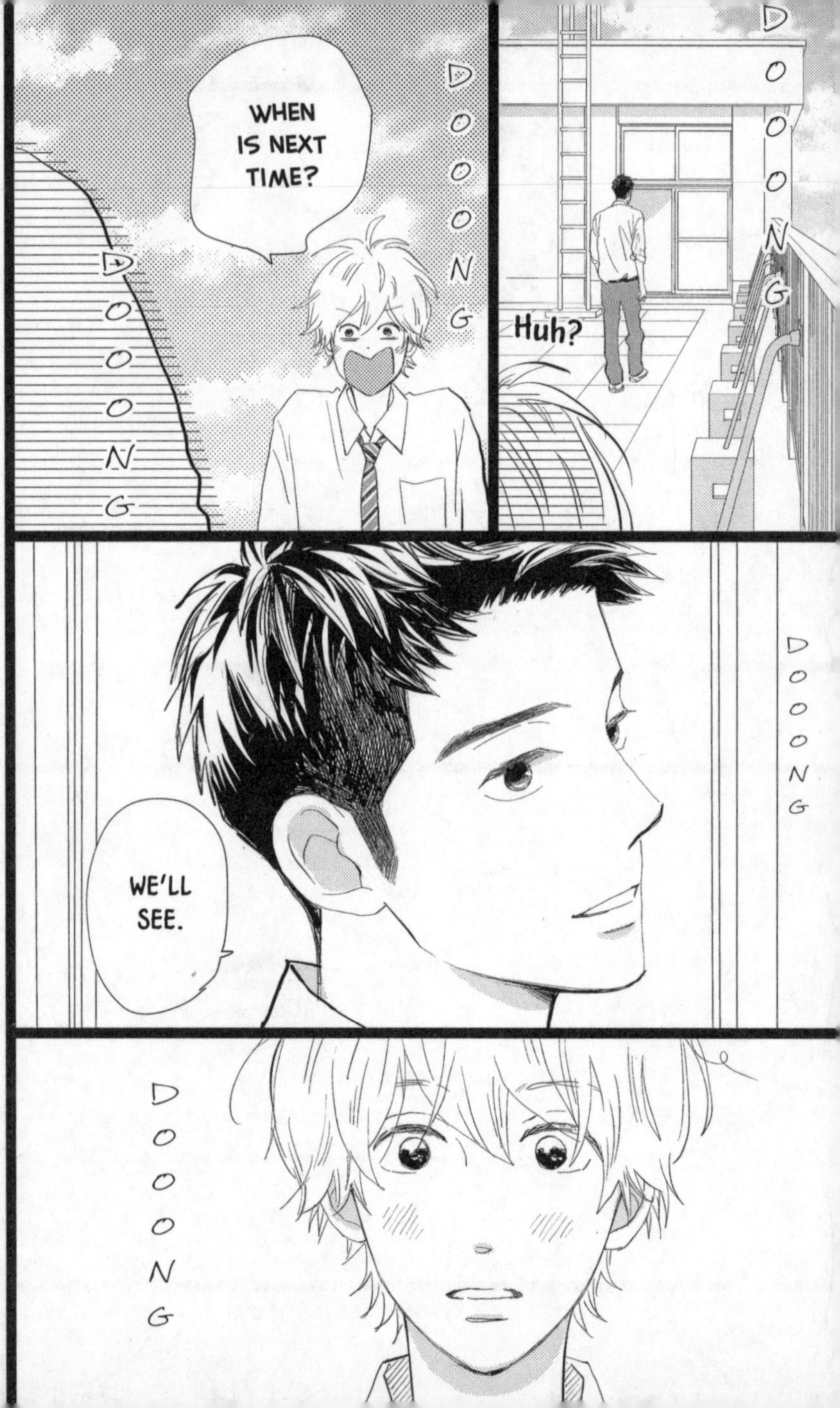
DOOONG
Huh?
DOOOONG
WHEN IS NEXT TIME?
DOOOONG
DOOOONG
WE'LL SEE.
DOOOONG

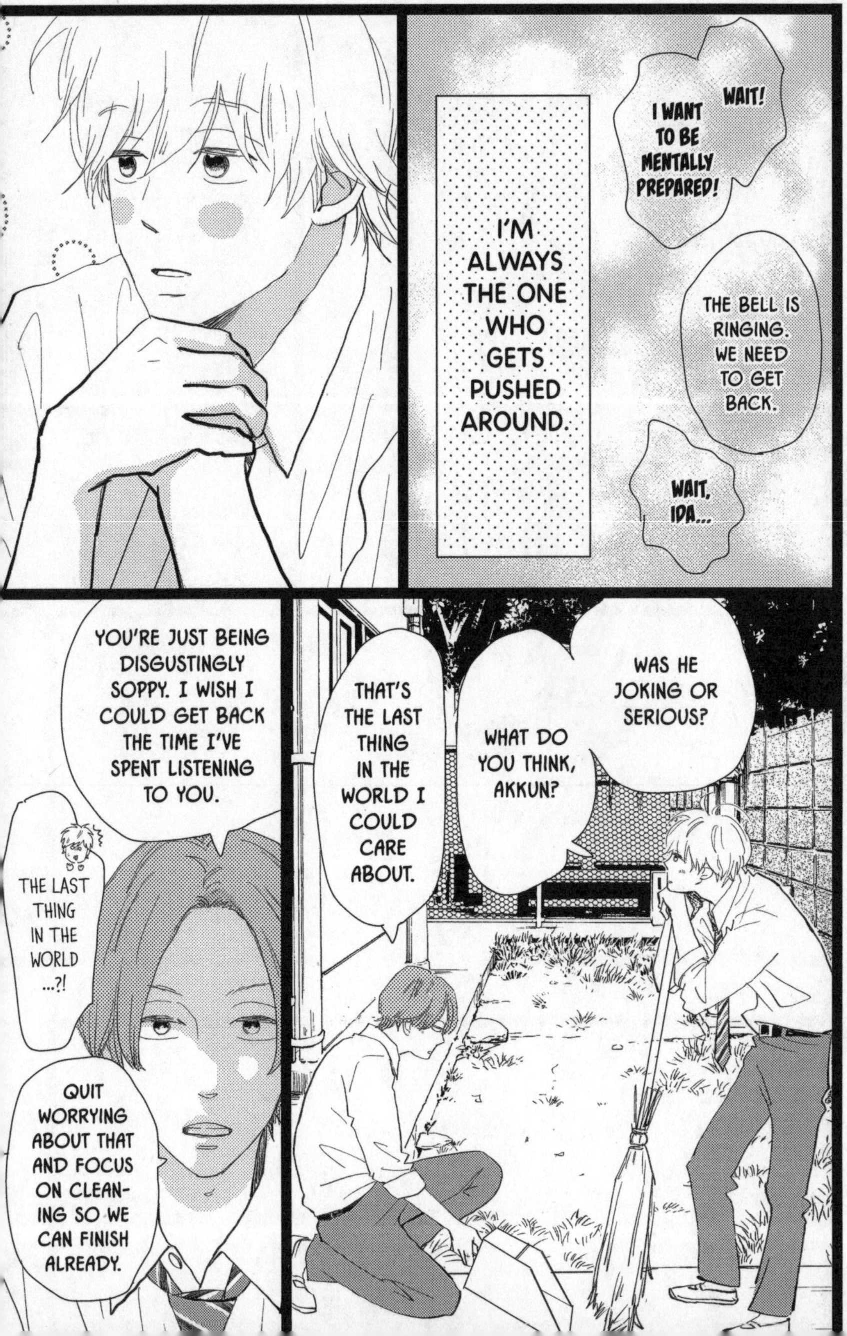
WAIT! I WANT TO BE MENTALLY PREPARED!
THE BELL IS RINGING. WE NEED TO GET BACK.
WAIT, IDA...
I'M ALWAYS THE ONE WHO GETS PUSHED AROUND.
WAS HE JOKING OR SERIOUS?
WHAT DO YOU THINK, AKKUN?
THAT'S THE LAST THING IN THE WORLD I COULD CARE ABOUT.
YOU'RE JUST BEING DISGUSTINGLY SOPPY. I WISH I COULD GET BACK THE TIME I'VE SPENT LISTENING TO YOU.
THE LAST THING IN THE WORLD ...?!
QUIT WORRYING ABOUT THAT AND FOCUS ON CLEAN-ING SO WE CAN FINISH ALREADY.

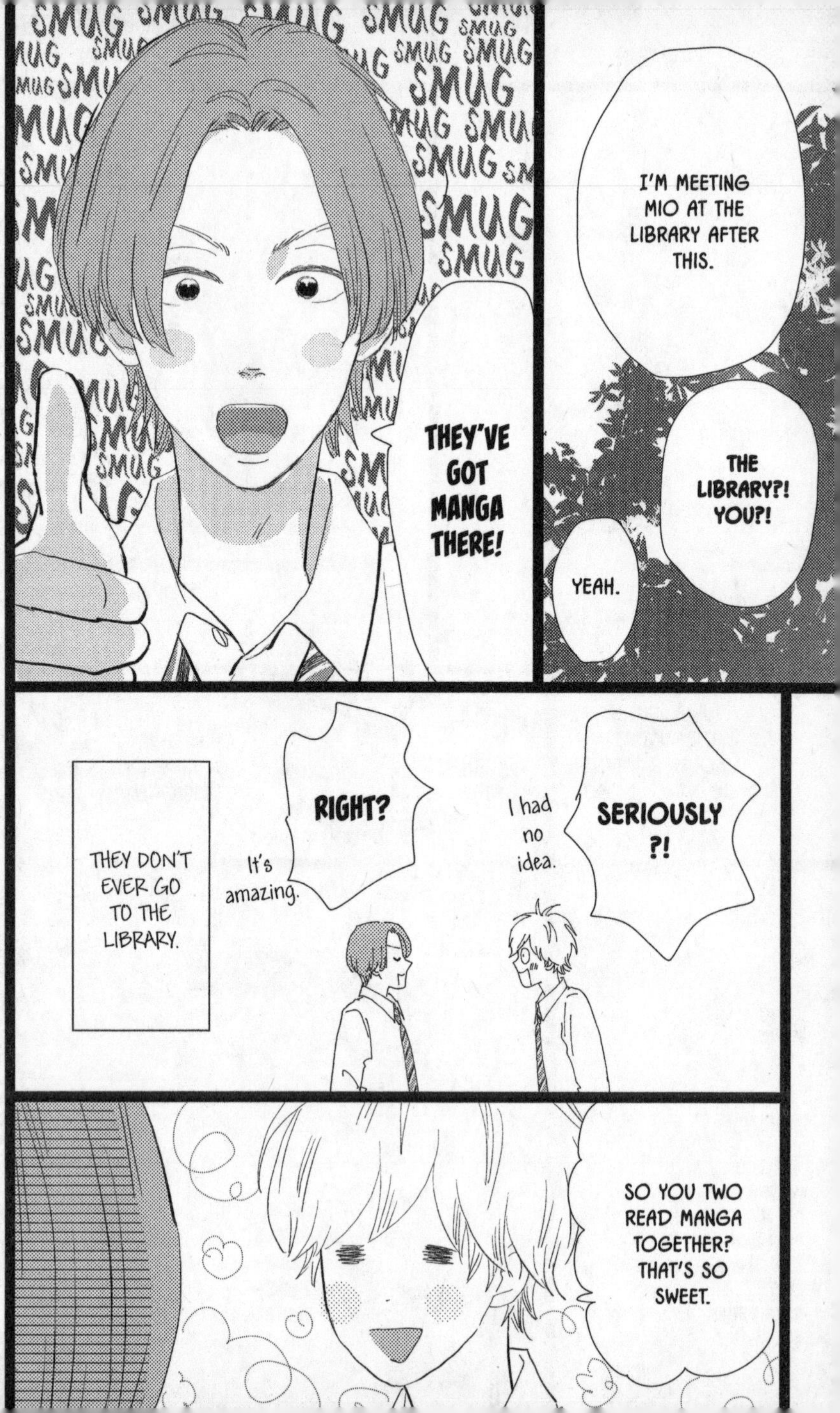
I'M MEETING MIO AT THE LIBRARY AFTER THIS.
THE LIBRARY?! YOU?!
YEAH.
SMUG SMUG SMUG SMUG SMUG SMUG SMUG SMUG SMUG
THEY'VE GOT MANGA THERE!
SERIOUSLY?!
I had no idea.
RIGHT?
It's amazing.
THEY DON'T EVER GO TO THE LIBRARY.
SO YOU TWO READ MANGA TOGETHER? THAT'S SO SWEET.

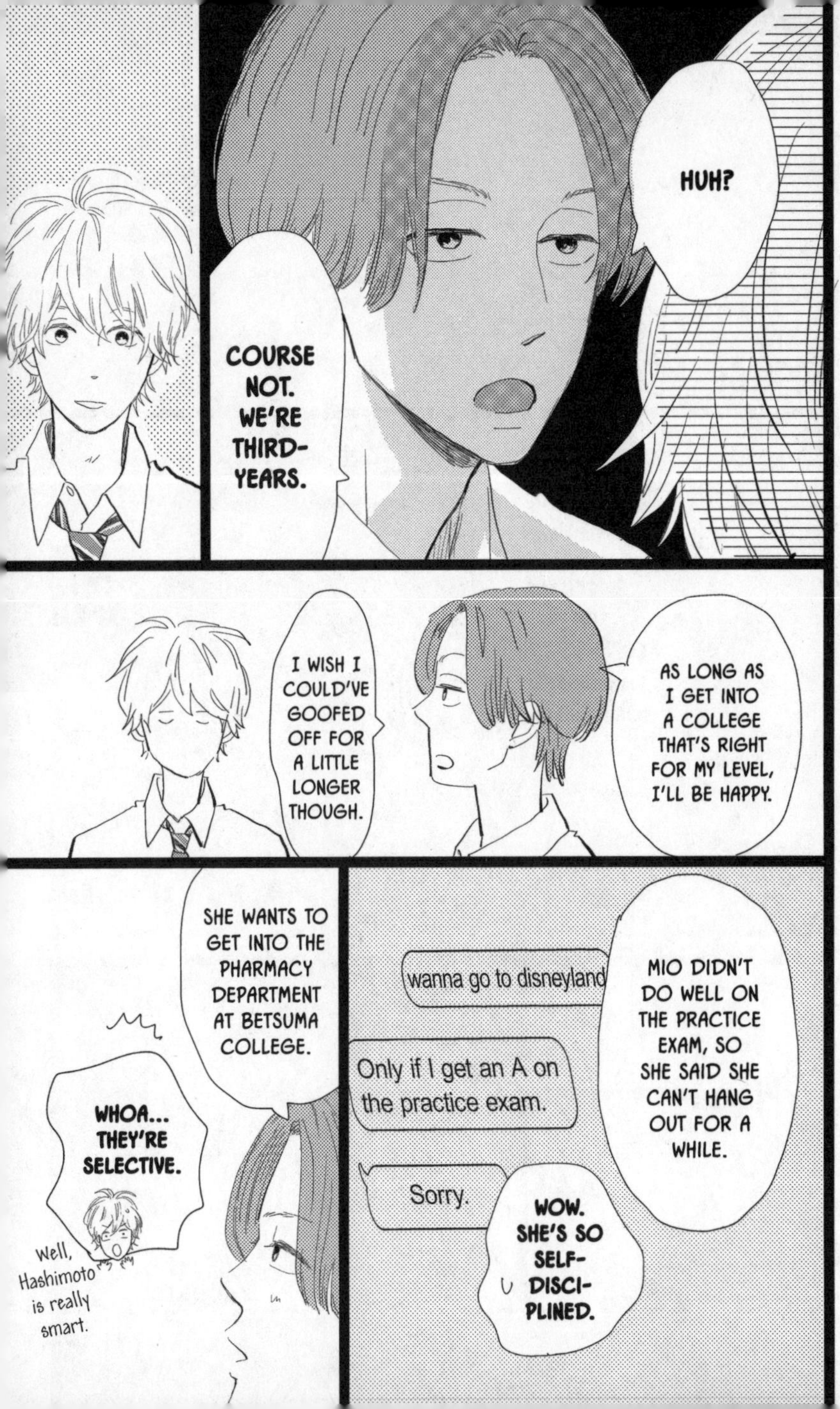
HUH?
COURSE NOT. WE'RE THIRD-YEARS.
AS LONG AS I GET INTO A COLLEGE THAT'S RIGHT FOR MY LEVEL, I'LL BE HAPPY.
I WISH I COULD'VE GOOFED OFF FOR A LITTLE LONGER THOUGH.
MIO DIDN'T DO WELL ON THE PRACTICE EXAM, SO SHE SAID SHE CAN'T HANG OUT FOR A WHILE.
wanna go to disneyland
Only if I get an A on the practice exam.
Sorry.
WOW. SHE'S SO SELF-DISCIPLINED.
SHE WANTS TO GET INTO THE PHARMACY DEPARTMENT AT BETSUMA COLLEGE.
WHOA... THEY'RE SELECTIVE.
Well, Hashimoto is really smart.

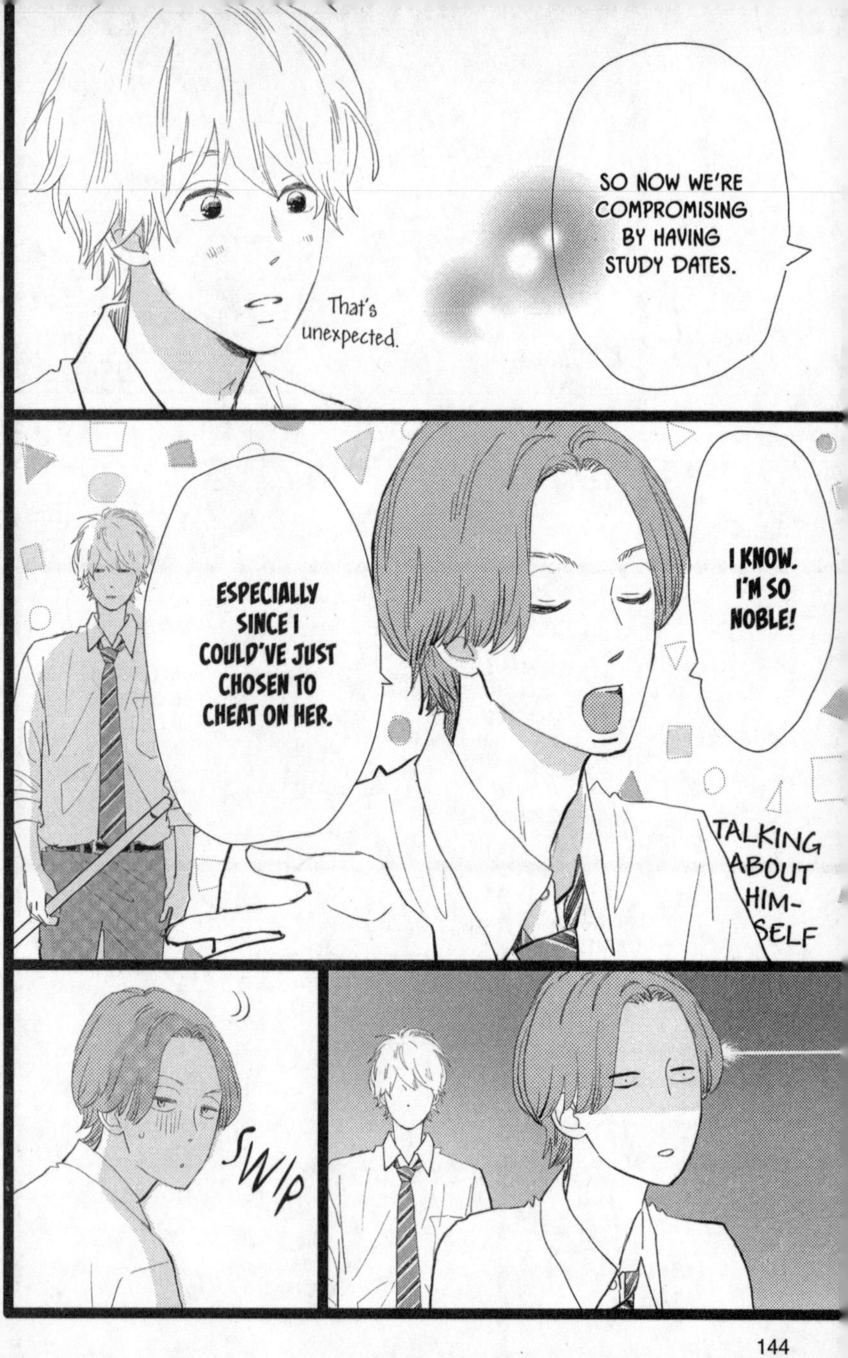
SO NOW WE'RE COMPROMISING BY HAVING STUDY DATES.
That's unexpected.
I KNOW. I'M SO NOBLE!
ESPECIALLY SINCE I COULD'VE JUST CHOSEN TO CHEAT ON HER.
TALKING ABOUT HIM-SELF
SWIP

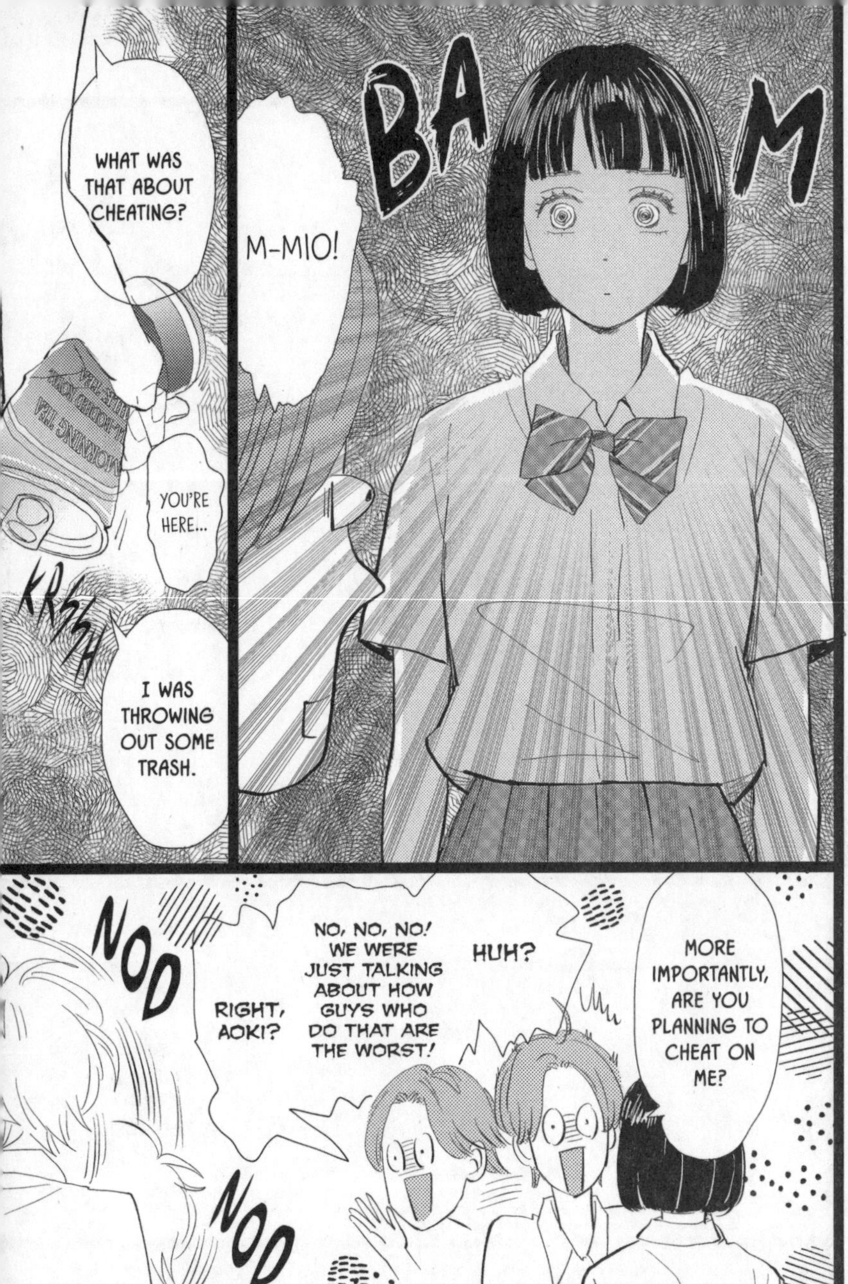
BAM
M-MIO!
WHAT WAS THAT ABOUT CHEATING?
YOU'RE HERE...
KRSSH
I WAS THROWING OUT SOME TRASH.
MORE IMPORTANTLY, ARE YOU PLANNING TO CHEAT ON ME?
HUH?
NO, NO, NO! WE WERE JUST TALKING ABOUT HOW GUYS WHO DO THAT ARE THE WORST!
RIGHT, AOKI?
NOD
NOD

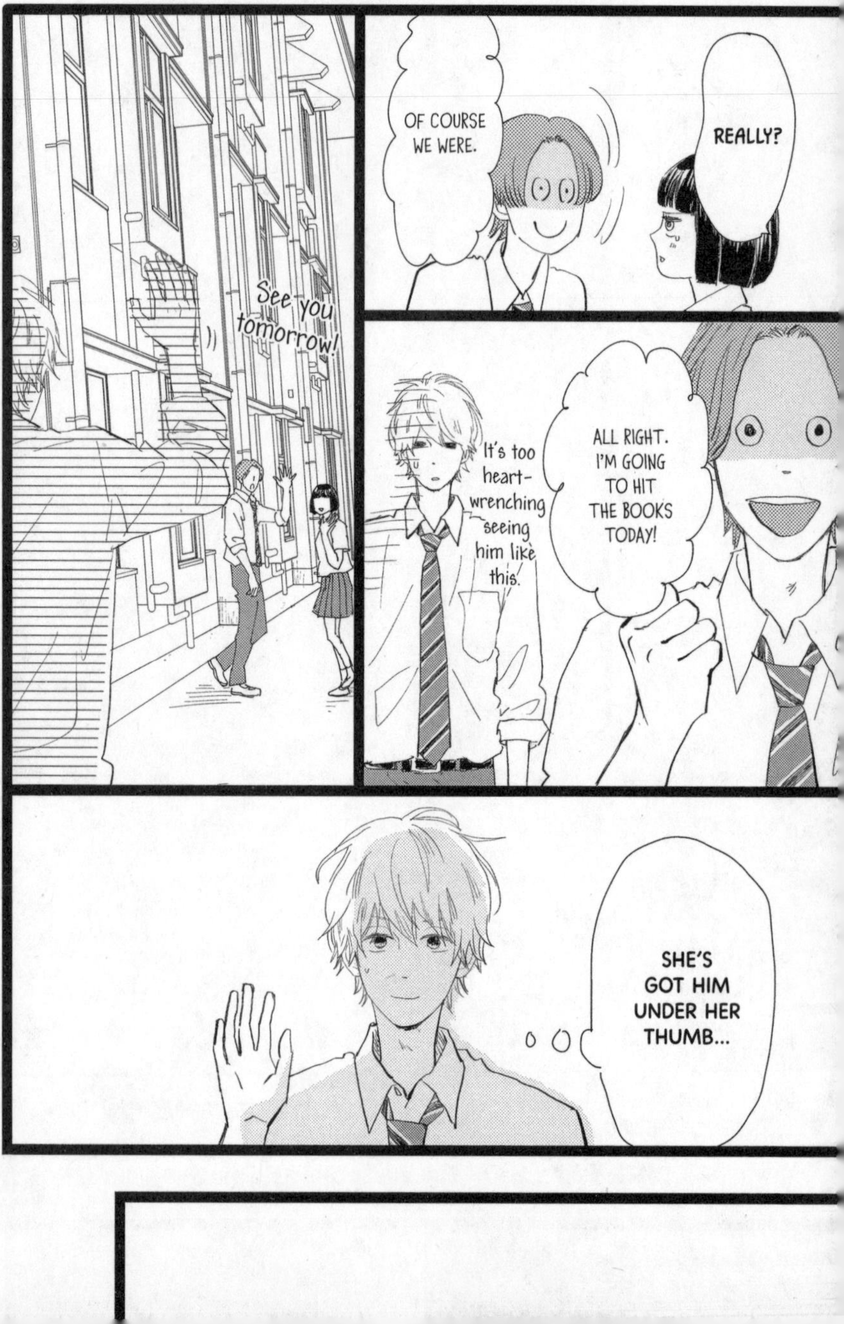
REALLY?
OF COURSE WE WERE.
ALL RIGHT. I'M GOING TO HIT THE BOOKS TODAY!
It's too heart-wrenching seeing him like this.
See you tomorrow!
SHE'S GOT HIM UNDER HER THUMB...

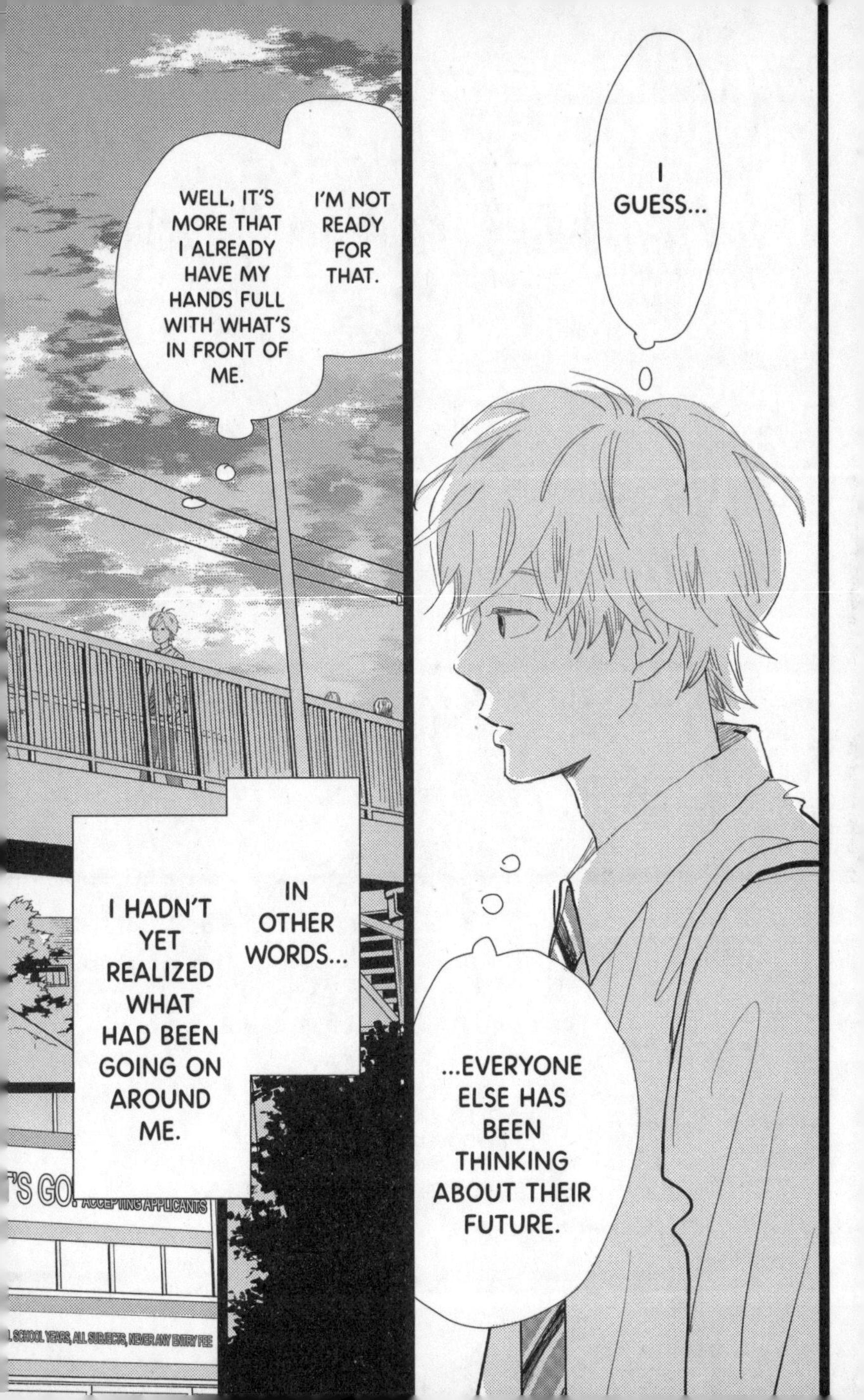
I GUESS...
...EVERYONE ELSE HAS BEEN THINKING ABOUT THEIR FUTURE.
I'M NOT READY FOR THAT.
WELL, IT'S MORE THAT I ALREADY HAVE MY HANDS FULL WITH WHAT'S IN FRONT OF ME.
IN OTHER WORDS...
I HADN'T YET REALIZED WHAT HAD BEEN GOING ON AROUND ME.
ACCEPTING APPLICANTS
SCHOOL YEARS, ALL SUBJECTS, NEVER ANY ENTRY FEE

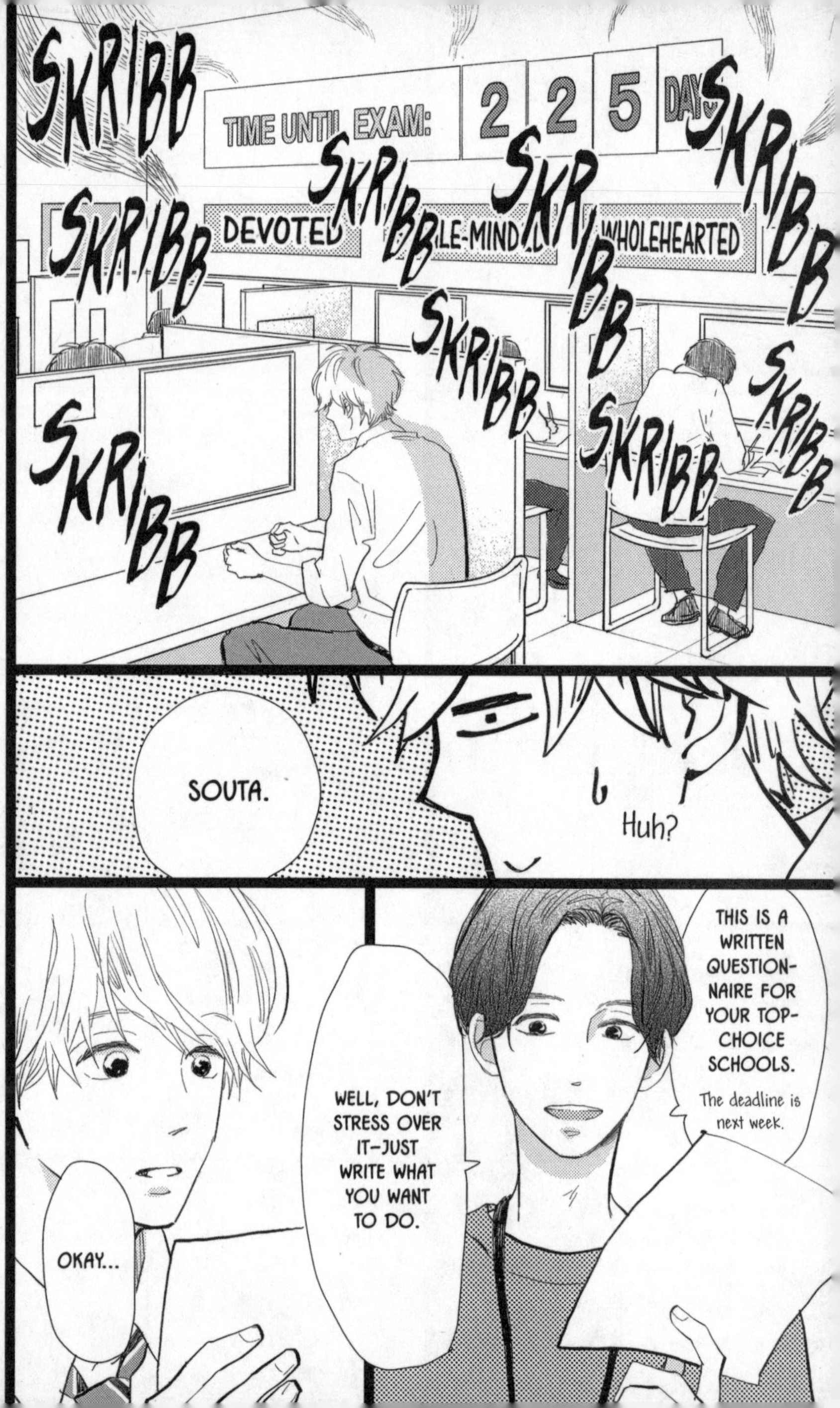
TIME UNTIL EXAM: 2 2 5 DAY
SKRIBB
SKRIBB
SKRIBB
SKRIBB
SKRIBB
SKRIBB
SKRIBB
SKRIBB
SKRIBB
DEVOTED
LE-MIND
WHOLEHEARTED
SOUTA.
Huh?
THIS IS A WRITTEN QUESTION-NAIRE FOR YOUR TOP-CHOICE SCHOOLS.
The deadline is next week.
WELL, DON'T STRESS OVER IT—JUST WRITE WHAT YOU WANT TO DO.
OKAY...

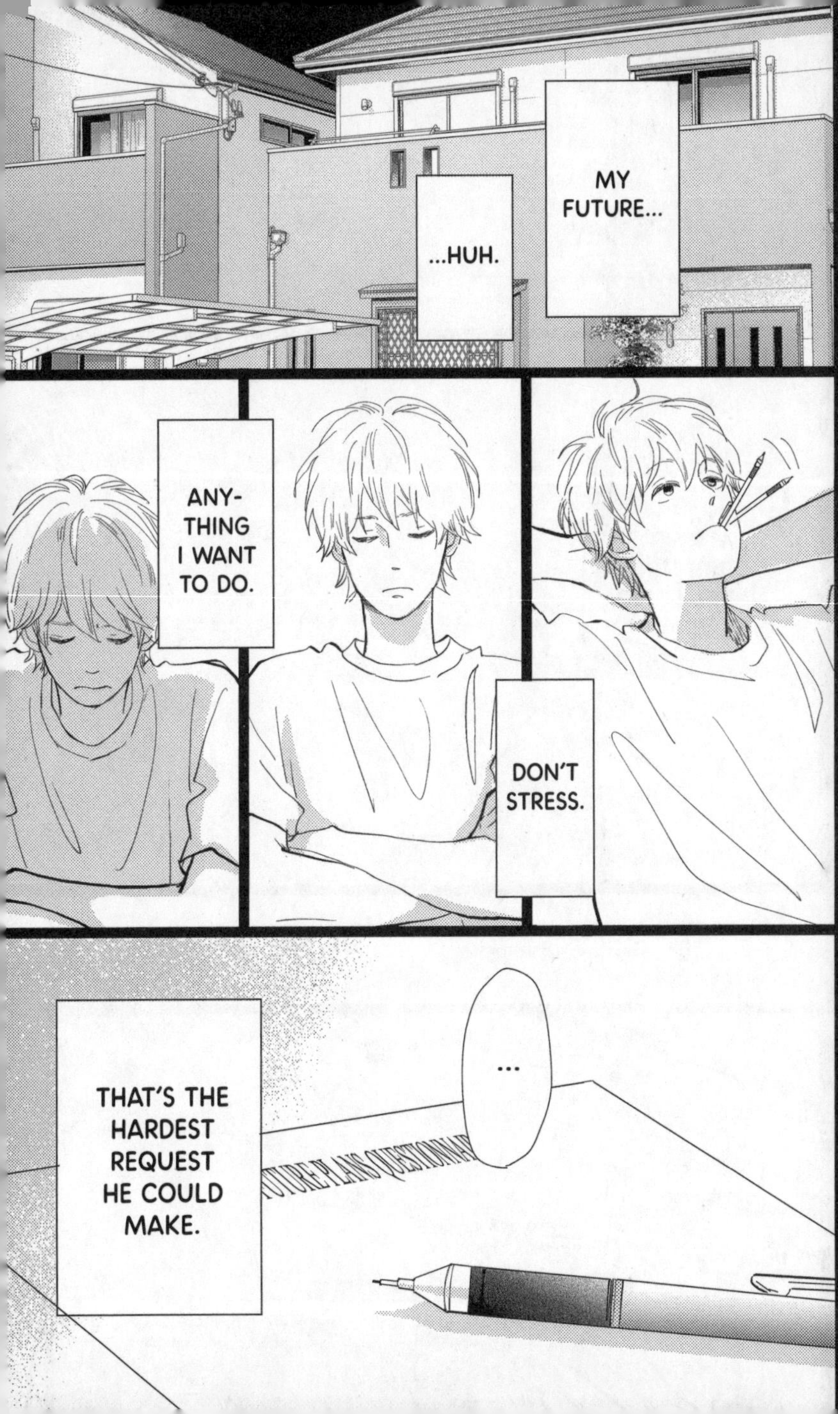
MY FUTURE...
...HUH.
DON'T STRESS.
ANY-THING I WANT TO DO.
...
THAT'S THE HARDEST REQUEST HE COULD MAKE.

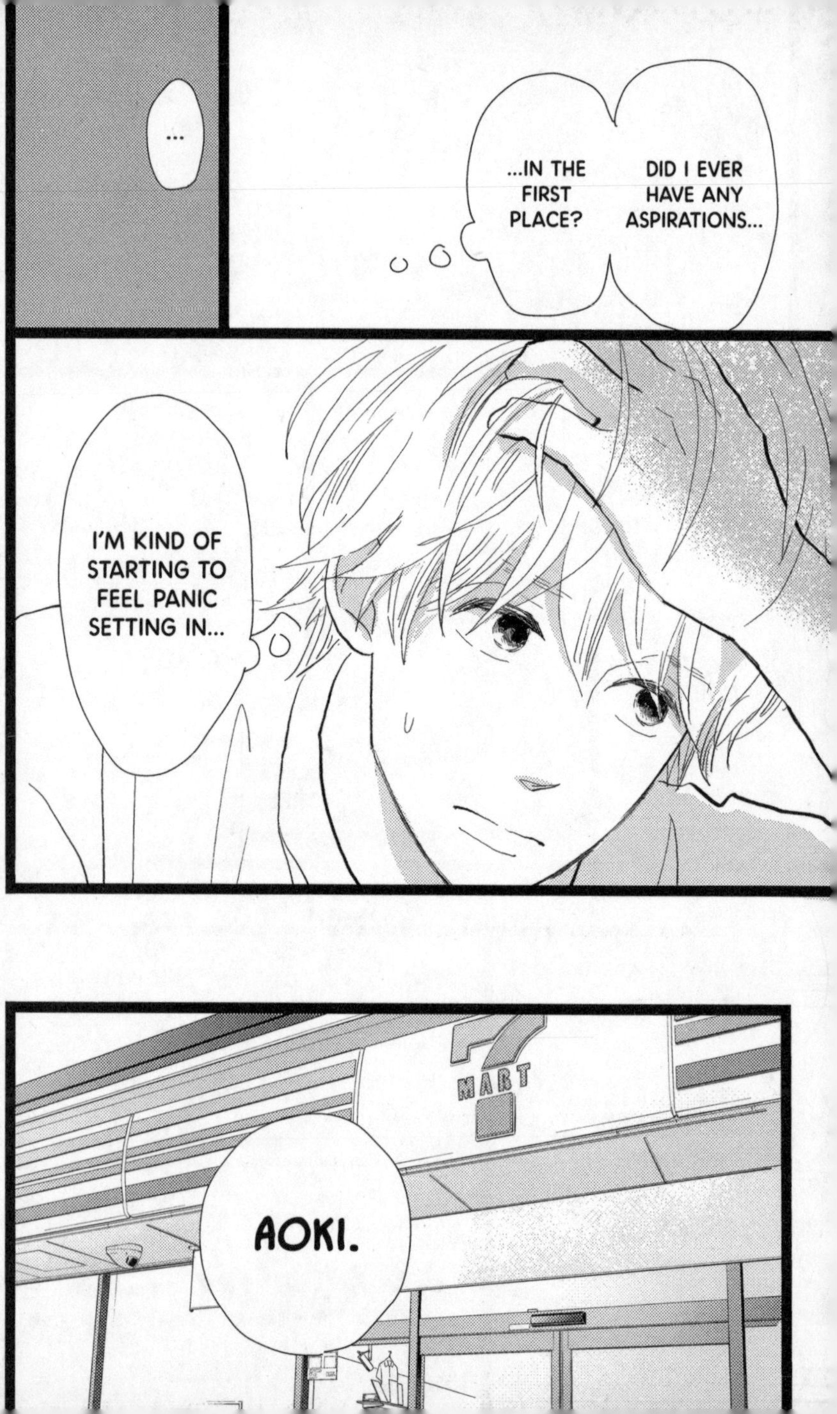
DID I EVER HAVE ANY ASPIRATIONS...
...IN THE FIRST PLACE?
...
I'M KIND OF STARTING TO FEEL PANIC SETTING IN...
MART
AOKI.

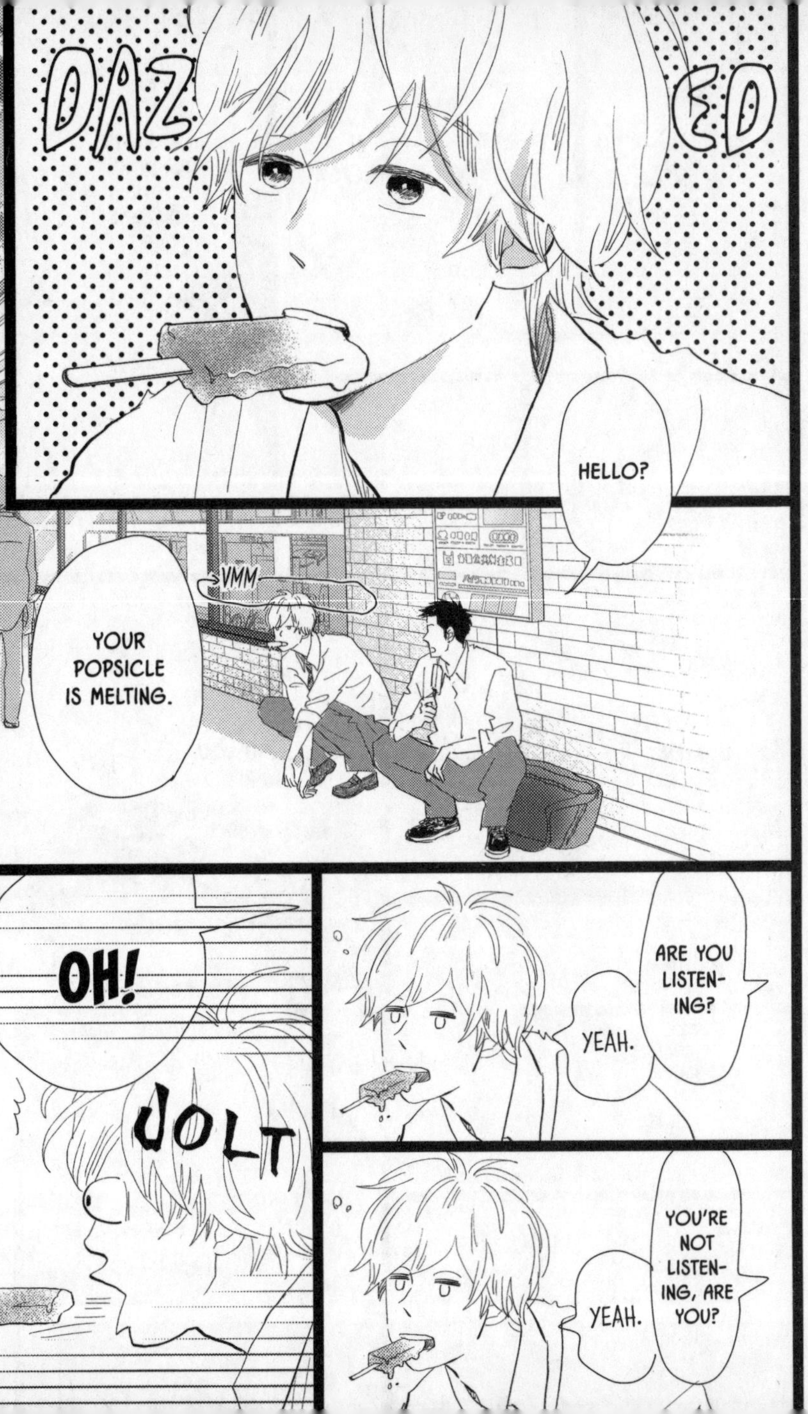
DAZED
HELLO?
VMM
YOUR POPSICLE IS MELTING.
ARE YOU LISTENING?
YEAH.
YOU'RE NOT LISTENING, ARE YOU?
YEAH.
OH!
JOLT

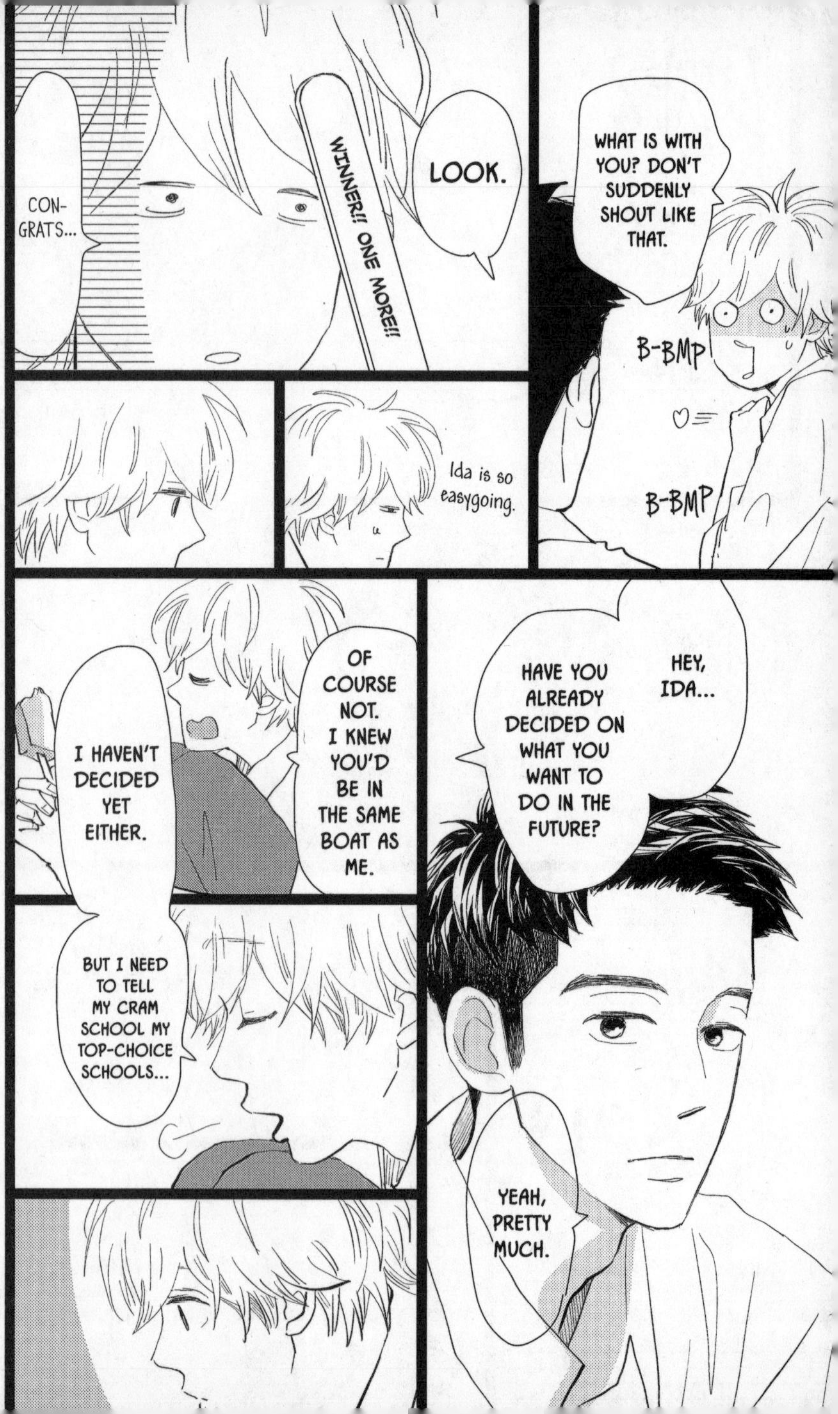
WHAT IS WITH YOU? DON'T SUDDENLY SHOUT LIKE THAT.
B-BMP
B-BMP
LOOK.
WINNER!! ONE MORE!!
CON-GRATS...
Ida is so easygoing.
HEY, IDA...
HAVE YOU ALREADY DECIDED ON WHAT YOU WANT TO DO IN THE FUTURE?
YEAH, PRETTY MUCH.
OF COURSE NOT. I KNEW YOU'D BE IN THE SAME BOAT AS ME.
I HAVEN'T DECIDED YET EITHER.
BUT I NEED TO TELL MY CRAM SCHOOL MY TOP-CHOICE SCHOOLS...

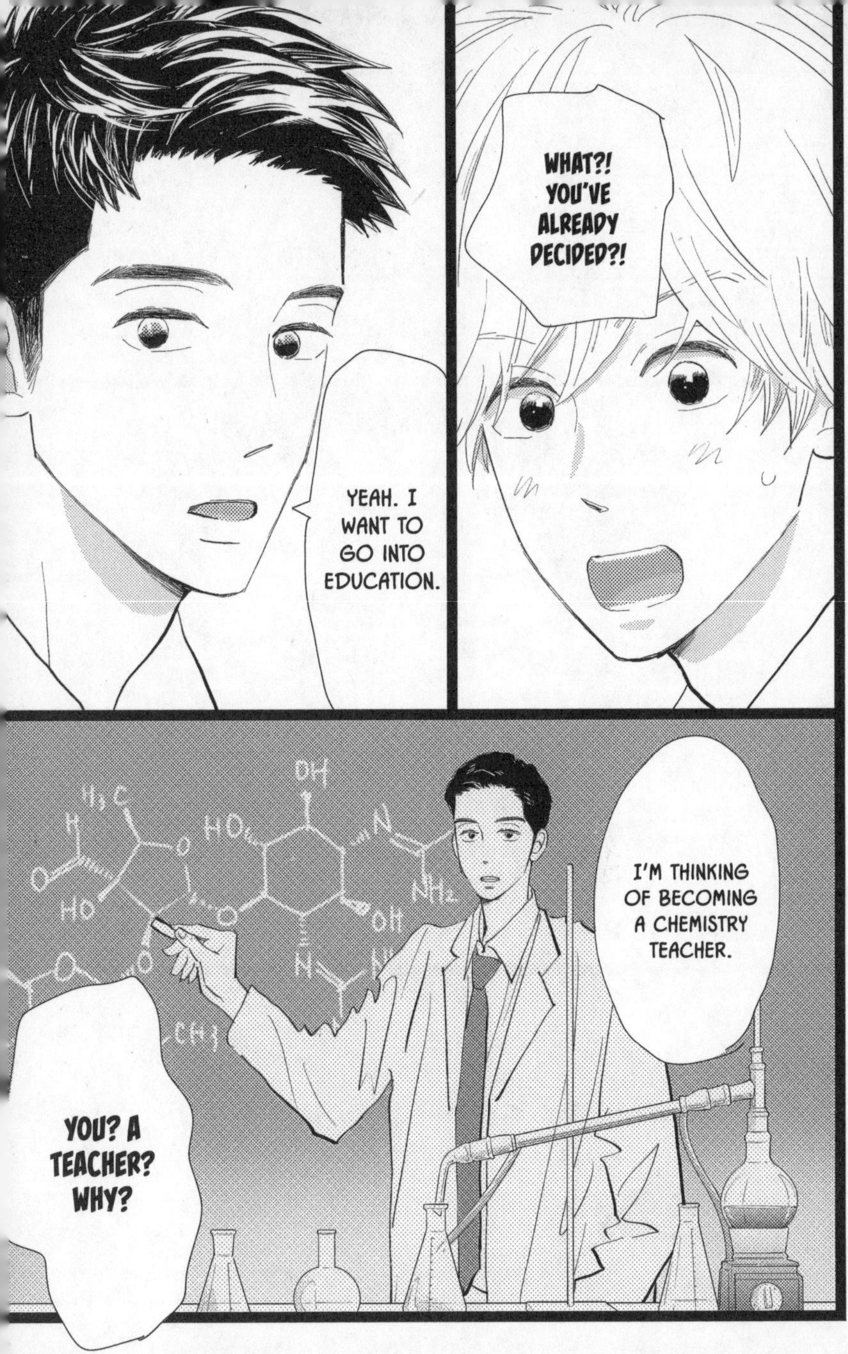
WHAT?! YOU'VE ALREADY DECIDED?!
YEAH. I WANT TO GO INTO EDUCATION.
I'M THINKING OF BECOMING A CHEMISTRY TEACHER.
YOU? A TEACHER? WHY?

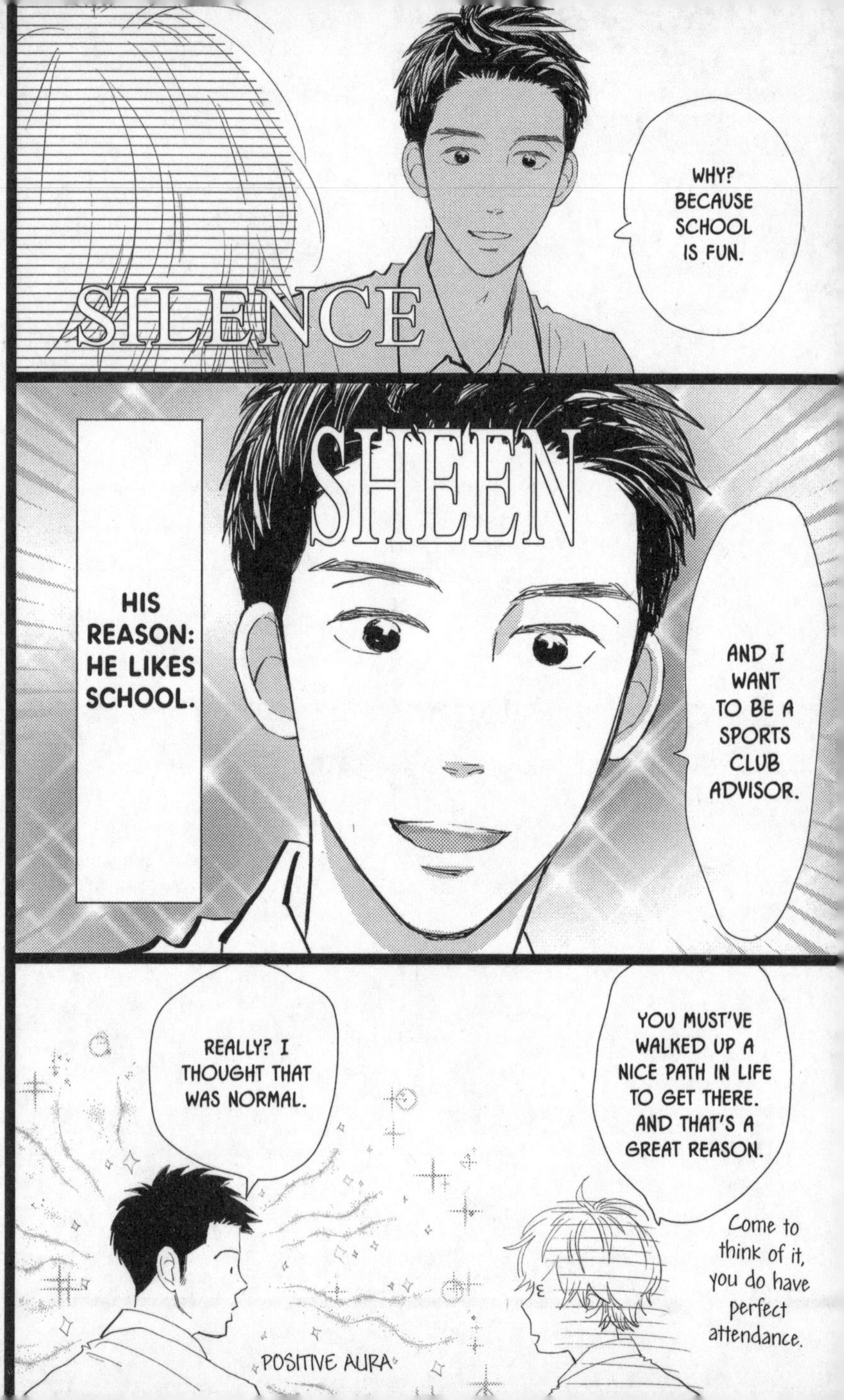
WHY? BECAUSE SCHOOL IS FUN.
SILENCE
AND I WANT TO BE A SPORTS CLUB ADVISOR.
SHEEN
HIS REASON: HE LIKES SCHOOL.
YOU MUST'VE WALKED UP A NICE PATH IN LIFE TO GET THERE. AND THAT'S A GREAT REASON.
Come to think of it, you do have perfect attendance.
REALLY? I THOUGHT THAT WAS NORMAL.
POSITIVE AURA

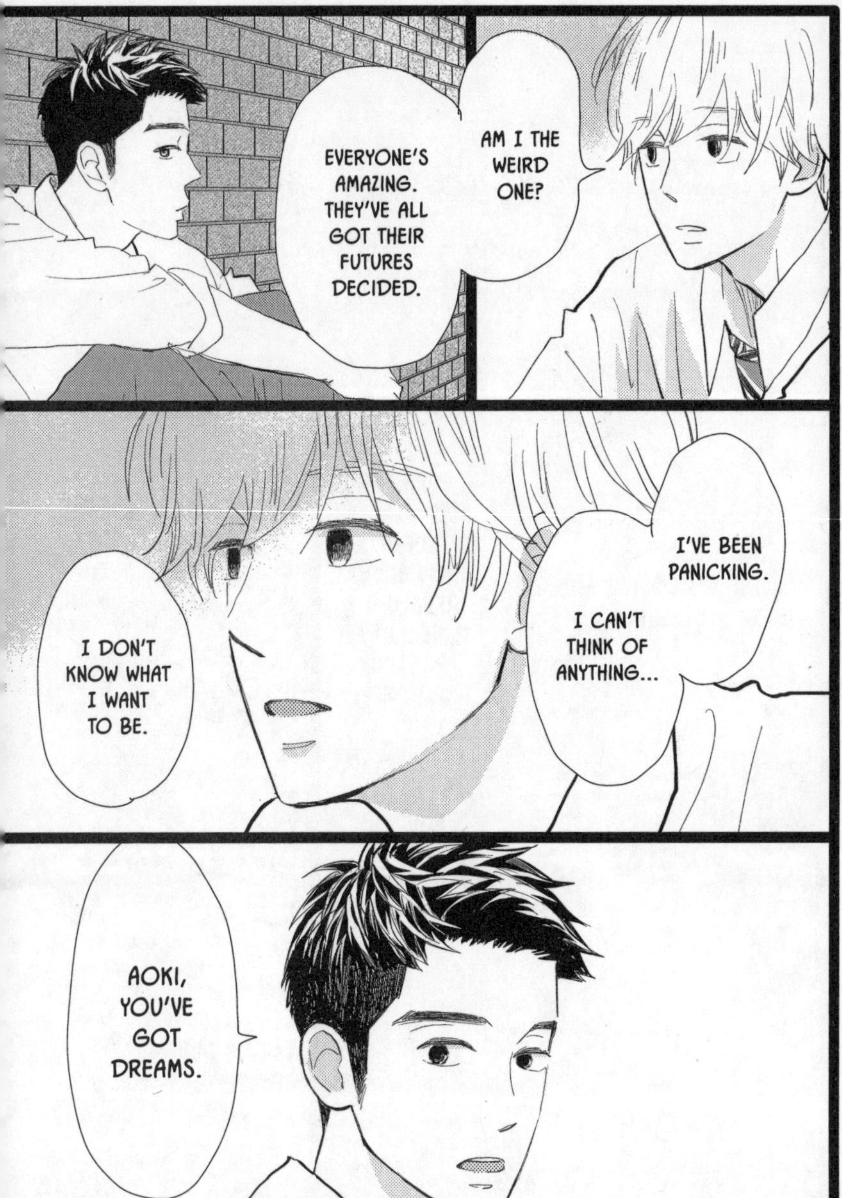
AM I THE WEIRD ONE?
EVERYONE'S AMAZING. THEY'VE ALL GOT THEIR FUTURES DECIDED.
I'VE BEEN PANICKING.
I CAN'T THINK OF ANYTHING...
I DON'T KNOW WHAT I WANT TO BE.
AOKI, YOU'VE GOT DREAMS.

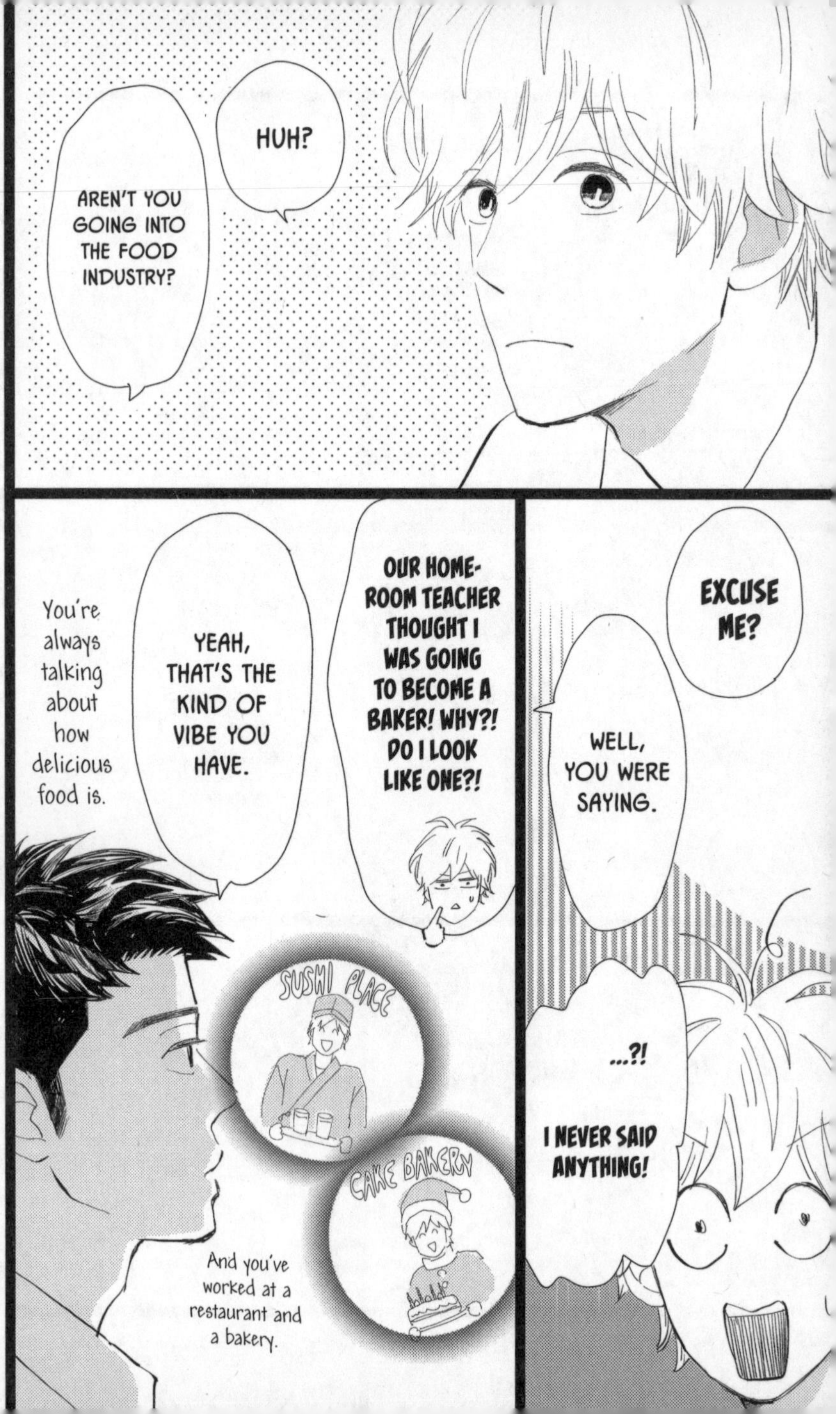
HUH?
AREN'T YOU GOING INTO THE FOOD INDUSTRY?
EXCUSE ME?
WELL, YOU WERE SAYING.
...?!
I NEVER SAID ANYTHING!
OUR HOME-ROOM TEACHER THOUGHT I WAS GOING TO BECOME A BAKER! WHY?! DO I LOOK LIKE ONE?!
YEAH, THAT'S THE KIND OF VIBE YOU HAVE.
You're always talking about how delicious food is.
SUSHI PLACE
CAKE BAKERY
And you've worked at a restaurant and a bakery.

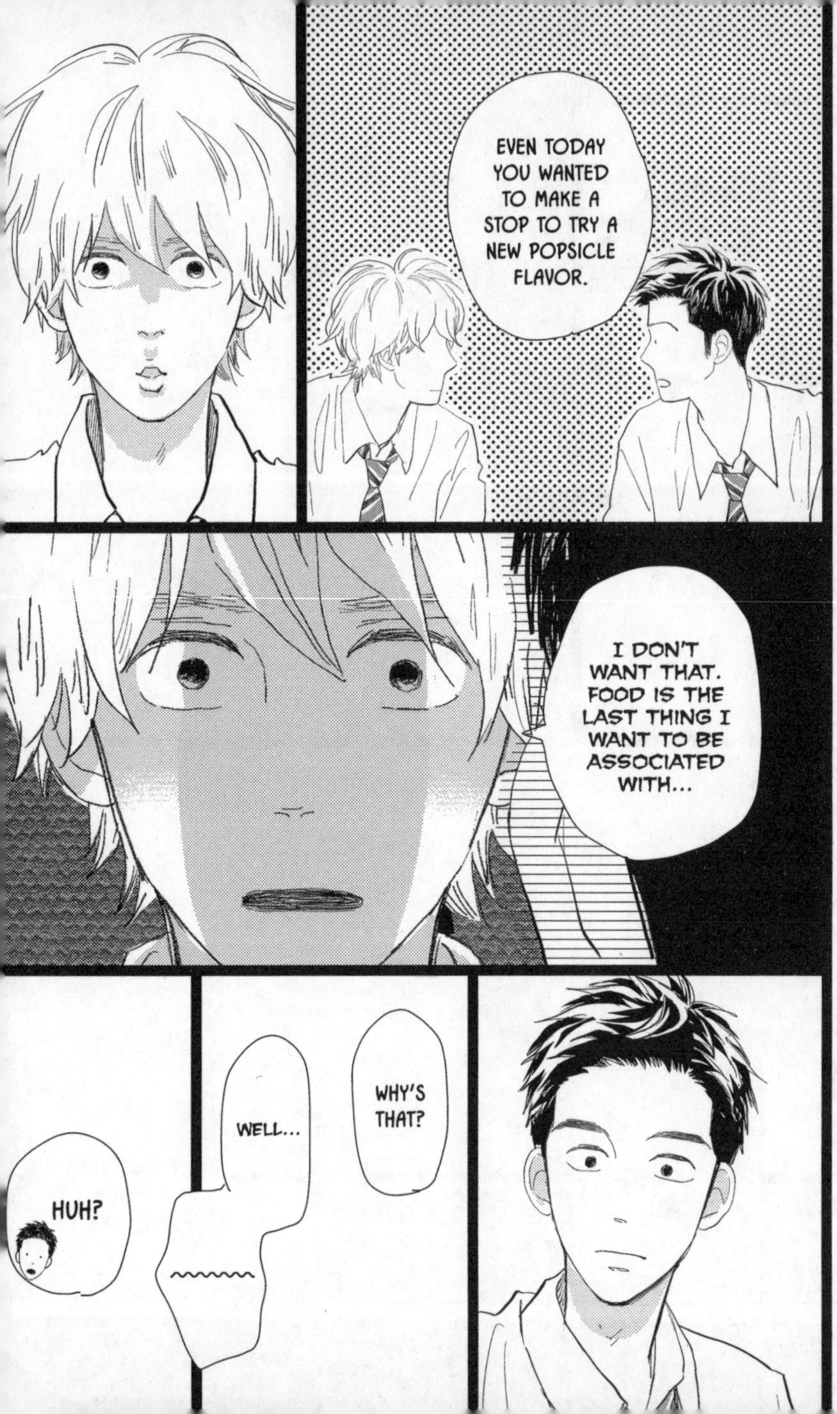
EVEN TODAY YOU WANTED TO MAKE A STOP TO TRY A NEW POPSICLE FLAVOR.
I DON'T WANT THAT. FOOD IS THE LAST THING I WANT TO BE ASSOCIATED WITH...
WHY'S THAT?
WELL...
HUH?

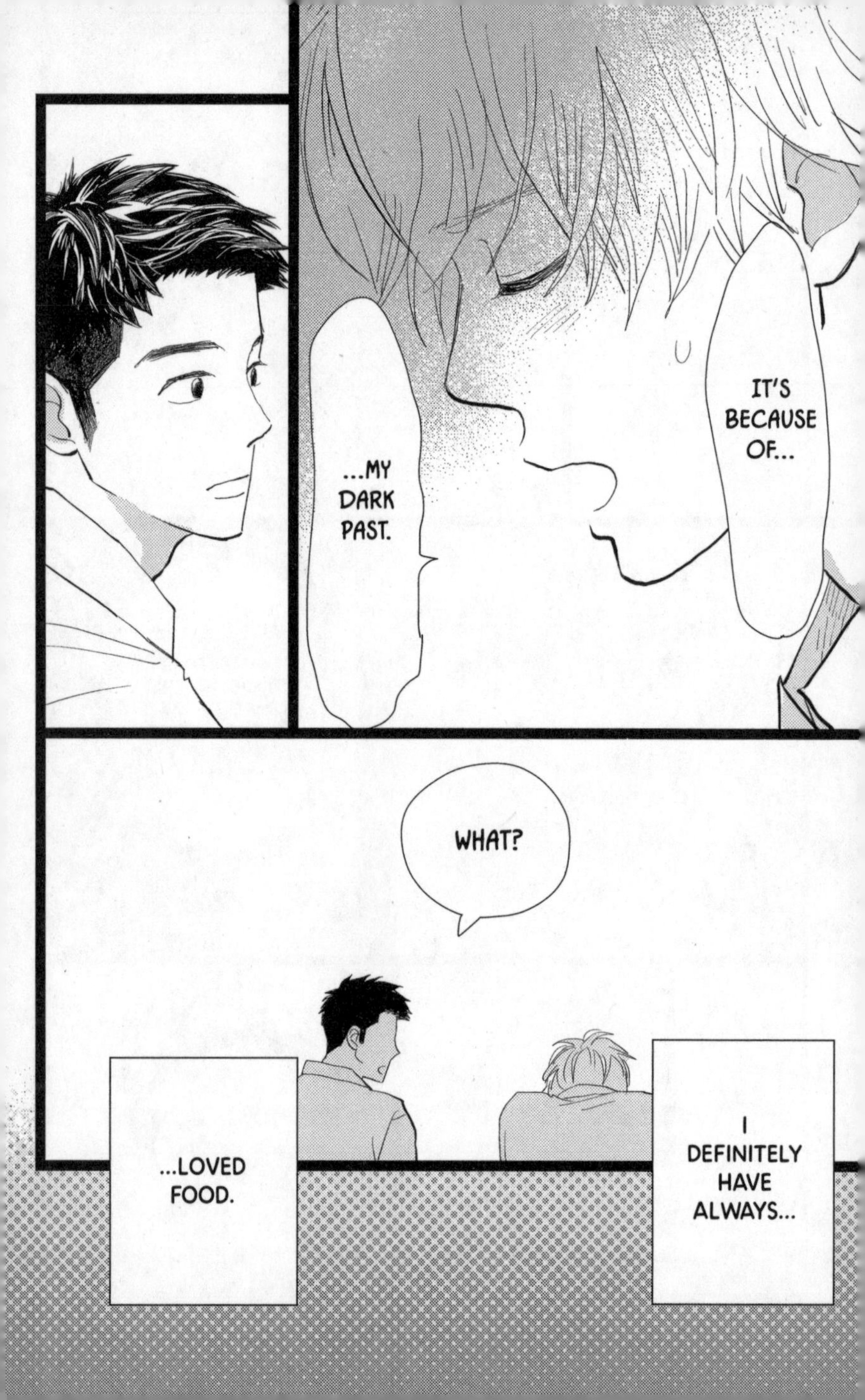
IT'S BECAUSE OF...
...MY DARK PAST.
WHAT?
I DEFINITELY HAVE ALWAYS...
...LOVED FOOD.

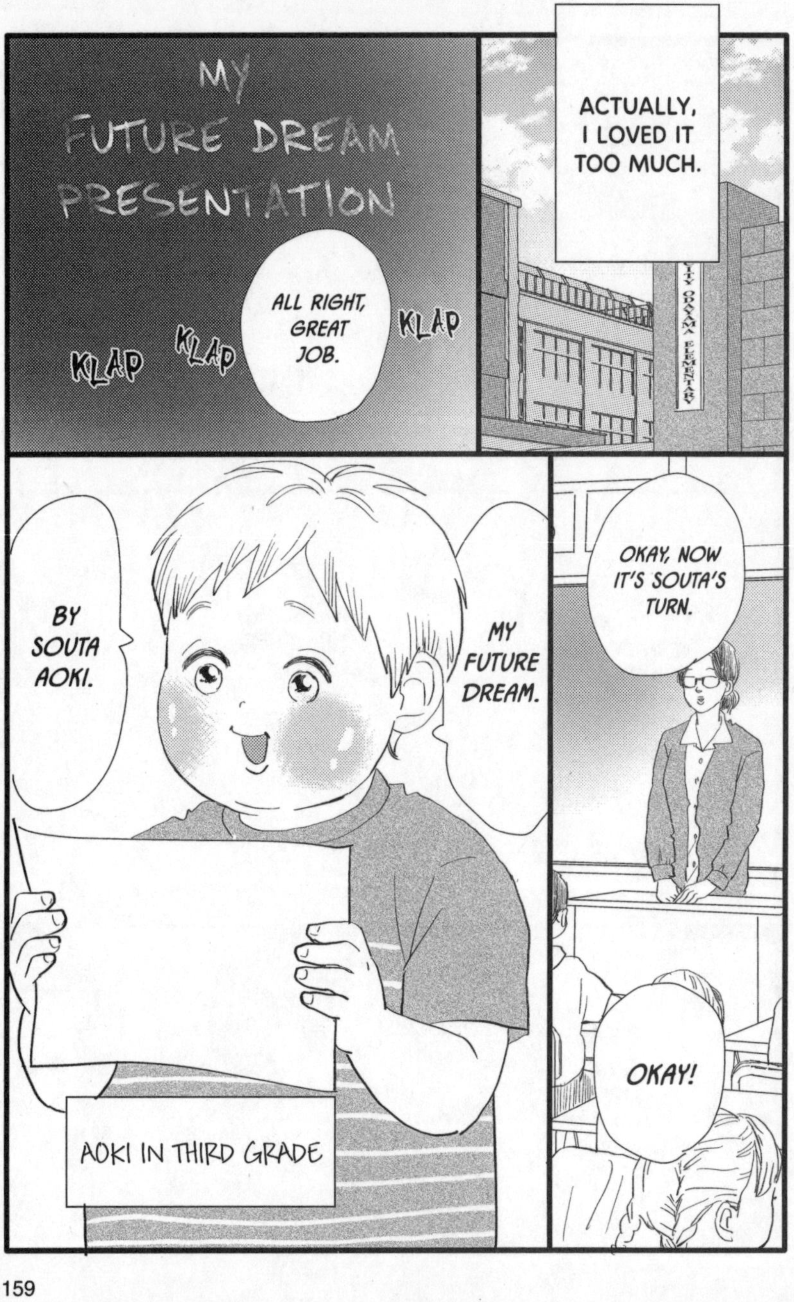

ACTUALLY, I LOVED IT TOO MUCH.
CITY ODAYAMA ELEMENTARY
MY FUTURE DREAM PRESENTATION
KLAP
ALL RIGHT, GREAT JOB.
KLAP
KLAP
OKAY, NOW IT'S SOUTA'S TURN.
OKAY!
MY FUTURE DREAM.
BY SOUTA AOKI.
AOKI IN THIRD GRADE

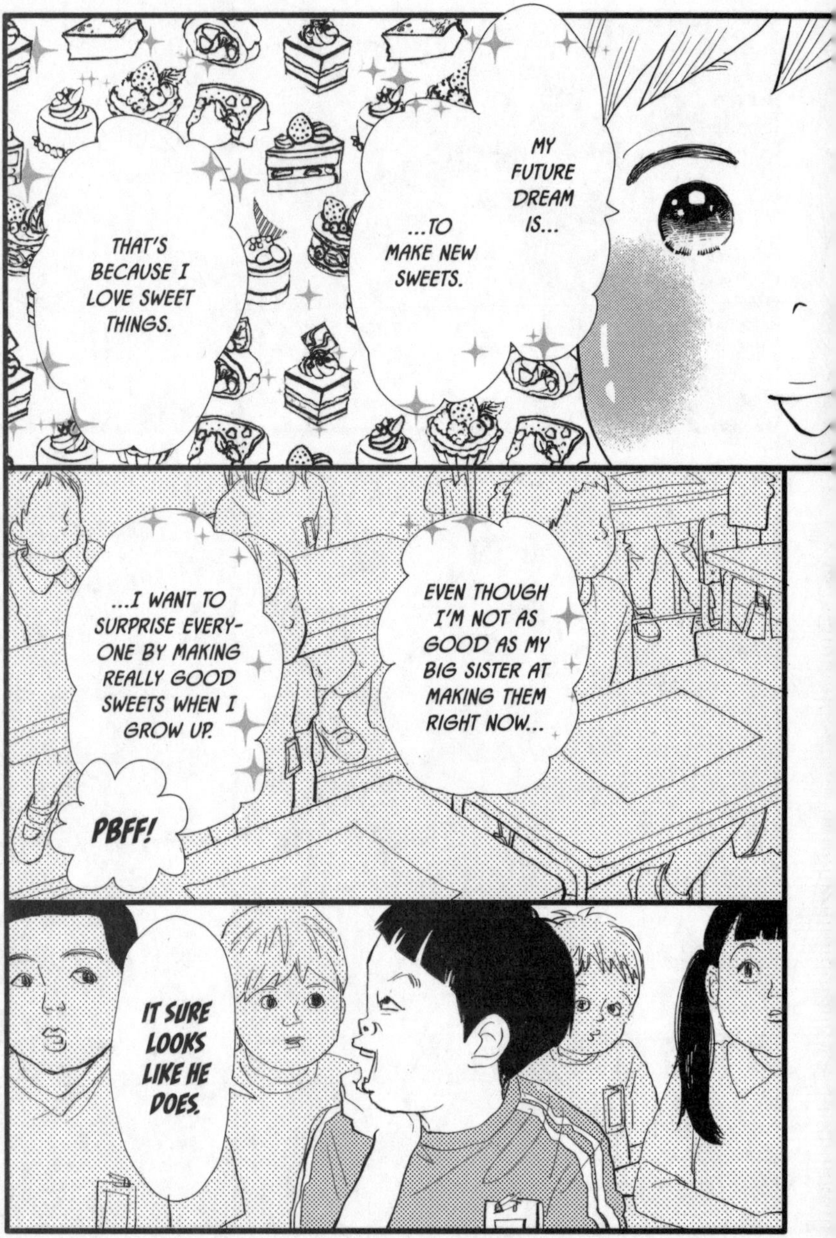
MY FUTURE DREAM IS...
...TO MAKE NEW SWEETS.
THAT'S BECAUSE I LOVE SWEET THINGS.
EVEN THOUGH I'M NOT AS GOOD AS MY BIG SISTER AT MAKING THEM RIGHT NOW...
...I WANT TO SURPRISE EVERY-ONE BY MAKING REALLY GOOD SWEETS WHEN I GROW UP.
PBFF!
IT SURE LOOKS LIKE HE DOES.

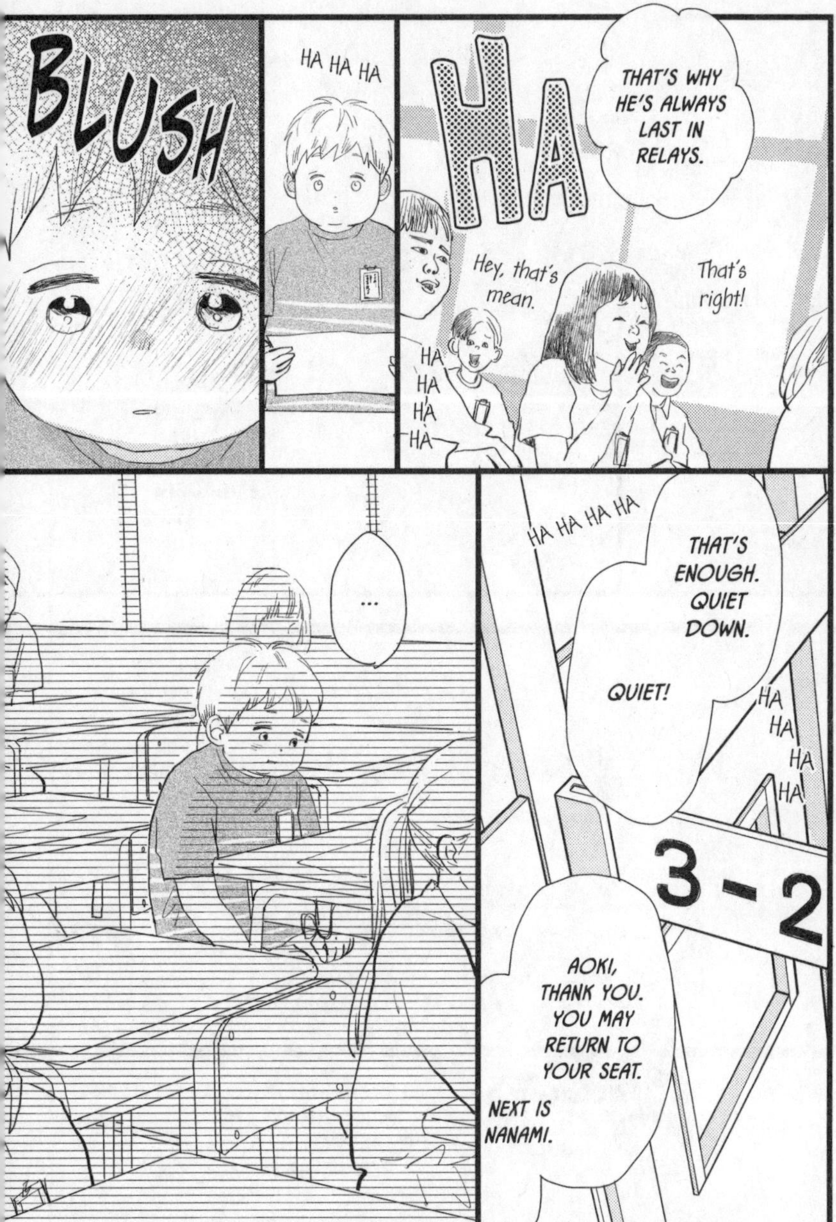
HA
THAT'S WHY HE'S ALWAYS LAST IN RELAYS.
Hey, that's mean.
That's right!
HA HA HA HA
HA HA HA
BLUSH
HA HA HA HA
THAT'S ENOUGH. QUIET DOWN.
QUIET!
HA HA HA HA
3-2
AOKI, THANK YOU. YOU MAY RETURN TO YOUR SEAT.
NEXT IS NANAMI.
...

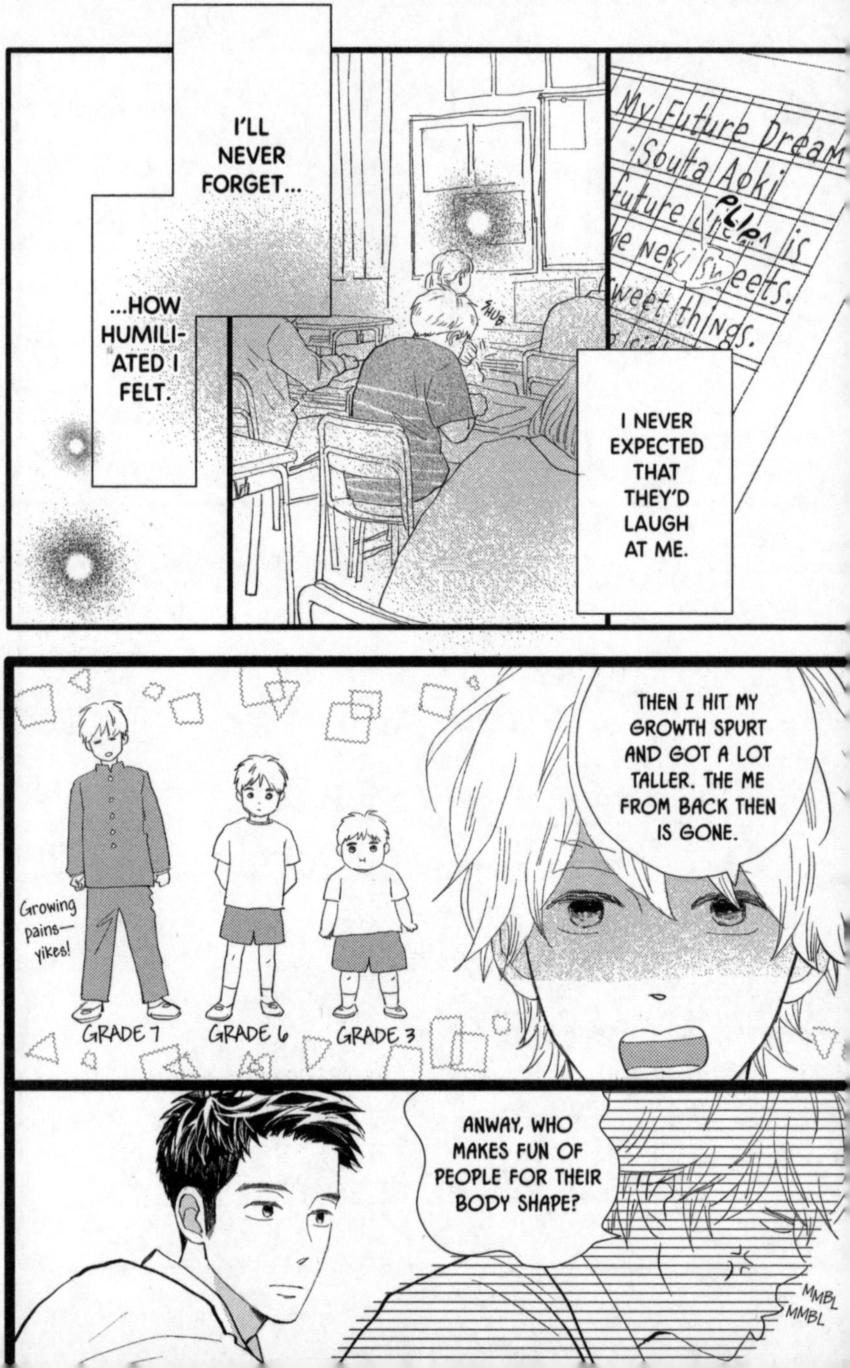
My Future Dream
Souta Aoki
sweet things.
I NEVER EXPECTED THAT THEY'D LAUGH AT ME.
SHUB
I'LL NEVER FORGET...
...HOW HUMILIATED I FELT.
THEN I HIT MY GROWTH SPURT AND GOT A LOT TALLER. THE ME FROM BACK THEN IS GONE.
GRADE 3
GRADE 6
GRADE 7
Growing pains—yikes!
ANWAY, WHO MAKES FUN OF PEOPLE FOR THEIR BODY SHAPE?
MMBL MMBL

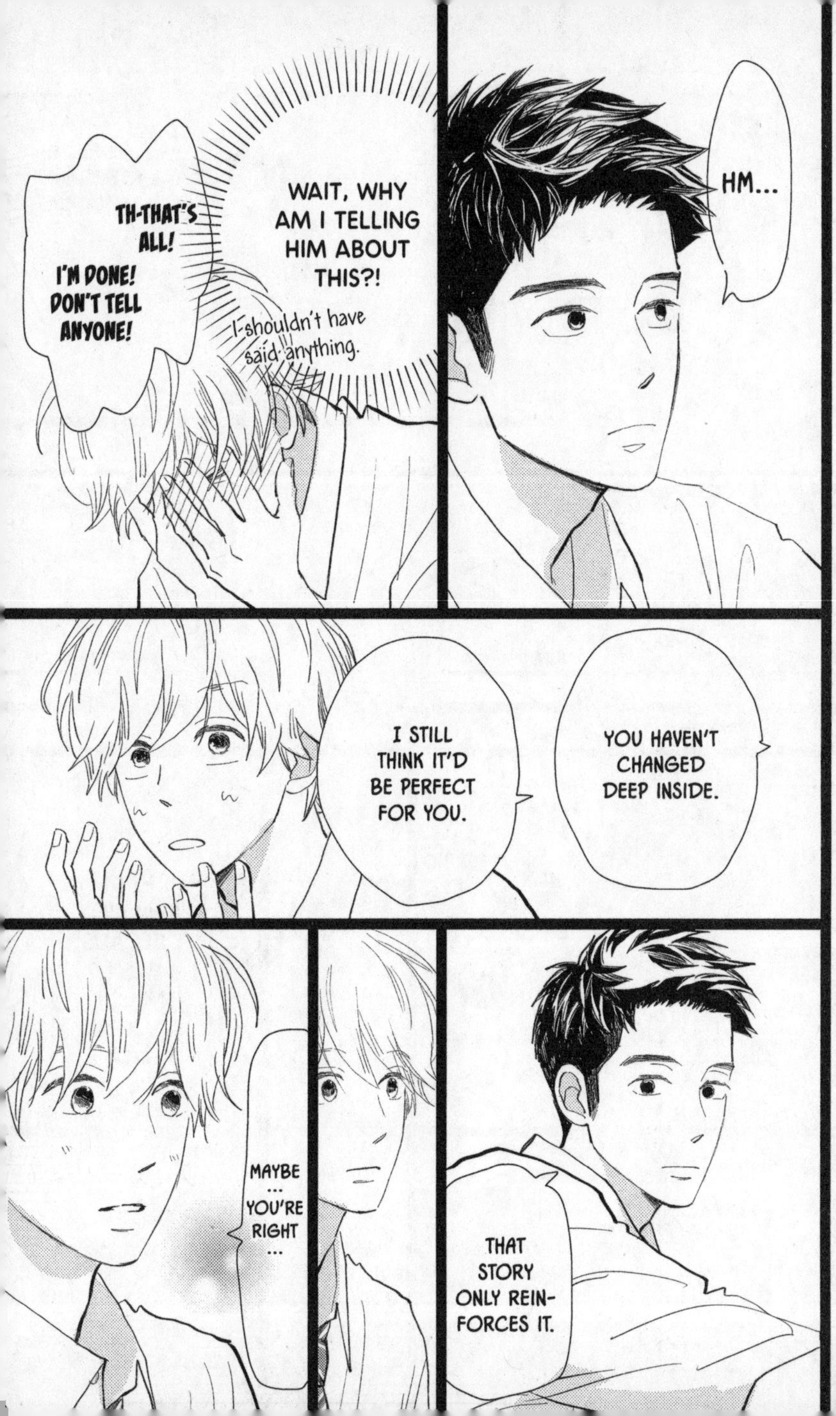
HM...
WAIT, WHY AM I TELLING HIM ABOUT THIS?!
I-shouldn't have said anything.
TH-THAT'S ALL!
I'M DONE! DON'T TELL ANYONE!
YOU HAVEN'T CHANGED DEEP INSIDE.
I STILL THINK IT'D BE PERFECT FOR YOU.
THAT STORY ONLY REIN-FORCES IT.
MAYBE ... YOU'RE RIGHT ...

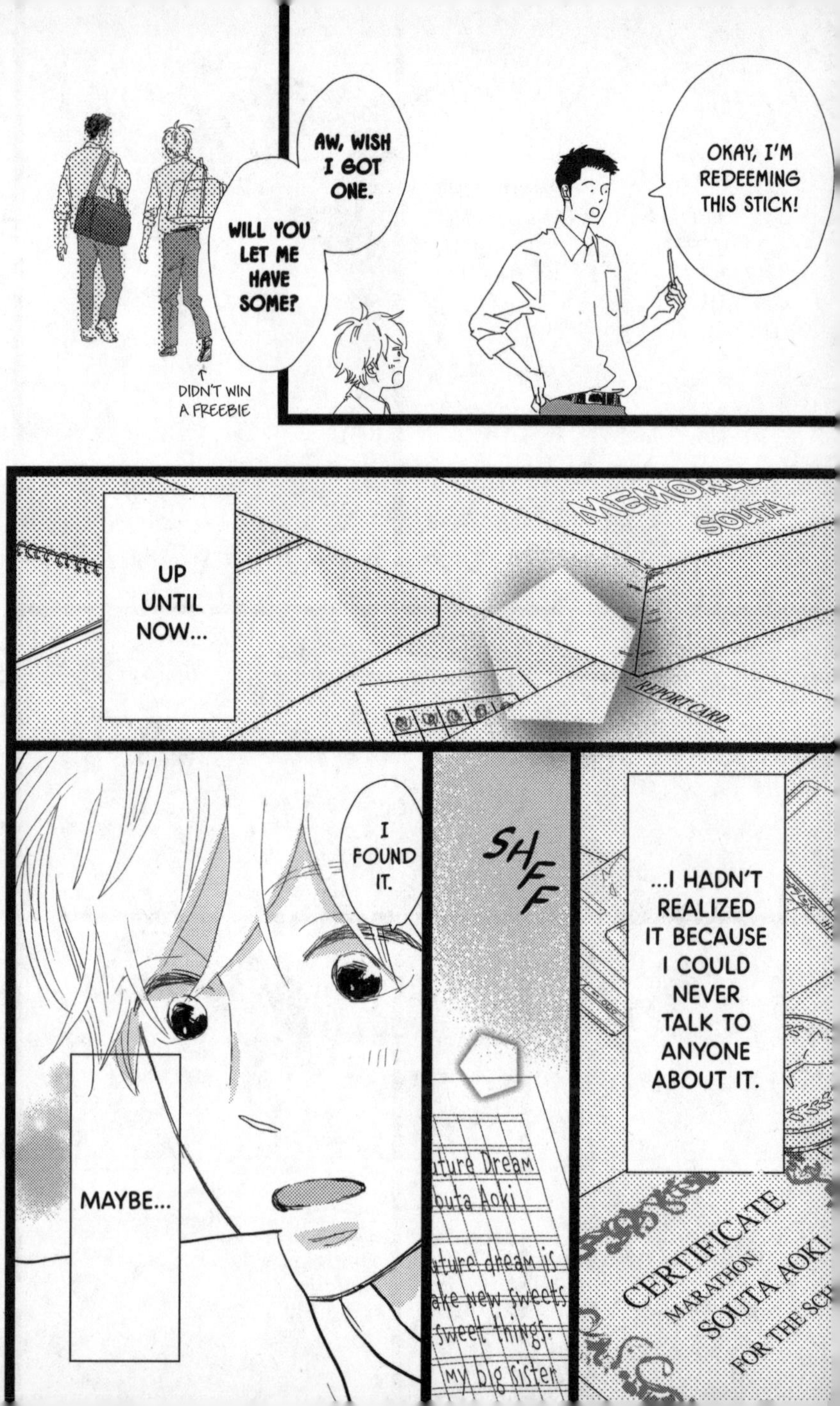
OKAY, I'M REDEEMING THIS STICK!
AW, WISH I GOT ONE.
WILL YOU LET ME HAVE SOME?
DIDN'T WIN A FREEBIE
UP UNTIL NOW...
SOUTA
REPORT CARD
...I HADN'T REALIZED IT BECAUSE I COULD NEVER TALK TO ANYONE ABOUT IT.
CERTIFICATE
MARATHON
SOUTA AOKI
SHFF
my big sister
I FOUND IT.
MAYBE...

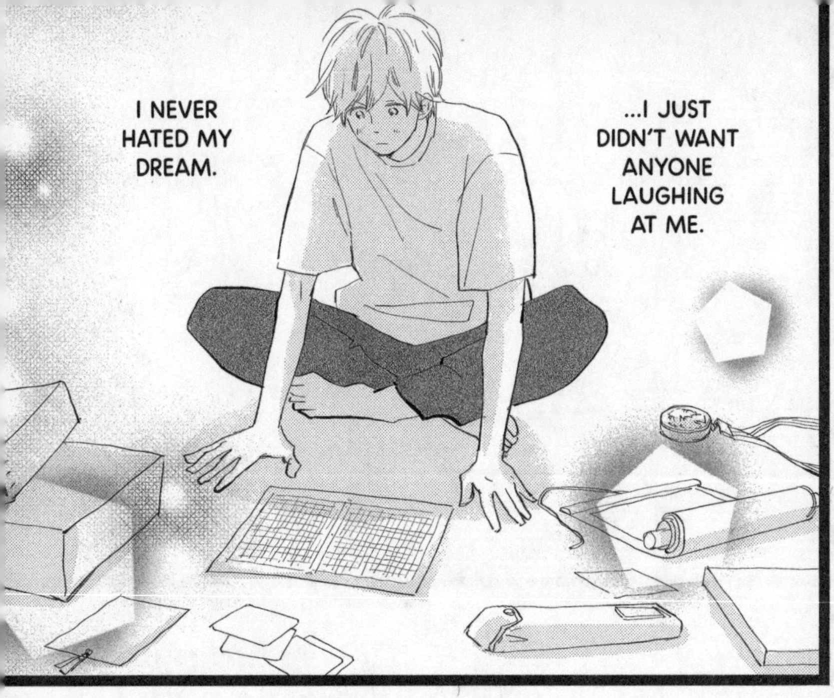
...I JUST DIDN'T WANT ANYONE LAUGHING AT ME.
I NEVER HATED MY DREAM.

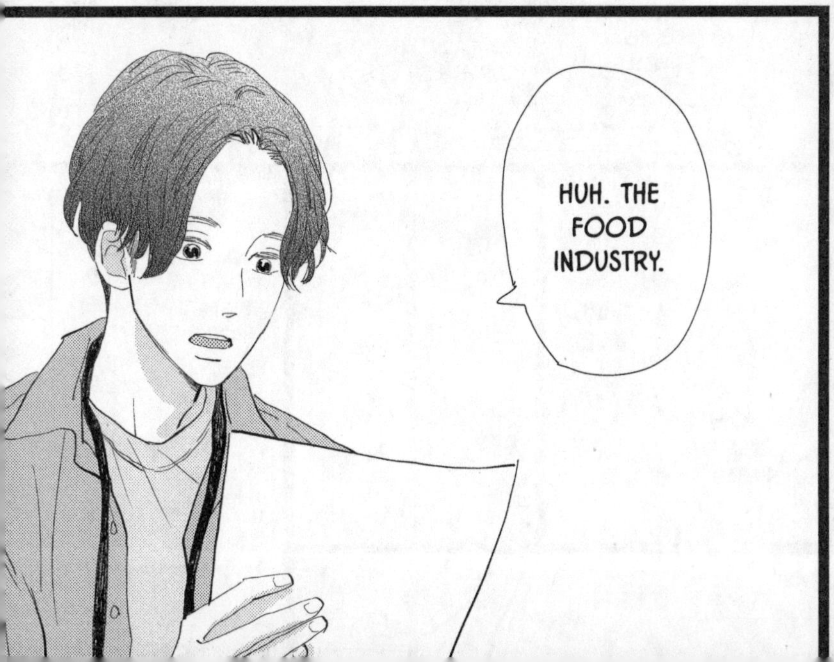
HUH. THE FOOD INDUSTRY.

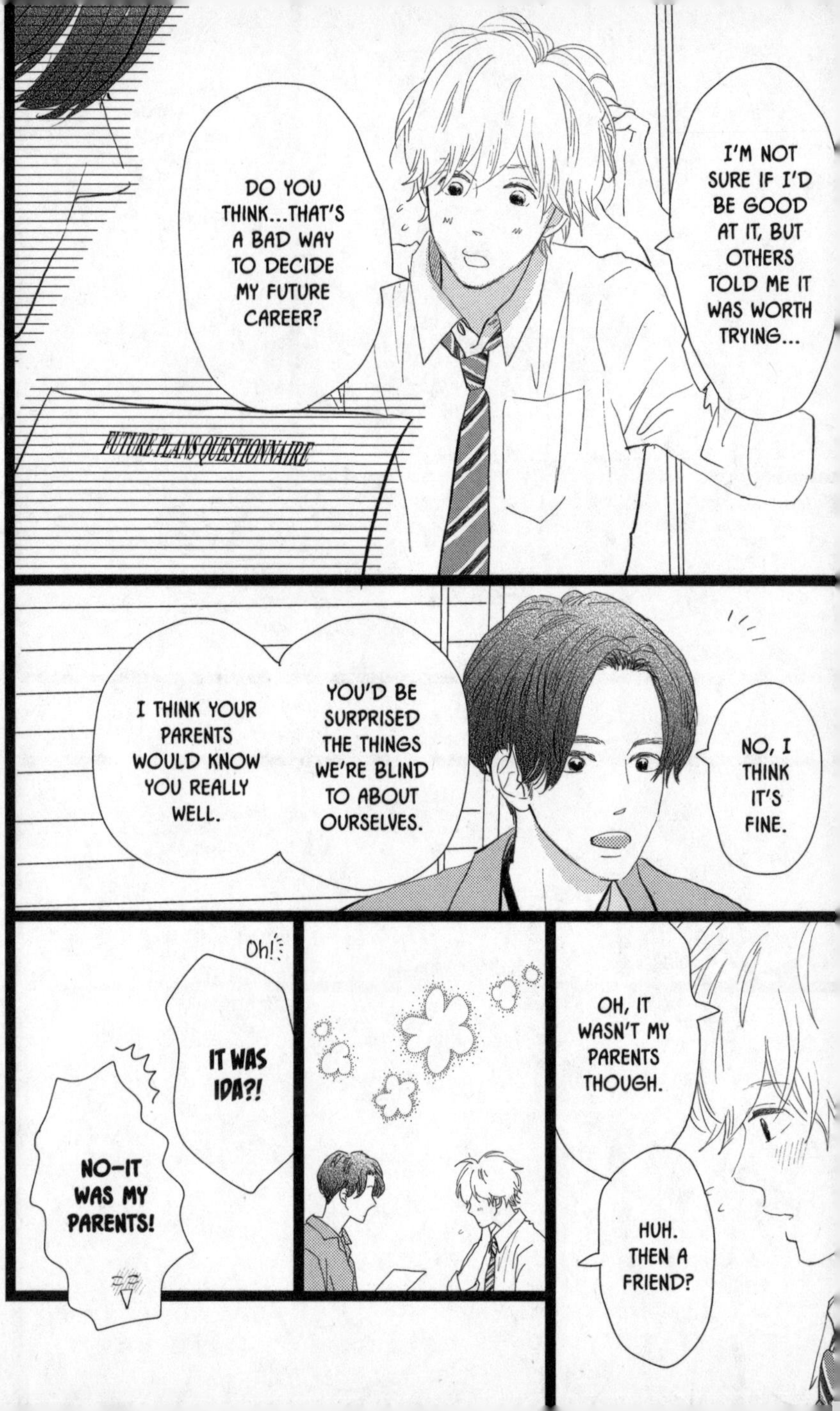
I'M NOT SURE IF I'D BE GOOD AT IT, BUT OTHERS TOLD ME IT WAS WORTH TRYING...
DO YOU THINK...THAT'S A BAD WAY TO DECIDE MY FUTURE CAREER?
FUTURE PLANS QUESTIONNAIRE
NO, I THINK IT'S FINE.
YOU'D BE SURPRISED THE THINGS WE'RE BLIND TO ABOUT OURSELVES.
I THINK YOUR PARENTS WOULD KNOW YOU REALLY WELL.
OH, IT WASN'T MY PARENTS THOUGH.
HUH. THEN A FRIEND?
Oh!
IT WAS IDA?!
NO—IT WAS MY PARENTS!

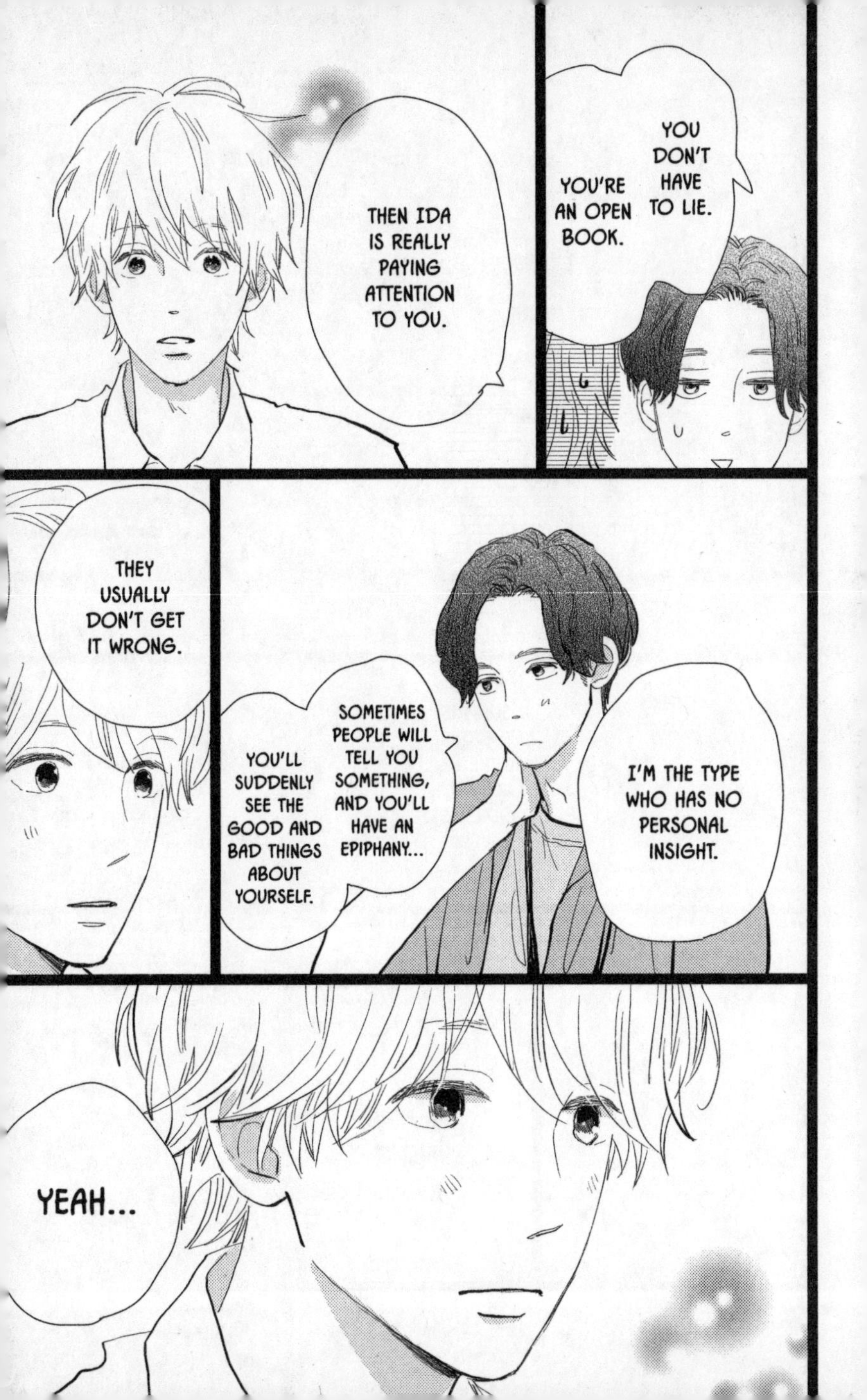
YOU DON'T HAVE TO LIE.
YOU'RE AN OPEN BOOK.
THEN IDA IS REALLY PAYING ATTENTION TO YOU.
I'M THE TYPE WHO HAS NO PERSONAL INSIGHT.
SOMETIMES PEOPLE WILL TELL YOU SOMETHING, AND YOU'LL HAVE AN EPIPHANY...
YOU'LL SUDDENLY SEE THE GOOD AND BAD THINGS ABOUT YOURSELF.
THEY USUALLY DON'T GET IT WRONG.
YEAH...

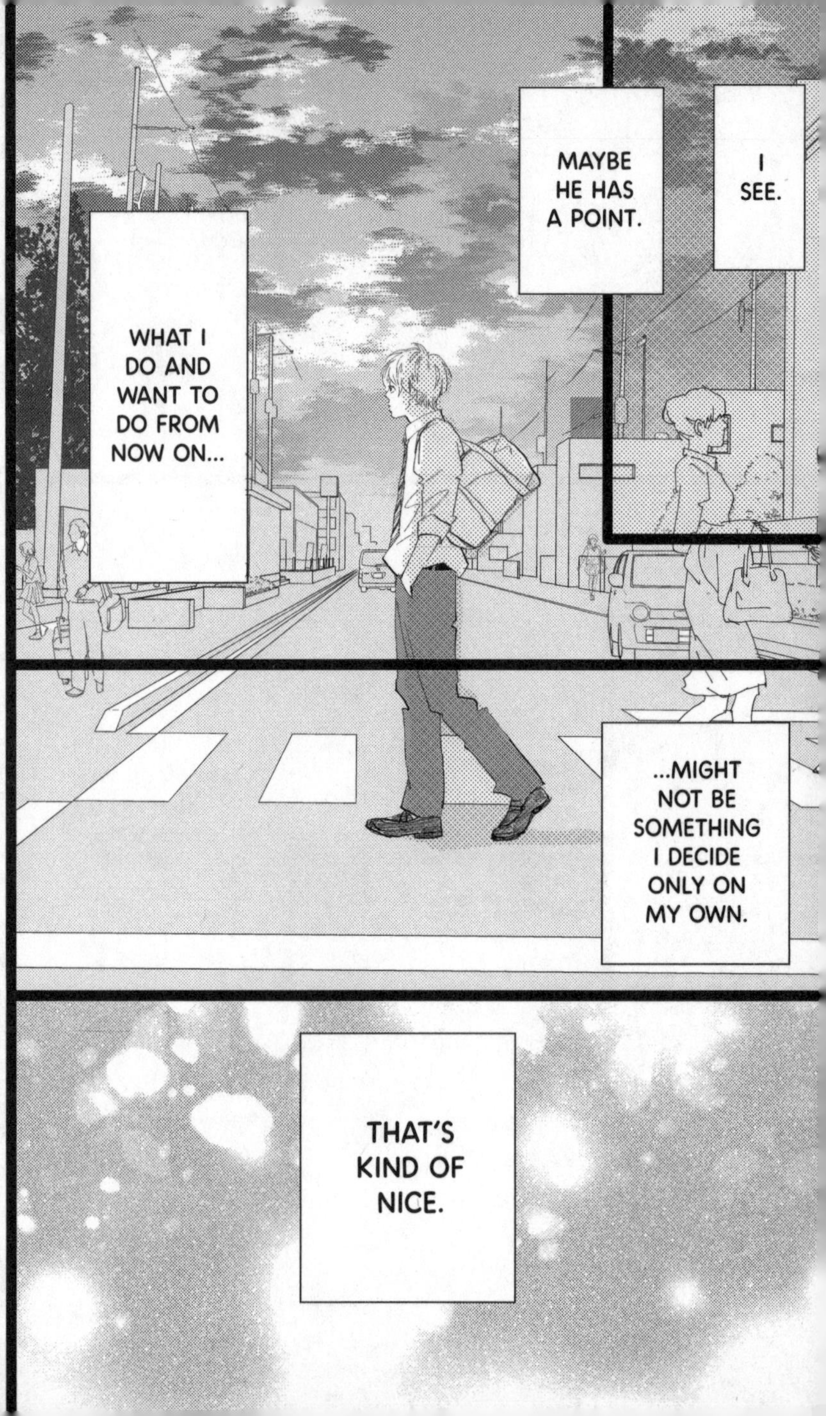
I SEE.
MAYBE HE HAS A POINT.
WHAT I DO AND WANT TO DO FROM NOW ON...
...MIGHT NOT BE SOMETHING I DECIDE ONLY ON MY OWN.
THAT'S KIND OF NICE.

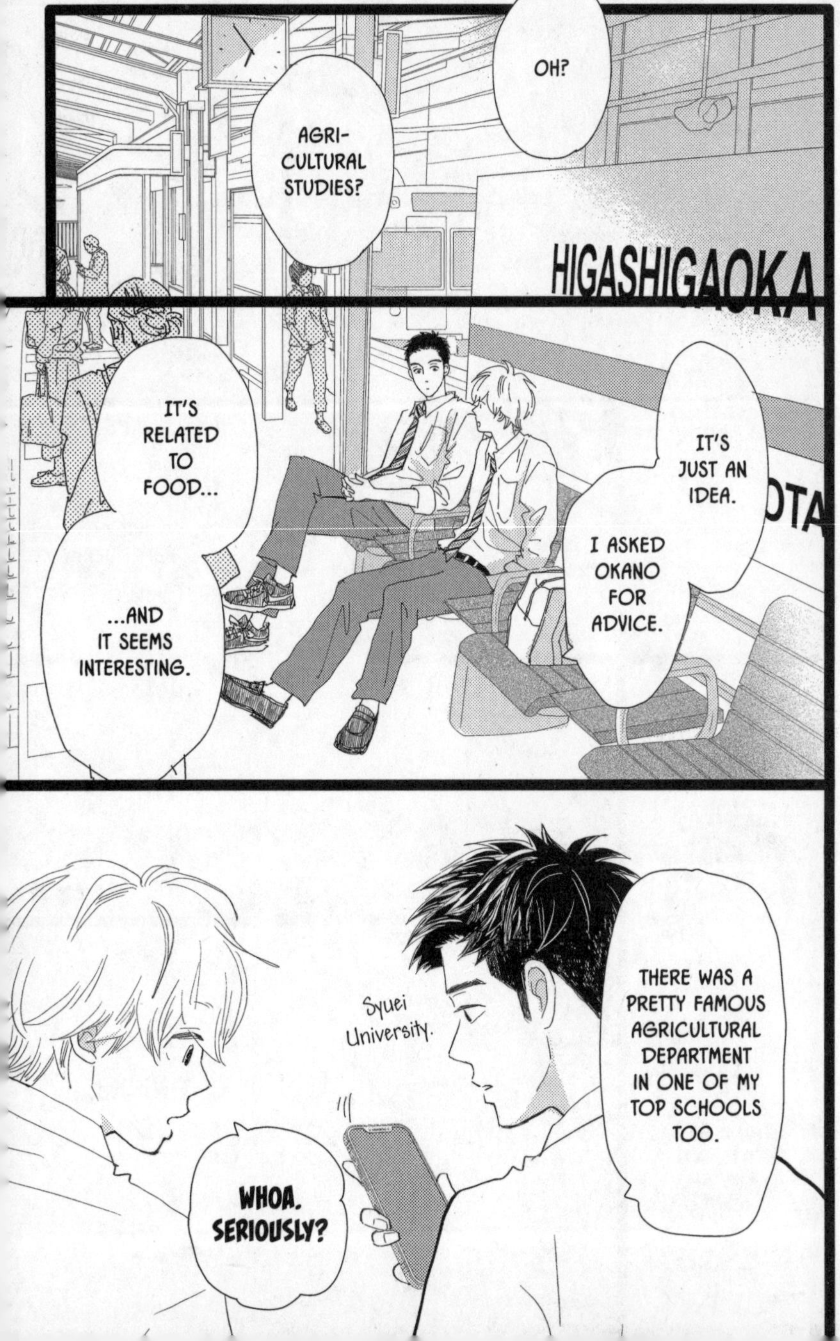
OH?
AGRI-CULTURAL STUDIES?
HIGASHIGAOKA
IT'S JUST AN IDEA.
I ASKED OKANO FOR ADVICE.
IT'S RELATED TO FOOD...
...AND IT SEEMS INTERESTING.
THERE WAS A PRETTY FAMOUS AGRICULTURAL DEPARTMENT IN ONE OF MY TOP SCHOOLS TOO.
Syuei University.
WHOA. SERIOUSLY?

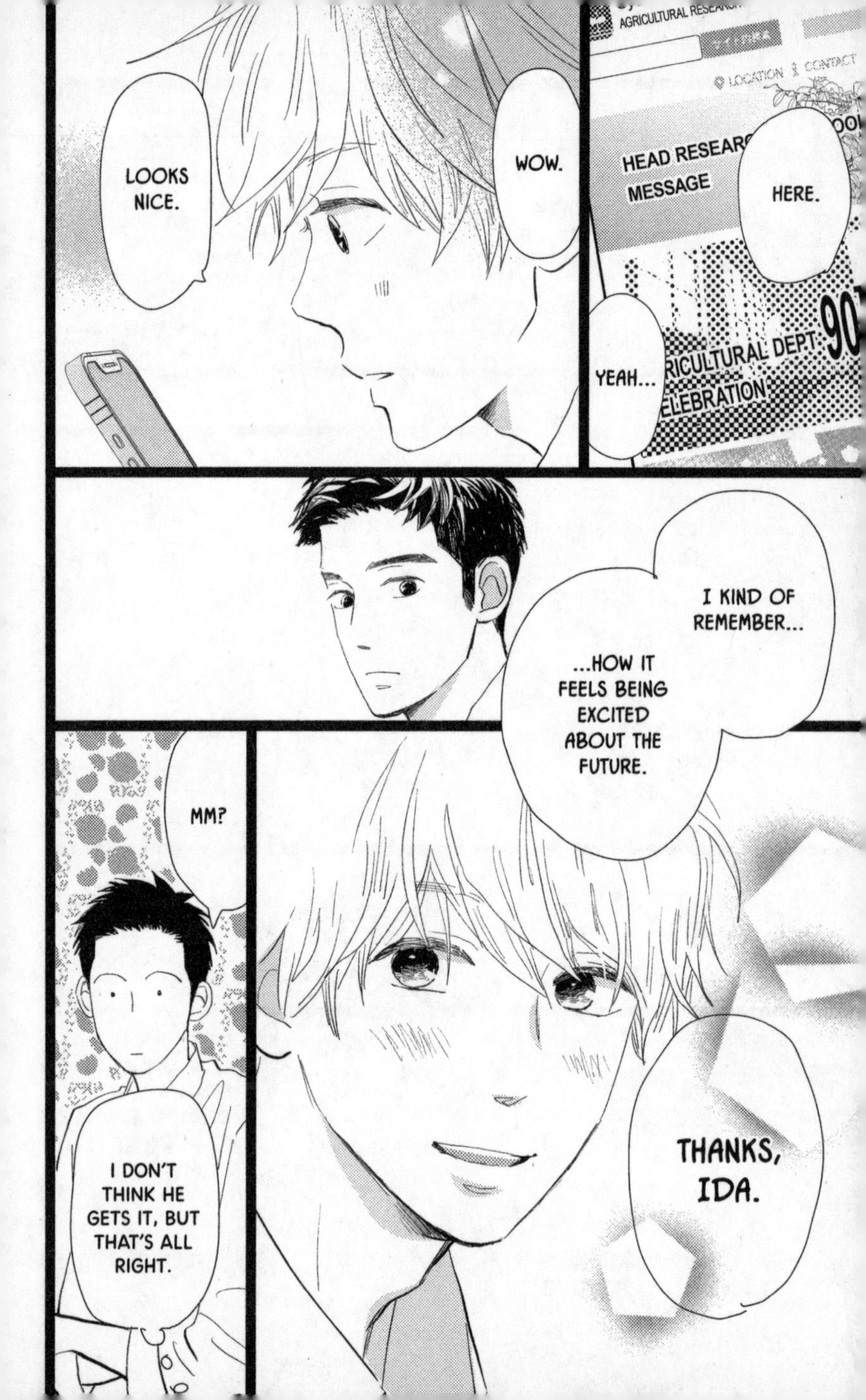
AGRICULTURAL RESEAR
LOCATION
CONTACT
HEAD RESEAR
MESSAGE
HERE.
RICULTURAL DEPT 90
ELEBRATION
YEAH...
WOW.
LOOKS NICE.
I KIND OF REMEMBER...
...HOW IT FEELS BEING EXCITED ABOUT THE FUTURE.
THANKS, IDA.
MM?
I DON'T THINK HE GETS IT, BUT THAT'S ALL RIGHT.

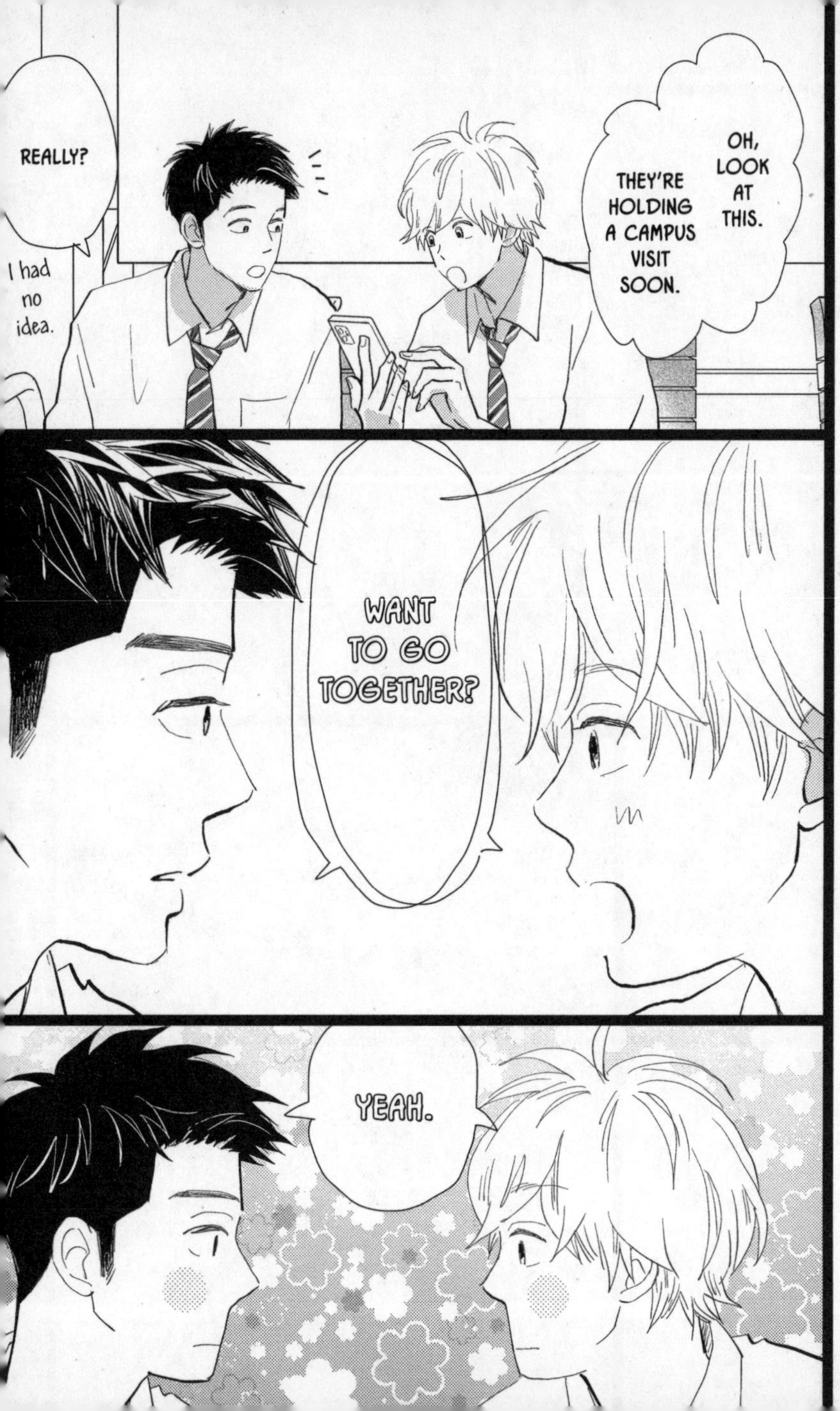
OH, LOOK AT THIS.
THEY'RE HOLDING A CAMPUS VISIT SOON.
REALLY?
I had no idea.
WANT TO GO TOGETHER?
YEAH.

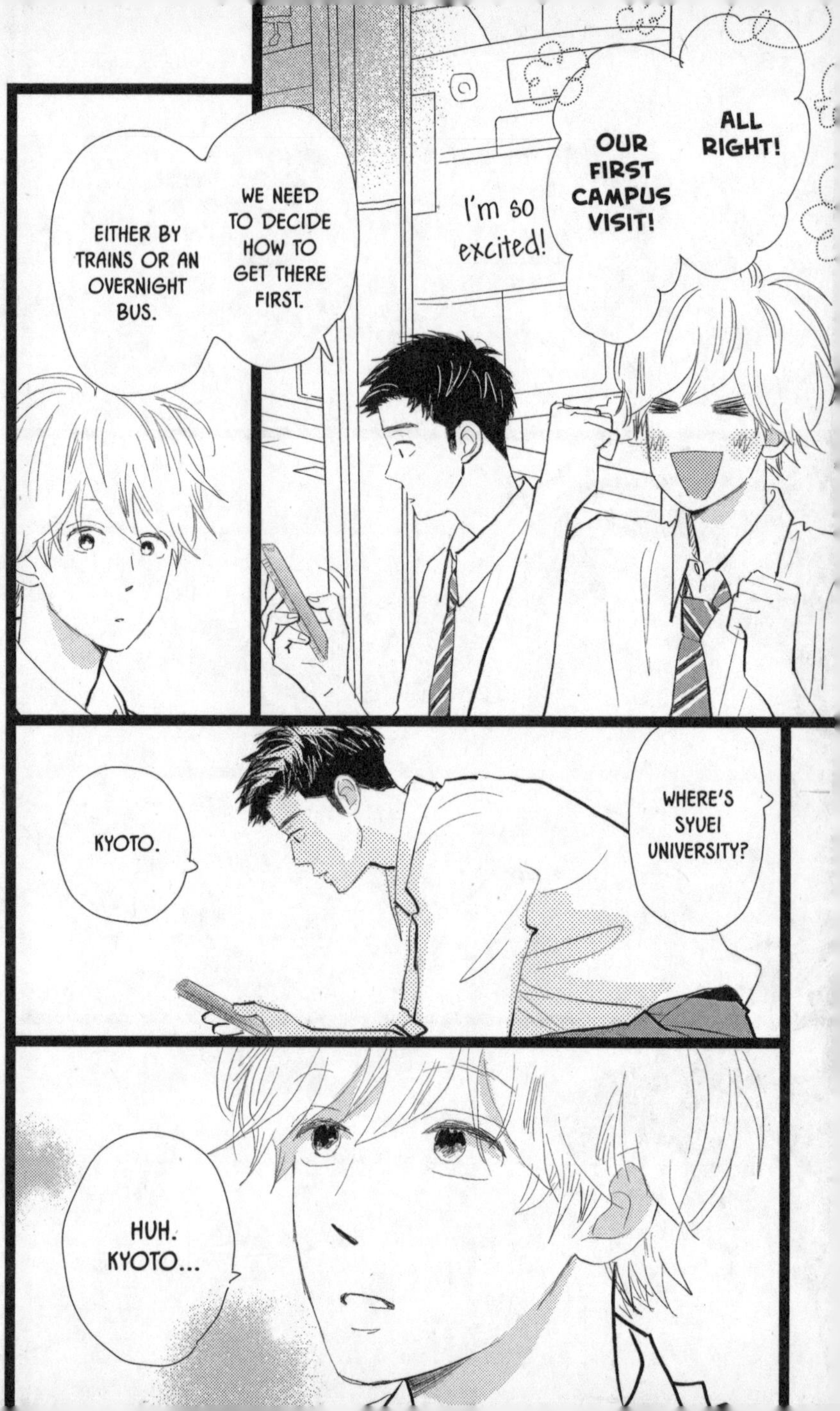
ALL RIGHT!
OUR FIRST CAMPUS VISIT!
I'm so excited!
WE NEED TO DECIDE HOW TO GET THERE FIRST.
EITHER BY TRAINS OR AN OVERNIGHT BUS.
WHERE'S SYUEI UNIVERSITY?
KYOTO.
HUH. KYOTO...

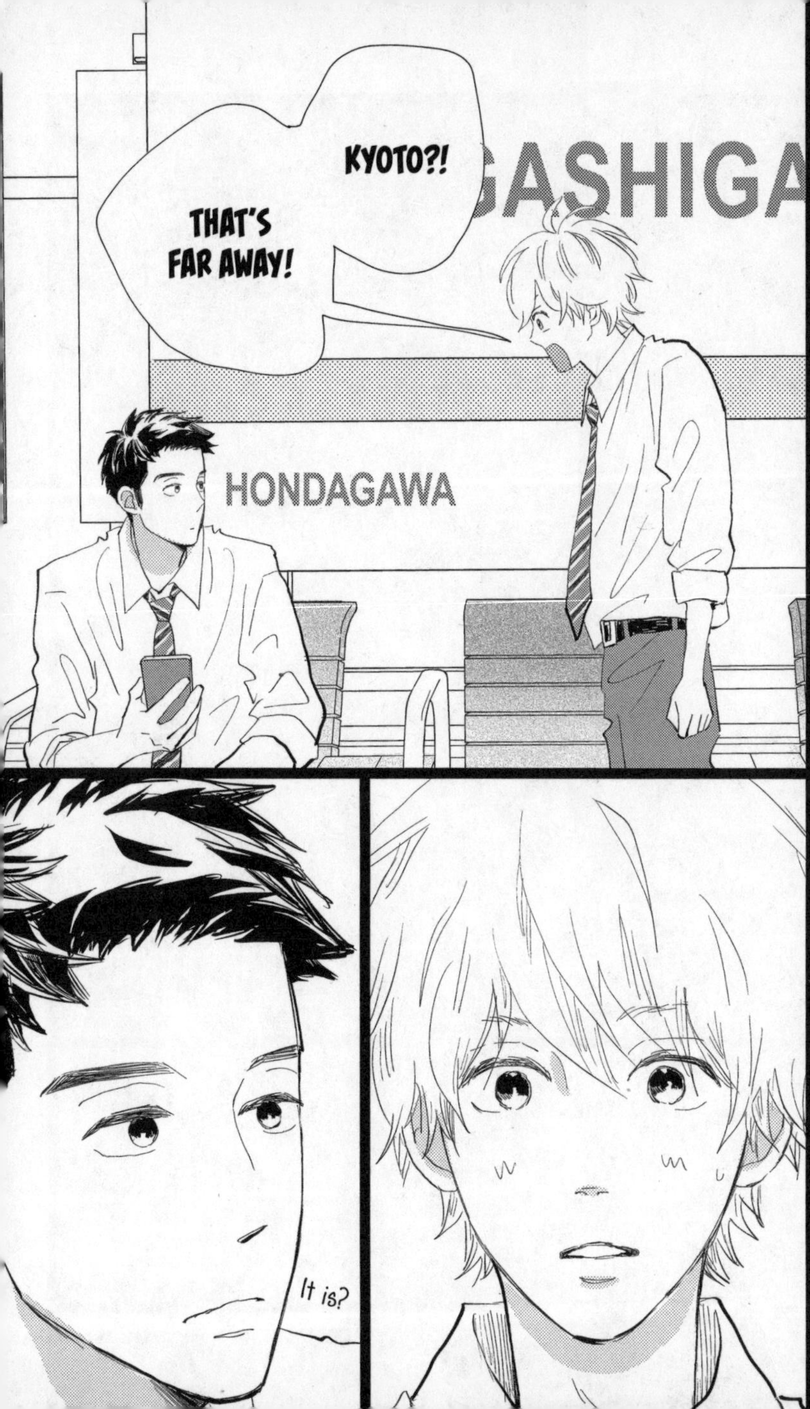
GASHIGA
KYOTO?! THAT'S FAR AWAY!
HONDAGAWA
It is?

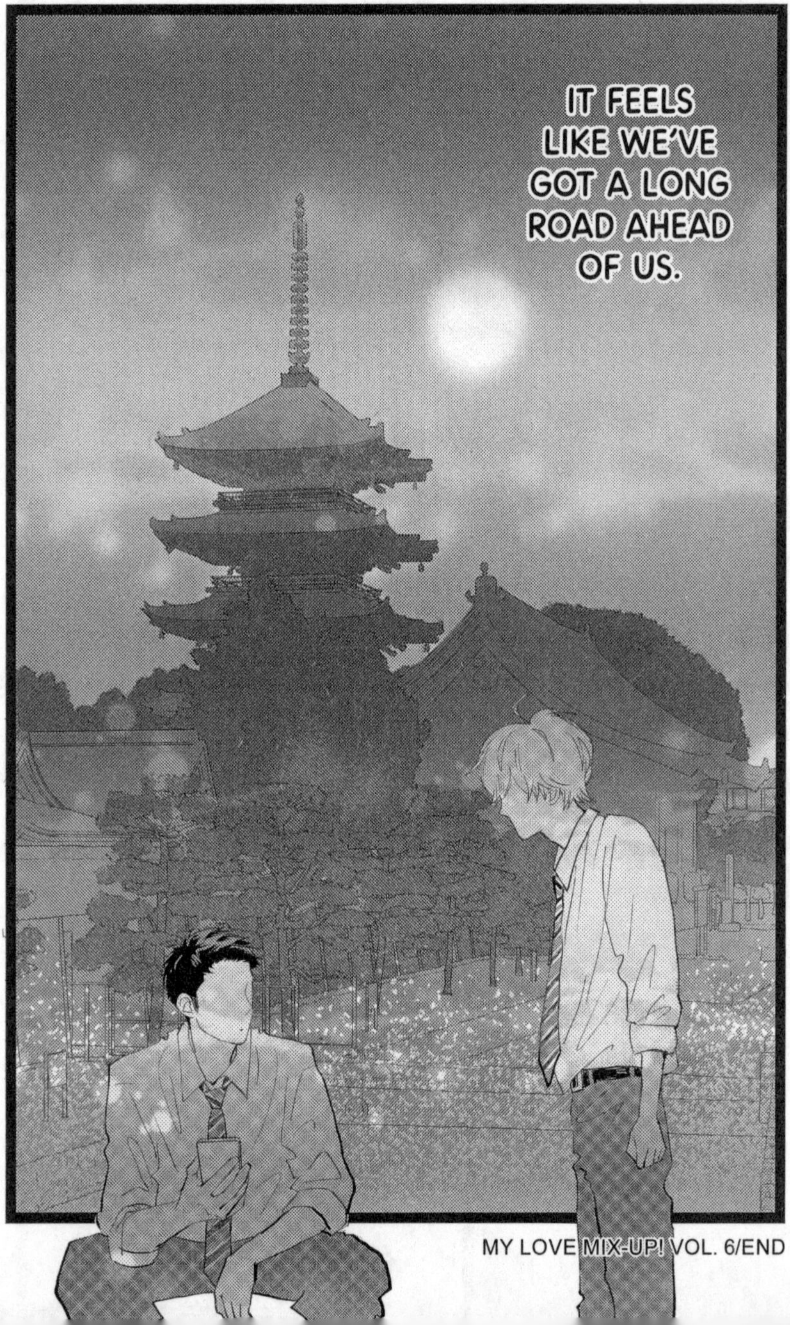
IT FEELS LIKE WE'VE GOT A LONG ROAD AHEAD OF US.

MY LOVE MIX-UP! VOL. 6/END

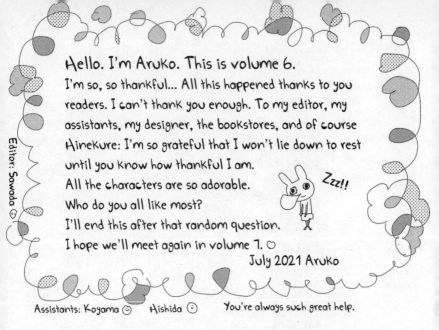

Editor: Sawada ☺

Hello. I'm Aruko. This is volume 6.

I'm so, so thankful... All this happened thanks to you readers. I can't thank you enough. To my editor, my assistants, my designer, the bookstores, and of course Hinekure: I'm so grateful that I won't lie down to rest until you know how thankful I am.

All the characters are so adorable.

Who do you all like most?

I'll end this after that random question.

I hope we'll meet again in volume 7. ○

Zzz!!

July 2021 Aruko

Assistants: Koyama ☺   Hishida ☺   You're always such great help.

Thank you for picking up *My Love Mix-Up!* volume 6.

Aruko Sensei, our editor, and all the readers—you've supported us continuously for two years of serialization. I'm so happy you're still with us and reading the manga even now. Thank you for everything. I'm going to work even harder. Also, Aoki and his friends are already in their last year of high school. I feel the same as I would seeing my own grandchildren grow up. Ida in particular seemed taciturn to me, so I had trouble getting him at first, but as I read Aruko Sensei's draft I low-key realized his gestures and expressions are lovely. Now I really like him a lot. I'm excited for you to see how charming the characters are in lots of different ways, like in the little theaters coming up. I hope to see you in the next volume.

Maybe it's not that Ida is taciturn so much that it's Aoki who's a busybody.

...

That's rude!!

I like summer because daylight lasts longer. But then I get exhausted really quickly. What to do?!

Aruko

Time keeps moving on, and volume 6 is already here. The change in the distance between the two on the cover is riveting and deeply poignant at the same time. Aruko Sensei, our editor, and all our readers—thank you for nurturing this story with me.

Wataru Hinekure

Aruko is from Ishikawa Prefecture in Japan and was born on July 26 (a Leo!). She made her manga debut with *Ame Nochi Hare* (Clear After the Rain). Her other works include *Yasuko to Kenji*, and her hobbies include laughing and getting lost.

Wataru Hinekure is a night owl. *My Love Mix-Up!* is Hinekure's first work.

My Love Mix-Up!

Vol. 6
Shojo Beat Edition

STORY BY
Wataru Hinekure
ART BY
Aruko

Translation & Adaptation/Jan Mitsuko Cash
Touch-Up Art & Lettering/Inori Fukuda Trant
Design/Yukiko Whitley
Editor/Nancy Thistlethwaite

Printed in the U.S.A.

Published by VIZ Media, LLC
P.O. Box 77010
San Francisco, CA 94107

10 9 8 7 6 5 4 3 2 1
First printing, January 2023

ratings.viz.com
RATED T TEEN

PARENTAL ADVISORY
MY LOVE MIX-UP! is rated T for Teen and is recommended for ages 13 and up. No cinnamon rolls were harmed in the making of this manga.

viz.com
shojobeat.com

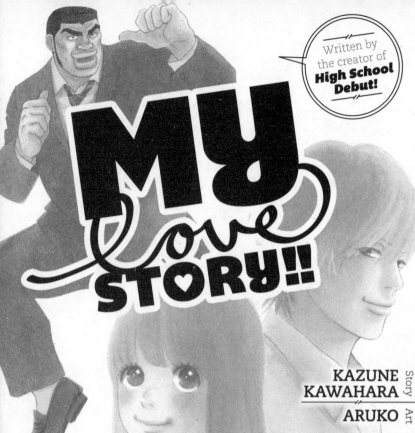

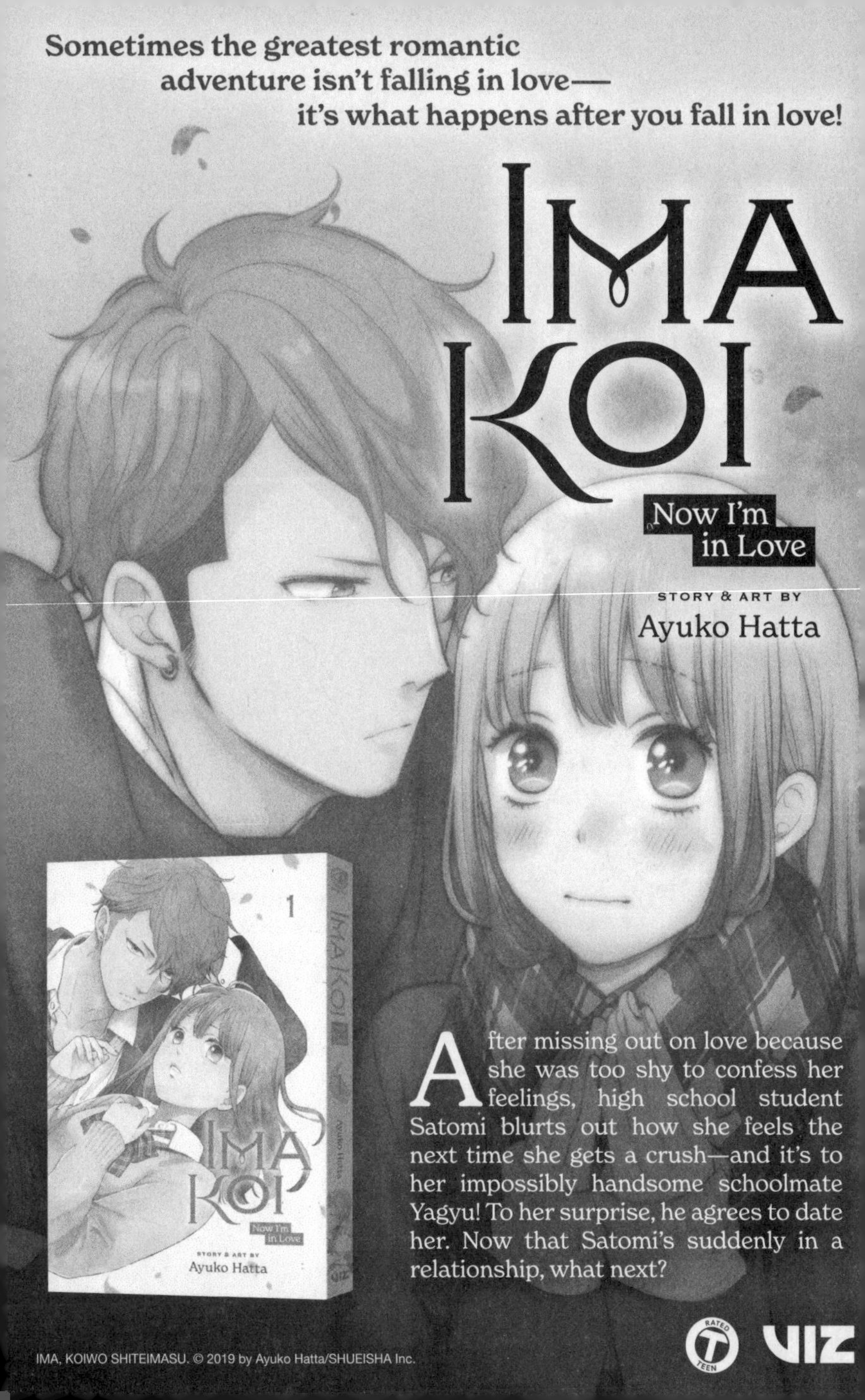
Sometimes the greatest romantic adventure isn't falling in love—it's what happens after you fall in love!
IMA KOI
Now I'm in Love
STORY & ART BY
Ayuko Hatta
1
IMA KOI
Now I'm in Love
STORY & ART BY
Ayuko Hatta
After missing out on love because she was too shy to confess her feelings, high school student Satomi blurts out how she feels the next time she gets a crush—and it's to her impossibly handsome schoolmate Yagyu! To her surprise, he agrees to date her. Now that Satomi's suddenly in a relationship, what next?
RATED T TEEN
VIZ
IMA, KOIWO SHITEIMASU. © 2019 by Ayuko Hatta/SHUEISHA Inc.

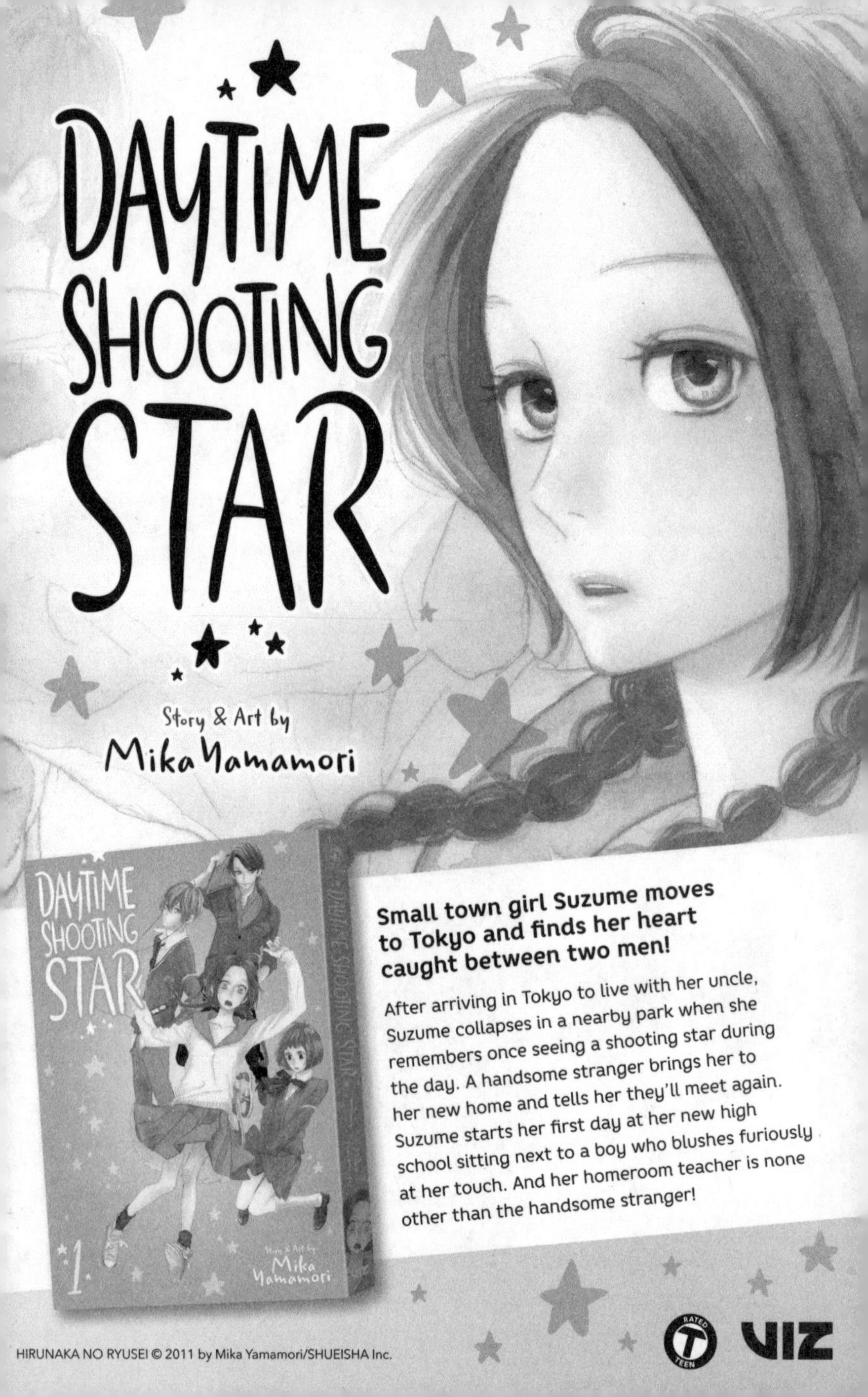
DAYTIME SHOOTING STAR
Story & Art by
Mika Yamamori
DAYTIME SHOOTING STAR
1
Story & Art by Mika Yamamori
Small town girl Suzume moves to Tokyo and finds her heart caught between two men!
After arriving in Tokyo to live with her uncle, Suzume collapses in a nearby park when she remembers once seeing a shooting star during the day. A handsome stranger brings her to her new home and tells her they'll meet again. Suzume starts her first day at her new high school sitting next to a boy who blushes furiously at her touch. And her homeroom teacher is none other than the handsome stranger!
RATED T TEEN
VIZ
HIRUNAKA NO RYUSEI © 2011 by Mika Yamamori/SHUEISHA Inc.

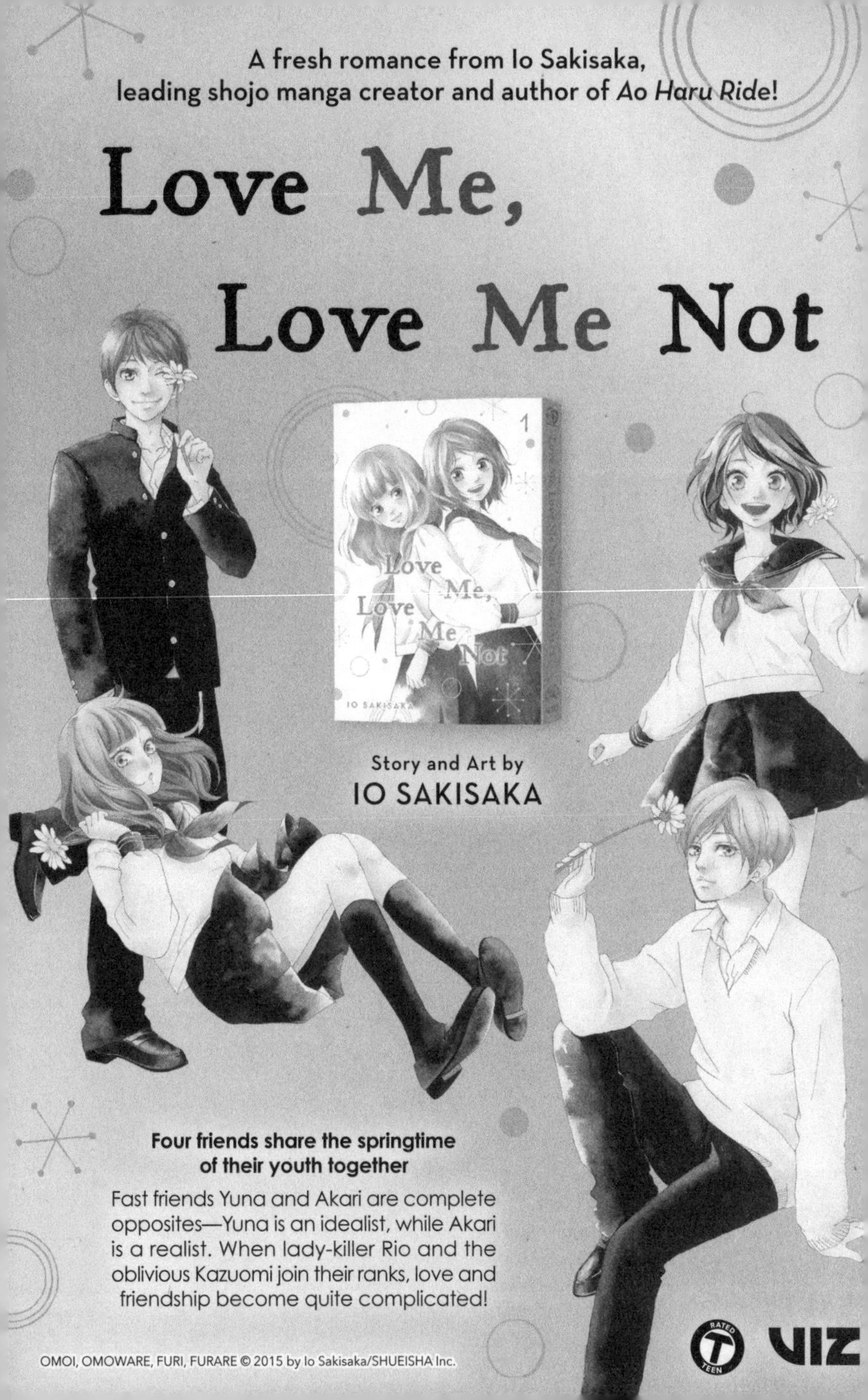
A fresh romance from Io Sakisaka,
leading shojo manga creator and author of *Ao Haru Ride*!
Love Me,
Love Me Not
1
Love Me, Love Me Not
IO SAKISAKA
Story and Art by
IO SAKISAKA
Four friends share the springtime
of their youth together
Fast friends Yuna and Akari are complete opposites—Yuna is an idealist, while Akari is a realist. When lady-killer Rio and the oblivious Kazuomi join their ranks, love and friendship become quite complicated!
RATED T TEEN
VIZ
OMOI, OMOWARE, FURI, FURARE © 2015 by Io Sakisaka/SHUEISHA Inc.

SHORTCAKE CAKE

STORY AND ART BY
suu Morishita

**An unflappable girl and a cast of
lovable roommates at a boardinghouse
create bonds of friendship and romance!**

When Ten moves out of her parents' home
in the mountains to live in a boardinghouse,
she finds herself becoming fast friends with
her male roommates. But can love and
romance be far behind?

VIZ

Stop!
You may be reading the wrong way.

In keeping with the original Japanese comic format, this book reads from right to left—so action, sound effects, and word balloons are completely reversed to preserve the orientation of the original artwork. Check out the diagram shown here to get the hang of things, and then turn to the other side of the book to get started!

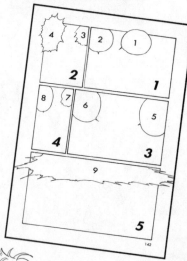